Dependent Growth: Foreign Investment and the Development of the Automotive Industry in East-Central Europe

Petr Pavlínek

Dependent Growth: Foreign Investment and the Development of the Automotive Industry in East-Central Europe

Springer

Petr Pavlínek
Department of Geography and Geology
University of Nebraska at Omaha
Omaha, NE, USA

Department of Social Geography and Regional Development
Faculty of Science, Charles University
Prague, Czechia

ISBN 978-3-319-53954-6   ISBN 978-3-319-53955-3 (eBook)
DOI 10.1007/978-3-319-53955-3

Library of Congress Control Number: 2017932538

Printed on acid-free paper

This Springer imprint is published by Springer Nature
The registered company is Springer International Publishing AG
The registered company address is: Gewerbestrasse 11, 6330 Cham, Switzerland

Preface

This book focuses on the rapid development of the automotive industry in East-Central Europe (ECE) since the early 1990s, which has been driven by large inflows of foreign direct investment. It summarizes a substantial part of my work on the ECE automotive industry during the period between 2011 and 2015. Field research, in the form of company questionnaires and interviews, for the topics presented in this book started in 2009. I am also drawing on my previous work on the ECE automotive industry that goes back to 1995. Since the beginning of my academic career, I have always been interested in understanding how particular social and economic processes operate on the ground in the concrete conditions of particular firms, places and regions. This grounded approach is reflected and presented in my work on the ECE automotive industry.

The chapters in this book draw on my previously published research articles and one book chapter. All of them have been edited, updated and in some cases expanded for this book. In particular, Chap. 1 is based on Pavlínek, P. (2015) Foreign direct investment and the development of the automotive industry in central and eastern Europe. In: Béla Galgóczi, Jan Drahokoupil, Magdalena Bernaciak (eds) Foreign investment in eastern and southern Europe after 2008: Still a lever of growth? ETUI, Brussels, pp. 209–255. Chapter 2 draws on Pavlínek, P. (2015) The impact of the 2008–2009 crisis on the automotive industry: Global trends and firm-level effects in Central Europe. *European Urban and Regional Studies,* 22(1):20–40, doi: 10.1177/0969776412460534, published by SAGE Publications. Chapter 3 was originally published by Oxford University Press as Pavlínek, P. and J. Ženka (2011) Upgrading in the automotive industry: Firm-level evidence from Central Europe, *Journal of Economic Geography* 11(3):559–586, doi:10.1093/jeg/lbq023. Chapter 4 was originally published as Pavlínek, P. (2012) The Internationalization of Corporate R&D and the Automotive Industry R&D of East-Central Europe. *Economic Geography* 88(3):279–310, doi: 10.1111/j.1944-8287.2012.01155.x. It is being reprinted by permission of Taylor & Francis Ltd. Chapter 5 originally appeared as Pavlínek, P. and P. Žížalová (2016) Linkages and spillovers in global production networks: Firm-level analysis of the Czech automotive industry. *Journal of Economic Geography* 16(2):331–363, doi: 10.1093/jeg/lbu041, published by

Oxford University Press. Finally, Chap. 6 is based on Pavlínek, P. (2016) Whose success? The state-foreign capital nexus and the development of the automotive industry in Slovakia. *European Urban and Regional Studies* 23(4):571–593, doi: 10.1177/0969776414557965, published by SAGE Publications. I want to express my gratitude to these publishers for their permission to use my previous work here. I also want to thank Jan Ženka and Pavla Žížalová for their permission to use the articles they have originally coauthored (Chap. 3 in the case of Jan Ženka and Chap. 5 in the case of Pavla Žížalová).

I would like to thank all of the people that helped with the collection of data presented in this book. Jan Ženka and Pavla Žížalová helped organize the questionnaire in Czechia and Slovakia and participated in the company interviews in Czechia. Jan Ženka also helped with company interviews in Slovakia. Pavel Hurbánek and Miroslava Poláková helped with organizing company interviews in Slovakia that would not have been possible to complete without their help. I am grateful to Karel Hostomský for the production of maps for this book. I want to thank more than 150 company directors and managers in Czechia and Slovakia who were willing to be interviewed in the course of the research for this book. I also want to thank my son Adam Pavlínek for proofreading several chapters.

The research presented in this book would have been impossible to conduct without three research grants. In particular, I am grateful to the Czech Science Foundation for two research grants between 2009 and 2015 and to the European Commission for the 2008–2012 research grant that supported the fieldwork, two research assistants and my publication efforts, amongst other things. The preparation of this book was supported by a research grant from the Czech Science Foundation (grant number: 16-21076S).

I am most grateful to my wife Gabriela and children Adam and Sára for their continuing love, support and encouragement during the preparation of this book. This book is dedicated to the memory of my parents Ilona Pavlínková and Josef Pavlínek.

Omaha, NE and Prague, USA and Czechia
December 2016

Petr Pavlínek

Contents

List of Abbreviations

BAZ	Bratislava Automotive Works
CEE	Central and Eastern Europe
ECE	East-Central Europe
EU	European Union
FDI	Foreign direct investment
GM	General Motors
GPN	Global production network
GVC	Global value chain
IMF	International Monetary Fund
JV	Joint venture
LCV	Light commercial vehicle
NAFTA	North American Free Trade Agreement
PSA	PSA Peugeot Citroën
R&D	Research and development
RTR	Renault Technologie Roumanie
SMEs	Small- and medium-size enterprises
SUV	Sport utility vehicle
TNC	Transnational corporation
TPCA	Toyota Peugeot Citroën Automobile
VW	Volkswagen
WWII	World War Two

Chapter 1
Foreign Direct Investment and the Development of the Automotive Industry

Introduction

In an increasingly globalized economy, foreign direct investment (FDI) by transnational corporations (TNCs) is considered a major force in the economic development of less developed economies, including the economies of East-Central Europe (ECE) (e.g. Jindra et al. 2009).[1] In the early 1990s, it was argued that a successful 'transition' to capitalism in East-Central Europe (ECE) would depend on large FDI inflows for triggering the necessary industrial restructuring, modernization and successful economic development (e.g. Fischer and Gelb 1991; Dunning 1993; EBRD 1993). Consequently, ECE countries were urged to open up their economies to global capital (Gowan 1995). The automotive industry was at the forefront of this FDI-driven development strategy in which foreign TNCs took over the ECE automotive industry through heavy capital investment, restructuring it and incorporating it into European and global production networks in the 1990s and 2000s (Pavlínek 2002a, c; Pavlínek et al. 2009). The goal of this chapter is to analyze FDI in the ECE automotive industry, examining trends and patterns since the 1990s with a focus on the 2000s and especially the period after the 2008–2009 economic crisis.

The automotive industry has experienced major reorganization on a global scale since the early 1990s and now represents one of the most globalized industries (Dicken 2015). This reorganization involved the rapid expansion of core-based vehicle assembly companies and their principal suppliers into less developed countries, made possible by the liberalization of trade and FDI policies (Sturgeon et al. 2008; Sturgeon and Lester 2004; Humphrey and Memedovic 2003; Humphrey

[1] In this book, East-Central Europe (ECE) denotes the region composed of former state socialist countries located in Europe outside the former Soviet Union, which have automobile assembly plants, i.e. Bulgaria, Czechia, Hungary, Poland, Romania, Serbia, Slovakia and Slovenia. Central Europe (CE) denotes the region composed of Czechia, Hungary, Poland, Slovakia and Slovenia. Central and Eastern Europe (CEE) denotes the broader region composed of East-Central Europe and the European part of the former Soviet Union (Belarus, Estonia, Latvia, Lithuania, Moldova and Ukraine).

P. Pavlínek, *Dependent Growth: Foreign Investment and the Development of the Automotive Industry in East-Central Europe*, DOI 10.1007/978-3-319-53955-3_1

2000). This expansion was driven by the efforts of automotive lead firms to increase sales and production in rapidly growing, less developed countries. It took several distinct forms (Humphrey et al. 2000). Brazil, China, India and, more recently, Russia are examples of countries that have attracted major inflows of FDI in the automotive industry mainly because of their large market potential. India, China, and Russia are examples of "protected autonomous markets" in which governments eased restrictions on FDI while continuing to protect the national market and domestic producers. Brazil and Thailand are examples of "emerging regional markets" typified by the combination of trade liberalization and regional integration (Humphrey and Oeter 2000). These countries tend to see automotive FDI as a way of developing (e.g. China and India) or modernizing (e.g. Russia) their domestic automotive industry. In addition to market penetration, TNCs expanded their production in less developed economies in order to increase their competitiveness in more developed markets by shifting production to peripheral areas located close to the affluent markets of North America and Western Europe. Mexico, Spain and ECE are the best examples of such integrated peripheries that have been integrated through FDI into the traditional core areas of automotive manufacturing in North America and Western Europe (Humphrey and Oeter 2000; Layan 2000).

This chapter focuses on ECE as an example of an integrated periphery in the automotive industry. It argues that the 2008–2009 global economic crisis coincided with the end of the period of rapid expansion of the ECE automotive industry related to the opening up of ECE to foreign trade and FDI in the 1990s and the European Union (EU) membership in the 2000s. Although the FDI-driven development of the ECE automotive industry is continuing in the aftermath of the economic crisis, it is no longer predominantly based on building new greenfield factories but increasingly on consolidating the existing spatial structure of the automotive industry in the form of expanding profitable investments through reinvestment. This consolidation phase is typified by continuing process and product upgrading and by the much more selective and uneven functional upgrading of the ECE automotive industry (Pavlínek et al. 2009; Pavlínek and Ženka 2011). Although this upgrading is crucial for maintaining the competitiveness of the ECE automotive industry, it is unlikely to alter its peripheral position in the European automotive industry division of labor, which will continue to be largely based on low labor costs compared to the Western European automotive industry core. The pressure to control rising wages in the ECE automotive industry is likely to intensify through inter-plant competition, the intensification of the labor process in the form of process upgrading and also through the selective devaluation of national currencies. This chapter also argues that large inflows of FDI led to the restructuring and rapid development of the automotive industry in ECE countries at the expense of excessive foreign domination and control and possibly limiting the industry's potential for future economic development and for closing the gap between ECE and Western European economies.

I start with a discussion of the position of ECE in the global and European division of labor in the automotive industry. This is followed by an overview of FDI trends in the ECE automotive industry, including an evaluation of automotive FDI trends in individual ECE countries. Next, I consider the future prospects of automotive FDI and its long-term developmental effects in ECE. Finally, I summarize the main points in the conclusion.

The Global and European Context of Developments in the ECE Automotive Industry

The much delayed acquisition and rescue of Serbia's struggling automaker Zastava by the Italian Fiat company in January 2010 marked the final step in the foreign takeover of the ECE passenger car (henceforth car) industry by core-based automotive TNCs and its integration into the European automotive production system. The ECE automotive industry has been profoundly transformed since the end of state socialism (e.g. Pavlínek 2002a, c; Havas 2000; Pavlínek et al. 2009). In the late 1980s, the inefficient and obsolete ECE automobile producers were struggling to meet their domestic demand and produce competitive vehicles that would sell in the lowest and cheapest market segments in Western Europe (e.g. Nestorovic 1991). Twenty-five years later, the foreign-controlled export-oriented automotive industry of the ECE countries is playing an increasingly important role in their domestic economies when measured in terms of employment, production value and the share of total manufacturing (Table 1.1). It also plays a growing role in the European automotive industry as a whole. Overall production of cars more than quadrupled in ECE between 1989 and 2015, from 945,000 to 3.9 million units (Fig. 1.1). By 2015, ECE countries accounted for 21.2% of total European car output, compared with just 5.0% in 1990 and 3.9% in 1991 (OICA 2016).[2] The automotive supplier industry grew even faster than vehicle assembly because, in addition to supplying new

Table 1.1 The automotive industry (NACE 29) employment, production value and the share of automotive industry employment and production value of the total manufacturing production in car producing ECE countries as of 2014 and 2015

	Number of persons employed (2015)	Production value (€ mil.) (2015)	Share of employment in manufacturing total (2014)	Share of production value in manufacturing total (2014)
Bulgaria	30,838	918	3.3	3.0
Czechia	159,732	40,052	12.1	24.8
Hungary	88,532	25,005	12.2	24.9
Poland	178,274	30,539	7.1	10.8
Romania	168,689	14,433	12.7	18.3
Slovakia	66,356	24,183	13.1	32.7
Slovenia	12,746	2579	6.9	10.6

Source: Eurostat (2016)

[2] Together with Russia and Ukraine, ECE accounted for 27.8% of the total 2015 European production of cars (OICA 2016).

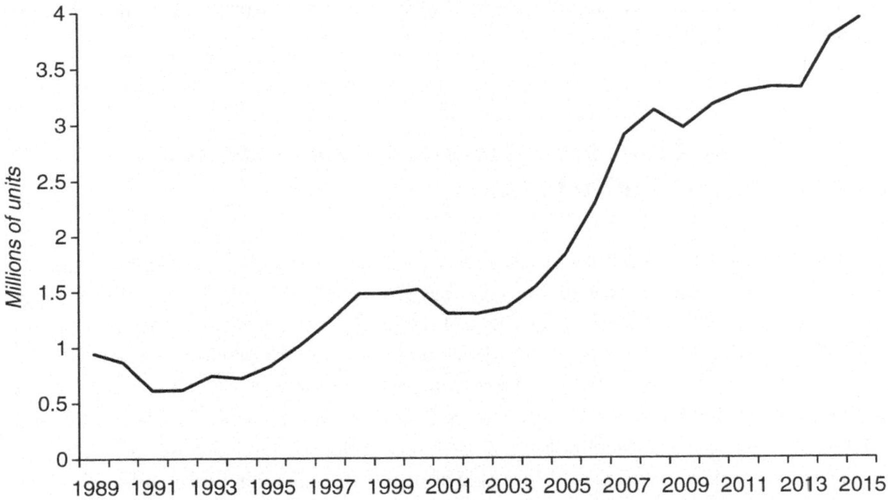

Fig. 1.1 Car production in East-Central Europe, 1989–2015. *Source:* Based on the data from national statistical offices (1989–2006), OICA (2016)

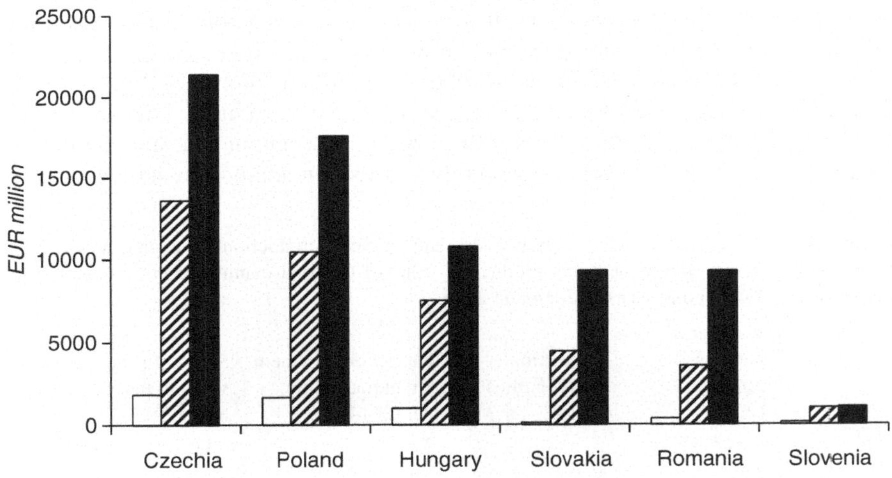

Fig. 1.2 The production value of manufacture of parts and accessories for motor vehicles in selected ECE countries, 1999, 2008 and 2015. *Source:* Based on the data in Eurostat (2016)

assembly plants in ECE, many supplier branch plants were established in ECE to supply West European assembly operations (e.g. Pavlínek 2003, Fig. 1.2).

The post-1990 ECE automotive industry transformation needs to be understood in the broader context of developments in the global automotive industry in the past three decades. The global automotive industry, one of the most globalized industries (Dicken 2015), has undergone major changes in the organization of production and, consequently, in the geography of production (Sturgeon et al. 2008; Sturgeon and Van Biesebroeck 2009; Lung 2004; Bailey et al. 2010). In particular, the concentration and consolidation of the automotive industry went hand in hand with its internationalization and a change in the methods of producing automobiles. Automakers vigorously pursued the so-called platform strategy to maintain large economies of scale, the traditional source of price competitiveness, while achieving economies of scope through the production of greater numbers of different models built on the same platform (e.g. Lung 2004). Automotive lead firms also consolidated their supplier base by introducing modular production and reducing the number of direct suppliers (e.g. Humphrey and Salerno 2000; Sturgeon et al. 2008). The most important module and Tier 1 suppliers were forced to establish production facilities wherever the automakers they supply assemble automobiles (the so-called follow supply or global supply) (Humphrey 2000; Humphrey and Memedovic 2003). To achieve this increased international presence, large suppliers engaged in a wave of mergers and acquisitions leading to the emergence of an elite group of 'global suppliers'. These were not only required to follow the automakers to foreign countries, but also had to increase their research and development (R&D) capabilities in order to participate in the development of modules, components and production technologies (co-design) with lead firms (Sturgeon and Lester 2004; Humphrey 2000; Humphrey and Memedovic 2003).

For the most part of the twentieth century, automotive production networks were organized predominantly at national scale (Dicken 2015). In the last three decades, however, automotive lead firms have increasingly organized their production networks on a macro-regional scale, encompassing for instance the whole EU or NAFTA (North American Free Trade Agreement) area (Bordenave and Lung 1996; Freyssenet and Lung 2000; Lung 2004; Sturgeon et al. 2008; Sturgeon and Van Biesebroeck 2009; Hudson and Schamp 1995). Cutthroat competition in the automotive industry is forcing lead firms to continuously design new strategies to keep their car production costs as low as possible. Various production and organizational strategies have been employed to achieve this goal, such as the use of lean production (Womack et al. 1990), a platform strategy (Lung 2004), modular production (Frigant and Talbot 2005; Frigant and Layan 2009) and the development of export-oriented production in low-cost countries to supply the markets of developed countries (Humphrey and Oeter 2000).

Export-oriented low-cost production plants have been established in peripheral areas located close to developed countries' markets such as Mexico (Humphrey and Oeter 2000; Sturgeon et al. 2010), Spain (Layan 2000) and ECE (Pavlínek 2002c). Additionally, compared to the saturated markets of developed countries with their predominantly replacement demand, demand from first-time buyers has been growing rapidly in such 'emerging' economies as China, India and Brazil (Liu and Yeung 2008; Liu and Dicken 2006; Humphrey 2003). This new demand, projected to continue growing strongly in the near future, reflects rapid economic growth and rising per capita incomes in these countries, combined with a rapidly growing population (with the exception of China).[3] The enormous market potential combined with political pressure to produce automobiles locally prompted large, mostly core-based, lead firms to establish assembly operations in these countries, in turn, contributing to extremely rapid production increases in these "peripheral markets", especially in China, since the mid-1990s.

Along with Mexico, ECE is a prime example of an "integrated peripheral market" (henceforth integrated periphery) (Humphrey and Oeter 2000) that has become a favorite manufacturing location for core-based automotive TNCs since the early 1990s following the period of swift liberalization of ECE economies in association with the 'shock therapy'. The existing inefficient and obsolete state-owned domestic automakers were unable to compete in the new market-based economic environment and became easy targets for takeovers by Western TNCs strongly encouraged by ECE governments (e.g. Pavlínek 2002c, 2006). For core-based automotive TNCs, ECE became an attractive low-cost production region located close to the Western European market. Central Europe has attracted the largest inflows of automotive FDI in the entire ECE since 1990, with the vast majority going into car assembly and the production of related components, fuelled by the region's proximity to the Western European market, low production costs, the prospect of early EU membership, its market potential, a skilled labor force, government investment incentives, liberal labor legislation, weak labor unions and a relatively well developed infrastructure (Pavlínek et al. 2009). Romania followed Central Europe in the 2000s, and Serbia, whose integration was stalled by the war and economic sanctions in the 1990s, followed in the 2010s.

The foreign takeover of the ECE automotive industry took on several forms and came in several waves of FDI. First were acquisitions of existing vehicle plants, most of which took place in the 1990s. Examples include VW's 1991 acquisition of the Czech Škoda and the Slovak BAZ, Fiat's 1992 takeover of the Polish FSM (Fabryka Samochodów Małolitrażowych), Daewoo's 1995 acquisition of the Polish FSO (Fabryka Samochodów Osobowych) and Renault's 1999 purchase of the Romanian Dacia (e.g. Pavlínek 2002c). Second, new greenfield assembly factories were established by core-based lead firms, starting with Suzuki in Hungary in 1990 and GM in Poland in 1995, with the majority being built in the 2000s, including Toyota Peugeot Citroën Automobile (TPCA—the joint venture of Toyota, Peugeot and Citroën) and Hyundai in Czechia; Kia and PSA Peugeot and Citroën in Slovakia; and Mercedes in Hungary (e.g. Pavlínek 2015; see Chap. 2). Third, key foreign suppliers followed foreign lead firms to ECE, setting up their manufacturing operations in countries where lead firms had established vehicle assembly operations in order to supply the most important components. Spatial proximity plays an important role in modular production and the just-in-time delivery of pre-assembled modules and crucial components (Frigant and Lung 2002; Larsson 2002; Pavlínek and Janák 2007).

[3] The population of less developed countries increased from 4.7 billion in 1997 to 6.1 billion in 2016. During the same period, the population of more developed countries grew from 1.1 billion to 1.25 billion (PRB 1997, 2016).

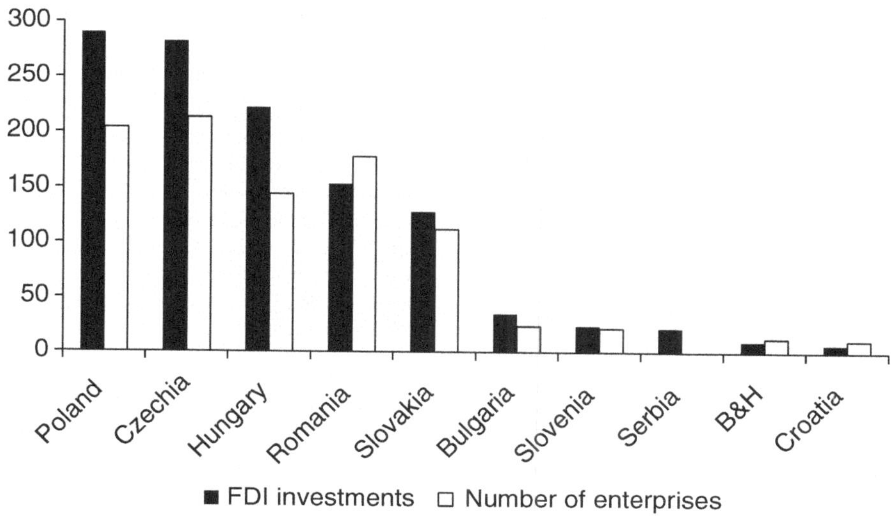

Fig. 1.3 The number of newly built foreign automotive supplier plants by country in ECE, 1997–2015 and the number of foreign-owned automotive industry enterprises in 2014. *Note:* The number of enterprises in Poland and Croatia as of 2013, the number of investments in Serbia in 1997–2009. *Source*: EY (2010), ERM (2016), Eurostat (2016)

Fourth, foreign component suppliers were attracted by low-cost production in ECE and invested heavily in both takeovers of domestic companies and in greenfield production sites (e.g. Pavlínek 2002b). Between 1997 and 2015, foreign suppliers built more than 1200 new plants in ECE (EY 2010; ERM 2016) and 921 foreign-owned automotive factories were operating in ECE in 2014 (excluding Serbia)[4] (Eurostat 2016) (Fig. 1.3). In addition to the possibility of supplying foreign-owned assembly plants in ECE, many foreign suppliers were attracted by low labor costs and set up plants in ECE to supply assembly plants in Western Europe. Overall, based on data from the national banks of individual countries, foreign companies invested more than €35 billion in the ECE automotive industry between 1990 and 2015.

As a result of large FDI inflows, the ECE automotive industry periphery has been very dynamic (e.g. Pavlínek et al. 2009; Pavlínek and Ženka 2011; Bernaciak and Šćepanović 2010; Domański et al. 2013; Sass and Szalavetz 2013). The ECE automotive industry has been restructured, modernized and expanded (e.g. Pavlínek et al. 2009; Bernaciak and Šćepanović 2010), local capabilities have been enhanced (Domanski and Gwosdz 2009) and a significant, although very uneven, upgrading has taken place (Pavlínek and Ženka 2011). This rapid development of the industry has been organized and directed from abroad and core-based automotive TNCs now fully control the ECE automotive industry through direct ownership of the vast majority of both assembly plants (Table 1.2) and key automotive suppliers. The high

[4]950 Including the Baltic states.

Table 1.2 Car assembly plants and produced models in ECE as of 2016

Country	Firm	Location	Models produced in 2016	2015 Output
Czechia	VW Group (Škoda Auto)	Mladá Boleslav	Škoda Fabia (hatchback & wagon); Octavia (sedan & wagon); Rapid, Rapid Spaceback; Seat Toledo	537,621
	VW Group (Škoda Auto)	Kvasiny	Škoda Kodiaq (starts 2016); Superb sedan & station wagon; Yeti; Seat Ateca	142,286
	Toyota Peugeot Citroën Automobile	Kolín	Citroen C1; Peugeot 108;Toyota Aygo	219,054
	Hyundai-Kia	Nošovice	Hyundai i30 hatchback (3 & 5 door), station wagon; ix20; Tucson/ix35	342,200
Hungary	Suzuki	Esztergom	Suzuki Swift; SX4 S-Cross; Vitara	185,533
	VW Group (Audi)	Györ	Audi A3 sedan, convertible; S3 sedan, convertible; TT coupe, roadster; TTS roadster, TTRS Q3 (starts in 2018)	160,206
	Daimler	Kecskemét	Mercedes B class; CLA	180,000
Poland	Fiat Chrysler	Tychy	Fiat 500; Lancia Ypsilon; Ford Ka (ended May 2016)	302,600
	General Motors (Opel)	Gliwice	Opel/Vauxhall Astra (K or new-generation) hatchback; Opel/Vauxhall Astra (J or previous-generation) sedan, GTC, GTC OPC; Cascada; Holden Astra GTC & VXR; Holden; Cascada; Buick Cascada	169,400
	VW Group (VW)	Poznań	VW Caddy; T6	170,800
	VW Group (VW)	Września	VW Crafter	0
Romania	Renault-Nissan-AvtoVAZ	Pitesti	Dacia Duster; Logan II; Logan II MCV; Sandero II	339,204
	Ford	Craiova	B-Max; EcoSport (fall 2017)	47,967
Serbia	Fiat Chrysler	Kragujevac	Fiat 500L; 500L Living	22,687

(continued)

Table 1.2 (continued)

Country	Firm	Location	Models produced in 2016	2015 Output
Slovakia	VW Group (VW)	Bratislava	Audi Q7, Q7 e-tron, SQ7; Bentley Bentayga; Porsche Cayenne (bodies in white; final assembly starts in 2018); VW Touareg; VW Up, e-Up; Seat Mii; Škoda Citigo	397,458
	PSA/Peugeot Citroën	Trnava	Citroen C3 Picasso; Peugeot 208	303,025
	Hyundai-Kia	Žilina	Kia Cee'd hatchback, wagon, coupe; Sportage; Venga	338,000
	Jaguar Land Rover (Tata)	Nitra	Land Rover Discovery (starts in 2018)	0
Slovenia	Renault-Nissan-AvtoVAZ	Novo Mesto	Renault Clio IV; Twingo III; Smart ForFour, Smart ForFour Electric Drive	129,428

Source: Automotive News Europe, annual reports and various other sources

Table 1.3 The percent share of foreign-controlled enterprises of different indicators in the automotive industry (NACE 29) by ECE countries as of 2014

	Production value	Gross investment in tangible goods	Number of persons employed	Value added at factor cost
Bulgaria	87	90	80	87
Czechia	95	92	83	92
Hungary	97	97	86	95
Poland	88	88	77	85
Romania	95	92	91	93
Slovenia	65	79	49	57
Slovakia	98	97	93	96

Source: Calculated by author from data in Eurostat (2016)

extent of foreign control over the ECE automotive industry is shown in Table 1.3. Slovakia, Hungary, Romania and Czechia had the highest share of their automotive industry controlled by foreign TNCs in 2014. The degree of foreign control was the lowest in Slovenia, reflecting its more cautious approach towards the privatization of its enterprises in the hands of foreign buyers. This almost total dependence on foreign capital is a sign of the weak and continuing peripheral position of ECE in the European automotive industry system despite its restructuring, modernization and upgrading. The position of ECE in the European automotive industry is in many respects similar to that of Mexico in the context of North America (Sturgeon et al. 2010).

Car production has increased in all ECE auto-producing countries with the exception of Serbia since 1990 (Fig. 1.4). Among the ECE countries that produced

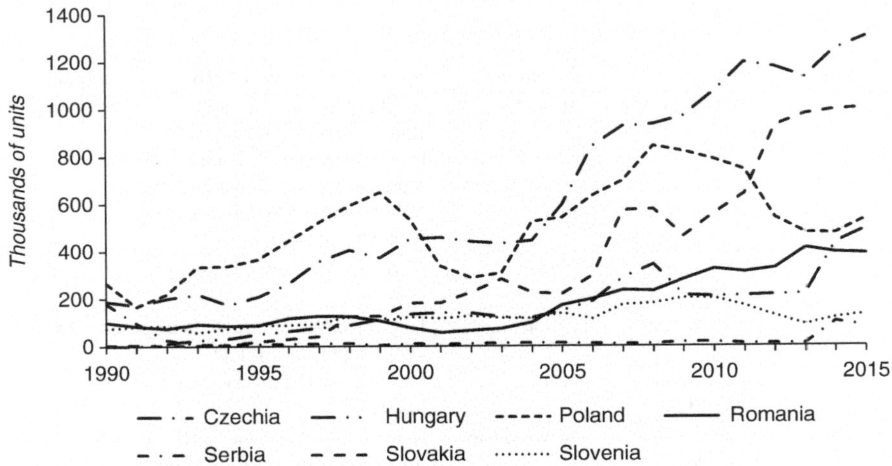

Fig. 1.4 Car production trends in ECE countries. *Source*: Based on 1997–2015 data in OICA (2016) and 1990–1996 data from the national statistical offices of individual countries

passenger cars before 1990, the greatest increase between 1990 and 2015 was in Czechia (+591%), followed by Romania (+287%) and Poland (+101%). Additionally, Hungary and Slovakia, which did not produce any passenger cars before 1990, became involved in car assembly in the early 1990s, and their output grew rapidly, with Slovakia becoming the second largest producer in ECE and the country with the largest car production per capita in the world. The production in Slovakia will further increase when Jaguar Land Rover opens its assembly plant in Slovakia in 2018 (see Chap. 6). In Serbia, production collapsed because of the war and economic embargo in the 1990s, and it has not fully recovered since. The growth in ECE passenger car production is projected to continue for the next few years. The existing assembly facilities of many carmakers are being expanded across ECE. The development of the automotive industry since 1990 has created a distinct automotive agglomeration in Central Europe (Fig. 1.5). It covers most of Czechia, western Slovakia, northwestern Hungary, and southwestern Poland and includes 23 vehicle assembly plants, 12 large engine factories and hundreds of other component production sites (Fig. 1.6). Geographic accessibility from Western Europe has been one of the underlying reasons behind the concentration of new plants and the expansion of the existing production facilities in this region.

ECE has two basic roles in the European automotive industry production system (Havas 2000; Pavlínek 2002c; Pavlínek et al. 2009): first and foremost is the high-volume production of standard car models; second is the low-volume assembly of luxury models and other niche market vehicles. Additionally, the ECE automotive industry has served as a testing ground for new production methods, which, if successful, are consequently introduced in core areas of the automotive industry such as Western Europe.

Fig. 1.5 Vehicle assembly plants and engine plants in East-Central Europe

Fig. 1.6 The distribution of vehicle assembly plants, engine plants and principal component suppliers in East-Central Europe

FDI Trends in the ECE Automotive Industry

Based on data from Eurostat, the FDI stock in the automotive industry (NACE 30) stood at €30.8 billion in ECE as of 2014, compared to €10.4 billion in 2003 (Fig. 1.7). Including Fiat's investment in Serbia, the total FDI stock exceeded €32 billion. The highest stocks were in Czechia (€10.6 bn in 2014) and Poland (€10.6 bn in 2015), followed by Hungary (€4.2 bn in 2015), Romania (€3.8 bn in 2015) and Slovakia (€2.9 bn in 2014). Slovenia's stock was €496 million and Bulgaria's €155 million (Fig. 1.8). However, Hungary's stock decreased from €6.5 billion in 2007 to negative €1.7 billion in 2011 partially because a large Audi investment in Hungary was transferred from manufacturing to other services for statistical and accounting purposes (Antalóczy and Sass 2014). Consequently, the real FDI stock in the ECE automotive industry was close to €35 billion in 2015 and significantly more if we include FDI in the closely related supplier industries, such as the production of tires, which are not classified within the narrowly defined automotive industry (NACE 29 and NACE 30). Together, Czechia and Poland attracted more than twice the amount of automotive FDI as the rest of ECE according to official national statistical data. The automotive FDI stock steadily increased between 2003 and 2007. It decreased during and after the 2008–2009 economic crisis, with the lowest point achieved in 2011, only to recover in 2012, suggesting that the negative effects of the economic crisis on FDI were only temporary. However, the FDI data for the entire ECE were affected by large fluctuations in the automotive FDI stock of Hungary. Without Hungary, the rest of the ECE automotive

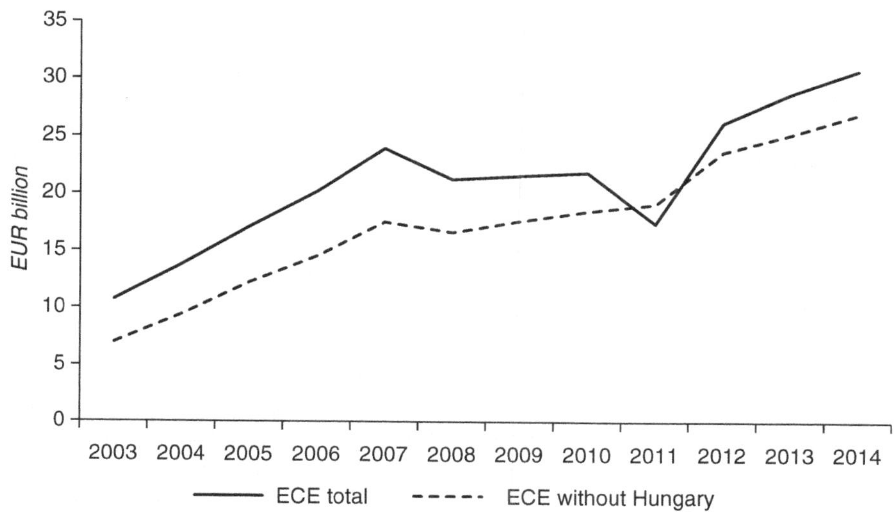

Fig. 1.7 Total automotive (NACE 29 + NACE 30) FDI stock in ECE (Bulgaria, Czechia, Hungary, Poland, Romania, Slovakia, Slovenia) and in ECE excluding Hungary, 2003–2014. *Source*: Based on data from Eurostat (2016) and national statistical offices of individual countries

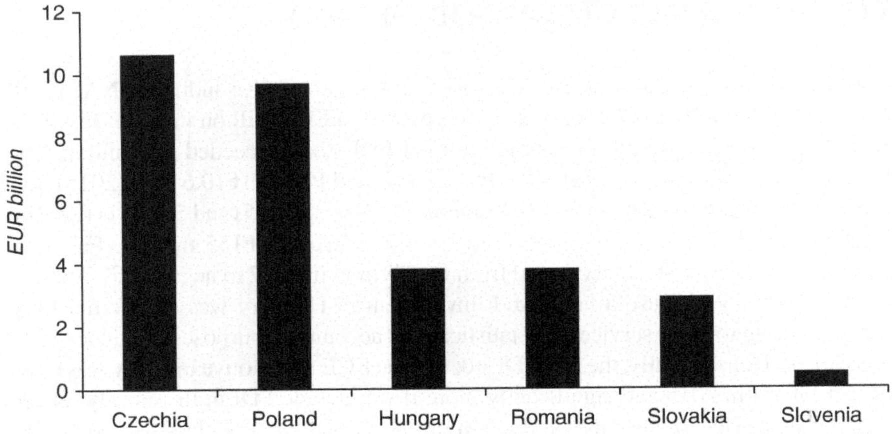

Fig. 1.8 FDI stock in the ECE automotive industry, 2014. *Note*: NACE 30: Manufacture of motor vehicles, trailers, semi-trailers and other transport equipment. *Source:* Based on data from Eurostat (2016)

industry recorded only a slight decrease in total FDI stock in 2008, which recovered in 2009. Overall, however, FDI stock increased more slowly during the 2008–2014 period than between 2003 and 2007 (Fig. 1.7).

Since the early 1990s, ECE countries were generally open to automotive FDI despite differences in national FDI policies (Drahokoupil 2009; Bartlett and Seleny 1998). However, since the late 1990s, ECE countries engaged in competitive bidding for flagship investments (Drahokoupil 2008; Kolesár 2006). Therefore, rather than attributing the leading positions of Czechia, Poland, Hungary and Slovakia to differences in their institutional environment compared to the rest of the region, it can be attributed to their relative geographical location with respect to the European automotive industry core and especially that of Germany. As of 2014, Czechia also had the highest automotive FDI stock per capita (€1012), followed by Slovakia (€536) and Hungary (€384), further underlining the importance of geographic location close to the Western European automotive market for the spatial distribution of large automotive FDI in ECE (Fig. 1.9).

FDI trends in the ECE automotive industry have largely been driven by the investment and location decisions of lead assembly firms (assemblers). These decisions triggered investment waves of their principal suppliers who followed them into ECE to meet the co-location requirements of modular production through follow sourcing (Sturgeon and Lester 2004; Frigant and Lung 2002; Pavlínek and Janák 2007). The construction of greenfield assembly plants began in the early 1990s in ECE but peaked in the 2000s before and shortly after EU accession. The establishment of new foreign-owned supplier factories peaked in 2004, though has since substantially declined, especially during and after the 2008–2009 economic crisis (Fig. 1.10). After 2009, automotive investment in ECE continued at a much

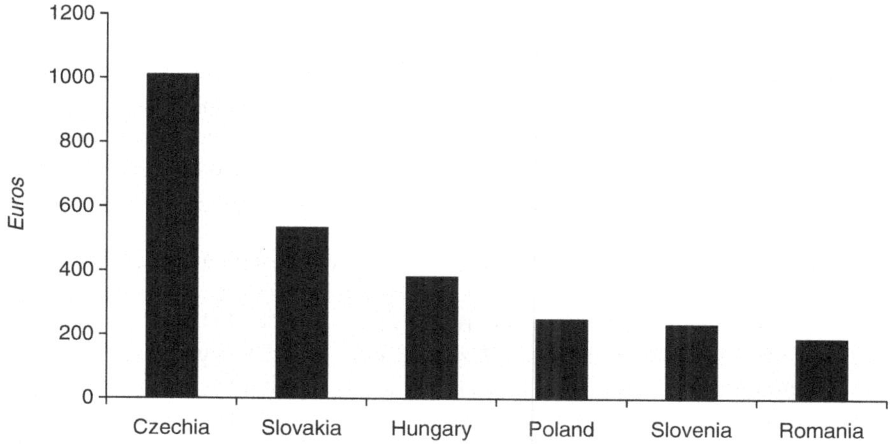

Fig. 1.9 Automotive FDI stock per capita (NACE 30) in ECE in 2014. *Source:* Based on data from the national banks of individual countries

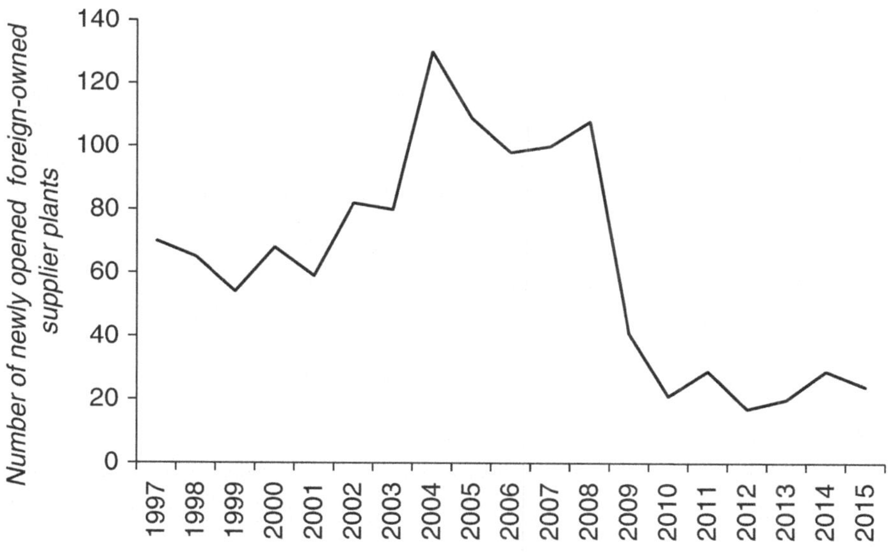

Fig. 1.10 The number of newly built foreign-owned supplier factories in ECE, 1997–2015. *Source*: Based on data from EY (2010), ERM (2016)

lower level than in the first half of the 2000s, with especially Western European investment declining well into 2013. Ernst and Young (EY 2014, p. 50) talk about "the end of the Central and Eastern European "miracle"". It is reasonable to assume that, at least for the time being, the period of rapid expansion of the automotive industry in ECE is over. We should not expect any new waves of greenfield assembly plant construction in ECE on the scale of the 2000s and associated investment waves in the automotive components industry in the foreseeable future, despite the 2015 decision of Jaguar Land Rover to build a new assembly factory in Slovakia. Instead, we should expect the consolidation of existing investments and, in some cases, their gradual expansion. Investment in the components industry is likely to continue at significantly lower levels than in the early 2000s and the period prior to the 2008–2009 economic crisis since automotive supplier networks are now already established in ECE.

To illustrate these trends in a national context, I will briefly analyze FDI trends in the ECE automotive industry, looking at the total FDI stock in the automotive industry of individual ECE countries. Based on automotive FDI, we can classify ECE countries into three categories. Czechia, Poland and Hungary form the first group, typified by the highest FDI stock in the automotive industry (Fig. 1.8). These three countries have benefited from their geographic proximity to Western Europe and especially Germany, low wages, FDI-friendly policies and industrial tradition. The second group includes Slovakia and Romania with lower automotive FDI stock than the first group, although Slovakia has the second highest FDI stock per capita in the entire ECE (Fig. 1.9). Compared to the first group, Slovakia and Romania are latecomers that were not very successful in attracting large FDI inflows in their automotive industries in the 1990s but experienced rapid FDI growth in the 2000s because of their EU membership, FDI-friendly policies and lower wages than the first group (Pavlínek 2016). Finally, Slovenia, Serbia and Bulgaria form the third group, typified by low levels of automotive FDI compared to the first two groups. Relatively high wages compared to the rest of ECE and the country's small size explain the relatively low FDI stock and low FDI per capita in the Slovenian automotive industry. In the case of Serbia, the main reason for low levels of automotive FDI is related to its delayed economic liberalization and opening to FDI compared to the rest of ECE because of the war and economic sanctions in the 1990s. Throughout the 2000s, all ECE countries fiercely competed for new automotive FDI projects, offering large incentives, low taxes and other FDI-friendly policies (Pavlínek 2016; Drahokoupil 2009; see Chap. 6). National automotive FDI accounts illustrate that ECE continues to be attractive for automotive FDI after the 2008–2009 economic crisis, which is now mainly directed at expanding existing FDI projects. At the same time, parts of ECE, especially in Central Europe, have become less competitive in the most labor-intensive low-skill automotive assembly, such as the assembly of cable harnesses, because of rising wages, leading to the relocation of these manufacturing activities to cheaper locations such as Romania or North Africa (Pavlínek 2015). This underscores the importance of low wages for the future competitiveness of automotive manufacturing in ECE. The national level analysis also underscores the uneven nature of FDI inflows, contributing to the uneven development of the automotive industry and the uneven effects of the 2008–2009 economic crisis.

It is important to note that the following analysis has been negatively affected by the uneven quality and availability of statistical data provided by the national banks of individual ECE countries and by Eurostat, making the compilation of longer-

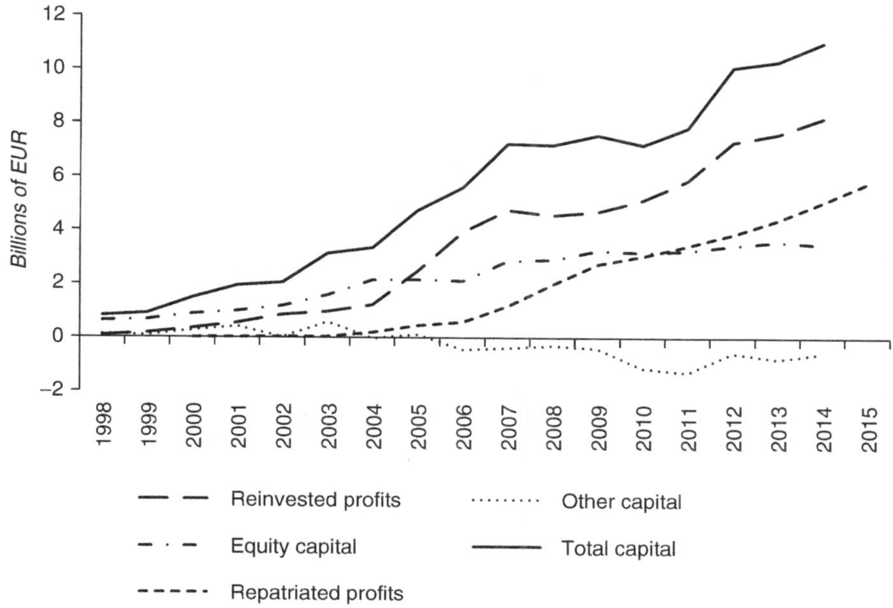

Fig. 1.11 FDI stock (1998–2014) and the stock of dividends transferred abroad (2000–2015) in the Czech automotive industry (NACE 29). *Source*: Based on data from CNB (2001–2016)

term trends and reliable international comparisons difficult, if not impossible. The quality of FDI data from ECE national banks was crosschecked against the Eurostat FDI database and found to be compatible. In the case of Czechia, Hungary, Slovakia and Slovenia, the definition of FDI is in line with IMF recommendations (BPM5). The Polish and Romanian methodologies also observe the 10% ownership criterion for defining FDI and record FDI flows on a directional basis. Poland also observes reverse capital investments.

Czechia

At €10.6 billion, Czechia had the ECE's highest FDI stock in the automotive industry (NACE 29 & 30: Manufacture of motor vehicles, trailers, semi-trailers and of other transport equipment) along with Poland as of 2014. The period between 1991 and 1998 was dominated by the Volkswagen (VW) investment in Škoda Auto and the related foreign takeovers of Czech automotive suppliers and new FDI greenfield projects by foreign suppliers of Škoda Auto (Pavlínek 2008; Pavlínek and Janák 2007). Automotive FDI stock increased steadily between 1998 and 2014 from €0.8 billion after the Czech government introduced a system of investment incentives in April 1998 (Pavlínek 2002b; Drahokoupil 2009) (Fig. 1.11). The fastest increase took place between 2003

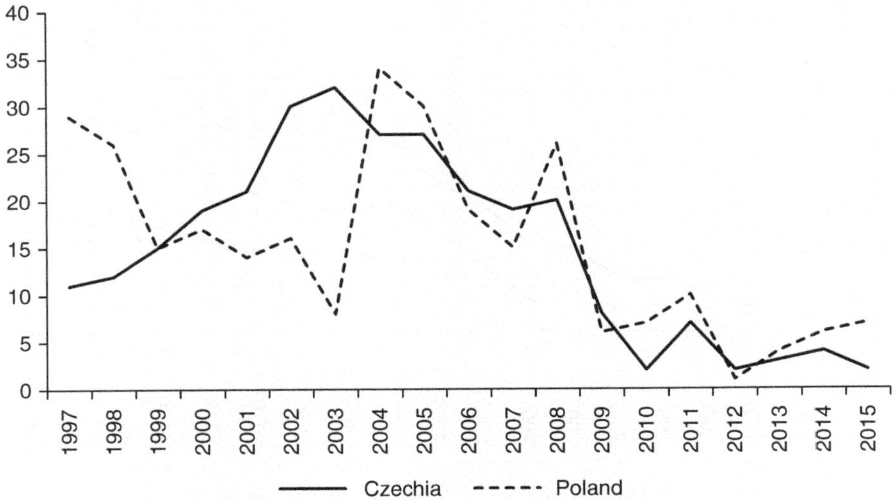

Fig. 1.12 The number of newly built FDI-based supplier factories in Czechia and Poland, 1997–2015. *Source*: Based on data from EY (2010) (1997–2009), ERM (2016) (2010–2015)

and 2007, with TPCA and Hyundai investing in new greenfield assembly plants and their principal Japanese and South Korean suppliers following suit (see Chap. 2 for details). FDI inflows stagnated during the economic crisis. Reinvested profits have been the most important source of new FDI. At the same time, however, the outflow of profits in the form of dividends transferred abroad has been steadily increasing since 2000, peaking in the economic crisis at €813 million in 2008. Between 2000 and 2014, EUR 5.8 bn were transferred abroad from the Czech automotive industry in the form of dividends paid to foreign parent companies (Fig. 1.11) (CNB 2001–2016). These general trends are also supported by data on new investments in the supplier sector. The post-1997 steady increase in the number of new supplier factories peaked in 2003, collapsed during the 2008–2009 economic crisis and did not fully recover after 2010 (Fig. 1.12). A 2009 survey of 263 companies in the broadly defined Czech automotive industry conducted by the author suggested that more than half of the surveyed companies (149 companies or 56.7%) stopped or postponed their investment plans because of the economic crisis. Among the 98 foreign companies that answered the question, the share of companies postponing their investments because of the economic crisis was 55.1%.

The effects of the economic crisis in the Czech automotive industry were significant, with the broadly defined automotive industry shedding 10% of its workers (Pavlínek and Ženka 2010; Pavlínek 2015). These job losses affected the whole industry, hitting both foreign and domestic companies regardless of their position in the automotive value chain. Of the 15 bankruptcies, plant closures and relocations during and immediately after the economic crisis, nine involved foreign-owned component suppliers (Pavlínek 2015, see Chap. 2 for details). 9187 jobs were lost, 8037 (87.5%) of which were in these nine companies. Given a more than 90% share of foreign companies in Czech automotive turnover and value added (Pavlínek and Žížalová 2016), foreign companies were not affected more by job losses than domestic companies.

The three largest job losses were in U.S.-owned companies. The largest was caused by Delphi Packard, a manufacturer of cable harnesses, relocating from Česká Lípa to the Romanian town of Sânnicolau Mare. Delphi Packard employed 3400 workers in Česká Lípa before the crisis in 2007 but began shedding workers in 2008. Then, in August 2010, it was decided the factory would close in May 2011. The remaining 1400 jobs were lost. Delphi Packard now supplies cable harnesses to Škoda Auto from Romania (interview on June 13, 2011). The company attributed its decision to close the plant and relocate production to high production costs, intense competition and terminated contracts with Audi and BMW. The second largest job loss was related to the relocation of AEES Czech Platinum Equity (previously Alcoa Fujikura), also a manufacturer of cable harnesses, to Romania due to lower labor costs in 2009. The plant, which employed 2200 workers in 2007, began to dismiss workers in 2008 because of lower demand for its cable harnesses from Škoda Auto. The factory was closed in 2009, shedding its remaining 733 workers (ERM 2016). The third largest job loss of 980 jobs involved the 2008 closure of a subsidiary of the US automotive sealing systems producer Henniges Automotive located in Ostrava.

Czechia continues to benefit from its geographic proximity to Germany, significantly lower labor costs than in Western Europe, a well-developed supplier base and increasing agglomeration economies. These factors are expected to contribute to the expansion of existing factories in the form of reinvested profits and attract additional FDI in the supplier sector in the foreseeable future. The latest major expansion was announced in March 2014 when VW, following a VW-wide competition, decided that a new large Škoda SUV (the Kodiaq) would be produced in Czechia. Škoda Auto invested €450 million in expanding its Kvasiny assembly plant in eastern Bohemia, creating 1500 jobs and attracting new component suppliers. The June 2014 decision by Nexen, a South Korean tire producer, to build its €829 million tire factory in Czechia (near the town of Žatec) represents the largest greenfield investment in the Czech automotive industry after the economic crisis and the third largest foreign investment in the country since 1993. Nexen's location decision suggests that Czechia continues to be attractive for new large FDI projects by global automotive suppliers.

Poland

As of 2014, Poland's total FDI stock in the broadly defined automotive industry (NACE 29 & 30) stood at €11.3 billion (€9.6 bn in NACE 29). Similarly to Czechia, Poland has benefitted from its geographic proximity to Germany and substantially lower labor costs (Pavlínek 2006). Between 1996 and 2015, annual inflows of FDI in the automotive industry were volatile and strongly affected by business cycles

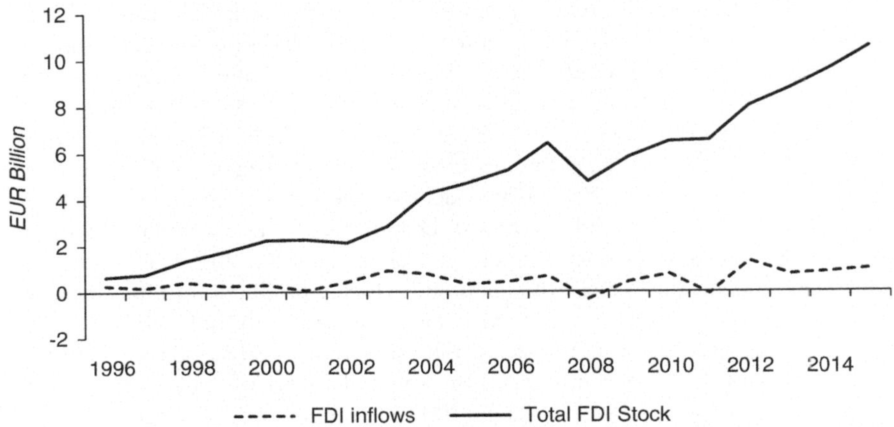

Fig. 1.13 FDI inflows and FDI stock in the Polish automotive industry (NACE 29), 1996–2015. *Source*: Based on data from NBP (2016) and Eurostat (2016)

and large investment projects. The greatest decrease in FDI inflows and FDI stock was recorded during the 2008–2009 economic crisis, with the FDI stock decreasing by more than €1.6 billion in 2008. The country recorded negative FDI inflows (minus €325 million), negative reinvested earnings (minus €213 million), a decrease in equity capital (by €68 million). After negative FDI inflows in 2011, the Polish automotive industry received record inflows of €1.3 billion in 2012 and FDI inflows and stocks continued to grow rapidly between 2012 and 2015 (Fig. 1.13). The number of newly built foreign components plants was similarly volatile (Fig. 1.12), peaking in 2004 at 34 and again in 2008 at 26. The lowest point was reached in 2012 and 2013 with one and four respectively (PIFIA 2013; EY 2010; ERM 2016).

Given the size of its automotive sector, the number of bankruptcies, closures, and relocations was low in Poland during the economic crisis. The most important examples of bankruptcies and closures included Toora Poland, which went bankrupt in 2008 (260 jobs lost); the International Automotive Components Group (IAC), which closed down its factory in Teresin and laid off 240 workers in 2009; and Leoni, which closed its Ostrzeszów factory and dismissed 500 workers in 2010. Only two important relocations took place during the economic crisis. Takata Petri closed down its Wałbrzych factory and relocated its production to Romania in 2009 (500 jobs lost) and Remy International relocated production from its Świdnica factory to Hungary and to its other facilities in Poland (200 jobs lost) in 2009 (ERM 2016).

Total vehicle output decreased in Poland by 38% between 2008 and 2013 (from 951 thousand units to 583 thousand units), mainly due to a 43.6% decrease in the output of cars (from 842 thousand to 475 thousand units), affecting all manufacturers in Poland (Fiat, GM Opel and FSO). At the same time, the output of commercial vehicles increased by 10.8% (11,200 units). After 2013, the total vehicle output started to recover and reached 661 thousand vehicles in 2015, of which 535 thousand were cars (OICA 2016). Poland has a more diversified automotive industry than its Central European neighbors. For example, compared to Czechia, Hungary, Slovakia and Romania, Poland is a major producer of commercial vehicles (126 thousand units in 2015, compared to 5367 in Czechia, 3650 in Hungary, zero in Slovakia and six in Romania). Compared to other ECE countries, Poland also relies more on the supplier sector than on vehicle assembly. This sector accounted for 60% of its automotive industry output and 43% of its exports in 2012, and 16 of the 40 engine factories of ECE, Russia, Ukraine and Belarus are located in Poland (PIFIA 2013).

In 2014, VW chose the Polish town of Września near Poznań for its new commercial vehicle factory, which will further strengthen Poland's specialization in the assembly of commercial vehicles and attract additional component suppliers to Poland. The VW investment is worth more than €800 million. Production started in the second half of 2016 and the planned annual production capacity of 100 thousand vehicles should be reached in 2019. In 2016, Daimler announced that it would build a €500 m engine factory in Jawor, while Toyota a $150 m transmission factory in Walbrzych that will produce transmissions for hybrid cars. The Polish automotive industry has overcome the economic crisis and is set to grow strongly in the near future based on the rebound in FDI inflows that will likely continue in the near future due to strong competitive advantages of Poland: its geographic location next to Germany, low labor costs, skilled labor, and a large domestic market.

Hungary

Hungary was the first ECE country to attract a foreign greenfield car assembly plant in 1990 (Suzuki), followed by Audi in 1994 and Mercedes-Benz in 2008. The country has become a favorite location for foreign automotive companies because of the presence of factors similar to those in the rest of ECE. In particular, the combination of its geographic proximity to Western Europe and low labor costs together with other factors such as investment incentives and flexible labor laws have attracted large automotive FDI. Automotive FDI stock increased rapidly before the 2008–2009 economic crisis from €866 million in 1998 to €6.4 billion in 2007. After 2007, however, FDI stock declined to minus €1.7 billion in 2011 before recovering to €2.5 billion in 2012 and €4.1 billion in 2015 (Fig. 1.14). According to data from the Central Bank of Hungary (CBH 2014), the automotive industry experienced a negative inflow of €7.8 billion in 2011 followed by an inflow of €4 billion in 2012. These unusual swings in the statistically reported automotive FDI stock and FDI inflows are difficult to interpret but they obviously have little in common with the actual situation because Hungary did not experience any such dramatic disinvestment in its automotive industry. On the contrary, over €4 billion were invested in the Hungarian automotive industry by foreign companies between 2009 and 2013 (CTCS 2014). This would suggest that the actual FDI stock in the Hungarian automotive industry is more than €10 billion, i.e. at a similar level as Czechia and Poland. As noted

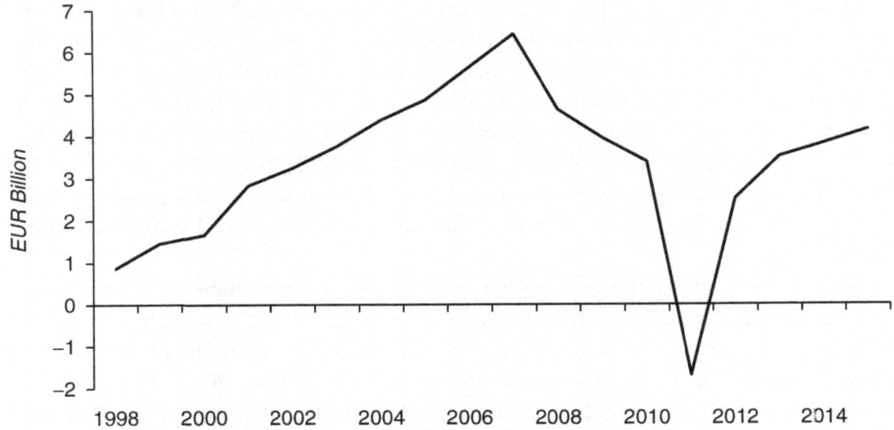

Fig. 1.14 FDI stock in the Hungarian automotive industry (NACE 29), 1998–2015. *Source*: Based on data from CBH (2016) and Eurostat (2016)

previously, about half of the dramatic decline in the FDI stock is attributable to the transfer of Audi's large FDI stock in Hungary (Audi alone has invested €8.14 bn in its factory in Györ since 1993) from manufacturing to other services in the form of a Hungary-based foreign-owned holding company established by Audi in 2011 (Antalóczy and Sass 2014).

The greatest job losses attributable to the 2008–2009 economic crisis took place in 2010 (Boros 2013) as automotive industry sales decreased on average by 30–40% (Antalóczy and Sass 2011) and the output of cars fell by 39% between 2008 and 2010 (from 342,359 units in 2008 to 205,571 in 2010 (OICA 2016). For example, Dräxlmaier laid off 450 workers in Mór, Denso cut 800 jobs in Székesfehérvár and Tyco Electronics 330 jobs in Esztergom. As in other ECE countries, Hungary has been increasingly threatened by the relocation of labor-intensive parts of the automotive value chain abroad. In 2012, for example, Remy Automotive Hungary relocated its production from Mezőkövesd to China, South Korea and Mexico (200 jobs were lost) and Car-Inside closed two factories in Jánosháza and Lenti and relocated their production to Bosnia-Herzegovina, resulting in 300 layoffs (ERM 2016). However, the number of relocations from Hungary has so far been low in the automotive industry. Sass and Hunya (2014) identified only four relocations between 2003 and 2011, significantly less than in the case of Czechia and Slovakia (Pavlínek 2015). At the same time, there have been over 60 relocations to Hungary from abroad in the automotive industry (Sass and Hunya 2014), although the 2007–2009 economic crisis saw a sharp decline in the number of newly built supplier factories by foreign companies (Fig. 1.15). The Michelin plant in Budapest closed in 2015 (ERM 2016).

Several large projects account for a high share of the large automotive FDI inflows after the 2008–2009 economic crisis. Mercedes-Benz's investment in its new assembly plant at Kecskemét (€800 million) was completed in 2012 and attracted 30–40 foreign suppliers to set up new factories supplying its production from Hungary. Examples

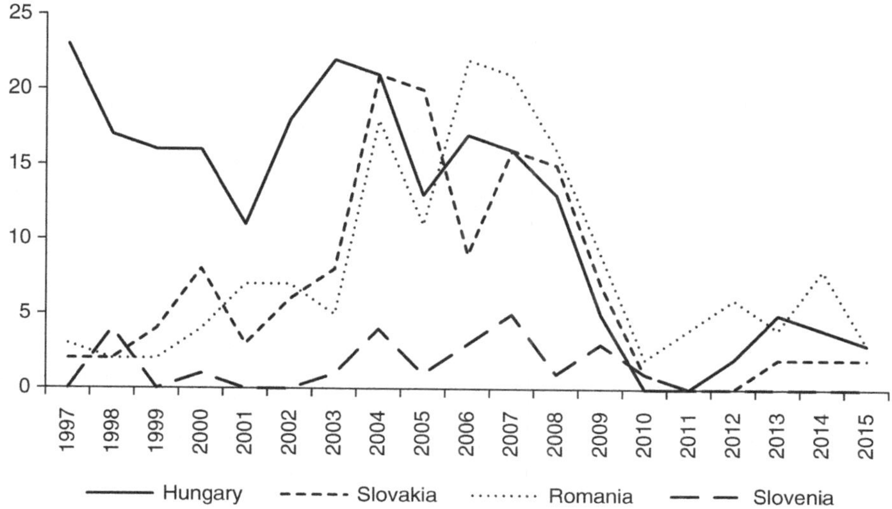

Fig. 1.15 The number of newly built FDI-based supplier factories in Hungary, Romania, Slovakia and Slovenia, 1997–2015. *Source*: Based on data from EY (2010) (1997–2009), ERM (2016) (2010–2015)

include Johnson Controls, Brose, Knorr-Bremse, Siemens, Magna, Dürr and Kuka. Ten of these suppliers are located within the Mercedes-Benz production complex at Kecskemét. In 2016, Mercedes-Benz announced that it would build a second factory in Kecskemét by 2020, investing an additional €1 billion and creating 2500 jobs. In addition to Mercedes-Benz and its suppliers, Hungary attracted several large automotive FDIs after the economic crisis, including major expansion projects by Opel, Audi and Hankook Tire. Opel invested €500 million in expanding its engine factory in Szentgotthárd, completed at the end of 2012. Opel also announced an additional €130 million expansion of its plant in 2013. In 2013, Audi completed a €900 million expansion of its vehicle assembly plant in Győr and is moving production of its Q3 compact crossover there from Spain, while Hankook Tire announced a €306 million expansion of its factory in Rácalmás in 2014.

These automotive investments suggest that Hungary has been more successful than all other ECE countries in attracting large volumes of automotive FDI after the 2008–2009 economic crisis. It is very likely that this success is, at least partially, related to the continuing low wages in the Hungarian automotive industry (Fig. 1.16). The Hungarian Forint was significantly devalued during the economic crisis, lowering Hungarian wages and making Hungary more attractive in the eyes of foreign investors. Compared to Poland, Hungary has a less militant labor force and better infrastructure. As with other ECE countries, Hungary has also vigorously competed for new FDI, offering attractive investment incentives. All these factors mean that Hungary will continue to be a very attractive location for automotive FDI in the foreseeable future as well.

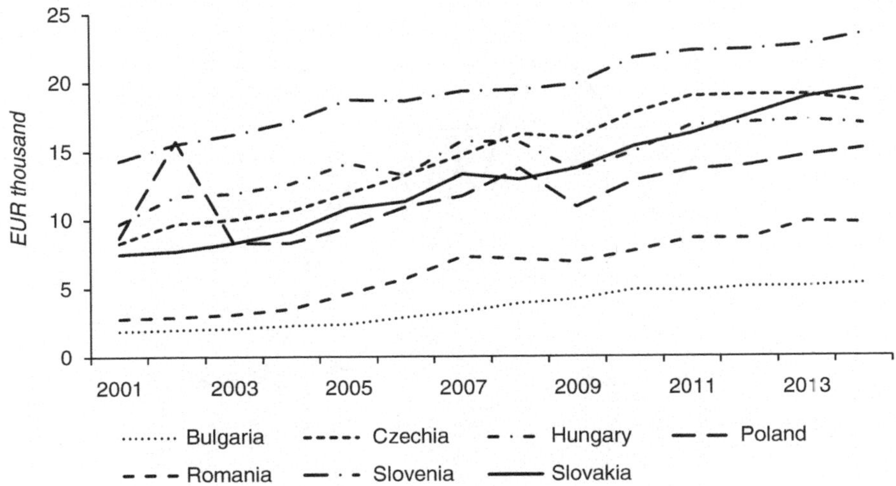

Fig. 1.16 Average personnel costs (personnel costs per employee per year) in the automotive industry (NACE 29) 2001–2014. *Source*: Based on data from Eurostat (2016)

Slovakia

Compared to the 1990s, Slovakia experienced a rapid increase in automotive FDI after 2000 by attracting greenfield assembly factories of PSA Peugeot Citroën to Trnava, Kia to Žilina and, most recently, Jaguar Land Rover to Nitra. These new assembly operations attracted large FDI by principal component suppliers. Additionally, VW substantially expanded its production in Slovakia after 2000, attracting a number of its most important suppliers as well (Pavlínek 2015, 2016). The number of new FDI projects in the supplier industry sharply increased in the early 2000s, peaking in 2004 and 2005 (Fig. 1.15). Automotive FDI stock increased from €448 million in 2003 to €3 billion in 2008 before declining to €2.4 billion in 2013 and recovering to €2.9 billion in 2014 (Fig. 1.17). This rapid increase in FDI inflows in the automotive industry was the outcome of policy changes in the late 1990s and early 2000s, which significantly increased the country's attractiveness in the eyes of foreign TNCs (see Chap. 6 for details). As a result of large FDI inflows, car production increased from 3453 units in 1990 to 180,706 units in 2000, 556,941 units in 2010 and one million in 2015 (OICA 2016; ZAP 2000). Consequently, Slovakia now has the largest per capita vehicle production in the entire world and is the second largest producer of cars in ECE after Czechia (Fig. 1.4).

The 2008–2009 economic crisis led to a 19.2% decrease in the output of cars and decreasing output in the entire supplier industry. FDI inflows slowed and the FDI stock declined. There were 13 bankruptcies, plant closures and relocations abroad in the Slovak automotive industry during and immediately after the economic crisis. Nine of these involved the labor-intensive assembly of cable harnesses, an area

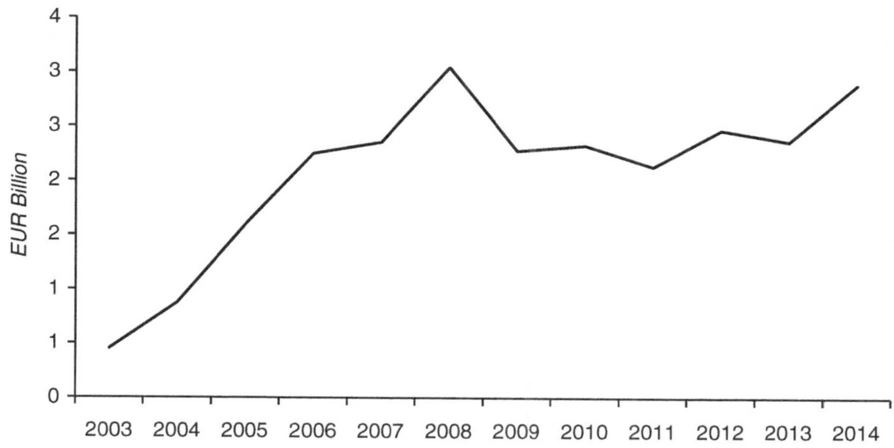

Fig. 1.17 FDI stock in the Slovak automotive industry, 2003–2014. *Source*: Based on data from NBS (2016) and Eurostat (2016)

especially sensitive to labor costs. For example, Delphi eliminated 1900 jobs in Senica between 2006 and 2010 and relocated the assembly of cable harnesses to Romania, Tunisia and Turkey between 2007 and 2011 (interview on June 13, 2011, Pavlínek 2015). In the wake of the economic crisis, Delphi created only 250 new jobs in Senica between 2012 and 2014 (ERM 2016). The second largest job loss in Slovakia was associated with the closure of Yazaki Slovakia in Prievidza in western Slovakia in 2010. At the time of its closure, the Japanese assembler of cable harnesses employed 1211 workers. Molex Slovakia closed its factory and eliminated 1000 jobs at Kechnec in eastern Slovakia in 2010, transferring cable harness production to its Chinese subsidiary. Similarly, the bankruptcy of Jas Elmont, a Slovak producer of cable harnesses located in Snina in eastern Slovakia, resulted in 1000 layoffs.

By 2011 the total output of the automotive industry had recovered to pre-crisis levels, with large production increases being recorded in 2012 and 2013 due to a major expansion of production at VW Slovakia and due to PSA and Kia each reaching full production capacity of 300,000 vehicles per year. In 2009, VW Slovakia won the VW concern-wide competition to assemble the smallest VW car (the VW Up!, Škoda Citigo and Seat Mii), launched in 2011. VW invested €308 m to increase the production capacity of VW Slovakia to 400,000 units, adding 1500 jobs and doubling its output (419,888 cars in 2012 and 397,458 in 2015 compared to 210,441 in 2011 and 104,300 in 2009) (VW 2016). A new €600 m welding plant was built in 2013 and VW Slovakia announced an additional €500 m investment in its Bratislava plant in January 2015 aimed at expanding the welding plant to produce bodies for the Bentley Bentayga SUV and Porsche Cayenne, and building a new assembly plant for Porsche Cayenne, which will add an additional 1000 jobs. Starting in 2017, the Cayenne will be completely assembled in Slovakia. VW invested almost €1.5 bn in Slovakia between 2012 and 2016 alone and the total 1991–2016 investment exceeded €2.5 bn.

However, based on the analysis of business announcements of new investments and the expansion of production in the Slovak automotive industry, FDI in the supplier industry did not pick up until 2013, with the lowest point reached in 2012. In 2014 and 2015, four new greenfield factories were announced by component suppliers while there were only three between 2010 and 2013 (ERM 2016; Fig. 1.15). The vast majority of new FDI is now flowing into the expansion of production, rather than the greenfield factories characteristic of the early- and mid-2000s. However, this situation is bound to change with the construction of the new assembly facility by Jaguar Land Rover to Nitra, which will attract the most important component suppliers of Jaguar Land Rover to the proximity of its plant.

As with other ECE countries, Slovakia will continue to benefit from its geographic proximity to Germany and the rest of the Western European automotive industry core, backed by its low wages and the aggressive investment promotion policy of the Slovak government. Compared to Czechia, Hungary and Poland, Slovakia has a distinct advantage in using the Euro, thereby eliminating currency exchange risks, something highly valued by foreign investors (2011–2015 interviews). However, as the Czech, Hungarian and Polish currencies devalued during and after the economic crisis, relative labor costs increased in Slovakia since it did not benefit from devaluation. While Slovakia had the lowest labor costs in the automotive industry Central Europe in the late 1990s and early 2000s, by 2014 its wages surpassed those of Hungary, Poland and Czechia (Fig. 1.16). It remains to be seen what effect this change will have on future inflows of FDI, though it is safe to conclude that Slovakia will be less competitive in attracting labor-intensive automotive production based on low labor costs than it was in the 2000s.

Romania

Romania's automotive FDI remained limited until the late 1990s despite selling 51% of the shares of Automobile Craiova to Daewoo (South Korea) in 1994. The purchase of Dacia by Renault in September 1999 and the subsequent development of Dacia as Renault's global low-cost brand in the 2000s transformed the Romanian automotive industry. This purchase was followed by a wave of investments by Renault's principal suppliers, peaking in 2006 and 2007 before the economic crisis (Fig. 1.15). Examples include Auto Chassis International, Valeo, Euro APS, Johnson Controls, Autoliv, Inergy, Euralcom, Michelin and Continental. By 2014, Renault had invested €2.2 billion in Dacia (Gillet 2014).

As opposed to Renault, Daewoo never achieved its ambitious plans in Craiova and declared bankruptcy in 1998, leaving the Craiova factory in limbo until 2006 when it was repurchased by the Romanian government. One year later, the government sold its 72.4% stake to Ford for €57 million. Ford promised to invest €869 million with the aim of producing 300,000 cars and 300,000 engines in the Craiova factory annually in exchange for state aid of €75 million (Lupu 2016). The engine plant was opened in 2012. In January 2013, Ford became the sole owner of the

Craiova plant and assumed full management control. It encouraged 40 of its most important European suppliers to set up operations in Romania and about 20 of them signed contracts with Ford. Examples of foreign suppliers which have already set up manufacturing operations in the proximity of the Craiova plant include Johnson Controls, Bamesa, Kirchoff Automotive, Leoni Wiring Systems and Gestamp Automoción.

However, the economic crisis slowed down Ford's progress in Craiova. Instead of mid-2009, assembly did not start until 2012 when only 30,591 B-Max minivans were produced. The expansion of the product portfolio to include a small car planned for 2010 did not materialize. In 2014, Ford produced 52,829 cars and 155,000 engines in Craiova (OICA 2016), well below the plant capacity of 300,000 vehicles. The vehicle output of the Craiova plant will increase after the start of the assembly of the new mini-SUV Ford EcoSport in the Fall of 2017, which should save the Craiova plant. Ford received the extension from the government to reach the originally promised production targets in exchange for state aid until the end of 2025 (Lupu 2016). The company invested €869 million in the Craiova plant between 2008 and 2012 (Butu 2016) and €1 billion by 2016.

Ford has been using its Craiova plant to extract concessions from workers in its other European plants by threatening to move production there. In 2014, for example, workers in Ford's Cologne plant agreed to a more flexible shift system and working hours after the company threatened to move production of its Fiesta model to Romania (Henning 2014). Workers' concessions in Cologne amount to USD 400 million in savings over the period 2017–2021 (ANE 2014). Despite low wages, Romania itself has not been spared of relocation threats by automotive lead firms. For example, because of rapidly rising wages at Dacia following the 2008 strike, Renault has repeatedly threatened to move production to Morocco where it started assembly of Dacia cars in a new factory in 2012. The average monthly salary at the Dacia Mioveni factory in Romania was about €900 in 2014 (€950 including bonuses) compared to €285 in early 2008 before the strike. This 170% increase between 2008 and 2014 compares with a 30% increase in inflation over the same period (Rosemain and Timu 2014). In 2016, Renault acted on its relocation threats and announced that starting in 2017, "some" production of the Dacia Logan MCV station wagon would be relocated from Romania to Morocco in 2017, citing the lack of capacity in the Pitesti plant (Ilie and Frost 2016).

The automotive FDI stock in Romania increased from €416 million in 2003 to €3.8 billion in 2015 (Eurostat 2016; NBR 2016; Fig. 1.18). Between 1997 and 2015, 154 new supplier plants were built in Romania (EY 2010; ERM 2016). The greatest increase took place before the economic crisis in 2006 and 2007. As in other ECE countries, there was a sharp decrease in the number of newly built supplier plants in 2008 and 2009 (Fig. 1.15). However, Romania continues to be attractive for relocations from other countries, including Central Europe. It benefits from EU membership and low wages. The 2014 average personnel costs per employee in the automotive industry were 87% lower in Romania than in Germany compared to 74% lower wages in Slovakia than in Germany, 75% in Czechia, 77% in Hungary and 79% in Poland (Eurostat 2016; Fig. 1.16). Not surprisingly, Romania attracted

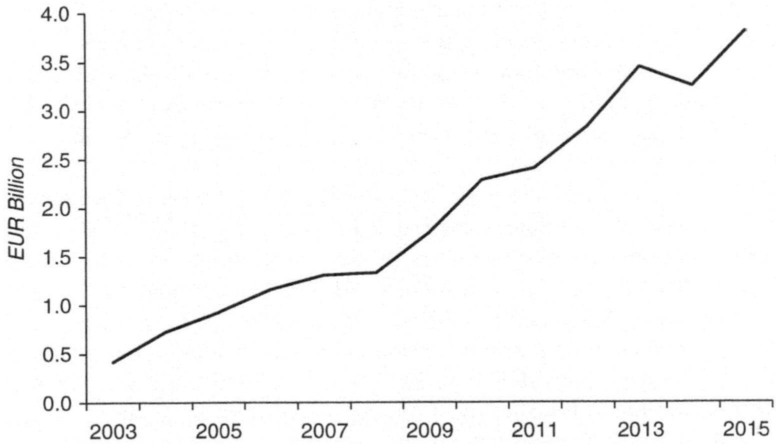

Fig. 1.18 FDI stock in the Romanian automotive industry, 2003–2015. *Source*: Based on data from NBR (2016) and Eurostat (2016)

by far the largest number (27) of new foreign-owned supplier plants among ECE countries between 2010 and 2015. Including 33 expansions of production, foreign firms pledged to create 29,106 new jobs in the automotive industry during this period (ERM 2016).

Despite production cuts and layoffs, Romania did not experience any relocations abroad, bankruptcies or closures in its automotive industry during and after the 2008–2009 economic crisis (ERM 2016). Instead, it benefited from relocations from other countries during this period. The prospects for further FDI in the Romanian automotive industry are very good because Romanian manufacturing wages continue to be almost 90% lower than in Germany and are also significantly lower than those in Central Europe. Romania will also continue to benefit from its EU membership. The poor quality of infrastructure in Romania has been the most significant obstacle for TNCs to fully exploit Romania's low wages and EU membership.

Slovenia

At €471 million as of 2015, Slovenia had the lowest automotive FDI stock of ECE countries with car assembly plants (Fig. 1.8). FDI stock in the automotive industry increased rapidly in the early 2000s before the 2007–2008 economic crisis, peaking in 2008 before declining by 38% in 2009 and 2010. Recovery began in 2011, peaking in 2013 and 2014 with the highest annual FDI inflows in the automotive industry since the early 1990s (Fig. 1.19).

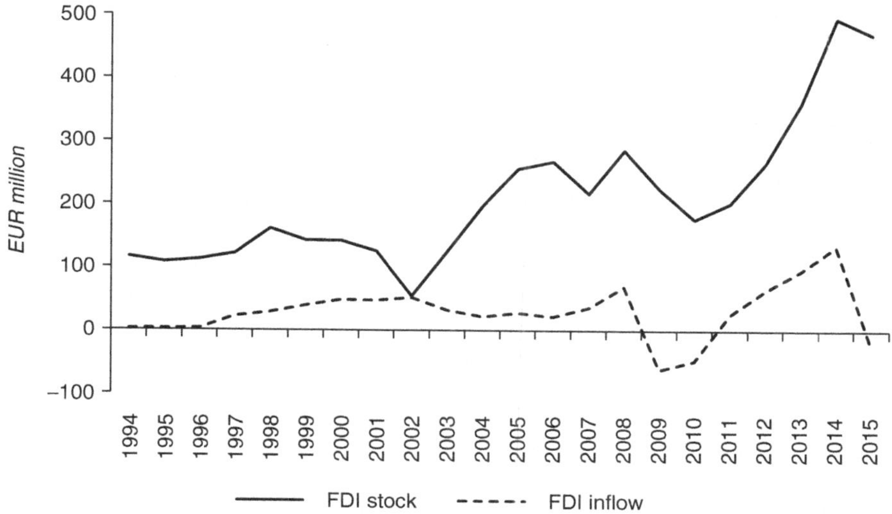

Fig. 1.19 FDI stock and FDI inflows in the Slovenian automotive industry (1994–2015). *Source*: Based on data from BS (2016) and Eurostat (2016)

Slovenia has only one car assembly plant (Revoz), located in Novo Mesto. Renault has been the majority shareholder of Revoz since 1991 and its sole owner since 2004. The assembly plant has an annual capacity of 220,000 units but has not been working at full capacity for many years. Its production peaked in the aftermath of the economic crisis in 2009 (202,570 units) and 2010 (201,039 units) as sales of small cars were boosted by government scrappage schemes introduced in France and other Western European countries in 2009 (OICA 2016; Stanford 2010; Pavlínek 2015). After 2010, the output declined to 93,700 vehicles in 2013 after which it started to recover. In 2015, 133,092 vehicles were assembled and a similar output was expected in 2016 (Fig. 1.4).

As in other ECE countries, Slovenia's automotive industry was hit by the 2008–2009 economic crisis, resulting in significant job losses. During and after the economic crisis, five automotive supplier plants, two of them Slovenian-owned, were closed between 2007 and 2014 with a total job loss of 1343. Two suppliers produced car seat covers and one made leather products for the automotive industry, suggesting a vulnerability of labor-intensive production in Slovenia to closure and relocation (ERM 2016). For example, Siemens closed its Transportation Systems factory in Maribor in 2009, laying off all 322 workers.

As of 2016, Renault invested €900 million in the Revoz assembly plant to assemble small Renault cars, such as the Clio and Twingo (STA 2016). Renault invested €150 million in 2013 and 2014 alone to launch production of the new Twingo and the four-seat Smart (Smart Forfour), a city car co-produced by Renault-Nissan and Daimler. It was supported by €22 million in state aid. Production was upgraded and expanded by about 25% from slightly over 600 cars a day to around 800 in December

2014. This production increase created about 450 new jobs in 2014 in addition to the 270 jobs created between March and June 2013 (STA 2014). However, in 2011 and 2012, 850 jobs were eliminated at Revoz and 600 jobs were cut in 2015 because of lower than expected demand for the Twingo and Smart Forfour (ERM 2016). Revoz employed 2100 workers in 2016. Only about 30% of the components for the Twingo are made in Slovenia, a percentage lower than that of large-volume assembly plants across ECE. This suggests that because of its low-volume production, the Revoz assembly plant has attracted fewer foreign component suppliers to Slovenia than other car assembly plants across ECE. Between 1997 and 2009 there were 23 investments in new automotive suppliers plants, less than 10% of the number of investments attracted by Czechia and Poland and also substantially less than the numbers of suppliers attracted to Slovakia and Hungary (Fig. 1.14). The assembly of the new Clio 4 will be launched in February 2017, which should boost the annual output of the factory to between 180,000 and 190,000 vehicles and increase employment by 300 to 500 workers (STA 2016).

Compared to other ECE countries, no new supplier factories have been built in Slovenia after the economic crisis (2010–2015). Slovenia is less attractive as a destination for automotive FDI than other ECE countries for two basic reasons. First, the low-volume production at Revoz makes it more difficult to convince foreign suppliers to co-locate their factories in the proximity of the Revoz plant. Second, relatively high Slovenian wages compared to other ECE countries make Slovenia less attractive as a destination for export-oriented FDI seeking low labor-cost locations. However, in 2016, Magna Steyr, an Austrian contract manufacturer owned by Magna, a Canadian industrial conglomerate, considered Slovenia as a potential location for its new assembly plant. Perhaps the most important reason for considering Slovenia was its geographic proximity to Magna Steyr's Graz plant in Austria, while having average personnel costs per employee in the automotive industry 61% lower than in Austria (Eurostat 2016). The starting wages in Revoz were €910 gross per month at the end of 2016 (STA 2016).

Serbia

Kragujevac-based Zastava was originally set up in 1955 based on a license purchased from Italy's Fiat company in 1953 (Pavlínek 2002a). Zastava closed the car assembly in 2008 after years of low production in the 1990s and 2000s (Fig. 1.4). In 2010, Fiat took over the Kragujevac Zastava plant on establishing the Fiat Automobili Srbija (FAS) (recently renamed to Fiat Chrysler Automobiles Serbia) joint venture between Fiat (67%) and the Serbian government (33%). Under the terms of the agreement, Fiat promised to invest €940 in the modernization of the factory in exchange for heavy subsidies from the Serbian government in the form of investment incentives and tax breaks. By the end of 2014, Fiat had invested €1.05 billion in the construction of a new assembly plant (SIEPA 2014). Despite the new assembly plant opened in April 2012, which assembles the small Fiat 500L model and has an annual capacity of 186,000 vehicles, car assembly remained at a low level in 2012 and 2013. Production increased in 2014 to 103,150 vehicles but declined to 82,630 in 2015 and 85,000 in 2016 (OICA 2016) because of slow sales of the 500L both in Europe and North America. Consequently, FAS employment decreased from 3100 to 2400 in 2016 after FAS canceled the third shift. Hundreds of jobs were also lost in component suppliers.

Low labor costs are FAS's greatest asset, being 80% lower than in Italy and starting at about 30,000 dinars ($360) a month. The average monthly wage of assembly workers was 34,000 dinars ($400) in 2013, a third of what Fiat paid its workers in Poland (Economist 2013). Fiat has attracted a number of foreign suppliers to the vicinity of the FAS plant and it claims that the local content is 67%. More than 60 foreign investors invested around €1.7 billion in the automotive industry as of 2014, including Michelin, Cimos, Bosch, Cooper Tires, Yura, Proma, MagnetiMarelli, Johnson Controls, PKC, Leoni, Draxmaier and Continental. This rapid development has been supported by the generous system of investment incentives from the Serbian government, which can reach 50% of the eligible costs for large companies, 60% for medium-sized companies and 70% for small enterprises (SIEPA 2014).

Future prospects for the development of the automotive industry based on foreign investment are very good. Serbia has a free trade agreement with both the EU and Russia and it is reasonable to expect its EU membership in the foreseeable future since accession negotiations with the EU formally started in January 2014. EU membership will further decrease potential political and economic risks for foreign investors. The country has been heavily investing in transportation infrastructure improvements and its very low labor costs are already attracting export-oriented labor-intensive automotive production from abroad. The average net monthly salaries in the automotive industry were €300 in 2013 (SIEPA 2014).

Bulgaria

Despite its distance from Western European markets and poor infrastructure, Bulgaria has also become increasingly targeted by automotive FDI mainly because of its EU membership, very low labor costs (Fig. 1.16) and low taxes. In 2014, average personnel costs per employee in the automotive industry were 93% lower in Bulgaria than in Germany, about 70% lower than in Central Europe and 45% lower than in Romania (Eurostat 2016). FDI stock in the automotive industry (NACE 29) was €153 million as of 2012 (Eurostat 2016). Between 1997 and 2015, foreign suppliers built 35 new plants in Bulgaria (EY 2010; ERM 2016) but the total number of enterprises in the automotive supplier sector was close to 100 in 2016 and this number has doubled since 2012. Foreign-owned suppliers employed over 33,000 workers in 2016 (Troev and Petrov 2016).

Bulgaria has been less successful in attracting car assembly operations. Rover's attempt to assemble semi-knockdown kits of Maestro hatchbacks and vans in Varna in a joint venture with the Bulgarian company Daru Group failed in 1996. Another attempt to assemble cars in Bulgaria failed 20 years later in Bahovitsa near Lovech when a joint venture of the Chinese car company Great Wall Motors and Bulgarian Litex Motors stopped the assembly of cars in January 2016 after only 4 years of operation. The total investment in the assembly plant was about €97 million with 90% being paid by the Bulgarian partner. The factory assembled cars for the Bulgarian market from kits shipped from China. Its cars were also sold in Romania, Macedonia and Serbia. Only about 4000 Great Wall cars were assembled in 2015, although the annual production capacity of the plant was 50,000 units, which was supposed to be reached by 2014.

Bulgaria has been desperately trying to attract a major car assembly factory for several years. The prospects of future FDI in the automotive industry are very good because Bulgaria has the lowest wages and taxes in the entire EU. For these reasons, Bulgaria is especially competitive in labor-intensive production of simple components that do not have to be delivered just-in-time to the European market.

Future Prospects of Automotive FDI in East-Central Europe and Its Long-Term Developmental Effects

Let us step back from the empirical details and address the more general questions regarding the development of the FDI-driven automotive industry in ECE. First, I will consider why ECE is set to remain attractive for automotive FDI. Second, I will address the long-term effects of FDI-driven development of the automotive industry for ECE countries and their position in the international division of labor.

The Continuing Attractiveness of ECE for Automotive FDI

Although the pre-2008–2009 economic crisis investment boom in the automotive industry is unlikely to be repeated, ECE will continue to be attractive for automotive FDI in the future due to a combination of favorable factors. The most important ones are the persisting wage gap between Western Europe and ECE, its geographic proximity to the affluent Western European markets and EU membership. In addition to the advantages of transnational economic integration, EU membership contributes to the ECE's economic and political stability.

Automakers need to make cars where they sell them on account of logistical reasons, political pressure and local content requirements (Sturgeon et al. 2008). This is what makes the relative geographic location of ECE so important to the European automotive industry. The political and economic instability east of the EU borders, increasing distance from the Western European markets and non-membership of the EU make a major shift of production capacity further east unlikely in the foreseeable future despite lower wages in countries such as Ukraine. Additionally, ECE countries have willingly engaged in the 'race to the bottom' by offering generous investment incentives and favorable conditions to foreign TNCs (e.g. Drahokoupil 2009; Pavlínek 2016).

Western European automakers have used threats to shift production from Western Europe to ECE to discipline and extract various concessions from their workers in Western Europe. Therefore, the continuing wage gap between the Western European and ECE automotive industry is of vital importance for automotive lead firms and for continuing investment in the ECE automotive industry. Although, some automotive industry 'experts' argue that wages are no longer an important location factor in the automotive industry (Bella 2013), the actual behavior of both assembly companies and component suppliers suggests otherwise. This is reflected in their location choices and also in the continuing pressure to maintain wages as low as possible even in the cheapest ECE locations through threats of relocations abroad. In Western Europe, automakers and component suppliers threaten workers with relocations to ECE; in Central Europe workers are threatened with relocations to Romania, Turkey or North Africa; while in Romania, workers are threatened with relocations to North Africa (Henning 2014; Rosemain and Timu 2014).

There have been a large number of relocations from Western Europe to ECE. To name just one example, Audi relocated its entire production of gasoline engines from Ingolstadt, Germany to Györ, Hungary, in the 1990s and 2000s after its German workers did not make sufficient concessions to satisfy demands for greater flexibility and lower wages. As a consequence, with its annual production of more than two million engines in 2015, Audi's Györ engine factory has become the world's largest engine plant. In 2016, Audi announced that it would relocate the production of its Q3 compact crossover car from Spain to Györ. In the case of Central Europe, relocations took place during and after the economic crisis, especially in the most labor-intensive segments of the automotive industry value chain, such as the assembly of cable harnesses (Pavlínek 2015).

The overall impact of the ECE automotive industry growth and relocations from Western Europe to ECE on West European automotive employment has been significant, with the number of persons employed decreasing by 10.4% (from 1.95 m to 1.74 m) between 2002 and 2015. While employment declined by 320,000 in Western Europe between 2002 and 2010, it increased by 117,000 between 2010 and 2015. At the same time, ECE employment increased by 396,000 (127%) between 2002 and 2015 despite the 2008–2009 economic crisis. Among the major ECE producers (Czechia, Hungary, Poland, Romania, Slovakia and Slovenia) employment grew from 303,000 in 2002 to 674,000 in 2015. The fastest growth was recorded in Slovakia (up 244% from 19,305 to 66,356) while the slowest was in Slovenia (up 76%) and Czechia (up 78%). As of 2015, the highest employment in the ECE automotive industry was in Poland (178,000), Romania (169,000) and Czechia (160,000) (Eurostat 2016). Additionally, employment quadrupled among minor ECE producers (Bulgaria and the Baltic states), going up from 5956 to 30,666 between 2002 and 2015 (Eurostat 2016). Although it is difficult to attribute exactly how much of the employment decline in Western Europe was directly related to growth in ECE, the inter-relationship is strong as automotive production was partially shifted to ECE from Western Europe (Fig. 1.20).

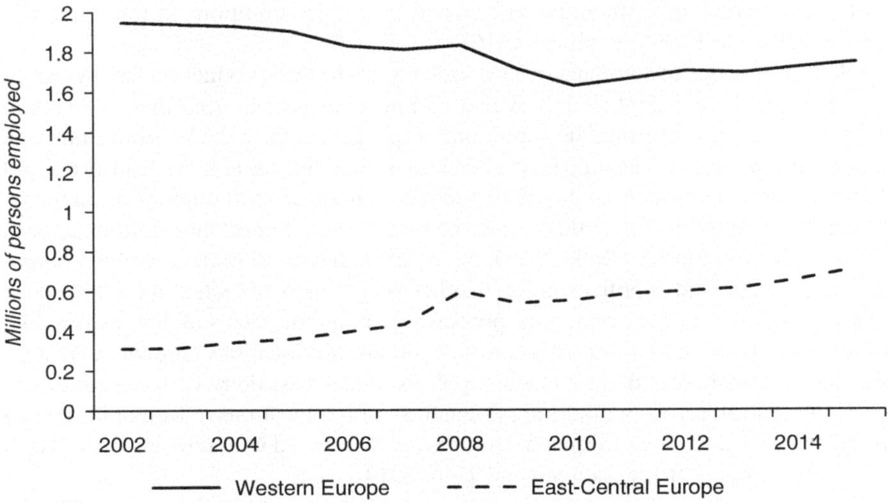

Fig. 1.20 Employment change in the European automotive industry, 2002–2015. *Note:* 2002–2007 data: NACE 34 (Rev. 1), 2008–2015 data: NACE 29 (Rev. 2). *Source*: Based on data from Eurostat (2016)

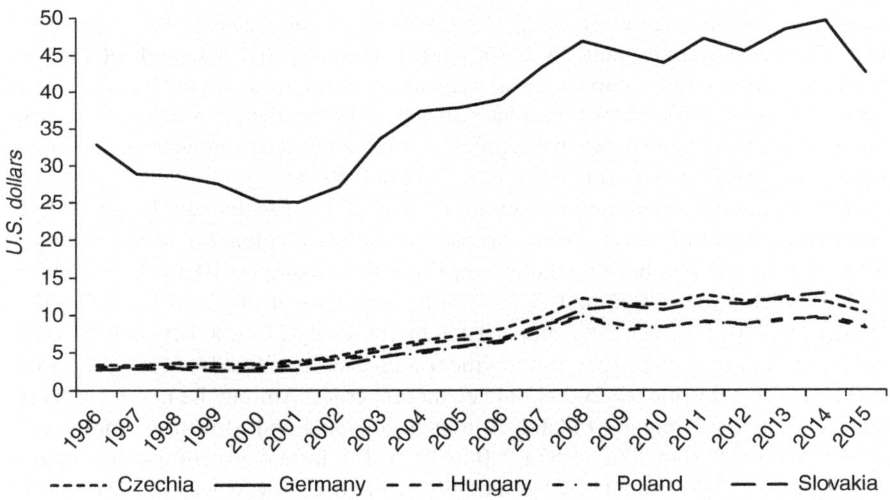

Fig. 1.21 Hourly compensation costs in manufacturing, in U.S. dollars, 1996–2015. *Source*: Based on data from Conference Board (2016)

The 1996–2015 development of hourly compensation costs in manufacturing suggests that the wage gap in the manufacturing industry between Western Europe and ECE is slowly narrowing (Fig. 1.21). In Czechia, Hungary, Poland and Slovakia, average hourly compensation costs in manufacturing as a percentage of German costs

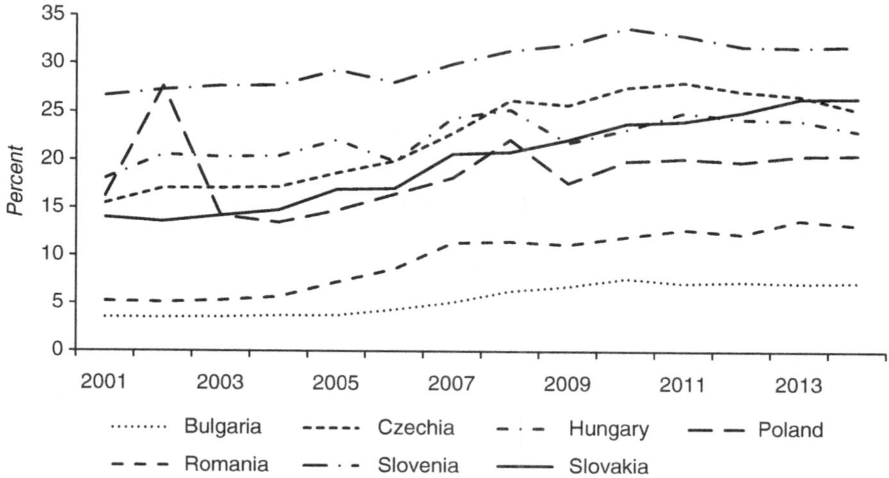

Fig. 1.22 Average personnel costs (personnel costs per employee) in the automotive industry (NACE 29) as a percentage of German levels (Germany = 100%), 2001–2014. *Source*: Based on data from Eurostat (2016)

ranged from 8.3% in Slovakia to 10.3% in Czechia in 1996. In 2015, they ranged from 19.4% in Hungary to 26.5% in Slovakia. In the automotive industry (NACE 29), the wage gap between ECE and Germany decreased in the 2000s before the 2008–2009 economic crisis but this trend slowed down considerably after 2010 (Fig. 1.22). This suggests that the graduate closure of the wage gap in the automotive industry between ECE and Germany is not necessarily an automatic and one-way process.

Relative to German levels, compensation costs in manufacturing increased most rapidly in Slovakia (from 8.3% to 26.5% between 1996 and 2015), compared to a slightly lower increase in Czechia (from 10.3% to 24.3%) and lower increases in Hungary (from 9.5% to 19.4%) and Poland (10.8% to 20.1%) (Conference Board 2016). The trends are similar in the automotive industry, where Slovak compensation costs grew the most rapidly of all the ECE countries between 2001 and 2014 (Fig. 1.22). Compared to its neighbors, Slovakia, a Eurozone member, cannot use currency devaluations to maintain its wage competitiveness. This rapid rise in Slovak industrial wages within two decades has undermined its wage competitiveness, one of its most important competitive advantages in the 2000s, and it might negatively influence future FDI inflows in the Slovak automotive industry (Pavlínek 2016). Automotive lead firms have attempted to slow down relative wage increases in Slovakia, trying to keep them at a minimum. In 2014, for example, VW Slovakia proposed a 4% cut in workers' salaries despite a low average monthly wage (€1400 in 2013) and €170 million profits earned by VW Slovakia in 2013 (SME 2014). PSA workers held several protests in Trnava in 2015 because PSA refused to raise salaries in 2015 after a 2-year salary freeze in 2013 and 2014 and because of the continuously increasing pace of work. The average monthly wage of PSA assembly line workers without bonuses was €665 as of April 30, 2015.

In Hungary, more than 7000 out of 11,411 Audi workers threatened to strike over low wages and long working hours in March 2016 (ANE 2016). Mercedes-Benz workers at Kecskemét held a 2-h strike over low pay in November 2016 after which Mercedes-Benz agreed to raise salaries by 10% in April 2017 and another 10% in April 2018 (Than and Szakacs 2016). In Czechia, the Škoda unions staged several strikes over pay and working conditions over the years. Adversarial labor relations typify both Hyundai and TPCA and both companies offered well below average wages and poor working conditions at the start of their assembly operations in Czechia (Pavlínek 2008). In addition to low wages, which both companies attempt to keep as low as possible, workers in Hyundai have also protested the increasing pace of work and requirements to work extra shifts on Saturdays without advance notice (iDnes 2015). Along with the strike of Dacia workers over pay in Romania in 2008 and other workers' strikes and protests across ECE, the frequent unwillingness of automotive firms to raise wages without being pressured in ECE suggests the importance of continuing low labor costs for foreign automotive TNCs in ECE. Consequently, the wage adjusted labor productivity in the automotive industry is significantly higher in ECE than in Western Europe (Eurostat 2016). For example, in 2014, it was 416% in Hungary, 360% in Czechia, 279% in Slovakia, 236% in Poland and 224% in Slovenia for the manufacture of motor vehicles (NACE 29.1), compared to 152% in Germany, 120% in France and 183% in Spain (Eurostat 2016).

Wages in the automotive industry of ECE countries have not been growing more rapidly also becasue of the relatively weak position of labor compared to that of capital in ECE (Bohle and Greskovits 2006). Union membership, which used to be more or less universal during the period of state socialism before 1990, decreased rapidly after 1990 to below 20% across ECE. In the automotive industry, however, any generalizations about the role of labor unions and industrial relations are difficult to make because of differences in the corporate cultures of TNCs from different countries and also because of legal and institutional differences in individual countries of ECE. Drahokoupil et al. (2015) demonstrated these differences among foreign assembly firms. On one side are German firms represented by Volkswagen Group, such as Škoda Auto, which transferred their relatively good industrial relations from the German automotive industry to their assembly factories in ECE. On the other side are Asian automakers, represented by Japanese and South Korean firms, such as Magyar Suzuki, that are typified by adversarial relations with labor unions and high levels of employment instability and insecurity, especially for temporary workers.

Long-Term Effects of FDI-Driven Automotive Industry Development in ECE

Since the early 1990s, the automotive industry has become a dominant industrial sector across ECE, significantly increasing its share of total exports, industrial production and job creation. In Slovakia, the automotive industry directly accounted for 12% of total production and indirectly for 17%, 4% of total value added, 26% of exports and 20% of imports in 2012 (ZAP 2013; Luptáčik et al. 2013). In 2015, it employed 80 thousand workers directly and an additional 120,000 indirectly and accounted for 43% of total manufacturing industry revenues and 35% of exports (Sario 2016). In Czechia, the narrowly defined automotive industry (NACE 29) accounted for 28.7% of manufacturing industry revenues, one-third of manufacturing exports and 14% of manufacturing industry employment in 2015, employing 155,365 workers (compared to 153,869 in 2008) (MIT 2014). In Poland, the narrowly defined automotive industry accounted for 8.6% of the total gross value added and employed 172,000 workers in 2015. The broadly defined automotive industry employed 362,200 workers in 2012. The automotive industry accounted for 15.9% of total Polish merchandise exports in 2015 (PAIA 2016). There were 2819 automotive industry companies in 2012 (KPMG 2013). In Hungary, the automotive industry accounted for 30.4% of total industrial output, more than 10% of GDP and 20% of total exports in 2013, while the broadly defined automotive industry employed 143,699 workers in 2015 (HIPA 2016).

These data for individual ECE countries confirm the increased importance of the FDI-based automotive industry for economic growth in ECE in the 1990s and especially in the 2000s, contributing to capital formation, driving exports and creating tens of thousands of new jobs. At the same time, however, the dependence of ECE economies on the externally owned and controlled automotive industry has increased and this dependence is likely to grow further in the future since FDI inflows in the automotive industry are set to continue, although they are likely to be smaller than in the 2000s.

To evaluate the potential long-term effects of the externally owned and controlled automotive industry on ECE economies, we can turn to economic geography, students of which have analyzed the effects of FDI on regional economies in the peripheral regions of Western Europe and in Canada since the 1970s (Firn 1975; Dicken 1976; Britton 1980; Hayter 1982; Schackmann-Fallis 1989; Amin et al. 1994; Phelps 1993). These studies point out the long-term structural costs of external ownership and control of economic activities for peripheral regions in the form of 'truncated development'. Externally owned manufacturing branch plants usually play a distinct role in a corporate hierarchy, being concentrated on routine manufacturing activities while lacking strategic and high value-added functions, such as decision-making powers about strategic planning, investment, product portfolio, market research and research and development (R&D) competencies. These functions remain concentrated in corporate headquarters or specialized R&D facilities in prosperous core regions (e.g. Britton 1980; Hayter 1982; Hayter and Watts 1983; Schackmann-Fallis 1989). In the case of foreign investment, these high value-added functions tend to remain concentrated in the home countries of principal investors while routine manufacturing functions are developed in host economies. For example, Hayter and Watts (1983: 171) summarized the truncation argument as follows:

> ...[I]n the long run branch plants are counter productive to regional development goals... because branch plants bring primarily unskilled jobs, limit local autonomy over investment decision making, arrest export potential in high technology goods, and, by relying on corporate rather than local linkages, increase import dependency on goods, services and technology.

Ultimately, truncated development contributes to value transfer from peripheral to core regions, making it more difficult for the affected regional economies to close the development gap with more developed core regions because of its negative effects on their indigenous growth potential (e.g. Schackmann-Fallis 1989). In the 1990s, the truncation and branch plant economy literature conclusions were challenged by arguments that branch plants were transformed into 'performance/networked branch plants' with greater autonomy and more functions and competencies than traditional branch plants (Phelps 1993; Amin et al. 1994). This has especially been the case in the automotive industry due to the changes in the organization of production and supplier relations experienced in the 1980s and 1990s (Womack et al. 1990). However, these changes have been limited and are insufficient to significantly alter the position of performance/networked branch plants in the corporate hierarchy and its spatial division of labor (Pike 1998; Dawley 2011). Furthermore, the positive changes affected the minority of branch plants (Dicken et al. 1994). As such, the problems associated with truncation and the branch plant economy persisted in the peripheral regions of Western Europe (Pike 1998).

Are the findings of the truncation literature relevant for the current situation in ECE? Truncation and truncated development were already observed in ECE after the first wave of FDI in the early 1990s (e.g. Grabher 1994, 1997; Hardy 1998). More evidence of economic and regional development risks related to large FDI inflows and their potential long-term structural costs was provided in the 2000s. For example, in the context of the ECE automotive industry it was argued that FDI potentially had both positive and negative effects on host economies (Pavlínek 2004). While FDI often leads to increased production, exports and job creation, wage increases, improvements in labor productivity and competitiveness, growth in real income and tax base, and spillovers to domestic companies, it can also lead to the downsizing of production, labor shedding and transfer of R&D abroad at the enterprise level in addition to a number of potential negative local and regional developmental effects. These include, for example, a dependency on foreign capital, external control, the poaching of skilled workers from domestic companies, the crowding out of domestic companies through deskilling and the development of a dual economy.

At the national level, questions have been raised about the long-term economic effects of large automotive FDI inflows on domestic economies. For example, in the mid-1990s Ellingstad (1997) warned of the development of what he calls the 'maquiladora syndrome" in ECE, a reference to the problems related to the rapid growth of a foreign capital-dominated manufacturing industry in Mexico and pointing to a number of FDI effects described by the truncation literature. State-based competition over large FDI projects in the automotive industry (regulatory arbitrage) has led to major state expenditure on investment incentives to attract strategic investors. These incentives are a form of state subsidy paid to foreign companies often at the expense of spending on education, domestic R&D, indigenous companies and other sectors of the domestic economy, and which contribute to the 'race to the bottom' in ECE (e.g. Bohle 2006; UNCTAD 1998; see Chap. 6).

It has also been argued that large foreign investors gained a disproportionate influence over state economic and education policies in ECE in the form of 'corporate capture' (Pavlínek 2016; Phelps 2000, 2008). Nölke and Vliegenthart (2009) have further developed this line of thought, arguing that a new distinct basic variety of capitalism, what they call a dependent market economy, has emerged in ECE. Such an economy differs from liberal market economies and coordinated market economies, the two dominant varieties of capitalism, through its greater dependence on foreign capital. This external dependence is its most important feature (see also Vliegenthart 2010). However, Nölke and Vliegenthart (2009) do not address the potential long-term consequences of this external dependency for ECE economies, with the exception of the threat of potential relocation "further east". As I have already noted, the relocation threat in the ECE automotive industry is greatest in the most labor-intensive and low-skilled manual operations, such as the assembly of cable harnesses (Pavlínek 2015; Pavlínek et al. 2009), while the potential for large-scale relocations of vehicle assembly operations from ECE is low in the foreseeable future. This is because of local content requirements, political pressure to produce within the EU, logistic reasons, transportation costs and large sunk costs in new investments.

There are already signs that the long-term effects of the industry's dependency on foreign capital, which will be discussed in the following chapters of this book, will be very similar to those described by the truncation literature: concentration on routine assembly operations, the weak development of R&D functions (see Chap. 4; Pavlínek 2012) and other strategic functions in foreign subsidiaries (see Chap. 6; Pavlínek and Ženka 2016), limited spillovers from foreign to domestic companies (see Chap. 5), the weak development of domestic companies, their limited upgrading and subordinate and dependent position in automotive GPNs (see Chaps. 3 and 5). All these factors will strongly influence the long-term prospects of the ECE automotive industry for catching-up with the more developed Western European automotive industry core.

It is important to realize that both foreign and domestic companies are important for successful economic development in the contemporary globalizing economy since both contribute to value creation and capture in different ways. Therefore, ECE governments should focus more on the long-term and sustainable development of the domestic automotive industry through targeted strategic industrial policies mitigating the overwhelming dependence on foreign capital. Greater investment in human capital in the form of high quality technical education and job training should attract more FDI in high value-added activities and contribute to the gradual upgrading of the ECE's position in the automotive industry's division of labor.

Conclusion

The ECE automotive industry has been integrated into the European and global automotive industry since 1990 mainly through the investment and trade activities of foreign TNCs. Foreign capital financed the restructuring of the existing ECE automotive industry and the build-up of new production capacity. Consequently, vehicle output more than quadrupled between 1990 and 2015, while the supplier industry grew even faster. In the contemporary global automotive industry, ECE represents a prime example of an integrated periphery made up of attractive production locations geographically close to large and affluent markets in developed economies and with significantly lower production costs, mainly because of lower wages. The high degree of integration of the ECE's automotive industry into the European production system and its overwhelming dependence on exports increased its vulnerability in the 2008–2009 economic crisis. The crisis led to declines in production and FDI inflows across the ECE automotive industry, although its effects, including post-crisis recovery, were geographically highly uneven.

Between 1990 and 2015, foreign automotive lead firms invested more than €35 billion in the ECE automotive industry, with the fastest increase in FDI stock taking place between 2000 and 2007. FDI inflows slowed during the 2008–2009 economic crisis and FDI stocks tended to decrease as foreign investors repatriated profits generated in ECE rather than reinvesting them. Although this decrease was only temporary and total FDI stock recovered by 2012, it suggests that the ECE automotive industry is vulnerable to increased profit repatriation and lower levels of investment during economic crises. Since investment by foreign lead firms in the ECE automotive industry is part of their profit-making behavior, we might expect that profit repatriation and the outflow of value from ECE will eventually exceed the volume of invested capital.

Individual automotive FDI country trends reflect the investment and location decisions of automotive lead firms, national differences in institutional environment, and the degree of success or failure in competitive bidding among ECE countries for large investment projects. Recent FDI trends suggest that ECE continues to be an attractive destination for automotive FDI. Although the large FDI inflows related to the construction of new assembly plants in the early and mid-2000s are unlikely to be repeated any time soon, ECE will continue to be attractive for automotive FDI as long as the wage gap between ECE and Western Europe persists. It will take many decades for ECE wages to catch up with wages in Western Europe at the current rate of wage increases.

Was there any alternative to the FDI-driven development of the automotive industry in ECE after 1990? Given the ECE's history of automotive industry underdevelopment throughout the entire twentieth century and the state of the ECE automotive industry at the end of the state socialist period in the late 1980s (Nestorovic 1991; Pavlínek 2002a), ECE countries were not in a position to pursue the successful development of an independent automotive industry. Attempts by domestic automakers to pursue independent development strategies, such as those by the Romanian Dacia and Russian AVTOVAZ in the 1990s and 2000s, were unsuccessful as these domestic automakers were unable to compete with the technologically more advanced production and vehicles of core-based TNCs (Pavlínek 2002c). Neither were ECE countries in a position to negotiate better terms for automotive FDI due to their small markets, similar factor endowments and strong competition over automotive FDI. As such, automotive TNCs were able to negotiate very favorable terms for their investment in ECE, often at the expense of ECE taxpayers and the subordination of state policies to the interests of foreign investors (Pavlínek 2016).

While FDI in the automotive industry strongly contributed to economic growth, job creation and the export competitiveness of ECE economies, it also significantly increased their dependence on the externally owned and controlled automotive industry. External control limits the potential economic benefits of the automotive industry for ECE economies because of truncation and because of limited opportunities for the development of an indigenous automotive industry. The long-term economic policies of individual ECE countries can be negatively affected by corporate capture, which tends to benefit foreign investors at the expense of domestic companies and population. Foreign ownership also undermines value capture in ECE and leads to value transfer from ECE to the core regions of the global automotive industry. The increased dependence of ECE economies on the automotive industry also increases their vulnerability to business cycles. In the long run, therefore, the development of the automotive industry in ECE will most likely be significantly more beneficial for foreign capital than for ECE economies and their population.

References

Amin A, Bradley D, Howells J, Tomaney J and Gentle C (1994) Regional incentives and the quality of mobile investment in the less favoured regions of the EC. Prog Plan 41, Part 1: 1–112.

ANE (2014) Ford will keep Fiesta production in Germany after cost-saving deal. Automotive News Europe. http://europe.autonews.com/article/20140610/ANE/140609836/ford-will-keep-fiesta-production-in-germany-after-cost-saving-deal. Accessed 24 Oct 2014

ANE (2016) Audi workers in Hungary threaten to strike over pay. Automotive News Europe. http://europe.autonews.com/article/20160330/ANE/160339993/audi-workers-in-hungary-threaten--to-strike-over-pay. Accessed 23 May 2016

Antalóczy K, Sass M (2011) The impact of the crisis on the Hungarian automotive industry. Rethinking development in an age of scarcity and uncertainty: new values, voices and alliances for increased resilience, University of York

Antalóczy K, Sass M (2014) Tükör által homályosan: a külföldi közvetlentőke-befektetések statisztikai adatainak tartalmáról [through a glass darkly: about the content of FDI data]. Külgazdaság 58(7–8):30–57

Bailey D, de Ruyter A, Michie J, Tyler P (2010) Global restructuring and the auto industry. Camb J Reg Econ Soc 3(3):311–318

Bartlett D, Seleny A (1998) The political enforcement of liberalism: bargaining, institutions, and auto multinationals in Hungary. Int Stud Q 42(2):319–338

Bella T (2013) Zabije nás nakoniec úspech našich automobiliek? SME. http://ekonomika.sme.sk/c/7028263/zabije-nas-nakoniec-uspech-nasich-automobiliek.html. Accessed 28 Dec 2013

Bernaciak M, Šćepanović V (2010) Challenges of upgrading: the dynamics of east Central Europe's integration into the European automotive production networks. Industrielle Beziehungen 17(2):123–146

Bohle D (2006) Neoliberal hegemony, transnational capital and the terms of the EU's eastward expansion. Cap Class 30(1):57–86

Bohle D, Greskovits B (2006) Capitalism without compromise: strong business and weak labor in Eastern Europe's new transnational industries. Stud Comp Int Dev 41(1):3–25

Bordenave G, Lung Y (1996) New spatial configurations in the European automobile industry. Eur Urban Reg Stud 3(4):305–321

Boros J (2013) Rising speed—Audi in Győr and Suzuki in Esztergom to produce new models as from this summer. Budapest Telegraph. http://www.budapesttelegraph.com/news/235/rising_speed. Accessed 14 Oct 2014

Britton JNH (1980) Industrial dependence and technological underdevelopment: Canadian consequences of foreign direct investment. Reg Stud 14(3):181–199

BS (2016) Direct investment 2015. Bank of Slovenia, Ljubljana

Butu AG (2016) Gov't Oks Ford investment in Craiova by 2025. Rom J. http://www.romaniajournal.ro/govt-oks-ford-investment-in-craiova-by-2025/. Accessed 21 Dec 2016

CBH (2016) Foreign direct investment—updated tables. The Central Bank of Hungary, Budapest

CNB (2001–2016) Přímé zahraniční investice [Foreign direct investment]. Annual publications. Prague, Czech National Bank

Conference Board (2016) International comparisons of hourly compensation costs in manufacturing, 1996–2015. The Conference Board, New York

CTCS (2014) A study on the Hungarian automotive industry. Canadian Trade Commissioner Service. http://www.enterprisecanadanetwork.ca/_uploads/resources/A-Study-on-the-Hungarian-Automotive-Industry.pdf. Accessed 13 Oct 2014

Dawley S (2011) Transnational corporations and local and regional development. In: Pike A, Rodriguez-Pose J, Tomaney J (eds) Handbook of local and regional development. Routledge, London, pp 394–412

Dicken P (1976) The multiplant business enterprise and geographical space: some issues in the study of external control and regional development. Reg Stud 10(4):401–412

Dicken P (2015) Global shift: mapping the changing contours of the world economy. The Guilford Press, New York

Dicken P, Forsgren M, Malmberg A (1994) The local embeddedness of transnational corporations. In: Amin A, Thrift N (eds) Globalization, institutions and regional development in Europe. Oxford University Press, Oxford, pp 23–45

Domanski B, Gwosdz K (2009) Toward a more embedded production system? Automotive supply networks and localized capabilities in Poland. Growth Chang 40(3):452–482

Domański B, Guzik R, Gwosdz K, Dej M (2013) The crisis and beyond: the dynamics and restructuring of automotive industry in Poland. Int J Automot Technol Manag 13(2):151–166

Drahokoupil J (2008) The investment-promotion machines: the politics of foreign direct investment promotion in central and Eastern Europe. Eur Asia Stud 60(2):197–225

Drahokoupil J (2009) Globalization and the state in central and Eastern Europe: the politics of foreign direct investment. Routledge, London

Drahokoupil J, Myant M, Domonkos S (2015) The politics of flexibility: Employment practices in automotive multinationals in Central and Eastern Europe. Eur J Ind Relat 21(3):223–240

Dunning JH (1993) The prospects for foreign direct investment in Eastern Europe. In: Artisien P, Rojec M, Svetličič M (eds) Foreign investment in central and Eastern Europe. St. Martin's Press, New York, pp 16–33

EBRD (1993) EBRD economic review: annual economic outlook. European Bank for Reconstruction and Development, London

Economist (2013) Manufacturing in Serbia: Balkan legacy. The Economist. http://www.economist.com/node/21588926. Accessed 29 Oct 2014

Ellingstad M (1997) The maquiladora syndrome: Central European prospects. Europe-Asia Studies 49(1):7–21

ERM (2016) European restructuring monitor: European restructuring database. European foundation for the improvement of living and working conditions

Eurostat (2016) Structural business statistics: annual detailed enterprise statistics—industry and construction. Eurostat

EY (2010) The central and eastern European automotive market: industry overview. Ernst & Young, Stuttgart

EY (2014) EY's attractiveness survey Europe 2014: back in the game. Ernst & Young, Stuttgart

Firn JR (1975) External control and regional development: the case of Scotland. Environ Plan A 7(4):393–414
Fischer S, Gelb A (1991) Issues in the reform of socialist economies. In: Coricelli F, Bossak J (eds) Reforming central and eastern European economies: initial results and challenges. The World Bank, Washington, DC, pp 67–82
Freyssenet M, Lung Y (2000) Between globalisation and regionalisation: what is the future of the motor industry? In: Humphrey J, Lecler Y, Salerno MS (eds) Global strategies and local realities; the auto industry in emerging markets. Basingstoke, Palgrave Macmillan, pp 72–94
Frigant V, Layan JB (2009) Modular production and the new division of labour within Europe: the perspective of French automotive parts suppliers. Eur Urban Reg Stud 16(1):11–25
Frigant V, Lung Y (2002) Geographical proximity and supplying relationships in modular production. Int J Urban Reg Res 26(4):742–755
Frigant V, Talbot D (2005) Technological determinism and modularity: lessons from a comparison between aircraft and auto industries in Europe. Ind Innov 12(3):337–355
Gillet K (2014) Dawn of the Dacia: how Romania's no-thrills car maker raced ahead. The Guardian. http://www.theguardian.com/business/2014/oct/21/dacia-romania-car-maker-europe-sales. Accessed 21 Oct 2014
Gowan P (1995) Neo-liberal theory and practice for Eastern Europe. New Left Rev 213:3–60
Grabher G (1994) The disembedded regional economy: the transformation of east German industrial complexes into western enclaves. In: Amin A, Thrift N (eds) Globalization, institutions and regional development in Europe. Oxford University Press, Oxford, pp 177–195
Grabher G (1997) Adaptation at the cost of adaptability? Restructuring the eastern German regional economy. In: Grabher G, Stark D (eds) Restructuring networks in post-socialism: legacies, linkages, and localities. Oxford University Press, Oxford, pp 107–134
Hardy J (1998) Cathedrals in the desert? Transnationals, corporate strategy and locality in Wroclaw. Reg Stud 32(7):639–652
Havas A (2000) Changing patterns of inter- and intra-regional division of labour: Central Europe's long and winding road. In: Humphrey J, Lecler Y, Salerno MS (eds) Global strategies and local realities; the auto industry in emerging markets. Basingstoke, Palgrave Macmillan, pp 234–262
Hayter R (1982) Truncation, the international firm and regional policy. Area 14(4):277–282
Hayter R, Watts HD (1983) The geography of enterprise—a reappraisal. Prog Hum Geogr 7(2):157–181
Henning D (2014) Ford cologne: management and IG metall union blackmail workers. http://www.wsws.org/en/articles/2014/02/24/ford-f24.html. Accessed 24Oct 2014
HIPA (2016) Automotive industry in Hungary. Hungarian Investment Promotion Agency, Budapest
Hudson R, Schamp EW (1995) Towards a new map of automobile manufacturing in Europe? New production concepts and spatial restructuring. Springer, Berlin
Humphrey J (2000) Assembler-supplier relations in the auto industry: globalisation and national development. Compet Chang 4(3):245–271
Humphrey J (2003) Globalization and supply chain networks: the auto industry in Brazil and India. Global Networks 3(2):121–141
Humphrey J, Memedovic O (2003) The global automotive industry value chain: what prospects for upgrading by developing countries. UNIDO, Vienna
Humphrey J, Oeter A (2000) Motor industry policies in emerging markets: globalisation and the promotion of domestic industry. In: Humphrey J, Lecler Y, Salerno MS (eds) Global strategies and local realities; the auto industry in emerging markets. Basingstoke, Palgrave Macmillan, pp 42–71
Humphrey J, Salerno MS (2000) Globalisation and assembler—supplier relations: Brazil and India. In: Humphrey J, Lecler Y, Salerno M (eds) Global strategies and local realities: the auto industry in emerging market. Palgrave MacMillan, Basingstoke, pp 149–175
Humphrey J, Lecler Y, Salerno MS (2000) Global strategies and local realities: the auto industry in emerging markets. Palgrave MacMillan, Basingstoke
iDnes (2015) We are not numbered machines, unions say. The battle over pay set to start at Hyundai. iDnes. http://ekonomika.idnes.cz/hyundai-nabizi-lidem-3-3-rustu-mezd-odborum-je-to-malo-fys-/ekoakcie.aspx?c=A151207_145516_ekoakcie_suj. Accessed 7 Dec 2015

Ilie L, Frost L (2016) Renault will shift some Dacia output to Morocco from Romania. Automotive News Europe, 21 Sept

Jindra B, Giroud A, Scott-Kennel J (2009) Subsidiary roles, vertical linkages and economic development: lessons from transition economies. J World Bus 44(2):167–179

Kolesár P (2006) Race to the bottom? The role of investment incentives in attracting strategic automotive foreign direct investment in Central Europe. Central European University, Budapest

KPMG (2013) Condition of the automotive industry and its role in the polish economy: report by KPMG in Poland on the initiative of the polish automotive industry association. Polish Automotive Industry Association, Warsaw

Larsson A (2002) The development and regional significance of the automotive industry: supplier parks in western Europe. Int J Urban Reg Res 26(4):767–784

Layan J (2000) The integration of peripheral markets: a comparison of Spain and Mexico. In: Humphrey J, Lecler Y, Salerno MS (eds) Global strategies and local realities: the auto industry in emerging markets. Basingstoke, Palgrave Macmillan, pp 16–41

Liu WD, Dicken P (2006) Transnational corporations and 'obligated embeddedness': foreign direct investment in China's automobile industry. Environ Plan A 38(7):1229–1247

Liu WD, Yeung HWC (2008) China's dynamic industrial sector: the automobile industry. Eurasian Geogr Econ 49(5):523–548

Lung Y (2004) The changing geography of the European automobile system. Int J Automot Technol Manage 4(2/3):137–165

Luptáčik M, Habrman M, Lábaj M, Rehák Š (2013) The importance of automotive industry for the Slovak economy: empirical results. University of Economics in Bratislava, Department of Economic Policy, Bratislava

Lupu V (2016) Ford will manufacture a new model in Craiova, EUR 130m investments. Rom J. http://www.romaniajournal.ro/ford-will-manufacture-a-new-model-in-craiova-eur-130m-investments/. Accessed 21 Dec 2016

MIT (2014) Panorama zpracovatelského průmyslu ČR [Panorama of the Czech manufacturing industry]. Ministry of Industry and Trade, Prague. http://www.mpo.cz/dokument154179.html

NBP (2016) Foreign direct investment in Poland. National Bank of Poland, Warsaw. http://www.nbp.pl/homen.aspx?f=/en/publikacje/ziben/ziben.html

NBR (2016) Foreign direct investment in Romania 2015. National Bank of Romania and National Institute of Statistics, Bucharest

NBS (2016) Priame zahraničné investície, 2014 [foreign direct investment, 201]. National Bank of Slovakia, Bratislava

Nestorovic C (1991) The automobile-industry in the east—national and international strategies. East Eur Econ 29(4):34–85

Nölke A, Vliegenthart A (2009) Enlarging the varieties of capitalism: the emergence of dependent market economies in east Central Europe. World Politics 61(4):670–702

OICA (2016) World motor vehicle production by country and type, 1997–2015. Organisation Internationale des Constructeurs d'Automobile, Paris

PAIA (2016) Automotive industry, 2016. Polish Automotive Industry Association, Warsaw

Pavlínek P (2002a) Restructuring the central and eastern European automobile industry: legacies, trends, and effects of foreign direct investment. Post-Soviet Geogr Econ 43(1):41–77

Pavlínek P (2002b) The role of foreign direct investment in the privatisation and restructuring of the Czech motor industry. Post-Communist Econ 14(3):359–379

Pavlínek P (2002c) Transformation of the central and east European passenger car industry: selective peripheral integration through foreign direct investment. Environ Plan A 34(9):1685–1709

Pavlínek P (2003) Transformation of the Czech automotive components industry through foreign direct investment. Eurasian Geogr Econ 44(3):184–209

Pavlínek P (2004) Regional development implications of foreign direct investment in Central Europe. Eur Urban Reg Stud 11(1):47–70

Pavlínek P (2006) Restructuring of the polish passenger car industry through foreign direct investment. Eurasian Geogr Econ 47(3):353–377

Pavlínek P (2008) A successful transformation? Restructuring of the Czech automobile industry. Physica Verlag, Heidelberg
Pavlínek P (2012) The internationalization of corporate R&D and the automotive industry R&D of east-Central Europe. Econ Geogr 88(3):279–310
Pavlínek P (2015) The impact of the 2008–2009 crisis on the automotive industry: global trends and firm-level effects in Central Europe. Eur Urban Reg Stud 22(1):20–40
Pavlínek P (2016) Whose success? The state-foreign capital nexus and the development of the automotive industry in Slovakia. Eur Urban Reg Stud 23(4):571–593
Pavlínek P, Janák L (2007) Regional restructuring of the Skoda auto supplier network in Czechia. Eur Urban Reg Stud 14(2):133–155
Pavlínek P, Ženka J (2010) The 2008–2009 automotive industry crisis and regional unemployment in Central Europe. Camb J Reg Econ Soc 3(3):349–365
Pavlínek P, Ženka J (2011) Upgrading in the automotive industry: firm-level evidence from Central Europe. J Econ Geogr 11(3):559–586
Pavlínek P, Ženka J (2016) Value creation and value capture in the automotive industry: empirical evidence from Czechia. Environ Plan A 48(5):937–959
Pavlínek P, Žížalová P (2016) Linkages and spillovers in global production networks: firm-level analysis of the Czech automotive industry. J Econ Geogr 16(2):331–363
Pavlínek P, Domanski B, Guzik R (2009) Industrial upgrading through foreign direct investment in central European automotive manufacturing. Euro Urban Reg Stud 16(1):43–63
Phelps NA (1993) Branch plants and the evolving spatial division-of-labor: a study of material linkage change in the northern region of England. Reg Stud 27(2):87–101
Phelps NA (2000) The locally embedded multinational and institutional capture. Area 32(2):169–178
Phelps NA (2008) Cluster or capture? Manufacturing foreign direct investment, external economies and agglomeration. Reg Stud 42(4):457–473
PIFIA (2013) The automotive sector in Poland: sector profile. Polish Information and Foreign Investment Agency, Warsaw
Pike A (1998) Making performance plants from branch plants? In situ restructuring in the automobile industry in the United Kingdom. Environ Plan A 30(5):881–900
PRB (1997) 1997 world population data sheet. Population Reference Bureau, Washington, DC
PRB (2016) 2016 world population data sheet. Population Reference Bureau, Washington, DC. http://www.prb.org
Rosemain M, Timu A (2014) Dacia thrives as Europe's cheapest cars revive Romania. Bloomberg. http://www.bloomberg.com/news/print/2014-09-11/europe-s-cheapest-cars-reviving-romania-as-dacia-thrives.html. Accessed 21 Oct 2014
Sario (2016) Automotive sector in Slovakia. Slovak Investment and Trade Development Agency, Bratislava
Sass M, Hunya G (2014) Escaping to the east? Relocation of business activities to and from Hungary, 2003–2011. Institute of Economics, Centre for Economic and Regional Studies, Hungarian Academy of Sciences, Budapest
Sass M, Szalavetz A (2013) Crisis and upgrading: the case of the Hungarian automotive and electronics sectors. Eur Asia Stud 65(3):489–507
Schackmann-Fallis KP (1989) External control and regional development within the Federal Republic of Germany. Int Reg Sci Rev 12(3):245–261
SIEPA (2014) Serbia: automotive industry. Serbia Investment and Export Promotion Agency, Belgrade
SME (2014) Volkswagen chce znížiť platy, odborárov zaskočil. SME. http://ekonomika.sme.sk/c/7074289/volkswagen-chce-znizit-platy-odborarov-zaskocil.html. Accessed 28 Jan 2014
STA (2014) Revoz announces 450 new jobs following production expansion. The Slovenia Times. http://www.sloveniatimes.com/revoz-announces-450-new-jobs-following-production-expansion. Accessed 26 Oct 2014
STA (2016) Cerar promises support for new Revoz projects. The Slovenia Times. http://www.sloveniatimes.com/cerar-promises-support-for-new-revoz-projects. Accessed 22 Dec 2016

Stanford J (2010) The geography of auto globalization and the politics of auto bailouts. Camb J Reg Econ Soc 3(3):383–405
Sturgeon TJ, Lester RK (2004) The new global supply base: new challenges for local suppliers in East Asia. In: Yusuf S, Altaf MAA, Nabeshima K (eds) Global production networking and technological change in East Asia. The World Bank and Oxford University Press, Washington, DC, pp 35–87
Sturgeon TJ, Van Biesebroeck J (2009) Crisis and protection in the automotive industry: a global value chain perspective. In: Evenett SJ, Hoekman BM, Cattaneo O (eds) Effective crisis response and openness: implications for the trading system. World Bank, Centre for Economic Policy Research, London, pp 285–305
Sturgeon T, Van Biesebroeck J, Gereffi G (2008) Value chains, networks and clusters: reframing the global automotive industry. J Econ Geogr 8(3):297–321
Sturgeon TJ, Gereffi G, Rogers KB, Fernandez-Stark K (2010) The prospects for Mexico in the north American automotive industry: a global value chain perspective. Actes du GERPISA 42(June):11–22
Than K, Szakacs G (2016) Mercedes will raise wages by over 20% at Hungary plant in next 2 years. Automotive News Europe. http://europe.autonews.com/article/20161212/ANE/161219991. Accessed 21 Dec 2016
Troev T, Petrov A (2016) Auto parts industry powers up. Financial Times, p 4, 29 Nov
UNCTAD (1998) World investment report 1998: trends and determinants. United Nations, New York
Vliegenthart A (2010) Bringing dependency back in: the economic crisis in post-socialist Europe and the continued relevance of dependent development. Hist Soc Res 35(2):242–265
VW (2016) Volkswagen Slovakia: facts and figures. VW Slovakia, Bratislava
Womack JP, Jones DT, Roos D (1990) The machine that changed the world. Rawson Associates, New York
ZAP (2000) Slovak republic automotive industry: statistics—yearbook 2000. The Automotive Industry Association of the Slovak Republic and the Slovak Chamber of Commerce and Industry, Bratislava
ZAP (2013) Základné informácie o automobilovom priemysle a jeho význame pre SR [basic information about the automotive industry and its importance for Slovakia]. The Automotive Industry Association of the Slovak Republic, Bratislava

Chapter 2
The Impact of the 2008–2009 Crisis

Introduction

The 2008–2009 economic crisis has been considered to be one of the most severe in modern history (Cattaneo et al. 2010). Various explanations, ranging from institutionalist and cultural to neoclassical and Marxist, have been presented, and geographers have emphasized the importance of spatial perspectives in a full understanding of the crisis (e.g. Gowan 2009; Harvey 2011; Martin 2011; Smith and Swain 2010). In the automotive industry, the impact of the crisis was more severe than in other economic sectors with the exception of housing and finance, and only the banking sector saw larger government intervention (Van Biesebroeck and Sturgeon 2010). Global vehicle production declined by 3.7% in 2008 and by 15.8% in 2009 (OICA 2016). Albeit unevenly, all segments of global vehicle production were affected by the crisis. This decline is hardly surprising given the automotive industry's sensitivity to business cycles. However, differences existed in the automotive output of different world regions. Since saturated vehicle markets of developed economies are typified by replacement demand, consumers tend to postpone purchases of new vehicles during periods of economic uncertainty (Dicken 2015). During the 2008–2009 crisis, the situation was exacerbated by worsening access to consumer credit, which has traditionally financed a high share of new vehicle purchases, especially in the United States. Consequently, saturated markets, including those in North America and Western Europe, have been hit the hardest by the crisis, despite government efforts to encourage consumer demand for new vehicles (Klier and Rubenstein 2010; Stanford 2010). The situation has been different in rapidly growing developing economies because of their steadily expanding new demand for vehicles. Although large developing countries, including China, India and Brazil, saw lower demand for new cars in 2008 and 2009 compared to 2007, their new vehicle sales continued to grow during the crisis (Van Biesebroeck and Sturgeon 2010; Cruz and Rolim 2010; OICA 2016).

Van Biesebroeck and Sturgeon (2010) argued that the crisis led to further consolidation of the supplier base as surviving smaller local suppliers were more

P. Pavlínek, *Dependent Growth: Foreign Investment and the Development of the Automotive Industry in East-Central Europe*, DOI 10.1007/978-3-319-53955-3_2

vulnerable to closure and bankruptcy than large "global" suppliers. So far, however, studies concerning the impact of the crisis in the supplier sector have been rare because reliable data about numerous automotive suppliers are difficult to collect. Therefore, the goal of this chapter is to analyze the crisis in the supplier sector at the firm-level and to evaluate to what extent the consolidation of the automotive supplier sector took place during the economic crisis. The case study focuses on Czechia and Slovakia, which together produced more than 1.8 million vehicles in 2011. Only Germany, France, Spain and Russia assembled more vehicles in Europe in 2011. The case study draws on unique data collected by the author via a survey of 274 Czech-based and 133 Slovak-based automotive firms in Fall 2009 and Spring 2010 and on 100 company interviews conducted with automotive firms in Czechia in 2010 and 2011 and 50 interviews conducted in Slovakia between 2011 and 2015.[1] The data suggest that the effects of the economic crisis in the Czech and Slovak supplier sectors were significant, although not as dramatic as originally thought. The economic crisis resulted in relatively few bankruptcies, plant closures and relocations among automotive suppliers in both Czechia and Slovakia. The firm-level analysis did not uncover any substantial differences between the effects of the economic crisis in the Czech and Slovak automotive industries.

This chapter begins with a brief discussion of the role of global production networks (GPNs) during the economic crisis. The second section reviews the 2008 and 2009 crisis in the global automotive industry, stressing its uneven geographic nature. The third section introduces the Czech and Slovak automotive industries as being part of a relatively new and rapidly growing periphery that was integrated into the European automotive production system in the 1990s and 2000s. The fourth section analyzes the general production and employment trends in the Czech and Slovak automotive industries during the economic crisis. The fifth section analyzes firm-level data about revenues, production and employment changes in the Czech and Slovak automotive industries during the 2008–2009 economic crisis. The sixth section investigates bankruptcies and relocations in the automotive industry of Czechia and Slovakia during the crisis. The main findings of the analysis are summarized in the conclusion.

Global Production Networks and the Economic Crisis

Geographers, amongst others, have applied their spatial perspective to better understand the uneven nature of the 2008–2009 economic crisis at various geographic scales (e.g. Martin 2011; Smith and Swain 2010). The 'varieties of capitalism' literature has also emphasized the variegated impacts of the economic crisis across ECE, which was influenced by different modes of growth and economic integration

[1] All interviews were conducted by the author and two members of his research team.

in the 1990s and 2000s (e.g. Drahokoupil and Myant 2010; Bohle 2009).[2] However, this literature largely limits its interest to national scale differences in various factors underlying the geographically uneven national economic performance during the different stages of the economic crisis. Myant and Drahokoupil (2012) present a more sophisticated approach to explain the vulnerability of individual countries to the economic crisis in ECE by considering different modes of integration of ECE countries into the global economy and emphasizing international integration through financial inflows and exports as the two most important channels transmitting the crisis into ECE. This approach still suffers from a national scale bias typical for the 'varieties of capitalism' literature (e.g. Bohle and Greskovits 2007; Farkas 2011), which limits our understanding of processes that are primarily organized at different geographic scales (e.g. Dicken 2015). However, it suggests that GPNs organized from outside the region constituted one of the principal transmission channels through which the crisis was transmitted into ECE economies. In other words, the incorporation of ECE producers in the externally organized GPNs increased the vulnerability of ECE to the economic crisis. This argument echoes the work of GPN and global value chain (GVC) scholars who have maintained that transnationally organized GPNs and GVCs were the principal mechanisms through which the economic crisis was transmitted around the world economy (Smith and Swain 2010; Cattaneo et al. 2010). One of the advantages of the GPN and GVC approaches is their focus on internationally organized production networks and value chains instead of national economies that makes it possible to analyze the economic crisis at the industry and firm levels (e.g., Cattaneo et al. 2010). This, in turn, allows for a more nuanced analysis of the uneven impacts of the economic crisis within particular industrial sectors, which might take into consideration differences between different groups of firms within the same sector depending, for example, on their position within the production network or value chain, their different ownership or their different size (e.g. Pavlínek and Ženka 2010). Such an analysis then allows for a better understanding of the resilience of particular types of firms to economic crises and their abilities to upgrade their position within GPNs and GVCs. At the same time, it also allows for the identification of the types of firms that are particularly vulnerable to systemic crises because of their limited opportunities to upgrade within the existing GPNs. Consequently, such firms might be more susceptible to downgrading, relocation or closure.

Since there are important differences in the way GPNs are organized in different industries (Gereffi et al. 2005), there are important differences in the resilience and vulnerability of different industrial sectors to economic crises and in the way the economic crisis has been transmitted through GPNs in these sectors (Cattaneo et al. 2010). We also need to consider national differences in institutional environment,

[2] In this chapter, ECE denotes the region composed of ten former state socialist countries, which are now EU members (Bulgaria, Czechia, Estonia, Latvia, Lithuania, Hungary, Poland, Romania, Slovakia, and Slovenia). Central Europe denotes the region composed of Czechia, Hungary, Poland, Slovakia and Slovenia.

which influence how a particular industrial sector is integrated into the global economy through GPNs.

The Uneven Nature of the 2008–2009 Economic Crisis as a Symptom of the Broader Geographic Shift in the Global Automotive Production

The global automotive industry is geographically organized in regional clusters of production networks nested in macro-regions (e.g. North America, South America and the European Union) or individual countries with large domestic markets (e.g. China, India) (Sturgeon et al. 2008, 2009). These regional clusters of production reflect the need for geographical proximity of the most important suppliers to assembly operations and the need of automotive lead firms to design and produce vehicles customized to consumer preferences in particular markets. They also reflect political pressures for local production and the need of automotive lead firms to meet various regulatory requirements that differ in contrasting parts of the world (Sturgeon et al. 2008). This strongly regional geographic structure of the global automotive industry (Humphrey et al. 2000; Carrillo et al. 2004) contributed to large differences in regional performance during the crisis as its effects have mostly been contained within the most important production regions and their respective countries (Van Biesebroeck and Sturgeon 2010).

At one extreme, North America,[3] which already experienced a decline in total vehicle production in 2006 and 2007, suffered a 16% drop in 2008 followed by an additional 32% decrease in 2009, representing the steepest production decline since the Great Depression and the deepest production decline of all world regions. Conversely, in 2010, North America experienced the strongest recovery with a 38.7% increase in vehicle production compared to 2009 (Fig. 2.1). At another extreme, Asia's vehicle production kept growing by 1.9% and 1.5% during 2008 and 2009. Sustained production in Asia during the economic crisis was mainly due to China, whose vehicle production increased by 7% in 2008 and by 45% in 2009 (OICA 2016). Fig. 2.1 also reveals that North America experienced 4 years of negative annual growth, and Europe experienced three between 2005 and 2010 compared to only one in South America and zero in Asia during the same period.[4] Production trends were also regionally uneven according to the individual segments of the automotive industry. During 2008–2009, global production declined across all vehicle segments (Table 2.1, OICA 2016). The European and North American automotive production declined across the board. In South America, only passenger

[3] In this chapter, North America is defined as the North American Free Trade Agreement (NAFTA) area composed of Canada, Mexico and the United States.

[4] Africa is excluded from this discussion because of its small vehicle output compared to other major world producing regions. Africa's 2011 vehicle production was 541,596, which was less than half of vehicle output of tiny Czechia (OICA 2016).

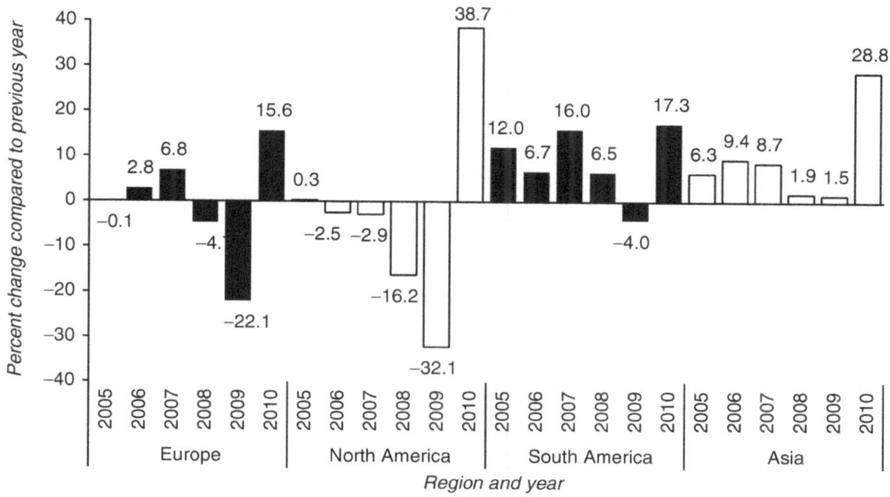

Fig. 2.1 Annual changes in vehicle production by main producing region, 2005–2010. *Source*: Calculated from data in OICA (2016)

Table 2.1 Percent change in output by world region during 2008 and 2009 compared to 2007

	All vehicles	Passenger cars	LCVs	Trucks	Buses
Europe	−25.8	−21.6	−44.4	−63.0	−36.7
North America	−43.2	−38.8	−46.2	−50.0	−22.7
South America	2.2	5.0	−6.3	−10.8	−9.2
Asia	3.4	4.4	−9.3	32.1	−49.9
Africa	−24.1	−15.3	−39.4	−38.8	26.6
World	−15.8	−10.4	−34.6	−5.6	−43.2

LCVs light commercial vehicles
Source: Calculated from data in OICA (2016)

cars did not decline, but the decline in the rest of automotive assembly was much smaller than in Europe and North America. In Asia, the decline was limited to LCVs and buses. A 50% decline in the assembly of buses in Asia was the largest of all world regions. At the same time, Asia's truck production increased by one-third. The extent of production decline in the individual segments of the automotive industry was strongly affected by the nature and extent of government intervention during the economic crisis (Stanford 2010; Van Biesebroeck and Sturgeon 2010).

The 2010 recovery was surprisingly strong, considering the lingering effects of the economic crisis especially in Europe and North America, although there were significant sectoral differences in the strength of output recovery (Table 2.2). The global vehicle production exceeded the 2007 pre-crisis level by 5.9% in 2010. The output of passenger cars and heavy trucks was higher in 2010 than in 2007, while

Table 2.2 Percent change in output by world region in 2010 compared to 2009

	All vehicles	Passenger cars	LCVs	Trucks	Buses
Europe	15.6	12.4	41.4	53.7	0.9
North America	38.7	28.5	48.5	19.4	−11.4
South America	17.3	12.8	34.0	37.2	33.2
Asia	28.8	28.2	28.0	36.7	22.3
Africa	18.0	21.0	12.6	9.6	0.0
World	25.8	22.2	38.9	37.2	17.2

LCVs light commercial vehicles
Source: Calculated from data in OICA (2016)

the output of LCVs and buses was lower (OICA 2016). The growth in output continued after 2010.[5]

The diverging production trends between more developed and less developed countries have been symptomatic of a general shift in output in favor of non-core areas of global automotive production caused by rapid production increases in less developed countries since the 1990s. The share of global vehicle production decreased in traditional automotive core countries from 66% to 36% between 1997 and 2010, while it increased outside the core from 34% in 1997 to 64% in 2010 (OICA 2016).[6] The United States and China illustrate different production trends since the mid-1990s and also different effects of the global automotive crisis of 2008 and 2009 between more developed and less developed countries (Fig. 2.2, see also Klier and Rubenstein 2010). Two types of less developed economies have particularly benefited from this shift. First are rapidly growing less developed countries that have (potentially) large domestic markets and might further benefit from regional economic integration. Examples of such "protected autonomous markets" include China, India and Brazil (Humphrey and Oeter 2000; Lung 2000; Cruz and Rolim 2010; Van Biesebroeck and Sturgeon 2010). Second are peripheral areas located close to large markets of developed regions that were integrated into production networks of traditional core areas of the automotive industry. Examples of such "integrated peripheral markets" include Mexico, Spain and ECE (Humphrey and Oeter 2000; Layan 2000; Pavlínek 2002a; Pavlínek et al. 2009: Sturgeon et al. 2010).

[5] Compared to 2010, in 2015 the total vehicle production increased by 17.0%, the output of passenger cars grew by 17.6% and the production of LCVs by 25.5%. The output of heavy trucks decreased by 18.8% and buses by 17.7% mainly because the 2015 figures for heavy trucks and heavy buses exclude the production of several EU countries and the output of Scania and Daimler trucks (OICA 2016).

[6] I consider the following countries to constitute the traditional global automotive industry core: France, Germany, Italy, Japan, Sweden, Britain and the United States. However, the contemporary global automotive industry core is composed of France, Germany, Italy, Japan, South Korea and the United States because the top 17 automotive transnational corporations (TNCs) in the world, each producing more than one million vehicles annually and collectively accounting for 85% of the total global vehicle production in 2008, were all based in these five countries (OICA 2016).

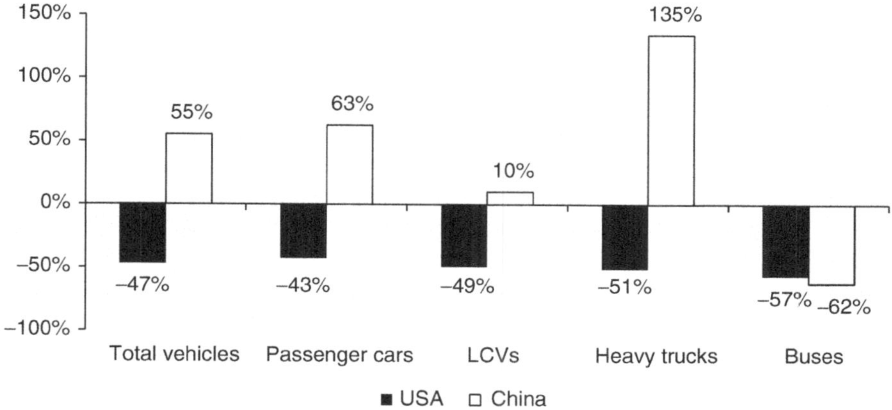

Fig. 2.2 Changes in vehicle output in the USA and China during 2008–2009 compared to 2007. *Source*: Calculated from data in OICA (2016)

ECE's Position in the European Automotive Production System

Since the early 1990s, the European automotive industry has been increasingly organized in trans-European rather than national production networks (Hudson and Schamp 1995). ECE represents an example of a peripheral region of the automotive industry that has been integrated into the European and global automotive GPNs through large inflows of FDI in the 1990s and 2000s (Pavlínek 2002a, b; Pavlínek et al. 2009). This peripheral integration has been organized and financed by foreign automotive lead firms through their profit-seeking strategies to enhance their overall competitiveness by exploiting the spatial division of labor in the European automotive industry. As a result, the ECE automotive industry is now owned and controlled by core-based TNCs. In order to maximize the advantage of ECE's cheaper and less organized labor, the role of the ECE automotive industry in the European production system has been threefold: the mass production of small passenger cars, the labor intensive low-volume production of luxury cars, and the experimentation with new production methods and flexible labor practices (Havas 2000: Pavlínek 2002a). The post-1990 development of the automotive industry in ECE has been strongly supported by favorable government policies based upon generous investment incentives to attract foreign assembly plants and foreign component suppliers. Central European countries have engaged in competitive bidding for automotive assembly plants and investments by large foreign suppliers (see Chap. 6).

Following the large investment by foreign assemblers and component suppliers, ECE's passenger car output increased five times between 1991 and 2011, from 608 thousand to 3.3 million units (3.4 million units of all vehicles). In 2011, ECE accounted for 19% of the total EU vehicle production and 21% of the EU passenger car output (OICA 2016). At the same time, however, the development of more value-added and higher-order functions, such as R&D competencies, has been limited in the ECE automotive industry. The opportunities for industrial upgrading have been mainly confined to process and, to a lesser degree, product upgrading, while functional upgrading has been much more limited (Pavlínek and Ženka 2011; Pavlínek 2012; Chap. 3). This situation is not surprising given the captive (or quasi-hierarchical) nature of automotive value chains in which power is concentrated in powerful lead firms. Lead firms use their power, among other things, to organize and govern hierarchical networks of component suppliers, and to control their chances for functional upgrading (Gereffi et al. 2005; Humphrey and Schmitz 2002, 2004). This transnational organization of automotive production networks has, at least theoretically, increased the vulnerability of ECE automotive operations and the vulnerability of regional and local economies specialized in the automotive industry, to economic crises as more simple and lower value-added production tends to be more susceptible to closure and/or relocation during economic downturns. The externally organized GPNs constituted the main transmission channels through which the crisis was transmitted into the ECE automotive industry. In the rest of this chapter, the analysis of the 2008–2009 crisis in the Czech and Slovak automotive industries will be presented.

Czech and Slovak Automotive Industries

In Czechia and Slovakia, the 2008–2009 economic crisis interrupted 15 years of rapid FDI-driven development of the automotive industry, which followed the trade and FDI liberalization of the early 1990s. The prospects of low-cost production, based upon the combination of low wages, geographic proximity to the west European market and strong governmental investment incentives, attracted large inflows of automotive FDI (e.g. Pavlínek 2002a, 2008; Pavlínek et al. 2009; Jakubiak et al. 2008). Czechia and Slovakia now rank among the important automobile producers within ECE and the entire EU, and their combined production of 2.3 million passenger cars in 2015 represented 59% of the ECE total and 12% of the EU total (OICA 2016). Czech passenger car production increased seven times from 188 thousand cars in 1990 to 1.3 million in 2015, and Slovak output increased from 3453 units in 1990 to one million in 2015 (Fig. 2.3). The production of automotive components increased even more rapidly than the assembly of cars as many foreign TNCs set up their export-oriented operations in Czechia and Slovakia to supply both locally-based assembly plants and assembly plants located in Western and Central Europe (e.g. Pavlínek and Janák 2007; Pavlínek and Ženka 2011; Chap. 1).

Different starting positions of the Czech and Slovak automotive industries in the early 1990s reflected differences in their previous development (e.g. Pavlínek and Smith 1998; Pavlínek 2008; Vagac 2000; see Chap. 6). In the 1990s, Volkswagen (VW) played the decisive role in the automotive industry of both countries through the acquisition and restructuring of the Czech Škoda assembler and launching the new production in the former BAZ factory (the Bratislava automobile works) in Slovakia. VW also pressured existing suppliers to substantially improve the quality

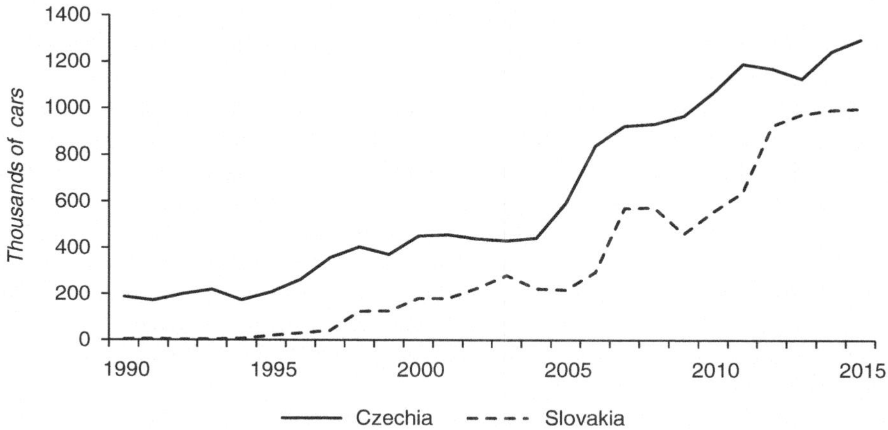

Fig. 2.3 Passenger car production in Czechia and Slovakia, 1990–2015. *Source*: Based on data from OICA (2016), AIA (2012)

and timing of supplied components and encouraged the follow sourcing by its Western European, mostly German, suppliers. These corporate strategies led to the restructuring and further development of the Czech and Slovak supplier industries (e.g. Pavlínek 2003, 2008). In the 2000s, Czechia and Slovakia attracted four additional greenfield passenger car assembly plants: the joint venture of Toyota, Peugeot and Citroën (TPCA) at Kolín (Czechia); Hyundai at Nošovice (Czechia); Kia at Žilina (Slovakia); and PSA Peugeot Citroën (PSA) at Trnava (Slovakia). In all four cases, the investments in assembly were followed by investments by foreign suppliers. As a result of this development, the automotive industry now represents the most important industrial branch in both Czechia and Slovakia, and its share of total manufacturing employment and output has been steadily increasing. In Czechia, the automotive industry had the highest share of revenues (19.4%) and exports of all manufacturing industry in 2009. The narrowly defined employment in the automotive industry increased from 58 thousand in 1994 (NACE 34) to 146 thousand in 2011 (NACE 29), accounting for 11.4% of total industrial employment in 2011 (CSO 2011).[7] In Slovakia, employment increased from six thousand in 1993 (NACE 34) to 51 thousand in 2010 (NACE 29) (SME 2011). The automotive industry accounted for 27.5% of total industrial revenues (74% of total manufacturing revenues) and 15.9% of industrial employment (46% of total manufacturing employment) in Slovakia in 2010. The share of the automotive industry of total industrial production reached 40% in 2013 and its share of GDP reached about 12% (Luptáčik

[7] NACE 34, used until 2008, refers to the NACE Rev. 1.1 classification of the automotive industry and NACE 29, introduced in January 2009, refers to its NACE Rev. 2 classification. These two classifications are not fully compatible because NACE 29 is 16.2% broader than the former NACE 34 when measured by value added. The reason is the addition of manufacture of electrical and electronic equipment for motor vehicles and manufacture of automobile seats to NACE 29 compared to former NACE 34.

et al. 2013). The more broadly defined automotive industry (NACE 29 – 30) employed 165 thousand workers in Czechia and 60 thousand workers in Slovakia in the middle of 2011 (CSO 2011; SSO 2011).

Although this rapid development of the automotive industry has been viewed as a success by both the Czech and Slovak governments and by industry analysts, it has significantly increased the dependence of the Czech and Slovak economies on the export-oriented automotive industry. In 2007, following Germany (11.7%) and Sweden (10.6%), Czechia had the third (8.8%) and Slovakia the fourth (8.0%) highest share of automotive employment (NACE 34) of total manufacturing employment in the European Union (Eurostat 2011). The Czech share increased to 12.0% by 2011 (CSO 2011) and the Slovak share increased to 15.9% by 2010 (SME 2011). Both countries also had high shares of employment in automotive components manufacturing (NACE 29.3) of the total manufacturing employment with Czechia at 8.6% in 2009 (MIT 2011) and Slovakia at 11.6% in 2010 (SME 2011). It has been argued that high degree of regional specialization increases regional economic instability (Ezcurra 2011; Baldwin and Brown 2004; Trendle 2006). This is also the case with externally controlled economies that are more vulnerable to disinvestment during economic crises (Dicken 1976). Therefore, the dependence on externally controlled export-oriented automotive manufacturing tends to make the Czech and Slovak economies vulnerable to plant closures and large scale layoffs in times of economic crises during which consumer demand for passenger cars may dramatically decrease. Therefore, the rest of this chapter investigates to what extent these arguments are empirically supported by the firm-level effects of the 2008–2009 economic crisis in the Czech and Slovak automotive industries.

General Effects of the Economic Crisis in the Czech and Slovak Automotive Industries

The effects of economic crises in peripheral regions of the automotive industry, such as ECE, depend on several factors. First is the degree of their dependence on exports to saturated markets since these markets are most likely to be affected by significantly lower sales because of their dominance by replacement demand for vehicles. Integrated export-oriented peripheral markets, including Mexico and ECE, would thus tend to be more affected than more isolated “protected autonomous markets” (e.g. China and India) (Humphrey and Oeter 2000) serving domestic markets, which are driven by new demand for vehicles. Second, product portfolio plays a role since different classes of vehicles are likely to experience different changes in consumer demand during economic crises. Third, the effects of economic crisis in peripheral locations also depend on corporate policies of core-based lead firms. On the one hand, they might be more likely to downsize production in foreign locations rather than their home countries because of domestic political pressures. On the other hand, they might be compelled to shift more production to foreign peripheral locations in order to reduce production costs and thus increase their competitiveness.

Table 2.3 Relative change in vehicle output by country and category in the broadly defined Central and East European automotive periphery between 2007 and 2009

	2007 Output	2009 Output	All vehicles	Passenger cars	LCVs	Trucks	Buses
Russia	1,660,120	725,012	−56.3	−53.5	−69.2	−61.2	−57.8
Turkey	1,099,413	869,605	−20.9	−19.5	−17.4	−76.1	−47.4
Czechia	937,648	983,243	4.9	5.6	−57.5	−65.6	−3.6
Poland	792,703	878,998	10.9	17.8	−45.6	134.4	35.7
Slovakia	571,071	461,340	−19.2	−19.2	N.A.	N.A.	N.A.
Ukraine	402,591	117,900	−70.7	−82.7	−79.8	−90.0	−84.8
Hungary	292,027	214,543	−26.5	−26.1	N.A.	−53.2	−79.1
Romania	241,712	296,498	22.7	19.3	128.2	21.3	−100.0
Slovenia	198,402	212,749	7.2	16.3	−57.9	N.A.	N.A.
Belarus	27,708	11,520	−58.4	N.A.	N.A.	−59.0	−51.4
Serbia	9903	16,738	69.0	98.4	−100.0	−28.6	−32.2
Total	6,233,298	4,788,146	−23.2	−20.3	−37.4	−61.7	−50.3

Note: N.A. refers to a particular category of vehicles not being produced in a particular country. *LCVs* light commercial vehicles
Source: Calculated from data in OICA (2016)

Fourth, the extent of governmental intervention, if any, in the automotive industry might influence the severity of the crisis. All these factors affected the course of the automotive industry crisis in ECE. At the national level, different combinations of these factors and particular national circumstances resulted in a highly uneven automotive industry crisis across the broader East European automotive periphery, composed of ECE, the non-EU European countries of the former Soviet Union (Belarus, Moldova, Russia and Ukraine) and Turkey (Table 2.3).

At first glance, data for passenger car production do not reveal any economic crisis in the Czech automotive industry in 2008 and 2009 because Czech vehicle output increased by 0.9% in 2008 and by 4.0% in 2009. The growth in output further accelerated in 2010 and 2011 with 9.5% and 11.5% increases, respectively (OICA 2016; AIA 2012). Together with Romania, Poland, Slovenia and Serbia, Czechia was only one of five European countries that recorded production increase in the output of passenger cars during the 2008–2009 crisis. Its 2010 production was 15% higher than its 2007 output (Fig. 2.3). However, this national-level measure of the impact of the economic crisis in the automotive industry is misleading for several reasons: it only considers passenger car assembly, ignoring the rest of the automotive industry, although passenger cars accounted for 99.4% of assembled vehicles in 2010; it only reflects domestic assembly, ignoring the changes in exports of components; and it is strongly affected by the fact that a newly opened Hyundai assembly plant in November 2008 was gradually increasing its output throughout 2009 and 2010. Firm-level data thus reveal a more complex picture as there were important differences among the individual assemblers (Table 2.4). Another indicator of the

Table 2.4 Annual output of Czech-based and Slovak-based vehicle factories, 2007–2011

	2007	2008	2009	2010	2011
Czechia					
Škoda Auto	622,811	603,981	528,585	576,362	673,127
TPCA	308,478	324,289	332,489	295,712	270,705
Hyundai	0	12,050	118,000	200,135	251,146
Tatra (trucks)	2431	2252	808	931	702
Avia (trucks)	737	485	283	479	600
Iveco (buses)	2698	3020	2526	2177	2972
SOR (buses)	418	368	427	478	543
Slovakia					
VW	248,700	188,000	104,300	144,510	210,441
PSA	180,000	190,000	205,000	186,150	205,000
Kia	142,371	197,800	152,400	229,500	252,000

Source: AIA (2012), 2011 interviews

extent of the automotive industry crisis in Czechia is the fact that during 2009, the three Czech-based passenger car producers assembled 383,000 passenger cars fewer than they had originally planned because production targets were not met by Škoda Auto and Hyundai (HN 2008). These pre-crisis plans were still not reached in 2011. Table 2.4 also suggests much more serious effects of the crisis in the truck industry compared to the passenger car industry. Tatra, the largest surviving Czech-based producer of heavy trucks, suffered a revenue decline of 45% and its production dropped by 64% in 2009. The company laid off half of its workers during the economic crisis, and its employment dropped from 4400 in June 2008 to 2280 at the end of 2009. Avia, the second (barely) surviving producer of medium trucks stopped its assembly line for 7 weeks between December 2008 and January 2009, and it operated only for 3 or 4 days per week in the first half of 2009. The company also dismissed almost half of its workforce during the economic crisis. The trends in the production of buses differed from both passenger cars and trucks (Table 2.4).

Based upon annual vehicle output, the Slovak automotive industry was hit harder by the crisis especially in 2009 when total vehicle production decreased by 19.9%. Despite the 20.7% increase in 2010, the 2010 output was still 2.5% lower than in 2007. As in Czechia, different assemblers were affected differently by the crisis (Table 2.4). Slovakia does not produce any trucks and buses.

Job losses were significant. In Czechia, 28,000 jobs, representing 17.2% of the automotive industry (NACE 29) total, were lost between the first quarter of 2008 and the third quarter of 2009. In the second quarter of 2011, there were still 17,000 fewer jobs than before the crisis despite the 15% increase in the passenger car output (CSO 2011). This suggests that the automotive firms rationalized production and became more efficient during the crisis. In Slovakia, employment in the broadly defined automobile industry (NACE 29 + 30) peaked in September 2008 at 61,078, and it reached the lowest point in June 2009 at 51,177, suggesting the loss of 9901 jobs or 16.2% of the pre-crisis employment.[8] After June 2009, employment began to recover, but with 59,768 workers as of July 2011, it still failed to reach pre-crisis levels (SSO 2011).

The firm-level effects of the crisis in the Czech and Slovak automotive industries were affected by institutional factors and government policies. Many European governments introduced various programs and incentives to support the automotive industry during the economic crisis in order to prevent plant closures and large-scale layoffs. These programs ranged from favorable loans, loan guarantees, wage subsidies and direct subsidies to various cash scrappage incentives (e.g. see Stanford 2010). The Czech government, however, did not implement any such program, and it only launched several active labor policy programs, which supported job training and worker education (see Pavlínek and Ženka 2010). Slovakia followed a different strategy by introducing the scrappage scheme for passenger cars. Consumers could receive up to a €1500 subsidy for the purchase of a new passenger car priced at less than €25,000. 44,200 Old cars were scrapped, but beyond environmental and safety improvements, the effect of this policy on the Slovak-based assemblers was negligible since the vast majority of new passenger cars replacing the old ones were not assembled in Slovakia. More importantly, both Slovak and Czech-based assemblers and component suppliers benefited from scrappage schemes introduced in their large markets, such as Germany, Britain, France and Italy in 2009.

Firm-Level Effects of the 2008–2009 Economic Crisis in the Czech and Slovak Automotive Industries

In order to evaluate the effects of the 2008–2009 crisis in the Czech and Slovak automotive industries, a survey was administered in Czechia at the end of 2009 and in Slovakia at the beginning of 2010 to collect firm-level data about changes in revenues, production, employment and investment plans in 2009 (during the past 12 months). The survey targeted firms with 20 or more employees and involved 800 firms in Czechia and 299 in Slovakia. It yielded a response rate of 35% (274 firms) in Czechia and 44% (133 firms) in Slovakia. The survey results show significant firm-level effects of the 2008–2009 economic crisis in both countries. Especially in Czechia, the survey results generally do not correspond with the overall growing assembly of automobiles in 2008 and 2009.

[8] Employment in the narrowly defined Slovak automotive industry (NACE 29) is unavailable. For the sake of comparison, job losses in the broadly defined Czech automobile industry (NACE 29 + 30) reached 27,210 or 15.2% of the pre-crisis employment. As opposed to NACE 29, Czech employment in NACE 30 increased during the economic crisis from 15,921 in the second quarter of 2008 to 16,674 in the third quarter of 2009 (CSO 2011).

Declines in Revenues and Production

Overall, 95% of the surveyed firms reported a decline in revenues in Czechia and 91% in Slovakia. Production decline affected 92% of the surveyed firms in Czechia and 80% in Slovakia. However, overall differences in declines in revenues and production between Czech and Slovak firms as a whole are not statistically significant and suggest that the firm-level effects of economic crisis were similar in the Czech and Slovak automotive industries, despite slightly greater declines in Czechia (Fig. 2.4).[9]

Differences in economic performance between foreign-owned and domestic-owned firms (henceforth foreign firms and domestic firms) during the economic crisis were statistically significant.[10] In Czechia, domestic firms experienced a statistically significant greater decline in revenues (t-Test, $P = 0.005$) and production (t-Test, $P = 0.043$) compared to foreign firms. In Slovakia, however, there were no statistically significant differences between foreign and domestic firms in declines in revenues and production during the economic crisis (Fig. 2.4). I was also interested to see whether the extent of involvement of firms in the automotive industry affected the degree of decline during the economic crisis. Firms were compared according to the share of automotive production among their total revenues. All firms were classified into five classes: 100% of automotive production, 75–99%, 50–74%, 25–49%, and 1–24% of automotive production. In Czechia, these groups of firms did not statistically differ in the extent of revenue and production decline. These results suggest that the automotive industry was not affected harder by the economic crisis than the rest of the manufacturing industry and that the effects of the crisis were universal across Czech manufacturing industry. In Slovakia, the results differed from those in Czechia. The five groups of firms according to the extent of their involvement in the automotive industry statistically differed in the extent of decline in revenues and in production (One-way ANOVA nonparametric test, $P = 0.005$ and $P = 0.003$). Further analysis of the t-Test revealed that firms with 75–99% of the automotive production suffered a greater production and revenue decline than firms fully dedicated to automotive production ($P = 0.001$ and $P = 0.004$) and firms with 1–24% of automotive production ($P = 0.001$ and $P = 0.001$). There was also a statistically significant greater decline in revenues in firms with 25–49% than in the firms with 1–24% of automotive production ($P = 0.019$). I was unable to find a plausible explanation for these differences.

Finally, the extent of decline in small- and medium-size enterprises (SMEs) and large firms was analyzed. In Czechia, 171 SMEs (250 employees and less) in the

[9] All unpaired t-tests were conducted at the 95% confidence interval.

[10] Among the Czech-based surveyed firms, there were 101 fully foreign-owned firms and 14 majority foreign-owned firms. There were also seven firms that were 50% foreign-owned. For the purposes of this chapter, I have considered these firms to be majority foreign-owned. There were 131 fully domestic-owned firms and two majority domestic-owned firms. In Slovakia, there were 56 fully foreign-owned firms, nine majority foreign-owned firms, including two that were 50% foreign-owned, 68 fully domestic-owned and one majority domestic firm.

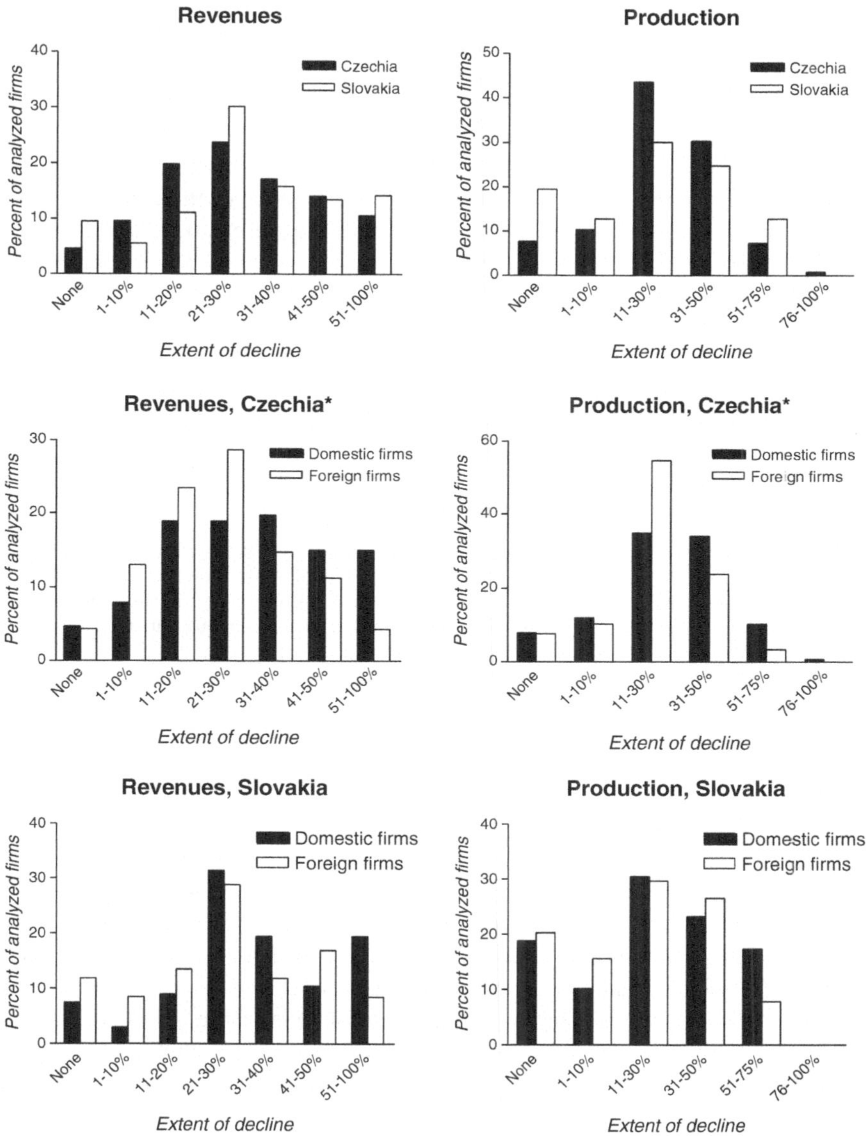

Fig. 2.4 Decline in revenues and production in Czech and Slovak automotive firms in the past 12 months during 2008 and 2009. *Notes:* An asterisk next to the title indicates a statistically significant difference between domestic and foreign firms as a whole in Czechia in decline in revenues (t-Test, P = 0.005) and production (t-Test, P = 0.043). Sample sizes (number of analyzed firms): Revenues: Czechia (N = 261), Slovakia (N = 125); Production: Czechia (N = 261) Slovakia (N = 133). Revenues, Czechia: 127 domestic, 115 foreign; Production, Czechia: 126 domestic, 117 foreign; Revenues, Slovakia: 67 domestic, 59 foreign; Production, Slovakia: 69 domestic, 64 foreign. *Source*: Author's 2009 automotive company survey conducted at the end of 2009 and early 2010

database were compared to 101 large automotive firms (more than 250 employees). The statistical difference in revenue decline between these two groups of firms was highly significant (t-Test, P = 0.0004). On average, SMEs experienced a greater decline in revenues than large enterprises. The statistical difference in production decline was not significant. However, 45% of SMEs suffered production decline greater than 30% compared to only 26% of large companies. In Slovakia, there were 31 large firms and 102 SMEs in the database. The differences in declines in revenues and production between large firms and SMEs were not statistically significant. However, 18% of SMEs suffered revenue declines of more than 50% compared to zero among larger firms, and declines of more than 30% were experienced by 50% of SMEs compared to only 22% of large firms. In terms of production, 41% of SMEs reported declines exceeding 30% compared to only 26% of large firms. This suggests a greater decline in revenues and production among SMEs compared to large firms in Slovakia. SMEs among automotive suppliers are generally found at the lower tiers of the supplier hierarchy. Company interviews revealed that these suppliers were particularly squeezed during the economic crisis. For example, a director of a Czech-owned automotive supplier argued that:

> We were forced to lower our prices by 10-20% after the crisis. Our prices always keep on going down. What cost 10 euros ten years ago costs 4 euros now. However, the greatest decrease was in the past three years during the economic crisis when we got really squeezed by assemblers. More or less, we were included in global sourcing together with the Chinese and Indians and assemblers squeezed everything out of us that was left (interview, July 8 2011).

Employment Effects

The employment effects of the economic crisis in the form of job losses were significant because 82% of the surveyed firms laid off permanent workers in Czechia compared to 71% in Slovakia. Before the economic crisis, both the Czech-based and Slovak-based automotive firms had increasing difficulties to recruit workers because of strong demand for automotive workers. This was due to the rapidly growing employment in the automotive industry following large inflows of FDI. At the same time, however, the traditional high-quality vocational training system disintegrated in both countries in the early 1990s. As a result, the supply of young skilled workers greatly diminished, and shortages became acute in the 2000s. In order to cope with surges in demand and with local labor shortages, firms increasingly relied on temporary workers. One-third of all surveyed firms in Czechia (33.6%) and one-fourth (27.7%) in Slovakia employed temporary workers between 2004 and 2009. In Czechia, many of these workers were recruited by work agencies from neighboring countries, including Poland, Slovakia and Ukraine. In some cases, Czech automotive companies began to recruit temporary low-skilled workers from more distant countries, such as Vietnam and Mongolia. Generally, however, the quality of this temporary labor force was poor, and temporary workers were first to lose their jobs during the economic crisis (2010 interviews). The difference between Czech and Slovak firms in the extent of the layoff of temporary workers was statistically significant (t-Test, P = 0.005), and Czech firms on average laid off a higher share of temporary workers than Slovak firms. Foreign and domestic firms did not significantly statistically differ in the extent of layoffs of temporary workers in both Czechia and Slovakia.

A different situation developed with respect to permanent workers. The dismissal of permanent workers is considered by firms to be a last resort strategy. As a result, the companies first typically reduced the working hours or working days of permanent employees to prevent their layoffs. As the result of these strategies, only 13% of the Czech-based surveyed firms laid off more than 30% of their permanent workers compared to 23% in Slovakia. However, the difference between Czech and Slovak firms in the extent of layoffs of permanent workers was not statistically significant, suggesting a similar extent of layoffs of permanent workers in both countries. In Slovakia, in order to prevent layoffs, VW Slovakia introduced flexible working time (the so called flexi account) in January 2009. In this system, workers are paid for work days during which they do not work because there is no work for them, but when demand recovers they are required to work those hours as overtime for which they have already been paid. The maximum deficit can reach 300 h per worker over 4 years. The flexi account was introduced by 60 additional firms in Slovakia because it allows them to keep workers at times of low demand (interview at VW Slovakia, June 14, 2011).

One of the interviewed managers described how his Czech-based company, which employs about 300 temporary workers, dealt with employment issues during the economic crisis:

> In 2008, we had to react to the crisis. We lost about 30% of our turnover. We did everything that was possible, first of all not using temporary workers supplied by external companies. Then we stopped using people with limited temporary contracts. We did not extend these contracts. The last possibility was to lay off some permanent workers, and we had to do it, too. But we resorted to that only at the beginning of 2009. Already in autumn 2009, the situation started to get better, so we started to take on people again. First, people from external companies, in order to be flexible, then slowly also permanent workers.[11]

Although in Czechia domestic firms experienced a statistically significant greater decline in revenues and production compared to foreign firms, there was not a statistically significant difference between domestic and foreign firms in terms of layoffs of permanent and temporary workers (Fig. 2.5). This suggests that domestic firms have been more reluctant to lay off workers than foreign firms during the economic crisis given their greater drop in revenues and production. It also suggests that foreign firms tend to be more flexible in using their labor force and react more quickly to changing market conditions. Thus, the situation in the Czech automotive industry would support the argument that foreign or domestic ownership may influence the propensity of firms to lay off workers during economic crises. In particular,

[11] Interview with a plant manager of the German-owned supplier of door systems and seat systems, November 16, 2010.

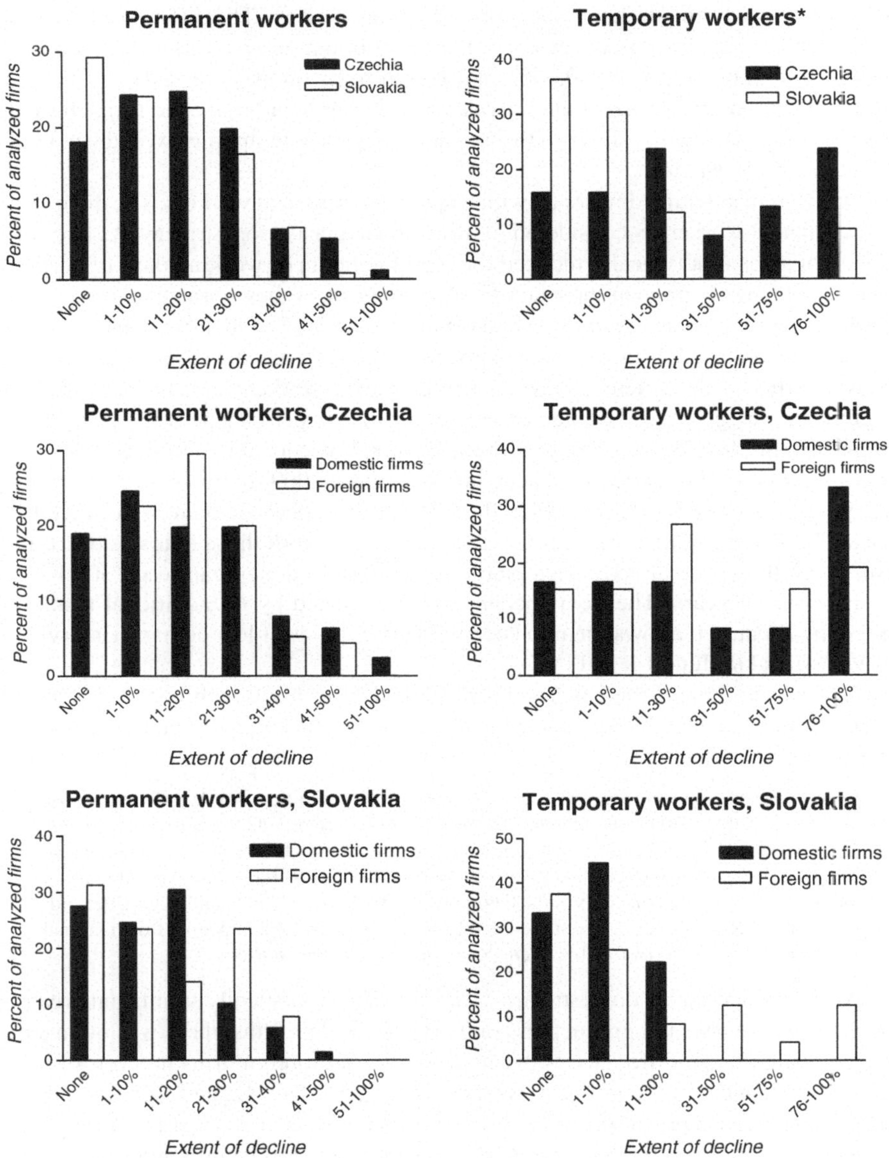

Fig. 2.5 Decline in permanent workers and temporary workers in Czech and Slovak automotive firms in the past 12 months during 2008 and 2009. *Note*: An *asterisk* next to the title indicates a statistically significant difference between Czech and Slovak firms as a whole in decline in temporary workers (t-Test, P = 0.005). Sample sizes (number of analyzed firms): Permanent workers: Czechia (N = 243), Slovakia (N = 133); Temporary workers: Czechia (N = 38), Slovakia (N = 33). Permanent workers, Czechia: 126 domestic, 115 foreign; Temporary workers, Czechia: 12 domestic, 25 foreign; Permanent workers, Slovakia: 69 domestic, 64 foreign; Temporary workers, Slovakia: 9 domestic, 24 foreign. *Source*: Author's 2009 automotive company survey conducted at the end of 2009 and early 2010

foreign firms are generally quicker to lay off redundant workers, when demand for their products declines (e.g. Pennings and Sleuwaegen 2000) because they tend to protect employment in their home country and attempt first to reduce labor costs in their foreign subsidiaries during an economic recession. In Slovakia, however, there was no statistically significant difference between foreign and domestic firms in the extent of layoffs of permanent workers and temporary workers during the economic crisis (Fig. 2.5).

In Czechia, the extent of involvement of firms in the automotive industry affected the extent of layoffs of permanent workers (One-way ANOVA nonparametric test, $P = 0.005$).[12] Given the fact that these groups of firms did not statistically differ in the extent of decline in revenues and production, it suggests that the automotive industry was not more greatly affected by the economic crisis than the rest of manufacturing industry and that the effects of the crisis were universal across the Czech manufacturing industry. However, the automotive industry and manufacturing industry as a whole were more seriously affected by job losses than the Czech economy as a whole during the economic crisis. Further analysis showed greater decline in permanent workers in firms involved 75–99% in automotive production than firms completely involved in automotive production ($P = 0.043$) and firms with the smallest share of the automotive production (1–24%) ($P = 0.010$). Firms with a 50–74% share of automotive production suffered a greater decline in permanent workers than firms with a 1–24% share of automotive production ($P = 0.043$). In Slovakia, the five groups of firms according to the extent of their involvement in the automotive industry statistically did not differ in the extent of layoffs of permanent workers.

Similarly, the statistical difference between SMEs and large firms in the decline in the number of permanent workers was insignificant. However, more SMEs were reluctant to dismiss their permanent workers compared to large companies. 45% of SMEs laid off less than 10% of their permanent employees compared to 26% of large firms. At the same time, 17% of SMEs dismissed more than 30% of their permanent workers compared to 7% of large firms.

As in Czechia, Slovak SMEs were more reluctant to shed permanent workers than large firms because 33% of SMEs did not dismiss any permanent workers compared to 19% of large firms. However, two-thirds of large firms (68%) shed less than 10% of their permanent workers compared to only half (50%) of SMEs. As in the case of Czechia, Slovak automotive SMEs were affected more seriously by the economic crisis because of their more vulnerable position in the automotive value chain and their greater dependence on lower value added activities. A high percentage of these firms in both countries are third-tier and second-tier automotive suppliers. The differences in decline in permanent workers were not statistically significant between SMEs and large firms in Slovakia.

[12] The decline in the number of temporary workers was not tested because of the small number of cases.

Bankruptcies and Relocations during the Economic Crisis

Another way to evaluate the effects of the economic crisis in the Czech and Slovak automotive industries is to analyze plant closures and relocations during the crisis period. It has been argued elsewhere that foreign companies are more likely to engage in disinvestment than domestic companies (Henderson et al. 2002; Dicken 1976) and, therefore, especially foreign subsidiaries, at the lowest levels of the value chain, are most susceptible to the risk of closure during economic crises. Small countries with open economies, such as Czechia and Slovakia, are especially vulnerable to relocation (Pennings and Sleuwaegen 2000). A high level of plant relocations and plant closures would also suggest a low degree of embeddedness of especially foreign automotive suppliers in Czechia and Slovakia. Generally, the most labor-intensive low-skill activities, the products with the lowest transportation costs, and limited significance in relation to just-in-time delivery, such as standardized cable harnesses, are most at risk of relocation. Pavlínek et al. (2009) argued before the crisis that the danger of large-scale relocations of automotive suppliers from Central Europe to lower-cost locations elsewhere was relatively low because of the increasing embeddedness of these firms in the region. Did their argument hold during the 2008–2009 economic crisis?

Overall, there were 15 bankruptcies and/or plant closures and five relocations abroad in the Czech automotive industry during and immediately after the economic crisis, which resulted in 9200 job losses (Table 2.5). In 13 cases these plant closures led to job losses of at least 100 workers each. Overall, however, the number of relocations was low during the economic crisis given the overall size of the Czech automotive industry, and it suggests a relatively high degree of embeddedness of automotive companies in Czechia. This is hardly surprising if one considers the importance of sunk costs, transportation costs, supplier links and the proximity of suppliers to assemblers in the contemporary automotive industry (see also Domański and Gwosdz 2009; Jürgens and Krzywdzinski 2009; Pavlínek et al. 2009). The data presented in Table 2.5 also suggest that both foreign and domestic firms were similarly affected by bankruptcies and plant closures in Czechia.

In Slovakia, at least 6928 jobs were lost because of plant closures and relocations in the automotive industry during the economic crisis (Table 2.6). The majority of jobs were lost in the labor-intensive assembly of simple cable harnesses. As of 2011, these activities were surviving in Slovakia in two settings. First were peripheral low-wage locations, such as eastern Slovakia. In 2011, the average monthly wage in the assembly of cable harnesses was €360 in eastern Slovakia compared to €550 in western Slovakia (2011 interviews). Second was the production of complex high value-added cable harnesses at Delphi Senica (main cockpit harnesses and main body harnesses) for luxury vehicles delivered in a just-in-time regime to VW Slovakia. Each of these cable harnesses is distinct, and they have to be delivered in 14 h after the order has been placed by VW Slovakia which requires spatial proximity.[13] Still, Delphi Senica had to resort to large-scale layoffs during the eco-

[13] Each cable harness assembled for VW-Group's luxury SUVs requires 10.5 h of work compared to 7 h required for Škoda Octavia and 5 h for Škoda Fabia.

Table 2.5 Largest bankruptcies, plant closures and foreign relocations in the Czech automotive industry during the economic crisis

Company	Location	Year	Products	Job loss	Ownership
Delphi Packard[a]	Česká Lípa	2011	Cable harnesses	3400	USA
AEES Czech Platinium Equity[b]	Stříbro	2009	Cable harnesses	2100	USA
Henniges Automotive	Příbor	2008	Sealing systems	980	USA
Faurecia Lecotex	Tábor, Počátky	2009	Seat cover cut and sew activities	564	France
Magneton	Kroměříž	2009	Car accessories	400	Czechia
Grammer	Horažďovice	2009	Automotive parts (head rests)	311	Germany
Akuma	Mladá Boleslav	2009	Car batteries	200	Italy
BTV Plast	Havlíčkův Brod	2009	Plastic automotive parts	200	Czechia
Johnson Controls[c]	Brno	2011	Efficiency division	200	USA
Bontaz-Centre[d]	Rokycany	2008	Valves, cooling nozzles, and injection parts	185	France
Dagro Plzeň	Plzeň	2009	Car upholstery and other interior components	170	Czechia
ACC	Rapotín	2009	Auto body parts	156	Czechia
Novak CV	Chomutov	2009	Seat inserts, covers and headrests	155	Czechia
Weisser&Griesshaber	Znojmo	2009	Plastic automotive parts	77	Germany
Connaught Electronic	Jiřice	2008	Automotive electronics	70	Ireland
SVA Holýšov	Holýšov	2009	Cable harnesses, moldings, welding	69	Czechia

Source: Compiled from ERM (2011), various newspapers, press reports and company web pages
Additionally, three Czech companies, each employing less than 20 workers that went bankrupt in 2008 and 2009 were identified: ACK Autopřívěsy in Rakovník, Aspekta Kovo in Plzeň and Precision Parts Manufacturing in Liberec

[a]Relocation to Romania

[b]Previously Alcoa Fujikura, relocation to Romania

[c]Relocation to Slovakia

Table 2.6 Largest bankruptcies, plant closures and foreign relocations in the Slovak automotive industry during the economic crisis

Company	Location	Year	Products	Job loss	Ownership
Yazaki[a]	Prievidza	2010	Cable harnesses	1211	Japan
Delphi[b]	Senica	2008–2010	Cable harnesses	1100	USA
Molex[c]	Kechnec	2010	Cable harnesses	1000	USA
Jas Elmont	Snina	2009	Cable harnesses	1000	Slovakia
SE Bordnetze[d]	Zlaté Moravce	2010	Cable harnesses	700	Japan
SEWS[e]	Topoľčany	2009	Cable harnesses	658	Japan
Kromberg&Schubert	Kolárovo	2009	Cable harnesses	614	Austria
Connect Systems[e]	Vráble	2010	Cable harnesses	130	Belgium
Kongsberg Driveline Systems	Vráble	2008–2009	Steering systems	180	Norway
FCT Electronic	Prešov	2008–2009	Cable harnesses	120	Germany
Promens	Nitra	2009	Plastic pressed components	100	Island
VAP	Prešov	2008	Automotive components	85	Slovakia
Saf-Holland	Zlaté Moravce	2009	Automotive components	40	Germany

Source: Compiled from various newspapers, press reports, company web pages and 2011 interviews
[a]Relocation to Tunisia
[b]1900 jobs eliminated between 2007 and 2011 and relocated to Tunisia, Romania and Turkey
[c]Relocation to China
[d]Relocation of 300 jobs to Nitra, Slovakia, 400 jobs eliminated
[e]Relocation to Romania

nomic crisis, and its number of workers was reduced from 2800 in 2006 to 900 by 2010. Only production for luxury SUVs survived at Senica, and even its future is uncertain. The assembly of more simple cable harnesses for PSA was relocated to Tunisia and for Mercedes to Romania and Turkey (interview on June 13, 2011).

Overall, the largest bankruptcies and relocations in both Czechia and Slovakia affected labor intensive, low-wage and low-skill assembly of cable harnesses. Although job losses were considerable, they were largely confined to a particular low-end segment of the automotive value chain. The 2008–2009 crisis did not lead to widespread relocations that would affect the automotive industry across the board. As such, it did not support the arguments about the "footlooseness" of the Central European automotive industry (Rugraff 2010).

Conclusion

The goal of this chapter has been to evaluate the effects of the 2008–2009 global economic crisis in the automotive industry in the context of the peripheral automotive production region. The analysis concentrated on a case study of the Czech and Slovak automotive industries as examples of "integrated peripheral markets." Both the Czech and Slovak automotive industries were negatively affected by the economic crisis. The vast majority of companies experienced significant declines in production, revenues and workers. However, with the exception of the labor intensive assembly of simple cable harnesses, the economic crisis did not lead to waves of bankruptcies or large-scale relocations of automotive suppliers from Czechia and Slovakia to cheaper production locations in foreign countries as some have feared. The low number of closures and relocations suggests a relatively strong embeddedness of the automotive firms in the Czech and Slovak economies. A high share of bankruptcies and relocations in the assembly of cable harnesses underscores the fact that Central European countries are no longer competitive in the export-oriented low-cost and labor intensive simple assembly of standardized components. Thus, the partial consolidation of the supplier base envisioned by Van Biesebroeck and Sturgeon (2010) did take place, although it was not limited to small domestic suppliers as they have argued. Instead, the consolidation also affected large foreign subsidiaries, especially in the assembly of cable harnesses. Suppliers were strongly squeezed by lead assembly firms during the crisis, which might further endanger future prospects of especially small domestic suppliers at the bottom of the supplier hierarchy.

This chapter has demonstrated the advantages of the firm-level analysis of the effects of economic crises, especially when compared to national-level approaches that would be limited to measuring changes in national levels of production and employment. The firm-level analysis revealed that the effects of the economic crisis were similar in the Czech and Slovak automotive industries despite very different national production trends during the crisis. This can be explained by the similar nature of the passenger car industries in these countries. Both the Czech and Slovak passenger car industries are predominantly specialized in the export-oriented assembly of small passenger cars and the production of automotive components. Insignificant differences between Czechia and Slovakia also suggest that the presence (in the case of Slovakia) or absence (in the case of Czechia) of active government policies to support the export-oriented passenger industry during the economic crisis had no significant effect on the extent of declines in revenues and production.

The employment effects of the economic crisis were extremely important because more than four-fifths of the surveyed Czech-based firms and more than two-thirds of the Slovak-based firms shed permanent workers, despite various efforts to maintain them. Among the surveyed Czech-based firms, domestic firms were worse affected by the economic crisis than foreign firms. This finding reflects the generally weaker and more vulnerable position of domestic firms in the automotive value chain because of their significantly smaller average size, their greater concentration among the third-tier and second-tier suppliers compared to foreign firms, and thus their greater reliance on the production of simpler and lower value-added components (see Pavlínek and Janák 2007). SMEs were more negatively affected by the economic crisis than large companies because of their less diversified production and their weaker and more vulnerable position in the automotive value chain.

The 2008–2009 crisis in the automotive industry exposed the dependence of the Czech and Slovak automotive industries on the West European automotive industry. The FDI-driven integration of Czech- and Slovak-based automotive firms into GPNs organized from abroad puts especially small domestic and foreign firms at the bottom of the supplier hierarchy in a weak, dependent and vulnerable position, with only limited chances for a successful upgrading. Because of the predominantly truncation effects of FDI in the ECE automotive industry (Britton 1980; Hayter 1982; Pavlínek 2012), the positive long-term regional development consequences of this type of captive value chain and the related industrial development are likely to be limited mostly to jobs in low value-added assembly operations in the supplier sector. The overwhelming foreign ownership and control contribute to the transfer of profits abroad and low value capture in ECE. Given this situation, it is clear that the future success of automotive industries in Czechia and Slovakia, as well as in ECE as a whole, will be closely tied with the continuing competitive success of the West European automotive industry.

References

AIA (2012) Production and sale of domestically produced vehicles. Czech Automotive Industry Association, Prague

Baldwin JR, Brown WM (2004) Regional manufacturing employment volatility in Canada: the effects of specialization and trade. Pap Reg Sci 83:519–541

Bohle D (2009) East European capitalism—what went wrong? Interv Eur J Economics Economic Policies 6(1):32–43

Bohle D, Greskovits B (2007) Neoliberalism, embedded neoliberalism and neocorporatism: towards transnational capitalism in Central-Eastern Europe. West Eur Politics 30(3):443–466

Britton JNH (1980) Industrial dependence and technological underdevelopment: Canadian consequences of foreign direct investment. Reg Stud 14(3):181–199

Carrillo J, Lung Y, van Tulder R (eds) (2004) Cars, carriers of regionalism? Palgrave MacMillan, Basingstoke

Cattaneo O, Gereffi G, Staritz C (2010) Global value chains in a postcrisis world: resilience, consolidation, and shifting end markets. In: Cattaneo O, Gereffi G, Staritz C (eds) Global value chains in a postcrisis world: a development perspective. The World Bank, Washington, DC, pp 3–20

Cruz MJV, Rolim CFC (2010) The Brazilian automotive industry in the BRICs context: the case of the metropolitan region of Curitiba. Camb J Reg Econ Soc 3(3):319–334

CSO (2011) Average registered number of employees by economic sector, 2000–2011. Czech Statistical Office, Prague

Dicken P (1976) The multiplant business enterprise and geographical space: some issues in the study of external control and regional development. Reg Stud 10(4):401–412

Dicken P (2015) Global shift: mapping the changing contours of the world economy, 7th edn. Sage, London

Domański B, Gwosdz K (2009) Toward a more embedded production system? Automotive supply networks and localized capabilities in Poland. Growth and Change 40(3):452–482

Drahokoupil J, Myant M (2010) Varieties of capitalism, varieties of vulnerabilities: financial crisis and its impact on welfare states in Eastern Europe and the commonwealth of independent states. Hist Soc Res 35(2):266–295

ERM (2011) European restructuring monitor. http://www.eurofou.europa.eu/emcc/erm/index.html, 2009.

Eurostat (2011) Structural business statistics

Ezcurra R (2011) Unemployment volatility and regional specialization in the European union. Reg Stud 45(8):1121–1137

Farkas B (2011) The central and eastern European model of capitalism. Post-Communist Econ 23(1):15–34

Gereffi G, Humphrey J, Sturgeon T (2005) The governance of global value chains. Rev Int Polit Econ 12(1):78–104

Gowan P (2009) Crisis in the heartland: consequences of the new wall street system. New Left Rev 55:5–29

Harvey D (2011) Crises, geographic disruptions and the uneven development of political responses. Econ Geogr 87(1):1–22

Havas A (2000) Changing patterns of inter- and intra-regional division of labour: Central Europe's long and winding road. In: Humphrey J, Lecler Y, Salerno MS (eds) Global strategies and local realities: the auto industry in emerging markets. Palgrave MacMillan, Basingstoke, pp 234–262

Hayter R (1982) Truncation, the international firm and regional policy. Area 14(4):277–282

Henderson J, Dicken P, Hess M, Coe N, Yeung HWC (2002) Global production networks and the analysis of economic development. Rev Int Polit Econ 9(3):436–464

HN (2008) First Czech Hyundai cars leaving Nošovice, (Ekonomika.IHNED.CZ). November 2, 2008. Accessed 11 Feb 2010 (in Czech)

Hudson R, Schamp EW (eds) (1995) Towards a new map of automobile manufacturing in Europe? New production concepts and spatial restructuring. Springer, Berlin

Humphrey J, Oeter A (2000) Motor industry policies in emerging markets: globalisation and the promotion of domestic industry. In: Humphrey J, Lecler Y, Salerno MS (eds) Global strategies and local realities: the auto industry in emerging markets. Macmillan and St. Martin's Press, Houndmills, pp 42–71

Humphrey J, Schmitz H (2002) How does insertion in global value chains affect upgrading in industrial clusters? Reg Stud 36(9):1017–1027

Humphrey J, Schmitz H (2004) Chain governance and upgrading: taking stock. In: Schmitz H (ed) Local enterprises in the global economy: issues of governance and upgrading. Edward Elgar, Cheltenham, pp 349–381

Humphrey J, Lecler Y, Salerno MS (eds) (2000) Global strategies and local realities: the auto industry in emerging markets. Palgrave MacMillan, Basingstoke

Jakubiak M, Kolesar P, Izvorski I and Kurekova L (2008) The automotive industry in the Slovak Republic: recent developments and impact on growth. Working Paper No. 29. Commission on Growth and Development, The International Bank for Reconstruction and Development/The World Bank, Washington, DC

Jürgens U, Krzywdzinski M (2009) Changing east-west division of labour in the European automotive industry. Eur Urban Reg Stud 16(1):27–42

Klier TH, Rubenstein JM (2010) The changing geography of north American motor vehicle production. Camb J Reg Econ Soc 3(3):335–347

Layan J (2000) The integration of peripheral markets: a comparison of Spain and Mexico. In: Humphrey J, Lecler Y, Salerno MS (eds) Global strategies and local realities: the auto industry in emerging markets. Palgrave MacMillan, Basingstoke, pp 122–148
Lung Y (2000) Is the rise of emerging countries as automobile producers an irreversible phenomenon? In: Humphrey J, Lecler Y, Salerno MS (eds) Global strategies and local realities: the auto industry in emerging markets. Palgrave MacMillan, Basingstoke, pp 16–41
Luptáčik M, Habrman M, Lábaj M, Rehák Š (2013) The importance of automotive industry for the Slovak economy: empirical results. University of Economics in Bratislava, Department of Economic Policy, Bratislava
Martin R (2011) The local geographies of the financial crisis: from the housing bubble to economic recession and beyond. J Econ Geogr 11:587–618
MIT (2011) Panorama zpracovatelského průmyslu ČR 2009 [Panorama of the Czech manufacturing industry 2009]. Czech Ministry of Industry and Trade, Prague
Myant M, Drahokoupil J (2012) International integration, varieties of capitalism and resilience to crisis in transition economies. Eur Asia Stud 64(1):1–33
OICA (2016) World motor vehicle production by country and type, 1997–2015. Organisation Internationale des Constructeurs d'Automobile, Paris (www.oica.net)
Pavlínek P (2002a) Transformation of central and east European passenger car industry: selective peripheral integration through foreign direct investment. Environ Plan A 34:1685–1709
Pavlínek P (2002b) Restructuring the central and eastern European automobile industry: legacies, trends and effects of foreign direct investment. Post-Soviet Geogr Econ 43:41–77
Pavlínek P (2003) Transformation of the Czech automotive components industry through foreign direct investment. Eurasian Geogr Econ 44(3):184–209
Pavlínek P (2008) A successful transformation? Restructuring of the Czech automobile industry. Heidelberg, Physica Verlag
Pavlínek P (2012) The internationalization of corporate R&D and the automotive industry R&D of east-Central Europe. Econ Geogr 88(3):279–310
Pavlínek P, Janák L (2007) Regional restructuring of the Škoda auto supplier network in the Czech Republic. Eur Urban Reg Stud 14(2):133–155
Pavlínek P, Smith A (1998) Internationalization and embeddedness in east-central European transition: the contrasting geographies of inward investment in the Czech and Slovak republics. Reg Stud 32:619–638
Pavlínek P, Ženka J (2010) The 2008–2009 automotive industry crisis and regional unemployment in Central Europe. Camb J Reg Econ Soc 3(3):349–365
Pavlínek P, Ženka J (2011) Upgrading in the automotive industry: firm-level evidence from Central Europe. J Econ Geogr 11(3):559–586
Pavlínek P, Domański B, Guzik R (2009) Industrial upgrading through foreign direct investment in central European automotive manufacturing. Eur Urban Reg Stud 16(1):43–63
Pennings E, Sleuwaegen L (2000) International relocation: firm and industry determinants. Econ Lett 67:179–186
Rugraff E (2010) Foreign direct investment (FDI) and supplier-oriented upgrading in the Czech motor vehicle industry. Reg Stud 44:627–638
SME (2011) Charakteristika strojárskeho priemyslu SR v roku 2010 [Slovak manufacturing in 2010]. The Slovak Ministry of Economy, Bratislava
Smith A, Swain A (2010) The global economic crisis, Eastern Europe, and the former soviet union: models of development and the contradictions of internationalization. Eurasian Geogr Econ 51(1):1–34
SSO (2011) Average registered number of employees by economic sector, 2000–2011. Slovak Statistical Office, Bratislava
Stanford J (2010) The geography of auto globalization and the politics of auto bailouts. Camb J Reg Econ Soc 3(3):383–405
Sturgeon TJ, Van Biesebroeck J, Gereffi G (2008) Value chains, networks and clusters: reframing the global automotive industry. J Econ Geogr 8:297–321

Sturgeon TJ, Memedovic O, Van Biesebroeck J, Gereffi G (2009) Globalisation of the automotive industry: main features and trends. Int J Technol Learn Innov Dev 2(1/2):7–24
Sturgeon TJ, Gereffi G, Rogers KB, Fernandez-Stark K (2010) The prospects for Mexico in the north American automotive industry: a global value chain perspective. Actes du GERPISA 42(June):11–22
Trendle B (2006) Regional economic instability: the role of industrial diversification and spatial spillovers. Ann Reg Sci 40:767–778
Vagac, L. (2000) The automotive industry in the Slovak Republic. South-East Europe review for labour and social affairs, No. 2, 143–72
Van Biesebroeck J, Sturgeon TJ (2010) Effects of the 2008–09 crisis on the automotive industry in developing countries: a global value chain perspective. In: Cattaneo O, Gereffi G, Staritz C (eds) Global value chains in a postcrisis world: a development perspective. The World Bank, Washington, DC, pp 209–244

Chapter 3
Upgrading

Introduction

One of the important aspects of the globalization of the automotive industry in recent decades has been a rapid increase in the assembly of automobiles and the related production of automotive components and parts outside the traditional core regions of automotive manufacturing. Two types of such areas have experienced this development. First are the peripheries of automotive core regions such as Mexico in the case of the North American core region and Spain and Central and Eastern Europe (CEE) in the case of the West European core region (Humphrey and Oeter 2000; Layan 2000; Lung 2000; Humphrey and Memedovic 2003; Dicken 2015; Dieter 2007; Pavlínek 2002a; Pavlínek et al. 2009). These peripheral areas have benefited from their lower production costs compared to core regions and their geographic proximity to the largest affluent developed world markets. Consequently, they have become attractive locations for export-oriented automotive manufacturing organized and financed by large automotive TNCs. By producing automobiles in lower-cost locations, automotive TNCs attempt to improve their overall competitiveness. Second, potentially large domestic markets of several rapidly growing "emerging economies", such as China, India and Brazil, have attracted market-capture FDI. Automotive FDI combined with governmental policies designed to support the development of domestic automotive manufacturing resulted in very rapid increases in the automotive production in these countries (e.g. Liu and Yeung 2008; Liu and Dicken 2006; Humphrey and Memedovic 2003; Carrillo et al. 2004; OICA 2016). These developments have been altering the geography of the automotive industry at various geographic scales. At the global scale, despite the continuing dominance of core regions in the global automotive industry, their share in the overall automotive output has been dramatically declining, while, at the same time, the share of less developed peripheral areas has been increasing.

The passenger car production grew from 718 thousand units in 1994 to 3.9 million in 2015 in ECE. Between 1997 and 2015, the share of ECE of the total European production increased from 7.9 to 21.2% and from 3.2 to 5.7% of the global passenger

P. Pavlínek, *Dependent Growth: Foreign Investment and the Development of the Automotive Industry in East-Central Europe*, DOI 10.1007/978-3-319-53955-3_3

car production (OICA 2016). Since the early 1990s, the ECE automotive industry has experienced rapid development based upon large inflows of FDI leading to its dramatic restructuring and growth in production (Chap. 1). In the process, the ECE automotive industry has been selectively reintegrated in the periphery of the European automotive production system. These processes have been largely limited to the passenger car production and the related manufacturing of automotive parts and components (Pavlínek 2002a, b, 2008; Pavlínek et al. 2009). The success of this development is typically measured by FDI inflows and rapid production increases. However, it has been argued that the position of the ECE automotive industry in the European automotive production system remains largely peripheral despite large FDI inflows and increases in output. This peripheral position has been typified by the large-volume production of small passenger cars, low-volume assembly of luxury passenger cars and special models from imported components, and by experimenting with new methods of work organization (e.g. Havas 2000; Pavlínek 2002a). Furthermore, the automotive industry of ECE is completely dominated by foreign TNCs through their direct ownership of all assembly plants and of the majority of especially higher tier component suppliers.

While the overall automotive production in ECE has increased, it is less clear to what extent these developments have affected the overall position of ECE-based automotive manufacturers (both foreign-owned and domestic-owned) in the European automotive value chain.[1] It is important to consider this position for several reasons. First, the position of firms in the automotive value chain affects their ability to produce, enhance and retain value. Second, it influences potential effects of the automotive industry for national and regional economies. Third, it largely determines the overall competitive position of firms in the automotive industry chain and, by extension, the overall locational stability or instability of automotive production in ECE. For these reasons, not only the firms themselves but also the ECE governments have been eager to promote improvement in the position of their automotive firms within the European and global automotive production networks.

In this chapter, I employ the concept of industrial upgrading to consider whether and to what extent the position of ECE automotive companies has been improving in the automotive value chain. I focus on the Czech automotive industry as an example of a country that has experienced a rapid increase in the passenger car output since the early 1990s and became an important European producer. In 2015, Czechia produced 1.3 m passenger cars (OICA 2016), representing the largest production volume in ECE and Eastern Europe as a whole. Within Europe, only five significantly larger countries (Germany, Spain, Britain and France) assembled more passenger cars than Czechia in 2015 (OICA 2016). As such, Czechia represents an excellent case to examine industrial upgrading in the ECE automotive industry. This chapter represents the first attempt to measure industrial upgrading in the ECE automotive industry at the firm level. It is based upon the quantitative analysis of the firm level data.

[1] Henceforth domestic-owned firms are referred to as domestic and foreign-owned firms as foreign.

The following section considers the concept of industrial upgrading. The third section explains the employed data and methodology. The fourth section evaluates the role of government policies in upgrading of the Czech automotive industry. The fifth section briefly reviews major developments in the Czech automotive industry followed by the discussion of results of empirical analysis in the sixth section. The seventh section considers changes in the relative position of Czechia in the European automotive value chains. The conclusion summarizes basic findings of the chapter.

Industrial Upgrading

One of the feasible responses of firms to maintain or increase their competitiveness in the increasingly globalized economy is to upgrade their production. Upgrading involves engaging in the production of higher value-added products, employing more efficient production strategies, and/or increasing the skill content of activities by firms (Humphrey and Schmitz 2002; Kaplinsky 2000; Porter 1990). In the global value chain (GVC) approach (e.g. Gereffi et al. 2005), the concept of industrial upgrading refers to the "process by which economic actors—nations, firms and workers—move from low-value to relatively high-value activities in global production networks" (Gereffi 2005). These processes operate at different geographic scales: within factories, within inter-firm enterprise networks, within local or national economies, and within macro regions at the international scale (Gereffi 1999). Industrial upgrading is vital for creating possibilities to enhance value and thus for creating possibilities for economic development (Henderson et al. 2002). Humphrey and Schmitz (2000, 2002, 2004a) have identified four different types of upgrading: process, product, functional and inter-sectoral. Process upgrading refers to the introduction of more efficient production methods and better technology leading also to the improved quality of produced goods and increased flexibility of producers. Product upgrading involves moving to the production of more sophisticated and higher value-added products. Functional upgrading is the process during which firms acquire new functions generating higher incomes or abandon old functions generating low incomes in the value-chain. Its goal is to increase the overall skill content of firm's activities. Inter-sectoral upgrading takes place when a firm uses its acquired production knowledge to move horizontally into new sectors. Additionally, Dunn et al. (2006: 21–3) have identified channel upgrading which refers to firms entering new higher value-added end markets in the value chain in order to lower their risk and increase sales volumes through diversification and receive higher prices for their products.

The automotive industry represents a typical example of producer-driven networks in which large industrial companies organize and coordinate investment-based vertical production networks of component suppliers (e.g. Gereffi 2001). A specific network organization and coordination is influenced by the differences in the competitive strategies of individual carmakers in different regions and markets and by the specific socio-political, cultural and institutional environment in which they operate

(Dicken 2015; Coe et al. 2004). Prospects of industrial upgrading of firms and clusters are strongly influenced by the type of value chain they are part of (Humphrey and Schmitz 2002, 2004a, b). The automotive industry represents a typical example of the so called quasi hierarchy in which lead firms drive the organization and regulation of the value chain through their corporate and market power.[2] The quasi hierarchy corresponds with captive value chains as one type of value chain governance identified by Gereffi et al. (2005). The power of lead firms over the value chain in quasi hierarchy and captive value chains allows them to determine which suppliers will be included or excluded from the value chain. It also allows them to often specify characteristics of components being supplied; the production, delivery and quality control processes to be followed by their suppliers; and control mechanisms to be employed (Humphrey and Schmitz 2002, 2004a; Coe et al. 2004). This situation differs significantly from the other types of relationships in value chains identified by Humphrey and Schmitz (2000, 2002, 2004a) (arm's length market transactions, networks and hierarchy) and by Gereffi et al. 2005 (markets, modular value chains, relational value chains and hierarchy). Humphrey and Schmitz (2002: 1023, 2004a: 355) argue that quasi hierarchical value chains offer favorable conditions for process and product upgrading but hinder functional upgrading of participating firms especially in less developed countries. Process and product upgrading among suppliers in quasi hierarchical (captive) networks is stimulated by process and product standards imposed by lead firms (assemblers) within their supplier networks. In the automotive industry, methods of "lean production" (Womack et al. 1990) tend to especially stimulate process upgrading by applying constant pressure on suppliers to cut the costs of their components, which requires frequent incremental improvements in production processes. Although beyond process upgrading, lean production alone is unlikely to lead to product and functional upgrading among suppliers (Isaksen and Kalsaas 2009), there have been additional changes in the organization of the automotive industry networks that affect upgrading prospects of suppliers. For example, in the contemporary model of assembler—supplier relations, the most important suppliers are required to become involved in R&D, thus acquiring new functions within the value chain. This situation is then favorable for functional upgrading. However, the question remains to what extent functional upgrading is limited only to certain individual tiers (such as Tier 1 suppliers) leaving other (lower) tiers with only limited chances for functional upgrading.[3] The fact that especially outside the automotive industry core Tier 1 suppliers are typically dominated by a small number of foreign TNCs, while domestic suppliers tend to be numerous in Tier 3 and Tier 2 (e.g. Pavlínek and Janák 2007), would then hinder

[2] Lead firms are powerful firms which set parameters followed by other firms in the production network, initiate the flow of new products through the production network, and organize and coordinate production networks in their respective industries (Humphrey and Schmitz 2004b; Sturgeon 2001). See, for example, Yeung (2009: 330–332) on lead firms in global production networks.

[3] See Humphrey and Memedovic (2003: 22) and Pavlínek and Janák (2007: 139–140) for an explanation of individual tiers in the automotive supplier hierarchy.

potential for functional upgrading of domestic suppliers in peripheral regions of automotive manufacturing.

The upgrading prospects particularly of smaller automotive firms at the bottom of the supplier hierarchy are limited because of highly concentrated firm structure in the automotive industry that creates high barriers of entry. Design specifications and requirements are determined by individual assemblers and are thus highly firm specific. This situation increases transaction costs for suppliers and makes their investment in production equipment and in product development more customer-specific, limiting their ability to develop unique products and technologies. The high product and process specificity makes such "captive" suppliers highly dependent on lead firms for their potential process and product upgrading and makes it difficult for them to switch to new customers. Consequently, there is little room for independent process and product upgrading and for improving the position of these small suppliers in the value chain (Sturgeon et al. 2009; Gereffi et al. 2005). However, the degree of product and process specificity depends on the complexity of supplied components, increasing with the increasing complexity of components and vice versa. Simple parts produced with simple technology tend to be less customer-specific and thus allow low-tier suppliers to supply multiple customers with similar products, which could potentially make them less 'captive'. However, their specialization in the production of simple, low value-added products under the relentless price squeeze from automotive customers typically leaves little resources to finance the development of unique products and technologies that would potentially improve the position of these firms in the value chain.

The chances for industrial upgrading at individual firms also strongly depend on the degree of their autonomy within production networks, which is strongly affected by unequal power distribution and power dominance within production networks and value chains (Henderson et al. 2002; Humphrey and Schmitz 2002). While not absolute, lead firms exercise a great deal of corporate power over production networks that they organize across different industries (Rutherford and Holmes 2008; Tokatli 2007; Coe and Hess 2005; Coe et al. 2004; Pickles et al. 2006; Yeung 2009; Sturgeon 2001). Lead firms may encourage process and product upgrading but discourage functional upgrading of their suppliers to prevent them from moving into core competency areas of lead firms, such as design and marketing, which are their greatest source of value capture, and which usually remain located in the core areas of the global economy (Tokatli 2007; Kaplinsky 2000; Schmitz and Knorringa 2000; Smith et al. 2002; Isaksen and Kalsaas 2009; Humphrey and Schmitz 2004a). However, one-sided interpretations of asymmetrical power distribution in production networks, emphasizing the power of lead firms over other network actors, tend to ignore the complex nature of power within production networks. To understand the effect of power relationships on the upgrading chances of local firms, these relationships need to be analyzed within local institutional contexts, which take into account their uneven nature in different regional and local settings (Pickles et al. 2006; Coe et al. 2004; Smith 2003; Smith et al. 2002; Henderson et al. 2002; Yeung 2005). For example, the opportunities for functional upgrading among smaller local suppliers are not only affected by the power of lead firms but also by the development of localized capabilities and competencies, which, among other things, depend on the education and skill level of the labor force, institutional settings, and cooperation with other firms.

In the automotive industry, power asymmetries favor assemblers and larger Tier 1 component suppliers over small and medium sized enterprises (SMEs), which account for the majority of Tier 2 and Tier 3 suppliers. The power of large assembly lead firms is reflected in their ability to decide which suppliers will be included in their supplier networks based on price, quality and timeliness of delivery, and also in their ability to pressure selected suppliers to engage in follow sourcing. The power of leading suppliers has increased through the wave of mergers and acquisitions among suppliers with complementary assets and advantages, reducing competition and leading to the emergence of global suppliers (Dicken 2003). Compared to the position of assemblers, global suppliers and Tier 1 suppliers in automotive production networks, the position of particularly small Tier 2 and Tier 3 local suppliers is generally weak, unless they posses unique technologies or highly specialized capabilities. This increasing power polarization in automotive industry production networks negatively influences the upgrading potential for small domestic SME suppliers, especially in less developed countries.

In the Czech automotive industry, the power of Škoda Auto especially over its small domestic suppliers was revealed during 33 interviews conducted with both domestic and foreign suppliers in 2000 and 2005. For example, the director of a foreign supplier of cloth for seat covers argued: "You must do whatever they [Škoda Auto] say because there is no other way" (Interview on 2 August 2000). And the director of a domestic supplier of rubber components argued:

> "Škoda Auto is a very demanding partner but it is not a good partner at all. Škoda is not behaving correctly to small local suppliers. It is clearly abusing its dominant position in the Czech market." (Interview on 28 July 2000).

Upgrading possibilities for domestic SMEs in less developed countries have also been affected by the changing sourcing strategies of transnational assembly firms. These lead firms increasingly relied on follow sourcing, which encouraged their established and trusted suppliers to set up manufacturing of components wherever they assembled cars (Humphrey 2000, 2003; Humphrey and Memedovic 2003). Follow sourcing contributed to the restructuring of the global automotive industry and the emergence of global suppliers, which, in addition to the geographical expansion and internationalization of their operations, significantly increased their competencies (Humphrey 2000; Sturgeon and Florida 2000; Sturgeon et al. 2008). It also had important implications for domestic automotive suppliers. Empirical evidence from Brazil and India shows that follow sourcing led to the marginalization of domestic component suppliers from Tier 1, as foreign Tier 1 suppliers started to exclusively supply the most important components and modules. Domestic suppliers were either sold or forced to form joint ventures (JVs) with foreign suppliers to maintain their position in the supplier hierarchy. Those who remained locally-owned usually supply simple components and parts with low-skilled labor. This situation undermined local engineering capabilities (Humphrey 2000, 2003;

Humphrey and Salerno 2000; Humphrey and Memedovic 2003). A similar marginalization of domestic suppliers took place in South Africa, where the combination of changing sourcing strategies of foreign assembly firms with the declining government protection of domestic suppliers, in the form of local purchasing requirements and tariff protection, led to falling numbers of domestic suppliers and of those using local technology in supply networks. Furthermore, upgrading of the domestic supplier sector was almost non-existent (Barnes and Kaplinsky 2000). The available evidence thus suggests that upgrading possibilities of particularly small domestic automotive suppliers could be very limited in less developed countries, outside the core areas of the global automotive industry.

Recent research on upgrading in the ECE automotive industry, to a large extent, supports the general trends identified by Humphrey (2000, 2003), Humphrey and Salerno (2000), Humphrey and Memedovic (2003) and Barnes and Kaplinsky (2000). Functional upgrading has indeed been very limited among domestic firms and selective functional upgrading has been taking place mostly among foreign firms. At the same time, however, research from ECE suggests that upgrading possibilities for local suppliers do exist, especially in terms of process and product upgrading (Domański and Gwosdz 2009; Jürgens and Krzywdzinski 2009; Pavlínek et al. 2009). At least in the context of the ECE automotive industry, the fear of "death of the local firm" (Barnes and Kaplinsky 2000) thus might be premature.

Industrial upgrading in the automotive industry outside the core regions can take several forms. Among assemblers, it may entail, first, product upgrading in the form of a shift from the assembly of small basic inexpensive models towards the production of larger, better equipped and, therefore, more expensive cars. However, the low-volume assembly of luxury and special models does not necessarily represent industrial upgrading in those cases when the production totally depends on know-how, machinery, and components supplied by the lead firm (e.g. Pavlínek 2002a; Havas 2000). Second, an increasing involvement in R&D activities by some assemblers, such as Czech Škoda Auto, represents an important source of functional upgrading. Third, the introduction of 'lean production', which, among other things, involved outsourcing of many activities that were previously conducted within assembly firms and the concentration on core competencies by assemblers, represents functional upgrading of assemblers.

Among suppliers, industrial upgrading involves the production of more sophisticated parts and components and, possibly, moving from the production of basic parts towards their assembly into components, and from the production of components to their assembly into modules. This type of product upgrading would then involve an improvement in the position within the hierarchy of automotive suppliers. For example, a former Tier 3 supplier can become a Tier 2 supplier or a former Tier 2 supplier can develop into a Tier 1 supplier. The second type of upgrading among suppliers is functional upgrading which involves the development of higher value-added activities and functions such as R&D, marketing and other service-related types of activities. However, as previously mentioned, functional upgrading in quasi hierarchical and captive value chains has its important limits and we might expect that only a very small number of selected suppliers actually experience it.

Additionally, because of enormous competitive and cost pressures in the automotive industry, all suppliers are under a constant pressure from assemblers and also higher-tier buyers within the value chain to engage in continuous process upgrading, leading to the production of higher quality and less expensive parts, components and modules.

Measuring Industrial Upgrading at the Firm Level

Industrial upgrading has usually been measured by the changing value and structure of exports from less to more developed countries and by analyzing a sequence of export roles of individual countries (e.g. Gereffi 1999; Bair and Gereffi 2003; Kaplinsky and Readman 2005). In the case of the ECE automotive industry, Pavlínek et al. (2009) evaluated industrial upgrading through changes in the structure of automotive exports of four ECE countries (Czechia, Hungary, Poland and Slovakia) based on the value-added of automotive products between 1998 and 2006. The major problem with this approach, as acknowledged by the authors, is that it does not tell us how much value is actually generated or added in the region. For example, the establishment of several export-oriented engine factories, which assemble engines from imported components, would result in export data suggesting major industrial upgrading through significantly increased exports of high value-added components. In reality, however, most of the value would be generated outside the region and the only value added in ECE would be in the form of assembly by low-cost labor. Pavlínek et al. (2009) also examine an increase in automotive R&D in ECE by looking at the growth and distribution of R&D centers, typically established by foreign companies. While this information is an important proxy measure especially for FDI-driven R&D in ECE, it does not provide any information about changes (if any) in the extent of R&D activities in the automotive sector as a whole and, in particular, in SMEs. Another weakness of this approach is that it could only be used for the analysis of upgrading at national or regional (NUTS III) levels because the structure of automotive exports is not available for individual firms. Moreover, as previously argued, the changing structure of automotive exports tells us nothing about how much value is actually generated in Czechia and it provides no information about functional upgrading of individual Czech-based firms.

A typical approach to evaluate upgrading at the firm level, especially by global production network (GPN) researchers, has been the collection and analysis of qualitative data from company interviews (e.g. Tokatli 2007; Smith 2003; Pickles et al. 2006; Grote and Täube 2006; Parthasarathy and Aoyama 2006; Rutherford and Holmes 2008; Domański and Gwosdz 2009; Jürgens and Krzywdzinski 2009; Isaksen and Kalsaas 2009). Although company interviews provide extremely valuable insights into processes of upgrading at the firm level, their results might be difficult to generalize because of the limited sample size and their often implicit focus on the most important firms in a particular industry. In this chapter, I develop an empirical, firm-level approach to analyze industrial upgrading at the firm level for the automotive industry as a whole. However, instead of analyzing the changing value and structure of exports, I analyze financial data and R&D indicators at the firm level. The main advantage of this approach is that it allows us to evaluate the extent of industrial upgrading in the industry as a whole and, at the same time, to compare its extent among individual firms and selected groups of firms. As such, it provides an alternative way for evaluating industrial upgrading at the firm level, which complements its qualitative analyses. In this chapter, I am specifically interested in the industrial upgrading of automotive firms (both domestic and foreign) located in Czechia. I concentrate on the processes of industrial upgrading at the firm level, which have important implications for upgrading processes at regional and national levels.

For this analysis, based on data collected by the Czech Statistical Office, I have constructed a unique database of 490 Czech-based plants employing more than 20 workers that were part of the automotive value chain in 2006. I have included not only companies classified in the NACE 34,[4] but also firms that are classified in other industrial sectors but are involved in the automotive value chain, such as companies from the rubber and plastic industries, electrical equipment and the iron and steel industry. I have collected the complete 1998–2006 data for 252 firms that existed during the entire 1998–2006 period and employed 159,281 workers in 2006. The remaining 238 firms, which employed 65,529 workers in 2006, were newly established during the 1998–2006 period, and, therefore, data for these firms do not cover the entire 1998–2006 period. The collected data included employment, output, value-added, wages and long-term tangible assets for the years of 1998, 2002, 2006 and 2007.[5] I have also collected R&D firm-level employment and R&D expenditures for the period of 1995–2007.

Firms and manufacturing branches within the automotive value chain are extremely diverse in terms of their capital, labor and R&D intensity, labor productivity and wages. The automotive industry is thus a network of technology-, capital- and labor-intensive industries, which have no common features except for the supplier linkages. Therefore, when evaluating industrial upgrading, we have to consider differences in the factor intensity (capital, labor) of production because they significantly influence values of industrial upgrading indicators.

To analyze industrial upgrading, I have employed four primary indicators (turnover per employee, factor productivity, wages and salaries per employee, R&D intensity) and five secondary indicators (capital intensity, value-added in production, labor productivity, capital productivity, and R&D employment) (Table 3.1). Seven of these measure the investment rate and profitability and the remaining two reflect the R&D intensity of production of individual firms. Capital intensity of production (capital-labor ratio) reflects a firm's investment into buildings, machinery and equipment. This type of investment can lead to an increase in labor productivity (through the embodied technological progress) as the result of process

[4] In order to ensure the data compatibility in time series, I am using the classification of industrial sectors based on the NACE 1.1 revision.

[5] With the exception of the 2007 employment data which was not available.

Table 3.1 Primary and secondary indicators of industrial upgrading

	Definition	Years measured	Type of upgrading
Primary indicators			
Turnover per employee	Turnover per employee	1998, 2002, 2006	Process, product
Factor productivity	Average of gross value-added per employee and gross value-added per unit of tangible assets	1998, 2002, 2006	Process, aggregate
Wages and salaries	Wages and salaries per employee and month	1998, 2002, 2006	Aggregate
R&D intensity	Share of total R&D expenditures in value-added	1995–2007	Functional
Secondary indicators			
Capital intensity	Tangible assets per employee	1998, 2002, 2006	Mostly process
Value-added in production	Share of value-added in turnover	1998, 2002, 2006	Mostly functional
Labor productivity	Gross value-added per employee	1998, 2002, 2006	Process, aggregate
Capital productivity	Gross value-added/tangible assets	1998, 2002, 2006	Process, aggregate
R&D employment	Share of R&D employment in total employment	1995–2007	Functional

Source: The author

upgrading (Sakellaris and Wilson 2004). However, an increase in capital intensity can result from the expansion of production that does not necessarily involve any significant upgrading. Therefore, I have not used capital intensity to measure the intensity of industrial upgrading, but to measure the contribution of capital investment to the increase in value-added. Capital-labor ratio also reflects sunk-costs (Pennings and Sleuwaegen 2000).

Turnover per employee, value-added in production, labor, capital and factor productivity are all strongly influenced by the factor intensity of production and, specifically, by its capital intensity (Ženka 2008). Capital-intensive industries exhibit the highest levels of labor productivity and low levels of value-added in production. Capital intensity is also high in the case of technology-intensive industries with high capital inputs and in the case of assembly type production (such as the manufacturing of motor vehicles—NACE 34.1). The correlation analysis of capital intensity and labor productivity between 2002 and 2006 conducted on the sample of 412 firms has shown no relationship between the growth in physical capital stock and labor productivity at the firm level. Therefore, I can use labor productivity to measure whether upgrading is taking place, but not the achieved level of upgrading. To measure the achieved level of upgrading, I have used "factor productivity" which is defined as the average of capital productivity and labor productivity,[6] and it measures the average amount of value-added per unit of labor costs and tangible assets. As a supplementary indicator, "capital productivity" is defined for our purposes as the value-added per unit of tangible assets. Factor productivity balances different influences on productivity in capital-intensive industries, technology-intensive industries and highly skilled labor-intensive industries by lowering the extremely high labor productivity of capital-intensive industries, while increasing it for labor-intensive industries and skill-intensive high-tech industries. It also reflects the real technology-intensity of production and value-added created by a particular firm. However, it does not measure functional upgrading, it has the same weaknesses as capital intensity described previously, and, its value can be strongly influenced by layoffs (Szalavetz 2005).

The share of value-added in turnover reflects the firm's ability to produce and retain value. Capital-intensive industries and assembly operations typically have the lowest share of value-added in turnover, while labor-intensive industries and skill-intensive high-tech industries have the highest share. Since the share of value-added in turnover tells us nothing about the skill content of production, I have only used it in combinations with other previously described indicators.

Increase in the "turnover per employee" reflects rising productivity in terms of firm's investment into modern technologies, automation of production, implementation of organization changes, management practices, and, also, a shift to the production of more expensive products. However, the turnover per employee measures only output. Its increased values may reflect neither product nor process upgrading in cases of highly efficient assembly plants importing sophisticated components and exporting final products without creating significant value-added during the assembly.

Wages and salaries per employee represent the most important indicator of the combined product, process and functional upgrading (what I call 'aggregate upgrading'). It reflects the value-added created by a particular firm, its labor skills, labor productivity and its functional upgrading. However, the growth in average wages is not necessarily related to increases in labor productivity since it is also influenced by regional differences in labor costs and it can be distorted by high managerial wages.

R&D intensity reflects the position of a particular firm in GVCs and it is considered to be the most important indicator of functional upgrading and technology intensity of production (e.g. Hatzichronoglou 1997). To elminate large annual changes in R&D expenditures, I have worked with their 3-year averages. I have also used R&D employment and its changes to evaluate the importance of R&D at the level of individual firms.

---

[6] Since the size units of labor and capital productivity are not comparable, I have calculated factor productivity in the form of an index, relating labor and capital productivity to the value of the Czech automotive industry as a whole.

Government Policy and Upgrading of the Czech Automotive Industry

Any analysis of upgrading in Czech automotive firms needs to be understood in the broader context of national economic regulation and policies. National governments retain their critical role in the systems of economic governance and regulation (Coe et al. 2008; Hudson 2004, 2008) and their role in the development of the automobile industry has been especially important (Dicken 2015). Governments' varying roles in industrial upgrading of different industries in different countries have been documented in the GPN and GVC literature (e. g. Gereffi 2009; Rutherford and Holmes 2008; Hess and Coe 2006; Hassler 2009; Liu and Dicken 2006), although the GVC analysis tends to focus on various forms of governance within the value chain, rather than on the role of government policies (e.g. Gereffi et al. 2005).

During the 1948–1989 state socialist period, the Czechoslovak government owned and commanded the automotive industry (see Pavlínek 2008 for details). The state reduced its role in the economy dramatically through liberalization, privatization and marketization policies, following the disintegration of the centrally planned economy after 1989 (e.g. Pavlínek 2002c). Since the early 1990s, different opinions about the government's role in economic development among major Czech political parties translated into inconsistent industrial policies. During periods of centrist and left-leaning governments (between 1990 and mid-1992, between 1998 and mid-2006 and after mid-2013), the government attempted to pursue industrial policies and it introduced incentives for foreign investors. During periods of right-leaning governments (between mid-1992 and 1997 and between mid-2006 and mid-2013), neoliberals rejected the need for industrial policy, questioned incentives for foreign investors, and dismantled or undermined existing policies in these areas. However, industrial policy was not pursued in any systematic manner, even during the period of its rhetorical government support between 1998 and 2006. Instead, it consisted of a number of uncoordinated measures pursued by individual departments of the Czech Ministry of Industry and Trade (MIT) and by the Czech Investment Promotion Agency (CzechInvest). Out of these measures, investment incentives were by far the most important and most expensive.[7] Even these uncoordinated measures were considered excessive by the right-wing Civic Democratic Party (CDP), which formed the government in 2006. It immediately abolished MIT's Department for Industrial Policy and reiterated its distaste for any industrial policy. CzechInvest's activities were significantly curtailed and its management replaced by inexperienced managers along party lines. The lack of political consensus about the role of the state in the economy undermined the government's role in nurturing the industrial strengths important for the 'strategic coupling' of GPNs and regional economies (Coe et al. 2004). Consequently, some of these industrial strengths have been significantly

[7]Additional measures that could be listed under the umbrella of industrial policy included R&D subsidies, export subsidies, subsidies for SMEs, subsidies for technology transfer, and various sectoral operational programs.

undermined in Czechia since the early 1990s. Perhaps, the best example is the disintegration of the successful system of vocational training in the early 1990s, which basically destroyed the supply of skilled labor for manufacturing companies, one of the former strengths of the Czech economy.

Despite being inconsistent and often contradictory, the government's role in upgrading the Czech automotive industry and its incorporation into GPNs has been crucial. Three influences have been especially important since the early 1990s. First was the JV agreement between state-owned Škoda passenger car producer and German Volkswagen (VW) in 1991, which triggered rapid upgrading in the Czech supplier industry through follow sourcing and by forcing domestic firms to upgrade the quality of supplied components. The government negotiated a clause protecting Škoda's Czech suppliers for a certain period from being replaced by foreign suppliers, after the JV was formed. This gave the domestic Škoda suppliers a limited time to upgrade or face exclusion from the Škoda supplier network. Follow sourcing was even more important, because 60 JVs and greenfield foreign-owned plants were set up to supply Škoda Auto by 1993. By 2005, the number of JVs among Czech-based Škoda suppliers had increased to 94 and the number of greenfield factories to 58 (see Pavlínek 2008 for details). Second was the government decision to offer generous investment incentives to foreign investors, beginning in 1998, which triggered a wave of automotive investments both in vehicle assembly, represented by new assembly plants built by Toyota Peugeot Citroën Automobile (TPCA) and Hyundai, and in the supply of automotive components. Between April 1998 and September 2016, the Czech government approved incentives for 319 automotive investments, promising to invest €10.9 billion and create 76,729 new jobs (CzechInvest 2016). Government support included corporate tax relief, job creation grants, training and re-training grants, and the provision of infrastructure and discounted land. This support is likely to remain vital in attracting FDI into the automotive industry in the future. Third was government support for technology and business support service centers, newly built or expanded by both foreign and domestic firms since 2001, which significantly contributed to the functional upgrading of subsidized firms. By 2009, 25 R&D centers and two business support service centers, which promised to create 1604 new jobs, had been offered investment incentives in the automotive industry. Six out of 25 investment incentives for R&D centers were granted to domestic firms (CzechInvest 2010). In addition to investment incentives, firms can deduct R&D costs from their tax base and apply for grants from the National Research Program. Corporate R&D is also supported by grants from EU structural funds, which support the development of education for R&D, development and upgrading of R&D infrastructure, and innovation projects in SMEs.

With the exception of the temporary protection of domestic suppliers negotiated in the Škoda-VW JV agreement, the government value creation and enhancement strategies benefited foreign TNCs, in particular, rather than domestic suppliers. Although domestic suppliers have been eligible for investment incentives, the minimum required investment of 200 million CZK (about 12 million USD) excluded the vast majority of them because of their small average size. The number of domestic firms eligible for investment incentives increased after the minimum required investment was significantly lowered. Out of 319 investments approved for government incentives between 1998 and 2016, 107 went to domestic companies (CzechInvest 2016).[8]

Thus, the upgrading of the Czech automotive industry benefited from government policies, although government support for manufacturing fluctuated significantly over the past twenty-five years. Such fluctuations in the extent of state involvement in the economy are common in capitalist states (e.g. Hudson 2001; Dicken 2015), although, in the case of Czechia, they have been exacerbated by political instability and infighting during the post-socialist transformation. The question remains how this erratic government policy towards the manufacturing industry will influence long-term prospects of the automotive industry in Czechia.

The Czech Automotive Industry

The narrowly defined Czech automotive industry (NACE 34) employed 118,454 workers in 2007 and 162,847 workers in in 2015 (NACE 29) (CSO 2016). However, my database shows that the actual employment in the Czech automotive value chain is significantly larger. Based on the 2006 firm-level data for all Czech-based automotive suppliers (not only in NACE 34), the Czech automotive industry employed 224,861 workers.[9] Employment in NACE 34 almost doubled between 1994 and 2007. This growth reflected a major employment increase in the production of components, where the number of jobs more than tripled between 1994 and 2007, while the employment in the assembly of cars and engines decreased by 4% during the same period. Employment in the assembly of passenger cars and engines increased significantly, but this increase was more than offset by the collapse of the Czech commercial vehicle industry and the related job losses in the 1990s and 2000s (Fig. 3.1).[10] Employment among automotive suppliers outside NACE 34 increased even faster (by 37,091 jobs) between 1998 and 2006 (Fig. 3.2). The rapid employment growth in the production of components reflected the increase in the assembly of passenger cars in Czechia from 173,586 units in 1994 to 931,298 in 2007 and 1.3 m units in 2015 and in the FDI-driven export-oriented manufacturing of automotive components, partially based on generous governmental investment incentives offered since April 1998 (Pavlínek 2008, 2002d; Pavlínek and Janák 2007). By

[8] However, this figure significantly overstates the number of incentives granted to domestic firms because CzechInvest lists many foreign firms, such as Škoda Auto, Honeywell, Mubea, Ronal, Johnson Controls, Hitachi, Faurecia and many more, among domestic firms (CzechInvest 2016).

[9] I am aware that this figure overstates the actual employment in the automotive value chain since auto suppliers are in many cases devoting only part of their production to automotive components. Unfortunately, precise data reflecting their degree of involvement in the automotive industry are not available.

[10] The Czech truck production declined from 37,686 units in 1989 to 850 units in 2015 (AIA 2016). The three most important truck producers and one bus maker shed more than 28,000 jobs between 1989 and 2006 (Pavlínek 2008).

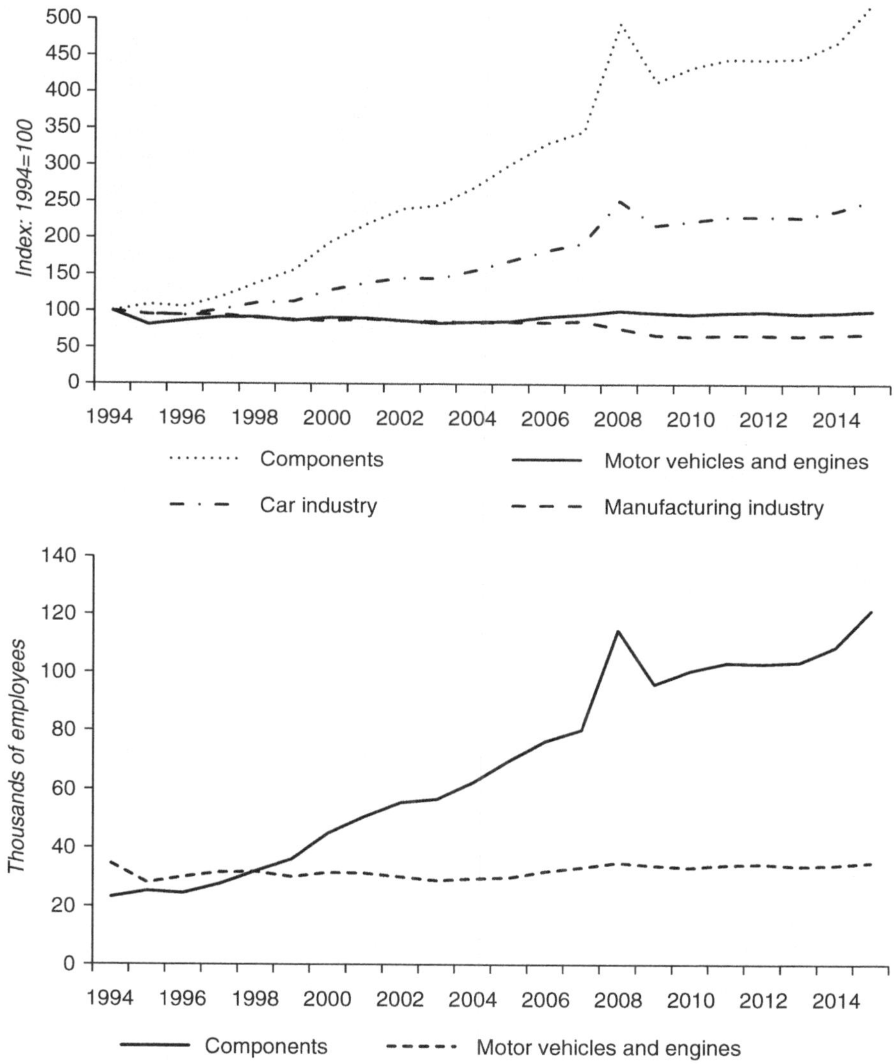

Fig. 3.1 Employment change in the narrowly defined Czech automotive components sector and in the production of motor vehicles and their engines (1994–2007: NACE 34.1, 2008–2015: NACE 29.1) (*top*) and the comparison of employment trends (*bottom*), 1994–2015. *Source*: Based on data in MIT (2001, 2008, 2015)

2009, three automakers assembled passenger cars in Czechia: Škoda Auto, TPCA, and Hyundai.

The employment increase in the automotive industry ran counter to the general employment trend in the Czech manufacturing industry as a whole, which lost 326 thousand jobs (20% of the total) between 1994 and 2015 (MIT 2008; CSO 2016;

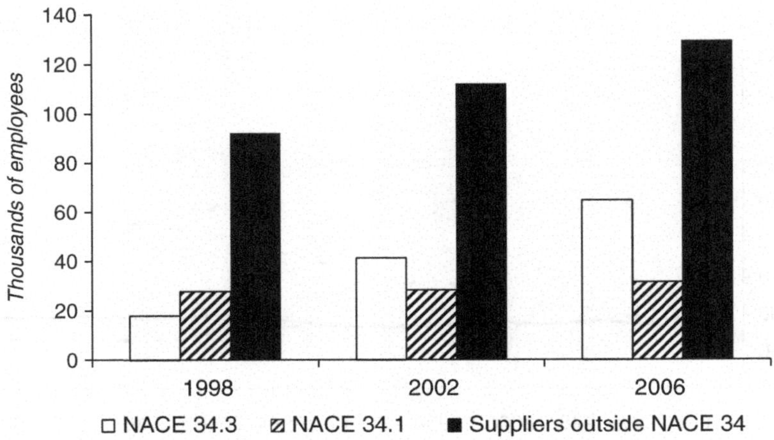

Fig. 3.2 Employment change according to different sectors of the broadly defined Czech automotive industry (NACE 34.1 = motor vehicles and their engines, NACE 34.3 = components). *Source*: Author's calculations based on various databases

Table 3.2 The development of basic indicators of the broadly defined Czech automotive industry, 1998–2006

	1998	2002	2006	2002 (1998 = 100)	2006 (1998 = 100)
Number of firms	265	412	490	155	185
Employment (thousands)	137.9	181.5	224.8	132	163
Turnover (bn. CZK)	266.7	439.8	676.2	165	254
Gross value-added (bn. CZK)	62.6	93.8	140.2	150	224
Total value of tangible assets (bn. CZK)	87.2	139.4	165.1	160	189
R&D personnel	3429	3896	4949	114	144
R&D expenditures (bn. CZK)	5.2	6.0	8.4	115	161

Notes: Includes firms with more than 20 employees, financial indicators are in constant prices
Source: Author's calculations based on various databases

Fig. 3.1). As a result, the narrowly defined automotive industry increased its share of the total manufacturing employment from 3.9% in 1994 to 14.3% in 2015. The automotive firms included in my broader database increased their share from 11.0 to 19.7% between 1998 and 2006. In addition to employment growth, the data in my database reveal rapid increases in output, value-added, physical capital stock, and R&D expenditures during the same period (Table 3.2). The output and value-added more than doubled. Apart from R&D expenditures, the employment grew least rapidly, resulting in significant gains in labor productivity and increases in the capital-labor ratio.

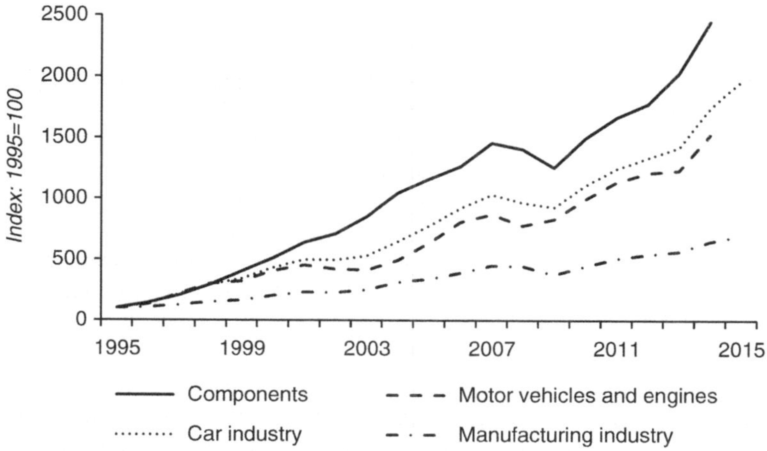

Fig. 3.3 Change in exports in the narrowly defined Czech automotive industry, 1995–2015. Based on current prices. *Source*: Based on data in MIT (2001, 2008, 2016)

The Czech automotive components industry experienced a radical FDI-driven restructuring in the 1990s and further in the 2000s based upon the transfer of Western know-how, production methods and the supply chain management policies of Volkswagen-owned Škoda Auto. As a lead firm, Škoda developed a strong pressure on its Czech-based suppliers in the early 1990s to dramatically raise the quality of their components. In the process, about two-thirds of Škoda's pre-1990 Czech suppliers were excluded from its supply chain (Pavlínek 2003, 2008). Overall, foreign assembly firms and components suppliers have invested more than ten billion EUR in the Czech automotive industry since 1990 (Chap. 1) and 76% of capital stock was foreign-owned as of 2008 (AIA 2016). Large capital investments led to significant increases in overall productivity and value-added in the automotive industry. Between 1998 and 2006, 20 companies with the highest capital investments accounted for 33% of newly created jobs, 50% of production increase and 48% of value-added increase in the Czech automotive industry. During the same period, these companies received 62% of the total investment into tangible assets.

Consequently, the structure of the Czech passenger car industry has changed significantly since the early 1990s. In the early 1990s, it was dominated by the production for the domestic market represented by a single assembler (Škoda Auto).[11] The components industry was thus overwhelmingly dependent on supplying Škoda. In the second half of the 1990s and in the 2000s, the Czech automotive industry diversified and lowered its dependence on Škoda. First, both foreign and successfully restructured domestic components suppliers significantly expanded exports, capitalizing on the lower-cost Czech labor force and the geographic proximity of the west European

[11] Tatra, a Czech truck producer, was engaged in the low volume assembly of its T700 luxury passenger cars in the 1990s. Their annual production peaked at 673 units in 1991 and completely ceased in 1998 (Pavlínek 2000).

automotive industry core to supply west European automakers (Fig. 3.3). Second, the low cost labor and relative geographic location combined with generous governmental investment incentives attracted a large number of foreign automotive suppliers not supplying Škoda to set up their operations in Czechia (Pavlínek and Janák 2007). Third, two new assembly plants, launched by TPCA and Hyundai in 2004 and 2008, respectively, and the corresponding follow supply by Japanese and South Korean suppliers further diversified the Czech automotive industry (Pavlínek 2008).

Based on my database, increases in the number of firms (from 265 to 490) and in their employment (from 137,928 to 224,810) suggest a major growth of the Czech automotive industry between 1998 and 2006.[12] Only 252 firms existed during the entire 1998–2006 period, while 238 new automotive firms were established. To better understand the newly established firms, I have analyzed the structure of 140 newly established companies employing more than 100 workers. These 140 foreign and domestic firms included 79 greenfield investments with 35,961 employees, and the companies that existed before 1998 but changed their ownership either by entering into a joint venture agreement with a foreign partner (four firms with 924 employees) or by being acquired by a foreign firm (ten firms with 7838 employees). The remaining 47 companies with 10,181 employees changed their names and registration numbers without any ownership changes. Altogether, these 140 largest newly established firms accounted for 74% (64,265) of newly created jobs in the broadly defined Czech automotive industry and received 60.5% (35.7 bn. CZK—about 1.9 bn. USD) of investment into tangible assets between 1998 and 2006. However, they generated only 42.1% of value-added and 16.6% of R&D expenditures, suggesting that a high share of automotive FDI went into the low value-added assembly production of parts and components. This type of FDI was thus largely responsible for the tripled value of production and value-added in production between 1998 and 2006. However, the newly established firms did not differ significantly from the existing ones in terms of capital intensity (higher by 4.9%). Their turnover per employee was higher (by 28.6%) and their labor productivity and average monthly wages were lower (by 11.1 and 8.9% respectively). They created only 546 R&D jobs and spent only 663 mil. CZK (35.4 mil. USD) in R&D expenditures, suggesting a low importance of R&D in the newly established firms.

1998–2006 Upgrading in the Czech Automotive Industry

Between 1998 and 2006, 92% of the Czech-based automotive firms recorded an increase in turnover per employee, 85% recorded an increase in labor productivity and all but three recorded an increase in wages. At the same time, more than half of all firms experienced either a decrease or no change in factor productivity, mostly resulting from the falling capital productivity caused by investment into tangible assets (Table 3.3). My data suggest that while the newly established firms were

[12] The Czech manufacturing industry as a whole lost 150,148 jobs in the same period.

Table 3.3 Indicators of industrial upgrading in the broadly defined Czech automotive industry, 1998–2006

	1998	2002	2006	2002 (1998 = 100)	2006 (1998 = 100)
Capital intensity	613	743	734	121	120
Turnover per employee	1875	2343	3007	125	160
Labor productivity	440	500	624	114	142
Capital productivity	0.72	0.67	0.85	94	118
Factor productivity index[a]				104	130
Wages and salaries	13.0	15.4	17.7	119	136
Share of R&D expenditures in value-added (%)	8.38	6.95	7.18	83	86

Notes: Includes firms with more than 20 employees, financial indicators are in constant prices, all indicators in thousands of CZK unless stated otherwise; see Table 3.1 for the definitions of terms
Source: Author's calculations based on various databases
[a]Factor productivity of the Czech automotive industry as a whole can only be expressed as a growth index

Table 3.4 Indicators of industrial upgrading of 252 firms that existed prior to 1998 and during the entire 1998–2006 period (newly created firms during the 1998–2006 period are excluded)

	1998	2002	2006	2002 (1998 = 100)	2006 (1998 = 100)
Turnover per employee	1908	2630	3518	138	184
Labor productivity	445	567	766	127	172
Capital productivity	0.71	0.67	0.94	94	133
Factor productivity index	98[a]	105[a]	117[a]	111	153
R&D employment (%)	2.5	2.5	2.7	100	109
R&D intensity (%)	8.6	6.9	6.3	79	73
Wages and salaries	13.0	17.2	21.5	132	165
Capital intensity	628	847	812	135	129

Notes: Includes firms with more than 20 employees, financial indicators are in constant prices, all indicators in thousands of CZK unless stated otherwise; see Table 3.1 for the definitions of terms
Source: Author's calculations based on various databases
[a]Czech automotive industry = 100

driving the job creation and rapid increases in output, an intensive upgrading was taking place especially in the group of 252 existing firms, which had existed before 1998 and most of them also before 1989. Compared to the newly established firms, the existing firms accounted for 73% of the total 1998–2006 increase in turnover, 79% increase in value-added, 56% increase in R&D employees and 92% increase in R&D expenditures. Both process and product upgrading was important in the existing firms, resulting in significant increases in turnover per employee, factor productivity and wages (Table 3.4). Unfortunately, the statistical analysis of financial indicators alone for individual firms does not allow us to distinguish between process and product upgrading since both are reflected in the data through increases in value-added productivity and factor productivity. Both labor productivity and factor productivity significantly increased between 1998 and 2006. The vast majority of firms (223 out of 252) recorded increases in labor productivity but less than half (121 out of 252) recorded increases in factor productivity.

Product upgrading among the Czech-based automotive suppliers was related to several developments between 1998 and 2006. First, Škoda Auto, which was the single assembler of passenger cars in Czechia until February 2005, was substantially increasing the assembly of more expensive and higher value-added models.[13] Consequently, Škoda's suppliers were required to supply higher quality and more expensive components. Second, as Škoda introduced modular production in the mid-1990s, Tier-1 suppliers were required to supply complex preassembled modules and integrated systems of components rather than individual components.[14] Third, to maintain their competitiveness, both in domestic and foreign markets, the Czech-based suppliers were pressured to produce more technology-intensive and, in many cases, also more complex and sophisticated components.

However, process upgrading represented the most intensive and most important type of upgrading. While product upgrading was very selective and was, to a large extent, limited to a relatively small group of especially Tier-1 suppliers (Pavlínek and Janák 2007), process upgrading was a necessary precondition for all automotive suppliers to maintain their competitiveness. Automotive suppliers are under a constant pressure from assembly firms and higher-tier suppliers in the automotive value chain to lower their production costs, while maintaining perfect quality of their products. This pressure forces suppliers to make large capital investments to purchase and employ better technology and machinery in production.

Functional upgrading was also highly selective when measured by changes in R&D employment and R&D expenditures. In 2006, 73% of all automotive firms had no R&D workers (compared to 76% in 1998) and only 7% employed more than 20 R&D workers. Between 1998 and 2006, 108 firms recorded an increase in the value of R&D expenditures, while 35 recorded a decrease. The ten automotive firms with the fastest growing R&D employment and expenditures accounted for 79% of the total increase in R&D expenditures and 87% of the total increase in R&D employment. The number of R&D employees grew by 44%, and the total value of R&D expenditures almost doubled in the Czech automotive industry between 1998 and 2006.

Industrial Upgrading in the Domestic and Foreign Firms

In the next step, I have analyzed differences between the domestic and foreign automotive firms. The number of domestic firms increased by 69% and of foreign firms by 104% between 1998 and 2006. Although there was exactly the same number of domestic and foreign firms (245 each) in 2006, the foreign firms were significantly

[13] The mid-sized Octavia was introduced in November 1996, the larger and more expensive Superb in September 2001, the modernized Octavia (Octavia II) in 2004 and the crossover Roomster in 2006.

[14] The first modular assembly plant was built by Škoda for the mid-sized model Octavia in 1997. The production of all subsequent models (the Fabia, Superb, Octavia II, Roomster, Yeti, Rapid and the Kodiaq) was based on modular assembly.

Table 3.5 Basic indicators of the domestic and foreign firms in the broadly defined Czech automotive industry, 1998–2006

	1998		2006		2006 (1998 = 100)	
	Czech	Foreign	Czech	Foreign	Czech	Foreign
Number of firms	145	120	245	245	169	204
Employment	58,521	79,407	65,875	158,935	113	200
Turnover (bn. CZK)	58.8	204.0	113.9	691.4	194	339
Value-added (bn. CZK)	17.3	44.1	29.6	137.4	171	311
Tangible assets (bn. CZK)	26.7	59.6	32.9	163.7	123	275
Wages and salaries total (bn. CZK)	7.9	13.7	13.7	43.1	174	314
R&D personnel	1044	2385	1251	3698	120	155
R&D expenditures (bn. CZK)	0.5	4.8	1.0	9.0	198	189

Notes: Includes firms with more than 20 employees, financial indicators are in constant prices
Source: Author's calculations based on various databases

larger, employing on average 649 workers compared to 269 workers in the domestic firms. The domestic companies thus accounted for only 29% of the total automotive employment. They accounted for only 14% of the total value of production and 18% of the value-added, suggesting their significantly lower turnover per employee and labor productivity compared to the foreign firms (Table 3.5).

Compared to the foreign firms, the domestic firms are typified by a lower capital and technology intensity, lower degree of automation of production and higher share of value-added in production. Their higher share of value-added in production results from lower labor productivity, and it is also caused by the foreign firms often engaging in the low value-added assembly production in Czechia.

The foreign firms recorded capital intensity higher by 106% and turnover per employee higher by 152% than the domestic firms in 2006. These large differences reflect a large FDI by the foreign firms in buildings, machinery and modern technologies. They also reflect a more efficient organization of production and management in the foreign firms. The differences in factor productivity and R&D employment were much smaller between the domestic and foreign firms (Table 3.6). Capital productivity was higher in the domestic firms because their fixed assets have already been written off.

The foreign firms are extremely heterogeneous in terms of their labor and factor productivity, capital intensity and R&D intensity. In 2006, Škoda Auto alone accounted for 24% of the total value-added of all foreign firms, and it created the higher total value-added than all 245 domestic firms combined. The differences among the foreign firms measured by the standard deviation were 115% higher in turnover per employee and 128% higher in capital intensity than the differences among the domestic firms. These large differences typify the highly selective nature of especially functional upgrading among the foreign firms.

Table 3.6 Indicators of industrial upgrading of the domestic and foreign firms in the broadly defined Czech automotive industry, 1998–2006

	1998		2006		2006 (1998 = 100)	
	Czech	Foreign	Czech	Foreign	Czech	Foreign
Turnover per employee	1005	2569	1728	4350	172	169
Labor productivity	295	556	449	865	152	156
Capital productivity	0.65	0.74	0.90	0.84	139	113
Factor productivity index[a]	78	115	83	108	146	134
R&D employment (%)	1.8	3.0	1.9	2.3	106	77
R&D expenditures/value-added (%)	2.8	10.8	3.3	6.6	115	61
Wages and salaries	11,190	14,415	17,287	22,605	154	157
Capital intensity	457	751	500	1030	109	137

Notes: Includes firms with more than 20 employees, financial indicators are in constant prices, all indicators in thousands of CZK unless stated otherwise; see Table 3.1 for the definitions of terms
Source: Author's calculations based on various databases
[a]Czech automotive industry = 100

Both the domestic and foreign firms recorded rapid increases in production, value-added, tangible assets and R&D expenditures between 1998 and 2006. However, all these indicators (except for R&D expenditures) show that the foreign firms grew much faster than the domestic automotive firms (Table 3.5). While the growth of the foreign firms was predominantly extensive, as documented by the decreasing value of R&D intensity and the decreasing share of value-added in production, the domestic firms recorded higher increases in several upgrading indicators, such as the turnover per employee, factor productivity, the share of R&D employment of the total employment and R&D intensity.

The largest difference between the domestic and foreign firms was in the total R&D expenditures. The domestic firms spent only 10% of the Czech automotive industry total in 2006, despite the fact that they accounted for 25% of the total Czech automotive R&D employment (Table 3.5). However, the R&D data for the foreign firms were strongly influenced by several automotive firms with the largest R&D expenditures and employment. The top five foreign companies accounted for 59% of the R&D employment and 68% of the R&D expenditures of the foreign firms' total in 2006. Škoda Auto alone accounted for 38% of the total R&D employment and 53% of the total R&D expenditures of the foreign firms.

Only 59 foreign firms recorded any R&D employment in 2006, compared to 23 in 1998, suggesting functional upgrading in 36 companies. However, 186 foreign automotive firms (76% of the total) had no R&D in Czechia in 2006. R&D employment increased in 44 foreign firms and the total R&D employment grew by 55% in the foreign firms between 1998 and 2006 (Table 3.5). R&D employment decreased in five companies, four of them formerly domestic firms, as the new foreign owners rationalized the existing R&D. Only one foreign company eliminated its R&D employment between 1998 and 2006.

There were 74 domestic automotive firms employing R&D workers in 2006 (30% of the total), compared to 39 in 1998, suggesting functional upgrading in 35 domestic firms. The total number of R&D employees in the domestic firms increased by 20% between 1998 and 2006 (Table 3.5). The R&D employment increased in 49 firms and decreased in 24 firms. There were 171 domestic automotive firms with no R&D in 2006 compared to 206 in 1998. Three domestic companies eliminated their R&D workforce between 1998 and 2006, while 37 launched R&D activities, suggesting a selective nature of functional upgrading among the domestic firms.

Changes in the Relative Position of Czechia in the European Automotive Value Chains

Did upgrading in the automotive industry have any effect on the relative position of Czechia in European automotive value chains? When compared to the sample of 18 European auto-producing countries between 1996 and 2006, the Czech automotive industry was the fastest growing with the exception of Slovakia. However, large increases in turnover are not necessarily associated with any industrial upgrading. To determine whether the position of Czech-based automotive firms has improved in GVCs, I have evaluated the development of R&D employment, R&D expenditures and the share of R&D expenditures in value-added for the automotive industry in Czechia relative to other European countries. In automotive R&D expenditures, the position of Czechia improved relative to all Western European countries for which the Eurostat data was available between 2001 and 2006 (Table 3.7). For example, while the R&D expenditures of the Spanish-based automotive firms were higher by 15% in 2001, they were 1% lower than the R&D expenditures of the Czech-based firms in 2006, despite Spain producing more than twice as many cars as Czechia in 2006. The Czech-based firms also began to narrow the gap in automotive R&D expenditures with semi-peripheral countries of the European automotive production system, such as France, Italy, Sweden and Britain, suggesting a gradual functional upgrading of the Czech-based automotive firms as a whole. While still enormous, the gap between Czechia and Germany has also narrowed between 2001 and 2006. Compared to other ECE countries, Czechia's automotive R&D expenditures were significantly larger than those of Poland and Hungary. Slovakia's automotive R&D expenditures were only at 0.5% and Slovenia's at 3% of the total Czech automotive R&D expenditures. These differences between Czechia and other ECE countries reflect the size and value of R&D at the Czech-based Škoda Auto. However, they also reflect the rapid development of automotive R&D centers in the early 2000s. In 2006, there were 14 automotive R&D centers employing more than 30 workers in Czechia. Only two were established before 1989 and one in the 1990s. The remaining 11 were launched in the 2000s (see Chap. 4). Although limited to a small number of firms, these R&D investments were responsible for functional upgrading and the gradual improvement in the relative position of the Czech

Table 3.7 Relative trends in business R&D expenditures, R&D employment, share of R&D expenditures in value-added, apparent labor productivity and wage-adjusted labor productivity for manufacture of motor vehicles, trailers and semi-trailers in selected countries between 2001 and 2013/2014, Czechia = 100

	R&D expenditures			R&D employment			R&D in value-added			Apparent labor productivity			Wage-adjusted labor productivity		
	2001	2006	2013	2001	2006	2013	2002	2006	2013	2001	2006	2014	2001	2006	2014
Czechia	100	100	100	100	100	100	100	100	100	100	100	100	100	100	100
Austria	143	103	185	77	67	79	156	123	374	366	286	239	71	75	73
Britain	551	132	821	290	107	334	83[a]	38	296	312	220	331	63	56	113
France	1482	892	763	993	561	366	163	200	326	320	187	149	65	50	49
Germany	6712	6509	6875	2967	2827	2477	279	344	488	348	250	244	54	50	62
Hungary	7	10	41	21	24	50	15	17	70	162	134	104	138	133	113
Poland	NA	10	52	NA	38	68	NA	20	55	103	89	73	71	108	89
Romania	1[b]	1	17	58	27	24	19	6	42	19	38	39	58	87	74
Slovakia	1	0	34	3	1	7	2	1	86	107	83	91	77	96	86
Spain	114	99	131	79	130	135	27[b]	39	87	245	181	167	63	63	71
Sweden	731	532	NA	377[c]	340	NA	348	342	NA	335	203	173	68	52	45

[a]2001
[b]2000
[c]2002

Notes: Apparent labor productivity = gross value added per employee, wage-adjusted labor productivity = apparent labor productivity by average personnel costs

Source: Calculated by the author from Eurostat (2009, 2016,)

automotive industry in the European automotive value chain. However, in contrast to the 2001–2006 period, the relative position of Czechia worsened with respect to both the majority of West European countries and the countries of ECE between 2006 and 2013 (Table 3.7). This reflects a less rapid growth in the automotive industry in Czechia than in other ECE countries, such as Slovakia and Romania, and the effects of the 2008–2009 economic crisis, which may have made foreign-controlled R&D more vulnerable to cuts than R&D in home countries (Chap. 2). However, the picture is less clear in terms of R&D employment and the share of R&D expenditure in value-added between 2002 and 2013.

The 2001–2014 trends in apparent labor productivity (gross value-added per employee) point towards the improving position of the Czech-based firms in the European automotive value chains. The Czech position improved with respect to all countries with the exception of Britain and Romania. These trends reflect the large capital investment in the Czech automotive industry and related process upgrading in the 2000s. The trends in wage-adjusted apparent labor productivity still show a gradually improving Czech position compared to most other countries between 2001 and 2006, but they also suggest that this improvement was being undermined by rapidly growing Czech wages.

Conclusion

In this chapter, I set out to develop a quantitative approach to measure industrial upgrading at the firm level and I tested my approach on the Czech automotive industry. The analysis of the firm-level data has revealed three important processes taking place in the Czech automotive industry between 1998 and 2006. First, the domestic firms were restructuring and modernizing their production to maintain or enhance their competitive position in the automotive supplier industry. Restructuring of the large domestic firms involved a significant labor shedding, which resulted in the increases in labor productivity and the growth in capital intensity of production in the domestic firms as a whole. Second, the foreign companies were rapidly expanding their production in Czechia, both through building new greenfield factories and enlarging the existing production between 1998 and 2006. As a result of this extensive growth, increases in production and employment of the foreign firms were faster than their increases in value-added, R&D employment and R&D expenditures. Third, both the domestic and foreign firms selectively engaged in product, process and functional upgrading. The rapid expansion of foreign firms was the single most important factor affecting the values of upgrading indicators in the Czech automotive industry as a whole.

My analysis thus revealed that, despite the predominantly extensive growth of employment and production, important processes of industrial upgrading were taking place in the Czech automotive industry between 1998 and 2006. It also showed that industrial upgrading was highly selective and very uneven. Although I was unable to statistically distinguish between product and process upgrading using financial indicators at the firm level, the statistical data show that both product and process upgrading played a very important role in the Czech automotive industry. Of these two, I have identified process upgrading as the most intensive and most widespread, being mainly responsible for the rapid increases in wages, labor and factor productivity at the firm level. The cutthroat competition in the automotive industry compels firms to continuously improve production processes to enhance their overall efficiency and productivity that allow them to keep prices low while achieving high product quality. Compared to the widespread process upgrading, product upgrading was taking place more selectively, and it was largely limited to firms in higher tiers of the supplier hierarchy.

Functional upgrading, measured by R&D expenditures and R&D employment, was also highly selective. It took place in only one-fifth of the analyzed firms and was most prominent in the ten largest firms that accounted for 80% of the total R&D expenditures in the Czech automotive industry between 1998 and 2006. My analysis showed that functional upgrading in the form of the development of strategic functions and R&D at the firm level can be statistically measured only indirectly by the wage level, value-added, labor productivity and factor productivity. These empirical results thus support the conclusions of Humphrey and Schmitz (2004a) about the limits of industrial upgrading in quasi hierarchical production networks, in which the conditions are favorable for process and product upgrading but much less favorable for functional upgrading. However, despite its highly selective character, functional upgrading was the most important process behind the gradual improvement in the position of the Czech automotive industry in the European automotive value chain. Although R&D intensity in the Czech automotive industry continues to be lower, by 100–200%, than in the core European countries and Sweden, it is comparable with smaller Western European countries, such as Austria, and it is higher than in other ECE countries.

While innovative, my case study of upgrading in the Czech automotive industry shows the limits of my quantitative methodological approach in measuring industrial upgrading at the firm level. In particular, I consider its inability to distinguish between product and process upgrading to be its most significant shortcoming. Statistical data for product upgrading at the firm level are unavailable and, therefore, need to be collected during company interviews or surveys. Obviously, because of the lack of available data, the quantitative approach alone is unable to evaluate all different types of industrial upgrading at the firm level and it should be combined with qualitative approaches.

Overall, my results show that, at least in Czechia, there is space for domestic automotive companies to participate in supplier networks dominated by foreign TNCs. This is reflected by an increase of more than two-thirds in the number of domestic automotive firms between 1998 and 2006. Thus, concerns about the "death of the local firm" (Barnes and Kaplinsky 2000), because of the exclusion of domestic suppliers from supplier networks dominated by foreign firms in the automotive industry in less developed countries, did not materialize in Czechia between 1998 and 2006.

Despite this significant, albeit very uneven, upgrading between 1998 and 2006, the mode of growth of the Czech automotive industry was highly problematic during this period and it typified its peripheral integration into the European and global production networks. The industry became almost totally dominated by foreign TNCs through their direct ownership of Czech-based assemblers and the largest component suppliers, and through power wielded over automotive GPNs by foreign-owned lead firms. The expansion of the automotive industry in Czechia was driven by TNCs, which were mainly looking for cheap export-oriented production sites and were supported by generous government investment incentives. Both new assembly plants built by TPCA and Hyundai produce small passenger cars, which are the most sensitive to labor costs, for the European market. The majority of newly built automotive component plants engage in the export-oriented assembly of low to medium value-added parts and accessories and they depend on the transfer of foreign technology, management systems and R&D from abroad. My analysis has shown that, despite government incentives, the development of automotive R&D was very limited in foreign subsidiaries and the vast majority of foreign investors did not develop any R&D functions in their Czech subsidiaries. I have also shown that the government played an important, although often very ambiguous, role in the development and upgrading of the Czech automotive industry. All these processes tend to reinforce the peripheral position of the Czech automotive industry in European value chains and production networks rather than improving it. This is the case despite the fact that the relative position of Czechia in European automotive value chains improved in the past decade and the gap between Czechia and less developed Western European countries, in particular, narrowed.

This domination of the Czech automotive industry by foreign companies affects how much value Czechia can capture in the automotive industry, due to profit transfers abroad, thereby undermining its overall economic benefits (Coe et al. 2004). It also affects the country's future economic development, because foreign companies are more likely to engage in disinvestment than domestic companies (Henderson et al. 2002; Dicken 1976). However, fears of potential relocation of automotive suppliers to lower cost countries from CE, as expressed by some authors (e.g. Rugraff 2010), have so far not been supported with evidence from CE, perhaps with the exception of extremely labor intensive assembly of components, such as cable harnesses. On the contrary, recent research points to the increasing embeddedness of the automotive industry in ECE (Domański and Gwosdz 2009; Jürgens and Krzywdzinski 2009). The future success of the Czech automotive industry will thus depend on the abilities of the Czech-based automotive firms to maintain or improve their position in European and global automotive production networks and value chains through upgrading their production processes, products and competencies. My analysis shows that the majority of the Czech-based foreign and domestic automotive firms have been consolidating their position in the European and global production networks and value chains, but any future improvement in this position will increasingly depend on the strategies and decisions of foreign TNCs, which now control the majority of the Czech automotive industry and its key players.

This will be the case especially if the Czech government continues its erratic industrial and economic policies in the future.

References

AIA (2016) Přehled výroby a odbytu vozidel domácích značek [Production and sale of domestically produced vehicles]. Czech Automotive Industry Association, Prague

Bair J, Gereffi G (2003) Upgrading, uneven development, and jobs in the North American apparel industry. Global Netw 3(2):143–169

Barnes J, Kaplinsky R (2000) Globalization and the death of the local firm? The automobile components sector in South Africa. Reg Stud 34:797–812

Carrillo J, Lung Y, van Tulder R (eds) (2004) Cars, carriers of regionalism? Palgrave MacMillan, Basingstoke

Coe NM, Hess M (2005) The internationalization of retailing: implications for supply network restructuring in East Asia and Eastern Europe. J Econ Geogr 5(4):449–473

Coe NM, Hess M, Yeung HW-C, Dicken P, Henderson J (2004) Globalizing regional development: a global production networks perspective. Tran Inst Brit Geogr 29:468–484

Coe NM, Dicken P, Hess M (2008) Global production networks: realizing the potential. J Econ Geogr 8(3):271–295

CSO (2016) Average registered number of employees by economic sector, 2000–2016. Prague, Czech Statistical Office

CzechInvest (2010) Incentives granted between April 1998 and 14 January 2010. CzechInvest, Prague

CzechInvest (2016) Incentives granted between April 1998 and 30 September 2016. CzechInvest, Prague

Dicken P (1976) The multiplant business enterprise and geographical space: some issues in the study of external control and regional development. Reg Stud 10(4):401–412

Dicken P. (2003) Global production networks in Europe and East Asia: the automobile components industries. GPN Working Paper 7. The University of Manchester, Manchester

Dicken P (2015) Global shift: mapping the changing contours of the world economy, 7th edn. Sage, London

Dieter H (2007) Transnational production networks in the automobile industry and the function of trade-facilitating measures. Notre Europe, Paris

Domański B, Gwosdz K (2009) Toward a more embedded production system? Automotive supply networks and localized capabilities in Poland. Growth and Change 40(3):452–482

Dunn E, Sebstad J, Batzdorff L, Parsons H (2006) Lessons learned on MSE upgrading in value chains. A synthesis paper. Microreport #71. USAID, Washington

Eurostat (2009) Structural business statistics.: Annual detailed enterprise statistics—industry and construction. Eurostat

Eurostat (2016) Structural business statistics: Annual detailed enterprise statistics—industry and construction. Eurostat

Gereffi G (1999) International trade and industrial upgrading in the apparel commodity chain. J Int Econ 48:37–70

Gereffi G (2001) Shifting governance structures in global commodity chains, with special reference to the internet. Am Behav Sci 44:1616–1637

Gereffi G (2005) The global economy: organization, governance, and development. In: Smelser NJ, Swedborg R (eds) The handbook of economic sociology, 2nd edn. Princeton, Princeton University Press, pp 160–182

Gereffi G (2009) Development models and industrial upgrading in China and Mexico. Eur Sociol Rev 25(1):37–51

Gereffi G, Humphrey J, Sturgeon T (2005) The governance of global value chains. Rev Int Polit Econ 12(1):78–104

Grote MH, Täube FA (2006) Offshoring the financial services industry: implications for the evolution of Indian IT clusters. Environ Plan A 38:1287–1305

Hassler M (2009) Variations of value creation: automobile manufacturing in Thailand. Environ Plan A 41:2232–2247

Hatzichronoglou T (1997) Revision of the high-technology sector and product classification. STI Working Paper. OECD, Paris

Havas A (2000) Changing patterns of inter- and intra-regional division of labour: central Europe's long and winding road. In: Humphrey J, Lecler Y, Salerno MS (eds) Global strategies and local realities: the auto industry in emerging markets. Palgrave Macmillan, Basingstoke, pp 234–262

Henderson J, Dicken P, Hess M, Coe N, Yeung HW-C (2002) Global production networks and the analysis of economic development. Rev Int Polit Econ 9:436–464

Hess M, Coe NM (2006) Making connections: global production networks, standards, and embeddedness in the mobile-telecommunications industry. Environ Plan A 38:1205–1227

Hudson R (2001) Producing places. Guilford, New York

Hudson R (2004) Conceptualizing economies and their geographies: spaces, flows and circuits. Prog Hum Geogr 28(4):447–471

Hudson R (2008) Cultural political economy meets global production networks: a productive meeting? J Econ Geogr 8:421–440

Humphrey J (2000) Assembler-supplier relations in the auto industry: globalisation and national development. Compet Change 4:245–271

Humphrey J (2003) Globalization and supply chain networks: the auto industry in Brazil and India. Global Netw 3(2):121–141

Humphrey J, Memedovic O (2003) The global automotive industry value chain: what prospects for upgrading by developing countries, sectoral studies series. UNIDO, Vienna

Humphrey J, Oeter A (2000) Motor industry policies in emerging markets: globalisation and the promotion of domestic industry. In: Humphrey J, Lecler Y, Salerno MS (eds) Global strategies and local realities; the auto industry in emerging markets. Palgrave Macmillan, Basingstoke, pp 42–71

Humphrey J, Salerno MS (2000) Globalisation and assembler-supplier relations: Brazil and India. In: Humphrey J, Lecler Y, Salerno MS (eds) Global strategies and local realities; the auto industry in emerging markets. Palgrave Macmillan, Basingstoke, pp 149–175

Humphrey J, Schmitz H (2000) Governance and upgrading: linking industrial cluster and global value chain research. IDS Working Paper 120. Institute of Development Studies, University of Sussex, Brighton

Humphrey J, Schmitz H (2002) How does insertion in global value chains affect upgrading in industrial clusters? Reg Stud 36(9):1017–1027

Humphrey J, Schmitz H (2004a) Chain governance and upgrading: taking stock. In: Schmitz H (ed) Local enterprises in the global economy: issues of governance and upgrading. Edward Elgar, Cheltenham, pp 349–381

Humphrey J, Schmitz H (2004b) Governance in global value chains. In: Schmitz H (ed) Local enterprises in the global economy: issues of governance and upgrading. Edward Elgar, Cheltenham, pp 95–109

Isaksen A, Kalsaas T (2009) Suppliers and strategies for upgrading in global production networks: the case of a supplier to the global automotive industry in a high-cost location. Eur Plan Stud 17(4):569–585

Jürgens U, Krzywdzinski M (2009) Changing east-west division of labour in the European automotive industry. Eur Urban Reg Stud 16(1):27–42

Kaplinsky R (2000) Globalisation and unequalisation: what can be learned from value chain analysis? J Dev Stud 37(2):117–146

Kaplinsky R, Readman J (2005) Globalization and upgrading: what can (and cannot) be learnt from international trade statistics in the wood furniture sector? Ind Corp Change 14(4):679–703

Layan J (2000) The integration of peripheral markets: a comparison of Spain and Mexico. In: Humphrey J, Lecler Y, Salerno MS (eds) Global strategies and local realities; the auto industry in emerging markets. Palgrave Macmillan, Basingstoke, pp 122–148

Liu W, Dicken P (2006) Transnational corporations and 'obligated embeddedness': foreign direct investment in Chinas automobile industry. Environ Plan A 38:1229–1247

Liu W, Yeung HW-C (2008) China's dynamic industrial sector: the automobile industry. Eurasian Geogr Econ 49(5):523–548

Lung Y (2000) Is the rise of emerging countries as automobile producers an irreversible phenomenon? In: Humphrey J, Lecler Y, Salerno MS (eds) Global strategies and local realities; the auto industry in emerging markets. Palgrave Macmillan, Basingstoke, pp 16–41

MIT (2001) Panorama zpracovatelského průmyslu ČR 2000 [Panorama of the Czech manufacturing industry 2000]. Czech Ministry of Industry and Trade, Prague

MIT (2008) Panorama zpracovatelského průmyslu ČR 2007 [Panorama of the Czech manufacturing industry 2007]. Czech Ministry of Industry and Trade, Prague

MIT (2015) Panorama zpracovatelského průmyslu ČR 2014 [Panorama of the Czech manufacturing industry 2014]. Czech Ministry of Industry and Trade, Prague

MIT (2016) Panorama zpracovatelského průmyslu ČR 2015 [Panorama of the Czech manufacturing industry 2015]. Czech Ministry of Industry and Trade, Prague

OICA (2016) World motor vehicle production by country and type, 1997–2015. Organisation Internationale des Constructeurs d'Automobile, Paris (www.oica.net)

Parthasarathy B, Aoyama Y (2006) From software services to R&D services: local entrepreneurship in the software industry in Bangalore, India. Environ Plan A 38:1269–1285

Pavlínek P (2000) Restructuring of the commercial vehicle industry in the Czech Republic. Post Sov Geogr Econ 41(4):265–287

Pavlínek P (2002a) Transformation of central and East European passenger car industry: selective peripheral integration through foreign direct investment. Environ Plan A 34:1685–1709

Pavlínek P (2002b) Restructuring the Central and Eastern European automobile industry: legacies trends and effects of foreign direct investment. Post Sov Geogr Econ 43:41–77

Pavlínek P (2002c) Domestic privatization and its effects on industrial enterprises in East Central Europe: the evidence from the Czech motor component industry. Eur Asia Stud 54(7):1127–1150

Pavlínek P (2002d) The role of foreign direct investment in the Czech automotive industry privatization and restructuring. Post Communist Econ 14(3):359–379

Pavlínek P (2003) Transformation of the Czech automotive components industry through foreign direct investment. Eurasian Geogr Econ 44:184–209

Pavlínek P (2008) A successful transformation? Restructuring of the Czech automobile industry. Physica Verlag, Heidelberg

Pavlínek P, Janák L (2007) Regional restructuring of the Škoda auto supplier network in the Czech Republic. Eur Urban Reg Stud 14(2):133–155

Pavlínek P, Domański B, Guzik R (2009) Industrial upgrading through foreign direct investment in Central European automotive manufacturing. Eur Urban Reg Stud 16(1):43–63

Pennings E, Sleuwaegen L (2000) International relocation: firm and industry determinants. Econ Lett 67:179–186

Pickles J, Smith A, Buček M, Roukova P, Begg R (2006) Upgrading, changing competitive pressures, and diverse practices in the East and Central European apparel industry. Environ Plan A 38:2305–2324

Porter M (1990) The competitive advantage of nations. The Free Press, New York

Rugraff E (2010) Foreign direct investment (FDI) and supplier-oriented upgrading in the Czech motor vehicle industry. Reg Stud 44:627–638

Rutherford T, Holmes J (2008) 'The flea on the tail of the dog': power in global production networks and the restructuring of Canadian automotive clusters. J Econ Geogr 8:519–544

Sakellaris P, Wilson D (2004) Quantifying embodied technological change. Rev Econ Dyn 7(1):1–26

Schmitz H, Knorringa P (2000) Learning from global buyers. J Dev Stud 37(2):177–205

Smith A (2003) Power relations industrial clusters, and regional transformations: Pan-European integration and outward processing in the Slovak clothing industry. Econ Geogr 79:17–40

Smith A, Rainnie A, Dunford M, Hardy J, Hudson R, Sadler D (2002) Networks of value, commodities and regions: reworking divisions of labour in macro-regional economies. Prog Hum Geogr 26:41–63

Sturgeon TJ (2001) How do we define value chains and production networks? IDS Bull 32(3):9–18

Sturgeon TJ, Florida R (2000) Globalization and jobs in the automotive industry. MIT-IPC-00-012. MIT Industrial Performance Center, Cambridge

Sturgeon TJ, Van Biesebroeck J, Gereffi G (2008) Value chains, networks and clusters: reframing the global automotive industry. J Econ Geogr 8:297–321

Sturgeon TJ, Memedovic O, Van Biesebroeck J, Gereffi G (2009) Globalisation of the automotive industry: main features and trends. Int J Technol Learning Innov Dev 2(1/2):7–24

Szalavetz A (2005) Physical capital stock, technological upgrading and modernisation in Hungary. Acta Oeconomica 55(2):201–221

Tokatli N (2007) Asymmetrical power relations and upgrading among suppliers of global clothing brands: Hugo Boss in Turkey. J Econ Geogr 7:67–92

Womack JP, Jones DT, Roos D (1990) The machine that changed the world. Rawson Associates, New York

Yeung HW-C (2005) Rethinking relational economic geography. Tran Inst Br Geogr 30:37–51

Yeung HW-C (2009) Regional development and the competitive dynamics of global production networks: an East Asian perspective. Reg Stud 43(3):325–351

Ženka J (2008) Riziko delokalizace zpracovatelského průmyslu Česka: regionální aspekty [Regional implications of delocalization risks in the Czech manufacturing industry]. Geografie 113(1):1–19

Chapter 4
Research and Development

Introduction

Important changes took place in the automotive industry in the 1990s and 2000s that have altered its geography at various geographic scales (e.g. Sturgeon et al. 2008; Carrillo et al. 2004; Lung 2004). At the global scale, vehicle assembly has been rapidly increasing in less developed countries located outside the traditional core areas of the automotive industry (Humphrey et al. 2000). Consequently, the share of the global vehicle production increased outside the core from 34.2% in 1997 to 64.5% in 2015, while it decreased in the core from 65.8% to 35.5% (OICA 2016). Less developed countries have become attractive production locations for the core-based TNCs for two basic reasons. First, a rapid economic growth in several large developing countries has led to increases in purchasing power and a growing demand for private cars. A perceived large future market potential in these countries (e.g. China, India, Brazil) prompted foreign automotive TNCs to build production capacity or form joint ventures (JVs) with domestic vehicle producers there (e.g. Liu and Yeung 2008; Liu and Dicken 2006; Van Biesebroeck and Sturgeon 2010). Second, peripheral areas surrounding the traditional core areas of the automotive production have become attractive because they combine lower production costs, geographic proximity to large and affluent core markets, and the advantages of regional economic blocs, such as the EU and the North American Free Trade Agreement. Examples include Mexico, Spain and, more recently, ECE (Layan 2000; Pavlínek 2002c).

The goal of this chapter is to investigate in the context of ECE whether and to what extent this increase in the automotive production outside traditional core areas has also led to the development of research and development (R&D) competencies. I argue that so far R&D development has been very limited in the ECE automotive industry and that, with some notable exceptions, foreign control over the ECE automotive industry and the spatial organization of international automotive R&D undermine the chances for a successful automotive R&D development.

P. Pavlínek, *Dependent Growth: Foreign Investment and the Development of the Automotive Industry in East-Central Europe*, DOI 10.1007/978-3-319-53955-3_4

This chapter draws on global production networks (GPN) and global value chains (GVC) perspectives (Coe et al. 2004, 2008; Gereffi et al. 2005; Henderson et al. 2002) to examine how automotive R&D in ECE was affected by the production increase from 0.6 to 3.9 million passenger cars between 1990 and 2015 in the context of corporate R&D internationalization. R&D is considered to be a crucial component of functional upgrading at the firm level, which is the process of acquiring new functions generating higher incomes and increasing the overall skill content of the firm's activities in the value-chain (Humphrey and Schmitz 2000, 2002, 2004a). Functional upgrading, along with industrial upgrading as a whole, therefore has a potential to improve the position of firms, regions and countries in GVCs and GPNs (Gereffi 1999; Gereffi et al. 2005) by creating possibilities for enhancing value and thus for economic development (Henderson et al. 2002).

Empirically, the chapter examines the changes in the automotive R&D activities in ECE and, in a greater detail, in Czechia to illustrate both the possibilities and constraints of automotive R&D development in peripheral locations of the European automotive production system. These possibilities and constraints are considered in the broader context of the internationalization of R&D in general and the automotive R&D in particular. This analysis combines quantitative and qualitative approaches. The national level statistical data are used to evaluate the importance of automotive R&D in individual EU countries. The case study of the Czech automotive R&D draws upon the combination of secondary firm-level statistical data with the primary data from a firm-level questionnaire and interviews conducted in 2000, 2005, and 2009–2011.

I start with a review of R&D internationalization and its nature in the automotive industry. There I demonstrate that corporate R&D generally and automotive R&D specifically remain highly geographically concentrated in the global economic core despite increased internationalization of R&D. Then, I discuss factors of FDI-driven R&D development in foreign locations from the GPN perspective. I argue that the chances of peripheral regions to attract sizeable FDI in R&D are limited and are most likely to take place when the strategic coupling between TNCs' needs and local/regional assets develops. Next, I evaluate the position of ECE automotive R&D in the European context. I stress very limited automotive R&D in ECE when compared to the West European automotive industry core. Finally, I analyze the Czech automotive R&D in a greater detail. There I emphasize the importance of external control of the Czech automotive R&D, its focus on development and technical support of production, small and fragmented nature of R&D in domestic firms, and the decreased complexity and sophistication of domestic automotive R&D between 1995 and 2007. Main findings are discussed in the Conclusion.

The Internationalization of Corporate R&D Through Foreign Direct Investment

Despite increasing economic globalization, R&D continues to be one of the least internationalized activities of TNCs (UNCTAD 2005; Reger 2004; Patel and Pavitt 1991).[1] Although FDI in R&D originated well before World War Two (Granstrand 1999; Kuemmerle 1999), it began to increase in the late 1970s and the early 1980s. The main reasons included the rapid expansion of overseas sales, distribution and manufacturing by TNCs and the need to support these foreign activities with development and design capabilities (Gerybadze and Reger 1999; Meyer-Krahmer and Reger 1999; Gassmann and von Zedtwitz 1998; Dicken 2015). FDI in R&D was driven by high-tech TNCs from small, highly-developed countries with small domestic markets and limited domestic R&D talent, including Switzerland, Sweden, Belgium and the Netherlands (Gassmann and von Zedtwitz 1998). American TNCs and TNCs from larger West European countries and especially Japan have been much slower to internationalize their R&D because of larger domestic markets and the larger pools of a scientific labor force (Ambos 2005; Archibugi and Iammarino 2002; Dunning and Wymbs 1999; Granstrand 1999; Le Bas and Sierra 2002; Meyer-Krahmer and Reger 1999; Reger 2004).

Since the degree of internationalization of R&D activities in most of the large R&D-intensive TNCs increased in the 1980s, 1990s (Gerybadze and Reger 1999) and 2000s (UNCTAD 2005), the "R&D globalization" rhetoric has become commonplace in the academic and business literature. This has been the case despite the fact that the processes of R&D internationalization have been geographically very uneven, both in terms of origins and destinations of FDI in R&D (Kumar 2001; Reger 2004). So far, FDI in R&D has largely been limited to the most developed core economies and a small group of rapidly growing semi-peripheral developing economies, including China, Taiwan, South Korea, Malaysia, Brazil and Mexico (Ambos 2005; Kumar 2001; Gassmann and von Zedtwitz 1999; von Zedtwitz and Gassmann 2002; Edler et al. 2002; Filippaios et al. 2009). Close to 70% of foreign-owned R&D-oriented subsidiaries were located in developed core economies in 2004 (UNCTAD 2005).[2] Some scholars have referred to this continuing geographic concentration as "non-globalization" rather than globalization of larger firms' R&D

[1] R&D is composed of basic research, applied research and development. In industry, basic research advances scientific knowledge without having specific immediate commercial applications in mind. Only a very low percentage of R&D performed by automotive firms is truly basic research. Applied research also advances scientific knowledge but for specific commercial objectives. Its goal is to apply scientific advances to specific products, processes and services. Development refers to the systematic use of the knowledge developed by research to advance production processes both in terms of methods of production and the nature of produced goods. It involves the new product design and development, including its adaptation to the local environment, the development of prototypes and the development of production processes (UNCTAD 2005).

[2] Henceforth domestic-owned firms are referred to as "domestic" and foreign-owned firms as "foreign".

(Patel and Pavitt 1991; Patel and Vega 1999). Others, referring to the triadic structure of the global economic core, have more realistically described the geographic distribution of foreign R&D as R&D "triadization" (Meyer-Krahmer and Reger 1999; Archibugi and Iammarino 2002; Edler et al. 2002; Reger 2004). Within the "Triad" itself, R&D is highly spatially concentrated (von Zedtwitz et al. 2004; Dalton and Serapio 1999; Meyer-Krahmer and Reger 1999). Because of this concentrated international dispersion (Ernst 2002) of R&D, it might be premature to talk about "the shift in the global distribution of innovation activities" (Schmitz and Strambach 2009, p. 232), especially given the fact that large differences in the degree of internationalization of R&D exist among different sectors, technology fields and individual companies (Reger 2004; Ambos 2005; Zander 1999).

In the 1970s and 1980s, geographers demonstrated that geographic distribution of industrial R&D and its patterns of concentration and dispersion were closely related to corporate hierarchy and organization of R&D (Malecki 1979, 1980; Howells 1990a, b, c; see also Hymer 1972; von Zedtwitz and Gassmann 2002). Different types of R&D activities of large firms differ in their degree of centralization and decentralization within the corporate hierarchy. While basic research tends to be centralized and located close to company headquarters, development work is typically decentralized to the plant level. Applied research is usually positioned between these two extremes by being decentralized to the individual product divisions. Basic or most strategic research tends to be the most geographically concentrated, while developmental work tends to be decentralized to the plant level and thus the most geographically dispersed.

This basic pattern of centralization and decentralization of different types of R&D activities of large TNCs, and the related pattern of their geographic concentration and dispersion, still holds today despite the increased R&D internationalization of the 1990s and 2000s. Knowledge and innovation do not easily disperse across international borders, and the internationalization of production is not automatically followed by the internationalization of R&D by TNCs (Ernst 2002). In deciding where to locate their R&D activities, TNCs have to balance opposing forces favoring R&D concentration and dispersion (Table 4.1). If TNCs conduct any R&D overseas at all, it is most likely development work. They are least likely to locate their most strategic research abroad. Additionally, the increased dispersion of corporate R&D overseas does not necessarily translate into an increased decentralization of corporate ownership and control of R&D. This is because internationally dispersed R&D units require increased coordination and management from TNC headquarters, which are typically located in TNC home countries (Gerybadze and Reger 1999; Filippaios et al. 2009). However, the degree of autonomy of foreign R&D units varies considerably, depending on the type of R&D network within individual TNCs (Gassmann and von Zedtwitz 1999).

In the 1980s, the internationalization of R&D led to its increased decentralization, which, in turn, led to the duplication of tasks and competency disputes among R&D units that often lacked the necessary size and resources to be efficient (Meyer-Krahmer and Reger 1999). Therefore, in the 1990s, highly decentralized TNCs, such as ABB, IBM, GM and Hoechst, centralized some corporate functions, such as financial and information flows within top management, in order to control the

Table 4.1 Forces promoting the geographic concentration and dispersion of corporate R&D

Forces promoting geographic concentration of R&D	Forces promoting geographic dispersion of R&D
Scale and scope economies in R&D	Customizing and tailoring parent company products and processes to foreign markets
Synergy effects	Providing technical support for host market factories
Better control over research results	International mergers and acquisitions
The need for personal interactions for certain types of R&D information (tacitness)	Tapping into scientific and technical talent and technological strengths of particular countries
Advantages of technical, social, cultural and organizational proximity for R&D communication and coordination	Monitoring new technological developments in foreign countries
The accumulated R&D experience in the home country (cumulativeness and path dependency)	Internal and external organizational decomposition of innovation activities
Difficulties of R&D internationalization, such as political risks in foreign countries, dangers of parallel development, high coordination and information costs, immobility of the best R&D personnel, high R&D wage costs in the core countries	Economic policies of host governments, such as local content requirements, investment incentives, protectionist barriers, and political pressures to establish or maintain local R&D units
	Advances in information and communication technologies

Sources: Author based on Ambos (2005), Le Bas and Sierra (2002), Cantwell et al. (2004), Carrincazeaux et al. (2001), Dalton and Serapio (1999), Edler et al. (2002), Ernst (2008), Florida (1997), Florida and Kenney (1994), Gassmann and von Zedtwitz (1998), Howells (1990a), Kuemmerle (1997, 1999), Lung (2004), Meyer-Krahmer and Reger (1999), Miller (1994), Patel and Vega (1999), Reger (2004), Schmitz and Strambach (2009), UNCTAD (2005), von Zedtwitz and Gassmann (2002), von Zedtwitz et al. (2004)

autonomy of their foreign R&D units. They also recentralized their internationally dispersed R&D into a small number of leading R&D centers in order to increase their control from corporate headquarters, reduce costs of their coordination and management, remove the duplication of tasks, and increase the overall efficiency of R&D (Gassmann and von Zedtwitz 1998).[3] To achieve these goals, TNCs strove to concentrate the core R&D activities for a particular product group or technology as much as possible in one location (Meyer-Krahmer and Reger 1999). At the same time that large and highly internationalized TNCs were centralizing their R&D, an organizational decomposition of the innovation process (Schmitz and Strambach 2009) began increasing, which holds the potential to alter the global geography of corporate R&D by making geographic dispersal of R&D easier.

[3] Continental AG represents an example of R&D centralization for these exact reasons in the automotive industry. Continental centralized its R&D from its overseas subsidiaries to its corporate R&D center in Hannover, Germany in the early to mid-1990s (interview with CEO of Barum Continental, November 12, 2010).

Although internationalization of R&D has traditionally been driven by demand side factors, more recently it has also expanded as a result of supply side factors (Table 4.1). In the early stages of their development, overseas R&D units typically concentrated on customizing parent company products and processes to the foreign markets in which they were located and on providing technical support for host market factories. The rationale for this demand-driven corporate R&D strategy has been explained by the product cycle model (Vernon 1966) and this strategy basically involves the transfer of knowledge from a TNC's central R&D facility to overseas R&D sites. The market reasons, or demand side factors, continue to be the most important motive for overseas R&D today (Ambos 2005; Edler et al. 2002; UNCTAD 2005; von Zedtwitz and Gassmann 2002; Patel and Vega 1999). However, the role of technology, or supply side factors, has increasingly influenced the location patterns of FDI in R&D, although its significance has been sectorally uneven (Florida 1997; Florida and Kenney 1994; Dalton and Serapio 1999). Increasingly, more overseas R&D units have specialized in a particular product or process R&D for the entire TNC, drawing on scientific and technical talent and technological strengths of particular countries (Howells 1990a; Florida and Kenney 1994; Dalton and Serapio 1999; Florida 1997; Cantwell et al. 2004; UNCTAD 2005; Edler et al. 2002; Kuemmerle 1997; Meyer-Krahmer and Reger 1999; Le Bas and Sierra 2002; Ambos 2005; Ernst 2008). Highly internationalized TNCs have thus increasingly established corporate-wide centers of R&D excellence overseas, with the mandate to generate knowledge and capabilities for the entire TNC, which are then transferred to TNC's headquarters and its central R&D facility (Reger 2004; Kuemmerle 1997). Supply side factors are therefore especially important for the internationalization of research, while demand side factors are crucial for the internationalization of development (von Zedtwitz and Gassmann 2002). Supply side factors are much more important in large highly developed economies because of their technological strength and the availability of large pools of scientific and technical labor (Florida 1997; Dalton and Serapio 1999). Less developed economies are not usually technologically strong, neither do they have a large R&D labor force. Demand-side factors have played a greater role in R&D internationalization strategies of West European TNCs compared to North American and Japanese TNCs, whose strategies have continued to be predominantly driven by the need to customize their products to foreign markets (Edler et al. 2002).

The Internationalization of Corporate R&D in the Automotive Industry

Although the general patterns of corporate R&D internationalization discussed so far apply to automotive R&D, the specific features of internationalization and geographic distribution of automotive R&D need further analysis in order to explain its spatial dynamics.

The automotive industry is one of the most important sectors in terms of total R&D expenditures (UNCTAD 2005; ACEA 2015), but its R&D was less internationalized than any other industrial sector by the mid-1990s, with the exception of the aerospace industry (Dunning and Wymbs 1999; Gerybadze and Reger 1999). Despite rapidly growing automobile production in less developed countries, the largest automotive TNCs conducted about three-quarters of automotive R&D in their home countries in the 1990s, with the rest being predominantly located in other developed economies (Gerybadze and Reger 1999; Zander 1999; Miller 1994). Although, the degree of R&D concentration and dispersion and R&D internationalization strategies of individual automotive lead firms (assemblers) differ considerably (Dias and Salerno 2004), the most important R&D strategies are a high degree of concentration near the home base or a partial dispersion close to assembly plants in the largest foreign markets (Miller 1994; Gassmann and von Zedtwitz 1999; Calabrese 2001). The automotive industry is an example of predominantly demand-driven R&D internationalization strategies because automobiles require regional and national product adaptation to satisfy customer preferences, road and climatic conditions, and government regulations in foreign markets (UNCTAD 2005). To deploy and implement technology developed at their main R&D centers, automotive lead firms have established regional development units in their main markets (von Zedtwitz and Gassmann 2002). In other words, the internationalization of automotive R&D has focused on development, while research remains concentrated near the home base of lead firms.

Automakers have traditionally faced the dual challenge of achieving economies of scale in production and R&D while, at the same time, maintaining their ability to design and produce automobiles customized to specific markets. Since the 1990s, the common platform strategy has been the most successful approach to achieve these two objectives. In production, the platform strategy allows car makers to achieve economies of scale by sharing common platforms (chassis and structure) and modules (mechanical subsystems) between different models. These standardized parts (lower-bodies) 'invisible' to the naked eye account for about 80% of the finished vehicle. At the same time, the visible parts (upper-bodies) remain distinct, differentiating one vehicle from another in the buyer's mind, thus allowing automakers to greatly expand their product range and achieve economies of scope (e.g. Lung 2004). The platform strategy and the efforts to minimize the number of platforms by lead firms have had important implications for automotive R&D. While R&D concerning platforms and modules has usually remained concentrated near the home base in the home countries of automotive lead firms, regional R&D centers specializing in the upper-bodies modifications have been established in the most important regional markets (Miller 1994). In countries with potentially very large markets, governments have greater bargaining power to mandate that lead firms establish R&D centers within a certain period following their investment in exchange for market access (e.g. Liu and Dicken 2006).

The role of suppliers in automotive R&D has increased as the Japanese-inspired assembler-supplier relationships became industry standard (Asanuma 1989; Patchell 1993; Sheard 1983). Lead firms now require co-design and co-location from their

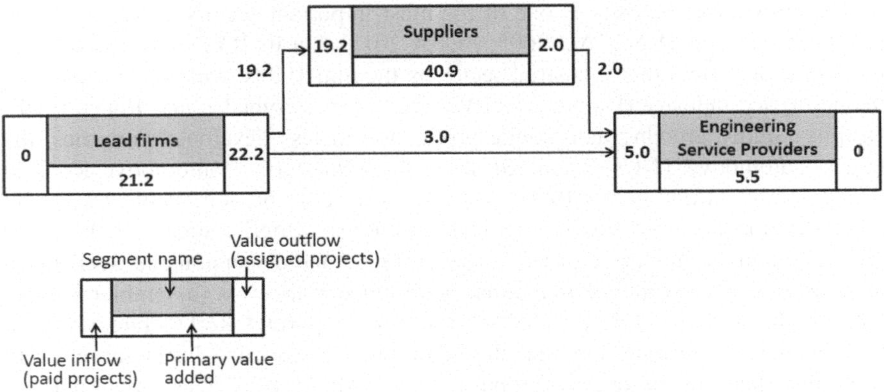

Fig. 4.1 Global automotive R&D value flow, 2005 (in billions of EUR). Note: Based on the financial data of 14 lead assembly firms and 107 selected suppliers, together accounting for about 90% of the global automotive industry's turnover. Source: Based on Dannenberg and Burgard (2007)

most important Tier One suppliers of advanced technology equipment and subassemblies (module and system integrators or Tier 0.5 suppliers). Consequently, automotive suppliers generally, and Tier 0.5 suppliers specifically, have increased their role in automotive R&D since the 1990s (Humphrey 2000, 2003; Humphrey and Memedovic 2003; Sturgeon and Lester 2004; Sturgeon et al. 2008; Lung and Volpato 2002; Volpato 2004; Van Biesebroeck and Sturgeon 2010). Suppliers accounted for about 40% of the total automotive industry's R&D in the early 2000s, and their share was predicted to increase to 60% by 2010 (ILO 2005). However, according to Dannenberg and Burgard (2007), suppliers' share of automotive R&D was already 61% between 2001 and 2005, twice that of lead firms' (31%), while engineering service providers accounted for the remaining 8% (Fig. 4.1). This growing share of R&D conducted by suppliers reflects the increase in R&D capabilities of especially Tier 0.5 suppliers that have become responsible for designing entire modules and their constituent components (Frigant and Layan 2009). R&D expenditures are strongly concentrated among the 100 largest suppliers, which accounted for 75% of the supplier industry total in 2005 (Dannenberg and Burgard 2007). To accomplish compatibility, increased interactions and close cooperation are necessary between Tier 0.5 suppliers, lead firms, for which particular modules are designed, and other Tier One suppliers responsible for the complementary modules (Frigant 2007; Frigant and Layan 2009). Such R&D cooperation is easier to achieve if suppliers have their design engineering facilities located close to R&D facilities of lead firms in order to facilitate the exchange of highly localized tacit knowledge (Howells 2002; Bathelt et al. 2004; Carrincazeaux et al. 2001). As opposed to codified or explicit knowledge, which is transmittable and does not require direct experience, tacit knowledge cannot be easily codified or articulated and, therefore, acquired and transmitted without direct experience and interaction.

The best way to communicate tacit knowledge is through demonstration and practice (Gertler 2003; Howells 1996, 2002). Consequently, the automotive R&D conducted by leading suppliers has become more spatially concentrated near lead firms' R&D sites in both North America and Western Europe (Sturgeon et al. 2008; Lung 2004; Frigant 2007; Van Biesebroeck and Sturgeon 2010). Since the most strategic R&D of lead firms has traditionally been located near company headquarters, this development then tended to increase the degree of concentration of the most strategic automotive R&D in the automotive industry core.

Tier 0.5 suppliers and leading Tier One suppliers have developed a three-tiered structure of their R&D facilities, which has influenced the geographic distribution of automotive R&D. As in the case of lead firms, the largest R&D centers are usually located in their home countries. These R&D centers concentrate on basic and applied research, which is not dedicated to a particular automaker or a particular model, and which involves the architecture of modules and their constituent components. The location of these suppliers' R&D centers close to lead firms' R&D facilities or assembly operations is not necessarily important. Ancillary R&D centers have been established by TNC suppliers outside their home countries in other leading car producing countries of the core regions (e.g. Japanese centers in the United States and Germany). Ancillary R&D centers ensure the integration of individual modules into the overall car architecture of individual lead firms and their specific platforms/models. As a result, ancillary R&D centers have become located close to lead firms' R&D centers to enable such integration since it requires a close cooperation, frequent interactions and the exchange of tacit information between the R&D of suppliers and lead firms. Finally, smaller technical centers have been set up for the purpose of technical coordination with lead firms in countries with a large volume production of components for local assembly (Frigant 2007). This R&D reorganization has meant that, in some cases, R&D activities previously carried out by Tier One suppliers in less developed countries (e.g. Brazil and India) have been relocated back to the automotive core countries (Humphrey 2000). Such R&D organization by Tier 0.5 suppliers is unfavorable for the development of their R&D activities in less developed countries, with the exception of smaller technical centers that support the local production of modules and its coordination with local assembly plants.

The pattern of corporate R&D organization in the contemporary automotive industry suggests that despite the significant internationalization of R&D, the chances are limited for countries located outside the global economic core to attract automotive R&D, unless they have very large markets and/or government regulations mandating lead firms to establish R&D centers. Even then, when less developed countries do attract automotive R&D, it will most likely be "end-stage R&D capabilities such as minor and peripheral design/process modifications" (Zhao et al. 2005: 144). It is within this broader context that we need to analyze and understand the position of ECE in the international automotive R&D networks and R&D division of labor.

Factors of Automotive R&D Development in Foreign Locations from the GPN Perspective

The GPN approach can be used to suggest the conditions under which FDI may lead to the development of R&D in host countries outside the core. However, I also emphasize that previous geographic research shows predominantly negative influences of FDI on R&D in peripheral regions.

GPN and GVC approaches analyze how GPNs and GVCs are organized and governed, how power is distributed within these networks, and how this organization and power distribution, along with institutional factors, influence the geographic location and distribution of interlinked value chain/production network activities (Sturgeon et al. 2008; Coe et al. 2008). The automotive industry is a typical example of the quasi-hierarchical or captive network governance typified by asymmetrical power relationships and competencies between lead firms and component suppliers (Humphrey and Schmitz 2002, 2004a; Gereffi et al. 2005). In captive networks, automotive lead firms exercise control over networks of transactionally dependent component suppliers wielding their corporate power. Lead firms decide which suppliers will be included in the production network and under what conditions, and they set parameters under which the entire network operates by determining and monitoring product specifications, quality control systems, and delivery systems and schedules. Exercising control over strategic functions within the captive production network, including R&D, allows the automotive lead firms to maintain their leading position within the network. Lead firms encourage process and product upgrading among their "captive" suppliers; however, they discourage functional upgrading, with the exception of their Tier 0.5 suppliers, to prevent suppliers from moving into lead firms' core competency areas, which are their greatest sources of value capture (Humphrey and Schmitz 2004a; Rutherford and Holmes 2008; Dedrick et al. 2010). Strategic functions, including strategic R&D, tend to be highly centralized and controlled by lead firms. As argued previously, the fact that automotive suppliers are now required to co-design and co-develop modules and components with lead firms (Humphrey 2000; Humphrey and Memedovic 2003; Volpato 2004) has tended to reinforce the spatial concentration of especially the most strategic automotive R&D near lead firms' R&D centers. At the same time, it limits R&D diffusion from core-based centers of automotive R&D to peripheral locations (e.g. Sturgeon et al. 2009).

Under this situation, I argue that one of the feasible strategies for a region to attract and develop automotive R&D functions is through "strategic coupling" of its R&D assets with the strategic needs of GPNs (Coe et al. 2004; Coe and Hess 2011; Yeung 2009a, b). Strategic coupling refers to "the dynamic processes through which actors in cities and/or regions coordinate, mediate, and arbitrage strategic interests between local actors and their counterparts in the global economy " (Yeung 2009b: 213). TNCs need to conduct their R&D at what they consider optimal locations that can serve their needs. Depending on the nature of R&D activities conducted overseas, TNCs need access to a sufficiently large supply of highly qualified scientists, engineers and technicians at optimal costs and also to the basic sources of science and marketing information in the form of universities, research institutes and trade associations (Dicken 2015; Carrincazeaux et al. 2001). In some cases, the acquisition of existing R&D in foreign locations may fit into strategic needs of TNCs by either supporting their expanding overseas production or tapping into the existing R&D capabilities. Regional R&D assets can take various forms, including highly localized concentrations of knowledge, particular labor market skills and expertise, favorable government policies towards R&D, strong institutional support for R&D, already existing R&D and innovative local and regional environments. Where such R&D assets have been developed, the potential for R&D growth is higher (Coe et al. 2004; Oinas and Malecki 2002; Martin and Sunley 2006; Martin 2010). However, the existence of previously developed R&D assets may not necessarily be enough to maintain existing R&D or to attract new R&D investment in a particular region or locality. In order to satisfy the changing needs of dynamic GPNs, the existing regional assets need to be actively maintained and further developed by regional actors (e.g. firms, regional and national institutions), to remain competitive. Furthermore, active firm-level strategies and national or regional policies are often necessary to attract external R&D to a particular region through corporate investment. Institutions thus play a crucial role in promoting innovation development strategies in "territorial innovation systems", variously conceptualized as national, regional and spatial innovation systems (e.g. Oinas and Malecki 2002; Lundvall et al. 2002; Howells 1999; Moulaert and Mehmood 2010). The empirical evidence supports the notion that well-developed innovation systems and their governance play an important role in successful economic development (e.g. Fagerberg and Srholec 2008). The role of the interlinked institutional spheres of university, industry and government, conceptualized as the "triple helix" of innovation, has particularly been stressed for innovation development in the national and regional contexts (e.g. Etzkowitz and Leydesdorff 2000; Etzkowitz 2003). However, because the "triple helix" has been conceptualized in the context of core economies, it cannot be applied well to non-core regions like ECE where industry-university and industry-government innovation links are underdeveloped (2009–2011 company interviews, see also Jensen and Tragardh 2004). Instead, I argue that FDI and TNCs' R&D strategies have played the dominant role in the development or lack of development of automotive R&D in ECE in the 1990s and 2000s.

It is important to keep in mind that innovation-oriented regional assets only become relevant for future R&D development if they meet the strategic needs of TNCs and their GPNs (Coe et al. 2004; Coe and Hess 2011), and if TNCs decide that it makes economic sense for them to exploit these assets in foreign locations. In most cases, however, TNCs only invest in production overseas, and non-production functions, including R&D, are not developed in foreign subsidiaries, undermining their potential for functional upgrading. Foreign subsidiaries then depend upon technology and R&D transfers from TNCs' R&D centers located elsewhere. These effects of foreign ownership and external control of industrial enterprises on domestic R&D capabilities, long recognized by geographers (e.g. Firn 1975; Dicken 1976), often result in what Britton (1980), Hayter (1982) and others called "truncation" (see also Schackmann-Fallis 1989; Massey 1979). Truncation refers to foreign-owned subsidiaries controlled from abroad that do not engage in R&D, which is, along with high-level technical and managerial jobs, centralized in TNCs' home countries. If any R&D is conducted in truncated companies at all, it is the lowest level development, which is directed at adapting foreign technology and products to local conditions and local markets. At the same time, innovation in domestic companies is also negatively affected by truncation because foreign technology, which is transferred to foreign subsidiaries from parent corporations, rarely spills over to domestic firms, and because truncated foreign subsidiaries tend to source only basic materials and services in host countries (Britton 1980). By limiting indigenous development, truncation contributes to industrial and technological underdevelopment in host economies (Hayter 1982; Britton 1980). The truncation argument has been supported by economic and econometric research on FDI effects in host economies, suggesting that FDI negatively affects domestic firms, including their innovation capabilities (e.g. Aitken and Harrison 1999; Konings 2001; Spencer 2008). It also resonates with Hymer's (1970, 1972) and dependency school's (e.g. Santos 1970) argument that large TNCs integrate less developed peripheral economies into the global economy in a dependent and disadvantageous position, which undercuts their development potential.

The ECE Automotive R&D in the European Context

In the following empirical analysis, I will address two theoretical questions. First, drawing on the truncation argument, I ask to what extent the FDI-driven growth of automotive assembly leads to the development of R&D functions in the context of the ECE automotive industry. Since capitalism is dynamic, and TNCs are constantly looking for ways to improve their competitiveness through organizational and technological innovations (Yeung 2007, 2009a), each round of investment may lead to the evolution of a new form of spatial division of labor (Massey 1979). Therefore, I ask whether the truncating effects of FDI on domestic R&D observed in the developed Western economies during the 1970s and 1980s have also developed in ECE during the 1990s and 2000s or, alternatively, whether changing investment strategies of TNCs and the internationalization of R&D have led to a significant increase in automotive R&D functions and competencies in ECE. Second, drawing on the GPN approach, I ask under what conditions FDI can lead to a successful automotive R&D development in host economies. Can we identify examples of successful strategic coupling between TNCs and regional R&D assets in the ECE automotive industry?

As a destination for foreign R&D, Central and Eastern Europe has played a marginal role compared to core regions of the global economy (UNCTAD 2005; Reger 2004; Pavlínek 2004). Its position in the global flows of R&D investment has also been less important compared to East Asia and similar to that of Latin America (Edler et al. 2002; Reger 2004). Inflows of FDI to Central and Eastern Europe, including FDI in R&D, were almost non-existent before 1990. They only grew significantly after the opening of Central and East European economies to foreign trade and investment in the early 1990s. Their gradual integration into the West European economy through foreign trade and FDI inflows intensified after the 2004 and 2007 EU accession of ten ECE countries, which lowered economic and political risks for TNCs and eased the trans-border flow of goods. The nature of this integration and the resultant position of ECE economies in the European division of labor, including corporate R&D, has predominantly been peripheral (e.g. Pavlínek et al. 2009). Nevertheless, ECE has several important advantages enhancing its potential for hosting foreign R&D. These include an increasing industrial production organized and controlled by foreign TNCs, growing markets, an educated but still significantly less expensive R&D and technical labor force than in Western Europe, and governmental R&D investment incentives. Perhaps, the most important advantages compared to other less developed regions are the geographic and cultural proximity of especially Central Europe to the West European economic core and the perceived political and economic stability of ECE related to the EU membership.

Before 1990, during the state socialist period, automotive R&D had been very limited in ECE. In the passenger car industry, only former East Germany and former Czechoslovakia produced indigenous passenger cars that were largely based on domestic technologies. But even there, a large part of product development was based on copying and reverse engineering of western products.[4] The rest of ECE relied on foreign licenses and foreign technology to assemble passenger cars (e.g. Havas 2000; Pavlínek 2002b). Consequently, with the exception of former East Germany and today's Czechia, indigenous automotive R&D capabilities were almost non-existent and did not extend beyond adapting Western technologies and licenses to local needs. Even the Czech and East German automotive firms were unable to conduct state of the art R&D and produce innovations that would prevent them from progressively falling behind developed countries' automotive firms.[5]

Because of large FDI inflows in the automotive industry since the early 1990s (Pavlínek 2008), the assembly of passenger cars more than quadrupled in ECE, and it increased more than six times in Central Europe between 1990 and 2015 (Pavlínek et al. 2009; OICA 2016). There were even larger increases in the production of automotive components for both local car assembly and for exports to Western Europe (e.g. Pavlínek 2003; Pavlínek and Ženka 2011). The ECE automotive industry has also experienced a significant upgrading of its products and production processes, especially in the 2000s. However, the development of automotive R&D has been very limited, reflecting only highly selective functional upgrading at the plant

[4] Interview with the former director of the Research Institute of Motorized Vehicles, Prague, August 12, 2010.

[5] In addition to automotive R&D conducted at vehicle assemblers, such as Škoda, former Czechoslovakia also had the centrally organized Research Institute of Motorized Vehicles in Prague. It employed about 630 workers in the 1980s. They conducted various research-related activities, such as the development of gearboxes. The number of workers at the Institute declined to about 100 after 1990, and the Institute was bought by German TÜV and transformed into a testing facility (interview with the former director of the Institute, Prague, August 12, 2010).

level (Pavlínek and Ženka 2011; Pavlínek et al. 2009; Lefilleur 2008). This is hardly surprising since a very limited firm-level functional upgrading is typical of quasi-hierarchical (captive) production networks, especially in less developed countries (Humphrey and Schmitz 2002, 2004a). Additionally, because of export-oriented strategies of automotive lead firms and small domestic markets, national governments of ECE countries have been in a weak bargaining position to persuade TNCs to establish higher level functions, like R&D facilities. However limited, the post-1990 development of automotive R&D in ECE has been driven by foreign TNCs and, in most cases, has concentrated on lower development functions, such as the technical support of production for local assemblers and product modifications for regional ECE markets.

Thus, while the automotive production has been partially decentralized from the West European automotive core to its ECE periphery since the 1990s, R&D has not followed the same trend but has remained highly concentrated in the West European core, particularly along a crescent-shaped axis that extends from the West Midlands in Britain through northern France, Belgium and southwest Germany and into northern Italy (Bordenave and Lung 1996; Lung 2004). Within this area, R&D is the most concentrated in Germany (Tables 4.2 and 4.3). When measured by automotive R&D expenditures, the position of core European countries in automotive R&D, especially Germany, actually strengthened between 1997 and 2013 (Table 4.2).[6] One of the reasons is that Japanese automotive R&D investment concentrated in the European core during the 1990s and 2000s. Germany attracted seven of 17 Japanese automotive R&D facilities established in Western Europe (JAMA 2010). With the exception of small technology centers, such as the one recently opened by Denso in Czechia, no large Japanese R&D centers are located in ECE, despite a significant development of manufacturing by the Japanese automakers and their suppliers there.[7]

[6] To compare automotive R&D in different EU countries, I have used data provided by the Eurostat Structural Business Statistics database for the narrowly defined automotive industry (NACE 34). In order to ensure the data compatibility in time series, I am using the classification of industrial sectors based on the NACE 1.1 revision up to 2007. Since this data is unavailable after 2007, I am using data for NACE Rev. 2 (C29) for 2013, which means that the 2013 data is not fully compatible with the pre-2008 data series. During the data analysis, I have found that some important automotive R&D establishments are not classified as NACE 34 and thus not included in the database. For example, Johnson Controls has an R&D center in the city of Trenčín of Western Slovakia, which is classified under NACE 73.1. It employed 377 workers in 2007. Its inclusion under NACE 34 would significantly affect automotive R&D data for Slovakia. Similarly, Ricardo Prague, which had 124 workers in 2007, is classified under NACE 74.2. MBtech Bohemia, which employed more than 160 researchers in Czechia in 2006 and 280 at three technology centers in Prague, Pilsen and Mladá Boleslav in 2010, is not included in the Eurostat database at all. All of these are stand-alone R&D centers not attached to a particular plant (see also Table 4.5), and I assume that they are classified the same way outside NACE 34 in all EU countries.

[7] Denso's technology center was opened in Liberec in 2007, and it represents the largest Japanese automotive R&D facility in Czechia. Its 40 workers are engaged in technical drawings, design and development of condensers, coolers, evaporators and other products for the parent company. It represents the lowest level of R&D facility in Denso's R&D hierarchy (interview with the company director on October 25, 2010).

Table 4.2 Trends in the automotive industry (NACE 34) R&D indicators in selected EU countries between 1997 and 2013

	R&D expenditures (mil EUR)				R&D personnel total				R&D personnel in employment (%)			
	1997	2002	2007	2013	1997	2002	2007	2013	1997	2002	2007	2013
Austria	124	311	324	463	1068	1775	2072	3066	4.1	6.3	6.1	10.2
Britain	924[a]	1360	1364	2053	7951[a]	8552[b]	9454	13,034	3.2[a]	3.9[b]	5.7	9.2
Czechia	81	175	290	250	2075	2536	3252	3898	3.3	2.8	2.7	2.8
France	1906	2677	3490	1908	18,883	26,671	30,912	14,249	6.8	9.4	5.3	6.1
Germany	9829[c]	13,621	17,587	17,187	73,447[c]	78,111	83,155	96,539	8.8[c]	8.9	9.8	11.9
Hungary	4	11	50	103	301[a]	990	876	1968	1.1[d]	2.7	1.6	2.7
Italy	748	688	1000	1453	9667	8440[a]	8833	13,952	5.1	4.5[c]	5.2	8.8
Poland	26	10	27	146	NA	975[e]	1118	2642	NA	0.9[e]	0.8	1.6
Romania	3.2[c]	0.6	35	130	825[c]	1468	1070	934	0.7[d]	2.1	1.7	0.7
Slovakia	2	0.7	3	42	153	112	72	276	0.5[d]	0.6	0.2	0.4
Spain	240[c]	294	254	85	3286[c]	3995[e]	3664	5277	2.1[c]	2.5[e]	2.4	4.0
Sweden	1201	1278	1537	NA	NA	9570	9567	NA	NA	13.0	11.2	NA

Notes: *NA* not available. The 1997–2007 data refer to the NACE Rev. 1 data, while the 2013 refer to the NACE Rev. 2 data, which makes them incompatible
Source: Eurostat (2016), national statistical offices of the selected EU countries
[a]1998
[b]2003
[c]1999
[d]2000
[e]2005

Table 4.3 The share of the individual EU vehicle producing countries of the EU's totals in automotive R&D expenditures, automotive R&D personnel, total vehicle assembly and total automotive employment in 2013

	R&D expenditures (%)	R&D personnel (%)	Vehicle assembly (%)	Automotive employment (%)
Germany	70.6	60.0	35.4	37.3
Britain	8.4	8.1	9.9	6.5
France	7.8	8.9	10.8	10.7
Italy	6.0	8.7	4.1	7.3
Austria	1.9	1.9	1	1.4
Spain	1.3	3.3	13.4	6
Czechia	1.0	2.4	7	6.4
Belgium	0.6	0.9	3.1	1.7
Netherlands	0.6	1.4	0.2	0.8
Poland	0.5	1.6	3.7	7.4
Hungary	0.4	1.2	1.4	3.4
Slovakia	0.3	0.2	6	2.8
Romania	0.2	0.6	2.5	6.3
Slovenia	0.2	0.3	0.6	0.6
Portugal	0.1	0.6	1	1.4
Total	*100.0*	*100.0*	100	100
Total CE	*2.5*	*5.8*	*21.2*	*20.7*
Total ECE	*2.7*	*6.3*	*18.7*	*26.9*

ECE East-Central Europe (Czechia, Hungary, Poland, Romania, Slovakia, Slovenia)
Source: Eurostat (2016), OICA (2016)

Germany accounted for more than two-thirds of the total EU automotive R&D expenditures in 2007 and for 71% in 2013.[8] High German shares of EU's automotive R&D expenditures (71%) and employment (60%) contrast with very low shares of ECE countries in 2013 (Table 4.3). Automotive R&D is more spatially concentrated in the West European core than the automotive production and employment. ECE's share of the total European automotive R&D expenditures is much lower than its share of the vehicle production and automotive employment (Table 4.3). ECE's figures thus underscore its specialization in more labor intensive automotive manufacturing, especially when compared with Germany. Lower-cost automotive R&D in ECE also reflects persistent wage differences between Western Europe and ECE. This large gap in automotive R&D between Germany and ECE is also revealed on a per capita basis and when compared with per capita vehicle assembly and employment (Table 4.4). In 2013, Czechia and Slovakia were producing more vehicles per capita than Germany, and the total Czech and Slovak automotive employment per capita was higher than that of Germany. While Slovakia's per capita vehicle assembly stood at 255% of the German level in 2013, its automotive R&D expenditures and employment were at 7.4% and 7.5% of the German levels.

[8] More recent data is not available.

Table 4.4 Per capita automotive R&D, production and employment data of ECE countries expressed as a percentage of German per capita levels and percentage share of individual countries of the ECE total in 2013

	R&D expenditures		R&D personnel		Vehicle assembly		Automotive employment	
	Share of ECE total	% of German per capita level	Share of ECE total	% of German per capita level	Share of ECE total	% of German per capita level	Share of ECE total	% of German per capita level
Czechia	38.5	11.2	38.2	31	33.1	152.1	23.9	132.8
Poland	20	1.6	25.9	5.7	17.2	21.6	27.5	41.6
Hungary	15.8	4.9	19.3	16.6	6.5	31.7	12.6	74.3
Romania	13.1	0.9	2.7	1.1	12	27.2	23.4	63.9
Slovakia	6.4	8.9	9.2	37.1	2.7	62.9	2.1	57.5
Slovenia	6.2	7.4	4.7	7.5	28.5	254.5	10.5	113.3
CE total	*86.9*	*4.3*	*97.3*	*11.7*	*88.0*	*48.7*	*76.6*	*67.3*
ECE total	*100.0*	*3.5*	*100.0*	*9.7*	*100.0*	*73.7*	*100.0*	*66.4*

Notes: In columns labeled as "% of German per capita level" Germany per capita levels = 100% and the national totals for each indicator for a particular country was divided by the population size of that country to obtain its value per capita. Countries ranked by the share of R&D expenditures
Source: Authors' calculations based on data from Eurostat (2016), OICA (2016)

The persistently marginal role of ECE countries in the European automotive R&D thus sharply contrasts with their increased importance in European automotive production and employment. This situation in ECE underscores my argument about the predominantly one-sided development of low-cost vehicle assembly in ECE, combined with underdevelopment of higher value-added functions, including automotive R&D and design, during the 1990s and 2000s.

High technological intensity of production, measured by R&D expenditures in value added, in Germany, Sweden and France (20–25%) in 2007 reflects their concentration on the development and production of high value added vehicles. The very low values in ECE countries (less than 2%), with the exception of Czechia, reflect the opposite (Pavlínek 2012). The declining values in Czechia, Poland, Romania and Slovakia show that FDI-driven increases in the automotive production and employment grew faster than R&D expenditures between 1997 and 2007. Core automotive industry countries tend to have a higher share of their R&D devoted to motor vehicles rather than to components. A high share of R&D dedicated to automotive components in Slovakia (100%), Poland (92%), Hungary (91%), Slovenia (70%) and Spain (49%) reflects their peripheral status in the European automotive system (Eurostat 2011). Low automotive R&D expenditures, combined with a high share of these expenditures devoted to automotive components, suggest the predominance of low level development work, concentrating on product modifications for local assemblers and the technical support of local production.

Using Oinas and Malecki's (2002) classification of spatial innovation systems, the vast majority of ECE automotive industry can be thus classified as adopter

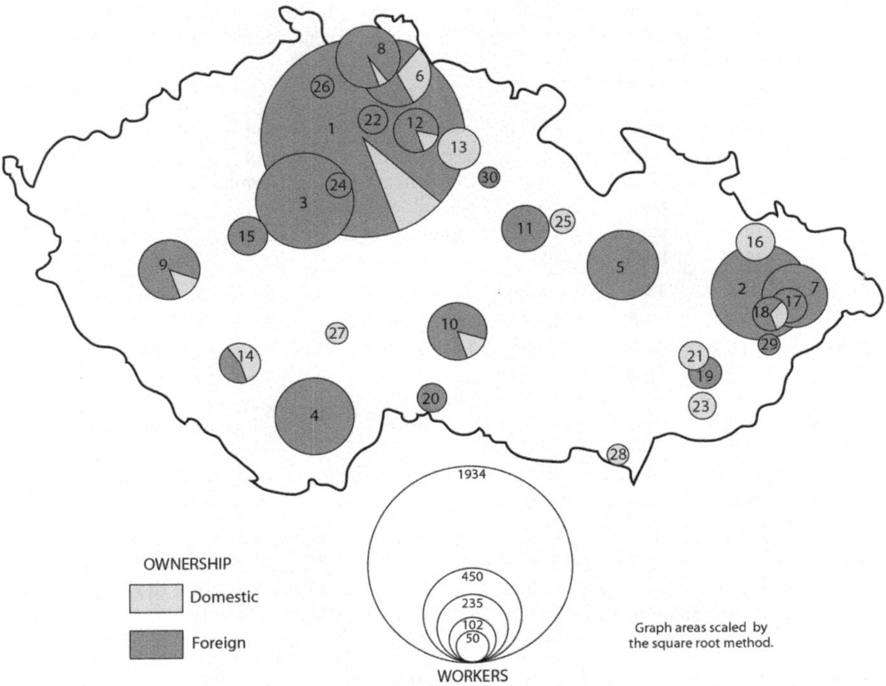

Fig. 4.2 The distribution of automotive R&D in Czechia by location with 20 or more R&D workers as of March 2011. Notes: 1 Mladá Boleslav, 2 Nový Jičín, 3 Prague, 4 České Budějovice, 5 Mohelnice, 6 Jablonec nad Nisou, 7 Kopřivnice, 8 Liberec, 9 Pilsen, 10 Jihlava, 11 Vysoké Mýto, 12 Jičín, 13 Hořice, 14 Strakonice, 15 Zdice, 16 Hradec nad Moravicí, 17 Frenštát pod Radhoštěm, 18 Valašské Meziříčí, 19 Otrokovice, 20 Dačice, 21 Kroměříž, 22 Bakov nad Jizerou, 23 Kunovice, 24 Brandýs nad Labem-Stará Boleslav, 25 Libchavy, 26 Česká Lípa, 27 Tábor, 28 Břeclav, 29 Vsetín, 30 Hradec Králové. Source: 2011 interviews

regions that have developed production oriented competencies mainly through technology and know-how transfer from the automotive industry core in the 1990s and 2000s. There are only a few regions of adapter activities, which are typified mainly by incremental innovations of the existing products and processes and by high levels of FDI. Two prime examples include the Mladá Boleslav region of Czechia, hosting Škoda Auto's R&D and R&D of its Tier 0.5 suppliers (Fig. 4.2) and the Bucharest-Pitesti region of Romania, hosting Dacia's R&D and R&D of its Tier 0.5 suppliers. ECE does not have regions of genuine innovators that develop radical innovations and best practices in the automotive industry. These are located in the core automotive regions of Western Europe, the United States and East Asia.

Czechia scored surprisingly well compared to the rest of ECE in both technological intensity of production (6.7%) and in having a high share of its automotive R&D

devoted to automobiles (75%) rather than components in 2007.[9] Table 4.4 also reveals the stronger position of Czechia than the rest of ECE countries in automotive R&D. In 2013, the Czech-based automotive firms accounted for almost 40% of ECE's R&D expenditures and employment, despite the fact that Czechia accounts for less than 12% of ECE's total population. This relatively greater role of R&D in the Czech automotive industry than in other ECE countries and the rest of the European automotive periphery warrants special attention.

Corporate R&D in the Czech Automotive Industry

The analysis of the Czech automotive R&D is based on three sources of data. First, it draws on a unique database of 476 Czech-based automotive firms with 20 or more employees in the broadly defined automotive industry (CSO 2010a). In addition to NACE 34 firms, it also includes firms which are part of the automotive value chain but are classified in other industrial sectors. Since the inclusion of data for entire firms that only have a small share of their production linked to the automotive industry would distort the dataset, each firm was assigned a weight based on the share of the automotive industry in its turnover. R&D data for the 1995–2007 and 2012–2014 periods were also provided by the Czech Statistical Office (CSO 2010b, 2016).[10] Second, I have collected more detailed information about the size and type of R&D and innovation activities at the firm level from 274 Czech-based automotive firms with 20 or more employees during a 2009 survey. Third, 125 company interviews were conducted with directors or top managers of automotive firms in 2000, 2005, and 2009–2011 to collect detailed information about the nature of R&D activities at the firm level. The interviewed companies are a representative sample selected from the database in terms of size, ownership and the position of firms in the supplier hierarchy.

The effects of shock therapy and privatization in the Czech automotive industry in the early 1990s have been analyzed elsewhere (Pavlínek 2002a, 2003). Their consequences for the Czech automotive R&D have been significant. The government-sponsored automotive R&D disintegrated as the government support ended and the demand for this type of R&D almost disappeared. Because of trade liberalization, domestic firms could freely buy modern technologies in the West. The horizontally integrated supplier sector around particular groups of components was fragmented during the hasty privatization (Pavlínek 2002a). This fragmentation took place at the time of the wave of mergers and acquisitions in the global components industry, leading to the emergence of large 'global suppliers' (Humphrey 2000; Sturgeon et al. 2008). In Czechia, the most important Škoda suppliers were taken over by the established Volkswagen's (VW) suppliers in the wave of JV agreements (see Pavlínek 2003, 2008). Consequently, five general scenarios of the post-1990 auto-

[9] More recent data is not available.

[10] More recent data is not available.

motive R&D development can be identified, four involving FDI in R&D, three of which involved acquisitions of domestic suppliers by foreign firms. First, after acquisition by a part-process TNC, the existing small-scale firm-level R&D was usually transferred from Czech subsidiaries to the R&D centers of their parent companies, which are typically located in Western Europe. Second, after acquisition by a conglomerate TNC, local small scale R&D was often maintained because of the existing local expertise. These cases have been rare, however. The third scenario is typified by the division of R&D labor at the corporate level after the acquisition, in which strategic R&D was concentrated in parent company's R&D center in Western Europe, while a lower level product or process development was conducted in Czech subsidiaries because of substantially lower R&D labor costs (Pavlínek 2004). Fourth, several foreign and domestic stand-alone engineering centers were established to provide design and development services to automakers, mostly Škoda Auto, and component suppliers. These facilities are typically located either close to the Škoda Auto's R&D and assembly facilities or in larger cities with the available R&D labor force (Table 4.5, Fig. 4.2). Finally, small-scale and low-level R&D was conducted by some surviving domestic suppliers that were not acquired by foreign TNCs. Between 2001 and 2009, the Czech government attempted to boost FDI in R&D by offering investment incentives to both foreign and domestic firms to establish or expand technology and business support service centers. In the automotive industry, the program involved 25 technology centers and two business support service centers, which promised to create 1604 new jobs, including 222 jobs in six R&D investments proposed by five domestic firms (CzechInvest 2010).

What accounts for a relatively stronger position of R&D in the Czech automotive industry compared to the rest of ECE? The Czech automotive industry differs from other ECE countries by the presence of corporate headquarters of Škoda Auto and its R&D center (Fig. 4.2). This single firm accounts for more than 75% of total R&D expenditures in the Czech automotive industry. Without Škoda, the Czech automotive R&D expenditures would be only slightly higher than those of Hungary, and would be thus comparable to other ECE countries. Škoda Auto is what I call a Tier Two lead firm (Pavlínek and Janák 2007). Tier Two lead firms have many attributes of lead firms as defined by GVC and GPN approaches, including an international production network, which they organize and control, the power to establish and coordinate the vertical network of their component suppliers, their own R&D, although it is limited, end-user sales, and end-user marketing (e.g. Gereffi et al. 2005; Coe et al. 2004; Henderson et al. 2002). However, Tier Two lead firms differ from what I call Tier One lead firms in one crucial aspect: they are foreign owned. Foreign ownership means that the ultimate corporate power over corporate decision making rests with their owners (Tier One lead firms), which significantly limits the corporate power of Tier Two lead firms.[11] Ultimately, it also limits their value cap-

[11] The decisions about any Škoda investment exceeding EUR 15 million are made at VW's headquarters. Škoda is involved in strategic planning but in "cooperation within the VW Group, and the parent company coordinates the strategic planning for its brands". VW's headquarters decide

Table 4.5 Stand-alone automotive engineering centers employing more than 30 workers in Czechia as of 2011

Company	Location	Country of investor	Employment	Year of launch	Field of expertise
MBTech Bohemia	Prague, Pilsen, Mladá Boleslav	Germany	280	1996	Car and engine components, electronic equipment, modules
Ricardo Prague	Prague	Britain	151	2000	Engines and transmissions
Aufeer Design	Mladá Boleslav, Ostrava	Czechia	133	2000	Car bodies, interior parts, electronics and pressing tools
Volke	Mladá Boleslav	Germany	106	1993	Automotive components
Swell	Hořice Mladá Boleslav	Czechia	104	1993	Construction and computing center for automotive components and engineering services
Ingersoll Rand	Prague	Ireland	90	2007[a]	Cooling technology for freight vehicles and large trailers, air-conditioning for mass transit buses and rail transport
Idiada	Mladá Boleslav, Liberec, Hradec Králové	Spain	90	2001	Automotive design, simulation, components and modules
Valeo Autoklimatizace	Prague	France	62	2002	Air-conditioning systems and control panels
Evektor	Kunovice, Mladá Boleslav, Kvasiny	Czechia	55	1996	Sheet metal and plastic automotive components
Rücker	Mladá Boleslav	Germany	51	1995	Automotive components, modules, complete systems

(continued)

whether Škoda's profits are transferred to headquarters or are reinvested at Škoda (Interview at Škoda Auto, Mladá Boleslav, June 30, 2005).

Table 4.5 (continued)

Company	Location	Country of investor	Employment	Year of launch	Field of expertise
EDAG CZ	Mladá Boleslav	Germany	30	2002	Product development

Source: Company interviews, web pages of individual companies
[a]The Institute of chemical technology, originally established in 1949, was acquired by Thermo King in 1992. It was relocated into a newly built R&D center in 2007 and employed 90 workers

ture potential and thus their potential contribution to economic development of their home countries.

Škoda Auto is fully owned by German VW and it is one of its four mass-market brands, together with VW, Audi and Seat. Before its takeover by VW, Škoda was developing its own cars, and in 1991 its R&D center employed 584 R&D workers. One of the conditions of Škoda's sale to VW set by the Czech government was the continuation of Škoda's in-house R&D (Pavlínek 2008). After the takeover, VW needed to upgrade the existing Škoda model (Favorit), support its production and observe the terms of the JV agreement. Škoda's R&D gradually expanded to meet these requirements. By 1995 the number of R&D workers increased to 899, and by 2015, to 1715. A new Škoda R&D center was opened in 2008 and its construction was generously subsidized with government investment incentives. The continuing expansion of R&D at Škoda took place for two main reasons. First, for marketing reasons, the appearance of Škoda models needs to differ from VW, Audi and Seat. Škoda has been given responsibility for designing the upper-bodies of its cars, while the common car platforms and lower-bodies for the entire VW Group are designed in Germany. As the number of Škoda models increased from one in the early 1990s to seven in 2016, design capabilities expanded accordingly. Second, after the takeover by VW, Škoda employed experienced engineers and designers who were substantially less expensive than their German counterparts, thus significantly lowering the cost of in-house R&D. Consequently, some routine development work, such as CAD (computer-aided design) operations, was transferred from Germany to Škoda in the 1990s (CzechInvest 1997). The platform strategy combined with labor cost differences have thus resulted in an R&D division of labor between Škoda and VW. Higher engineering functions related to platform development are mainly conducted in Germany, while Škoda's R&D focuses on the design of upper bodies for Škoda models, the adjustment of VW Group's platforms to use with Czech-sourced components, and the testing of Škoda models. Also, Škoda is responsible for the development of three-cylinder gasoline engines for the entire VW Group. Škoda's R&D has thus typical attributes of regional automotive R&D centers established by TNCs at mass production sites or large markets. The combination of previous R&D development, existing local R&D capabilities, a strong government policy and VW's strategic need for local R&D has led to the continuing development of R&D at Škoda after its acquisition.

The importance of Škoda for Czech automotive R&D is not just in its own R&D center. Since physical proximity, agglomeration tendencies and face-to-face contact continue to play an important role in automotive R&D (e.g. Boschma 2004, 2005; Carrincazeaux et al. 2001; Gertler 2003; Howells 2002; Lung 2004; Leamer and Storper 2001; Rodriguez-Pose and Crescenzi 2008a, b; Storper and Venables 2004; Weterings and Boschma 2009), Škoda's R&D has attracted significant automotive R&D, particularly from automotive engineering firms, into the proximity of its R&D center. These firms co-design and co-develop products and production processes with Škoda, and as a result, these engineering firms employed at least 425 R&D workers in the close proximity of Škoda's R&D center in Mladá Boleslav in March 2011 (Table 4.5, Fig. 4.2). Their co-location is Škoda's precondition for co-design and a long-term R&D cooperation (2011 interviews). Some of these engineering companies were asked to set up their offices within walking distance (less than 200 m) from Škoda's R&D center. Six out of the eleven largest Czech-based automotive engineering firms are located close to Škoda's R&D in Mladá Boleslav, and an additional three (MBTech Bohemia, Swell and Evektor) have smaller outposts there. In the case of MBTech and Swell, they established small local engineering offices despite having their main offices less than 70 km from Mladá Boleslav. Another of Škoda's preconditions for long-term R&D contracts with independent automotive engineering firms is that selected workers of these firms work directly at Škoda's R&D center although they are not paid by Škoda (interview March 3, 2011). Physical proximity of engineering firms to Škoda's R&D center makes it easier for these companies to achieve other types of proximity that are important for a successful coordination of R&D, including technical, social, cultural, cognitive, institutional and organizational proximity (Boschma 2005; Gertler 2003; Lung 2004).[12]

I argue that the development of R&D at Škoda represents an example of strategic coupling between regional assets and strategic needs of TNCs. In this particular case, regional assets in the form of regional R&D competencies, engineering traditions and a skilled labor force, based on the previous automotive industry development and government policies, have coupled with the strategic need of VW to develop a low-cost brand distinct from its existing brands. This successful coupling allowed VW to expand its economies of scope and scale through the development of the Škoda brand which, in turn, allowed VW to penetrate new markets in less developed 'emerging' economies, including Central and Eastern Europe, China and India, and to open new market niches in the established and saturated West European market. Regional competencies combined with VW's active development efforts led to the successful upgrading of production processes, products and functions at Škoda. This successful in-house upgrading was only possible through the concurrent upgrading of its network of Czech-based suppliers by the application of Škoda's power, which forced its local suppliers to upgrade their production processes and their products or face the exclusion from Škoda's supplier network (e.g. Pavlínek 2003, 2008). Additionally, VW used its corporate power to force its existing suppliers into follow

[12] I am aware that too much proximity may negatively affect the innovation process (see Boschma 2005; Torre and Rallett 2005).

supply in Czechia and its R&D partners into smaller scale follow co-design and co-location (Table 4.5). In turn, upgrading at Škoda Auto and its suppliers (Pavlínek and Ženka 2011), has had important consequences for regional development and for the Czech economy as a whole. Full regional economic benefits of these developments have been limited by the inability of Škoda to capture the entire value it creates and enhances because of its foreign ownership and its Tier Two lead firm status. For example, between 2004 and 2015, Škoda sent CZK 68 billion (about USD 3.4 billion) in dividends to VW's German general headquarters (Škoda-Auto 2004–2015).[13] Also, Škoda's development and production of high value-added, larger, more expensive and well-equipped models have reportedly been limited by VW because of the potential competition with expensive models made by VW and Audi.

Although the extent of Škoda's R&D is unusual in ECE, it is not unique. Renault has followed a similar strategy with its Romanian Dacia since the mid-2000s, intentionally using the successful model of VW towards Škoda. It built a large regional R&D center in Romania (Renault Technologie Roumanie—RTR) in order to design new vehicles, adapt engines and gearboxes and provide technical support of production. In 2007, a regional engineering and design center was opened in Bucharest. It employed 1400 workers. At the Pitesti assembly and powertrain plants, 500 workers provide engineering services and technical support. In 2010, a 300 worker test center for vehicles and powertrain components from the B0 platform used for Dacia Logan was opened in Titu. Together, RTR employed 2300 engineers in 2011 (which was fewer than the 3000 originally anticipated by Renault for 2009) to develop vehicles and powertrains and provide technical support for its plants in Central and Eastern Europe, Turkey and northern Africa. RTR is Renault's largest engineering center outside France, and Renault plans to develop it into its global R&D center for low cost cars (Renault 2007, 2010). However, a part of Renault's R&D for low cost cars still remains at Guyancourt, France because of the difficulties with its transfer to Romania. The first platform for Dacia Logan was derived from Renault Clio in France, but product development responsibility for Dacia has been gradually moved to Romania. Renault is currently developing a new specific platform for low cost cars (M0) and Dacia's R&D center plays a very important role in its development.[14] In this way, Renault has taken VW's strategy towards Škoda of localizing R&D in ECE further.

The second largest automotive R&D in Czechia is found at Varroc Lighting Systems (former Visteon-Autopal) located at Nový Jičín, which hosts Varroc's European technology centers for lighting and air-conditioning systems (Fig. 4.2). These R&D centers employed 380 R&D workers (engineers and technicians) in 2015 and were planning to add an additional 200 R&D workers in 2015 and 2016.

---

[13] The differences in value capture capabilities between the Czech-based Škoda Auto and the German based VW and Audi were revealed during the distribution of 2010 bonuses. The bonus of Škoda Auto workers (EUR 129) was less than 2% of Audi's (EUR 6500) and 3.2% of VW's (EUR 4000), suggesting a disproportionate value capture at Audi and VW compared to Škoda. Audi accounted for about half of VW Group's profits, VW for about one-third and Škoda for 6% in 2010. The main reason is the different value of cars assembled by these three assemblers. Audi's luxury cars are three times as expensive as Škodas (Kaláb 2011).

[14] Personal communication with Vincent Frigant, February 2, 2011.

The reason for the unusual location of these R&D centers in Czechia instead of the West European automotive core was the 1993 acquisition of Autopal by Ford. The development of the existing R&D was a precondition set by Autopal for its acquisition. Ford agreed because it did not have any R&D facilities for lighting technologies in Europe in the early 1990s and it could build upon the existing R&D capabilities at Autopal. In the words of former Autopal's CEO:

> In 1992, we negotiated our acquisition with three to five potential partners in both lighting and cooling technologies. At the end, we chose Ford because it was the only company ready to further develop our existing R&D, which was one of our key preconditions for privatization. Especially in lighting technology, we had a relatively small but very competent group of researchers here. In turn, our acquisition was an ideal opportunity for Ford, first, to exploit our competencies in cooling technologies, because vehicle air conditioning was just beginning to grow in Europe in the early 1990s. Then, air conditioning was installed in 10-15% vehicles compared to 70% today. Second, Ford did not have any production facilities in lighting technologies in Europe at that time. Our acquisition thus fitted very well into Ford's development strategy in Europe.[15]

The lighting technology R&D center was opened in 1995. It has a global mandate, and it conducts applied industrial R&D for other Varroc factories. R&D in cooling technologies was developed only after the takeover by Ford and is composed of two units (air conditioning/cooling and exchangers). As opposed to the lighting technology which has its main European R&D center at Nový Jičín, the main R&D center for cooling technologies is located in Germany.[16] Here, again, we see the coupling process between local assets in the form of existing R&D capabilities and potential embodied in local labor and the strategic need of Ford to develop R&D capabilities in Europe. Active R&D development strategies, which built upon the previous R&D development, have thus been an important factor of the successful R&D growth at both Škoda Auto and Varroc.

1995–2015 Trends in the Czech Automotive R&D

What is the overall situation in Czech automotive R&D? Czech automotive industry (NACE 29) accounted for 20% of total manufacturing R&D employment and for 21% of total manufacturing R&D expenditures in 2014 (CSO 2016). Three basic trends in the Czech automotive R&D can be identified from 1995 to 2007: the expansion of R&D employment, the growing share of R&D conducted by component suppliers, and the increasing share of R&D conducted by foreign firms. Between 1995 and 2007, the number of companies with at least one R&D worker almost tripled from 41 to 118, but most of these R&D activities were very small. Three-quarters of automotive firms employed no R&D workers in 2007 (Tables 4.6 and 4.7). R&D was dominated by foreign firms, which employed 82–87% of R&D

[15] Interview with the CEO of Visteon-Autopal, Nový Jičín, August 9, 2005.

[16] Interviews at Visteon-Autopal, Nový Jičín, September 9, 2010 and August 9, 2005.

Table 4.6 The distribution of firms based on the number of R&D workers in the broadly defined Czech automotive industry in 2007

	All firms		Foreign firms		Domestic firms	
R&D workers	Number	%	Number	%	Number	%
More than 20	27	6.1	21	9.2	6	2.8
5–19	43	9.6	17	7.4	26	12.0
1–4	48	10.8	13	5.7	35	16.1
0	328	73.5	178	77.7	150	69.1
Total	446	100.0	229	100.0	217	100.0

Note: Based on the weighted database of 446 firms with more than 20 employees
Source: CSO (2010b)

workers and accounted for 88–96% of R&D expenditures compared to the 13–18% employed and 4–12% spent by domestic firms (Figs. 4.2 and 4.3). This very strong position of foreign firms in Czech automotive R&D cannot be attributed simply to the dominant position of Škoda Auto because, even after excluding Škoda Auto from the database, foreign firms still accounted for 79% of total R&D employment in 2007 (Table 4.7). However, my research indicates that in many cases R&D activities of foreign companies (as well as of domestic companies) are limited to the technical support of production, and even a relatively large number of workers listed under R&D may translate in little or no actual development work. For example, the plant manager of Bosch Diesel, the second largest automotive employer in Czechia, with three plants in Jihlava and more than 6000 workers at the time of the 2005 interview, argued:

> We have no technical product development here. We have some production support, but it is just an outpost here. These workers are supporting production, but you cannot say that this is development. No. It is the support lab – around 30 workers. We need them for production – to explain things, to help, to support. But they do not develop anything. There are 1800 workers in our R&D center in Germany.[17]

R&D activities in domestic firms are very small (Table 4.6). Based on the weighted data of the broadly defined automotive industry, 45% of 67 domestic firms reporting R&D workers in 2007 (30 firms) employed three or fewer R&D workers, and only 14 domestic automotive firms employed more than ten. Only two domestic automotive firms employed more than 50 R&D workers in 2011 (Table 4.8). The average size of R&D based on the weighted number of R&D workers was 68 in foreign firms conducting R&D and 38 when Škoda Auto is excluded, compared to only eight in domestic firms. These data underscore the weak and fragmented R&D among domestic automotive firms. Such small scale R&D makes it very difficult for domestic firms to achieve economies of scale in R&D. Almost three-quarters of the Czech-based automotive firms conducted no automotive R&D, which is further evidence of their weak and vulnerable position in the automotive value chain (Table 4.6).

[17] Interview at Bosch Diesel, Jihlava, July 7, 2005.

Table 4.7 Foreign-owned automotive R&D centers employing more than 40 R&D workers in Czechia as of March 2011

Company	Location	Country of investor	R&D employment	Year of launch	R&D field of expertise
Škoda Auto	Mladá Boleslav	Germany	1509[a]	Before 1990	Development and testing of Škoda models
Visteon - Autopal	Nový Jičín	USA	450	Before 1990	Lighting and air-conditioning systems
Robert Bosch	České Budějovice	Germany	290	2005	Engine components, electronic accelerators, fuel modules
Hella Autotechnik	Mohelnice	Germany	235	2004	Lighting systems
Tatra	Kopřivnice	USA	175	Before 1990	Development and testing of Tatra trucks
Magna Exteriors & Interiors	Liberec	Canada	118	1992	Cockpit systems
Iveco CR	Vysoké Mýto	Italy	100	Before 1990	Development and testing of buses
TRW LucasVarity	Jablonec n N.	USA	100	2005	Braking systems
Continental Teves	Jičín	Germany	80	2005	Interior and braking systems
Automotive Lighting	Jihlava	Italy	80	1997	Headlight systems
Kostal CR	Zdice	Germany	70	2003	Electric interior modules
Continental Automotive Systems	Frenštát pod Radhoštěm	Germany	60	2006	Electronic systems, sensors, technical support of production
Bosch Diesel	Jihlava	Germany	57	1999	Engine pumps: testing and technical support of production
Barum Continental	Otrokovice	Germany	50	Before 1990	Tires: testing and technical support of production
Benteler	Jablonec n N.	Germany	47	2004	Chassis and safety systems
TRW DAS	Dačice	USA	40	2006	Steering systems
Denso	Liberec	Japan	40	2007	Condensers, coolers, evaporators

Source: Company interviews, company questionnaire, Škoda Auto (2011)
[a]2010. All R&D centers are co-located with manufacturing plants

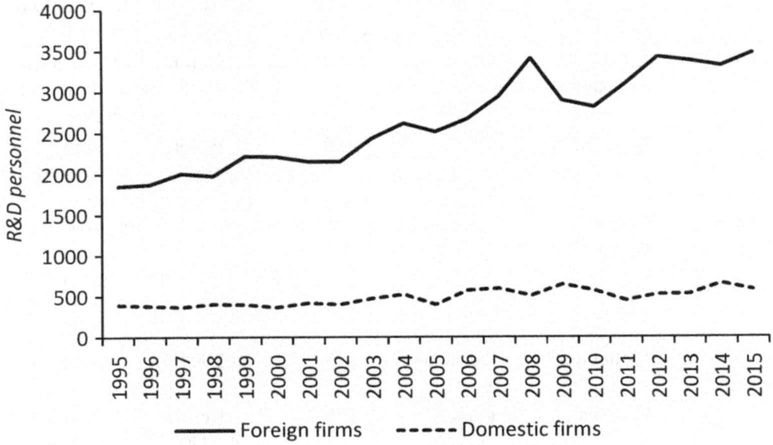

Fig. 4.3 Changes in automotive R&D employment in foreign and domestic firms in Czechia, 1995–2015 (1995–2004: NACE 34, 2005–2015: NACE 29). Source: Data from CSO (2010b, 2016)

The most important reason for the weak position of domestic firms is the fact that the largest domestic suppliers, who were more likely to have R&D functions, were taken over by foreign TNCs in the 1990s and early 2000s. Among Škoda suppliers, 94 JVs had been established between domestic suppliers and foreign companies in Czechia and Slovakia by 2005, the vast majority of them in Czechia.[18] Of 229 foreign suppliers, 178 with no R&D (78% of the total) are branch plants that rely on R&D and technology transfer from their parent companies. Since domestic firms cannot rely on R&D and technology transfer from parent companies, those with no R&D are limited to the production of simple standardized parts and components based on standardized technology, which does not require any development. Their main competitive advantage is the low cost production combined with the flexibility and speed of delivery.

In the broadly defined automotive industry, R&D expenditures increased by 79% and R&D employment by 61% between 1998 and 2007 (Table 4.9) because of significant FDI-driven expansion and the need of some suppliers to support their production with technological capabilities. The gap between foreign and domestic firms widened because both R&D expenditures and R&D employment grew more rapidly in foreign than in domestic firms (Figs. 4.3 and 4.4). Component suppliers increased their share of total automotive R&D employment from 30% to 54% and their share of total R&D expenditures from 18% to 28% between 1995 and 2007. Along with the growing number of component suppliers engaged in small-scale R&D activities, suppliers' increasing share of automotive R&D also resulted from the decrease in R&D conducted by domestic truck and bus makers. Overall, however, R&D employment and expenditures grew more slowly than automotive employment

[18] Interview at Škoda Auto, Mladá Boleslav, June 30, 2005.

Table 4.8 Domestic automotive firms with the largest automotive R&D in Czechia as of March 2011

Firm	Location	Employment	Year of launch	R&D field of expertise
Brano	Hradec n. M., Jablonec n. N.	118	1999	Door and cockpit systems
Evektor	Kunovice, Mladá Boleslav	55	1996	Sheet metal and plastic parts
ČZ	Strakonice	42	Before 1990	Turbochargers, fork-lift trucks, chains
SOR Libchavy	Libchavy	28	1992	Development/testing of buses
Naretec	Pilsen	24	2003	Acoustic, sheet-metal and plastic parts
Brisk Tábor	Tábor	22	1992	Spark plugs
GUMOTEX	Břeclav	21	Before 1990	Molded foam parts, interior components
AEV	Kroměříž	20	1991	Automotive electronics
Buzuluk	Komárov	16	Before 1990	Piston rings
TEDOM	Jablonec n. N.	16	Before 1990	Truck and bus engines
Tesla Blatná	Blatná	15	Before 1990	Cable harnesses
Vapos	Jičín	15	1996	Machine tools and production technologies
TMV Acoustics	Valašské Meziříčí	15	Before 1989	Speakers
Gumárny Zubří	Zubří	13	Before 1990	Components from molded technical rubber
Fortell	Lanškroun	8	2006	Plastic and metal products, injection forms, pressing tools

Notes: All R&D centers are co-located with manufacturing plants
Source: Company interviews, company questionnaire

and value added. As a result, R&D intensity decreased from 10.1% in 1998 to 5.6% in 2007, and the share of R&D personnel in total automotive employment decreased from 2.7 to 2.3%. The number of firms with no R&D workers increased from 208 to 328 between 1995 and 2007, but their share decreased from 81% to 73% of the total. The foreign domination of Czech automotive R&D has been gradually increasing as the share of R&D workers employed by foreign firms and their share of total R&D expenditures grew between 1995 and 2007 (Figs. 4.3 and 4.4).

However, the growth in R&D employment and expenditures is only a part of the story of the Czech automotive R&D between 1995 and 2007. A closer look at the firm-level data reveals a shift in the type and scale of R&D conducted by especially domestic firms. Because of the collapse of the Czech truck industry in the 1990s, the three truck assemblers (Tatra, Avia and LIAZ) shed 728 R&D workers (79%)

Table 4.9 The development of R&D indicators in the broadly defined Czech automotive industry between 1995 and 2007

	1995	1998	2002	2006	2007	2007 (1998 = 100)
Automotive industry employment	NA	91,391	128,902	168,867	172,331	189
Automotive industry value added	NA	46,999	79,066	136,499	150,009	319
Enterprises with R&D workers	49	53	64	119	118	223
R&D personnel	2428	2467	2585	3646	3972	161
R&D personnel with Master and Ph.D. degrees	747	734	981	1860	1998	272
R&D expenditures	2291	4735	6048	8573	8455	179
R&D personnel in employment (%)	NA	2.7	2.0	2.2	2.3	85
R&D expenditure in value added (%)	NA	10.1	7.6	6.3	5.6	56
R&D expenditure per employee	NA	51.8	46.9	50.8	49.1	95
Share of R&D personnel with Master and Ph.D. degrees (%)	30.7	29.8	38.0	51.0	50.3	169

Notes: Based on the weighted database of 476 firms with more than 20 employees, financial indicators are in constant prices, all indicators in thousands of CZK unless stated otherwise
Source: CSO (2010a, b)

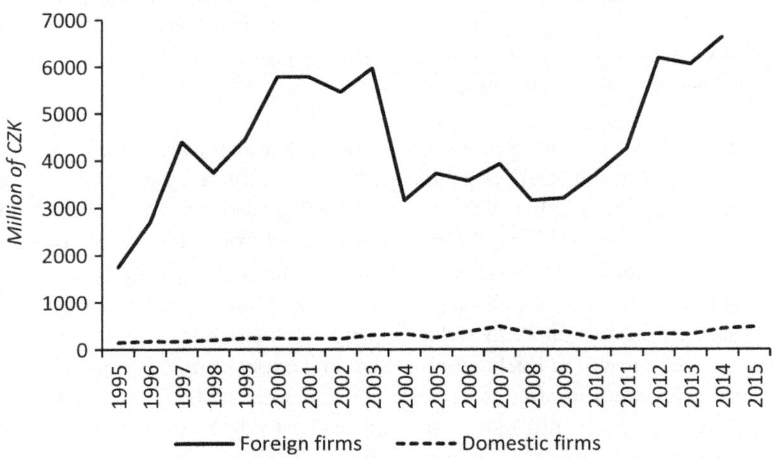

Fig. 4.4 Changes in automotive R&D expenditures in foreign and domestic firms in Czechia in current prices, 1995–2015 (1995–2004: NACE 34, 2005–2015: NACE 29). Source: Data from CSO (2010b, 2016)

between 1995 and 2011 (LIAZ went bankrupt in 2001). Iveco (former Karosa) bus manufacturer shed an additional 57 R&D workers. Thirteen domestic automotive firms with 15 or more R&D workers in 1995 shed more than two-thirds (904) of their R&D jobs between 1995 and 2011 (Table 4.10). Despite the growth in R&D employment and R&D expenditures in the passenger car industry, automotive R&D shifted away from a larger-scale R&D focusing on the development and design of complete vehicles to small scale development efforts and on the technical support of production. In short, the technological complexity of domestic automotive R&D decreased and domestic R&D capabilities in the automotive industry were significantly undermined during the 1995–2007 period.[19]

The Czech automotive R&D is dominated by several large foreign companies (Table 4.7), which is not unusual when compared to the situation in other countries (UNCTAD 2005). Five automotive companies with the largest R&D expenditures (Škoda Auto, Robert Bosch, Barum Continental, Visteon Autopal and Iveco) accounted for 80% of the total R&D expenditures in 2007. They also accounted for 81% of the increase in total R&D expenditures between 1995 and 2007. Five automotive companies with the largest R&D employment (Škoda Auto, Visteon Autopal, Robert Bosch, Hella Autotechnik, and Tatra) employed 60% of the total R&D personnel in 2007 (Table 4.7). Between 1998 and 2007, R&D expenditures per employee increased by 38% among assemblers, represented by Škoda Auto, Iveco-Karosa (buses), Tatra (heavy trucks) and Avia (medium-size trucks), and increased by 33% among narrowly defined suppliers (NACE 34.3). However, R&D expenditures decreased by 5% in the broadly defined automotive industry as a whole, reflecting its predominantly extensive growth during this period.

The educational level of R&D personnel improved as the share of R&D workers holding Masters and Ph.D. degrees increased from 31% to 50%. While researchers accounted for 75% of R&D personnel among assemblers, they accounted for only 22% among suppliers in 2007. The prevalence of less educated technicians among R&D personnel of suppliers suggests the focus of their R&D activities in technical support, adaptation, testing and development of automotive parts and components.

The 2009 survey provided additional insights into R&D activities at the firm level. Out of 274 firms, 109 firms employed at least one R&D worker, of which more than half (60) conducted technical support of production. Overall, 72% of those involved in R&D reported the development or modification of products for the Central and East European market (14 foreign and 35 domestic firms) and 45% for the Czech market (27 foreign and 45 domestic firms). Reported data showed that 13 firms (5%) conducted basic research while 21 firms (8%) developed products or technologies for their parent companies. However, Eurostat statistical data show the share of basic research of the total Czech automotive (NACE 34) R&D expenditures

[19] SOR Libchavy, a small domestic bus maker, is the only notable exception to this general trend. SOR used to produce agricultural machines before 1990 but moved into assembling buses of its own design in the 1990s (inter-sectoral upgrading). SOR had 29 R&D workers and assembled 478 buses in 2010 (interview, October 14, 2010).

Table 4.10 1995–2007 changes in R&D employment of domestic firms with the largest R&D employment in 1995

Firm	Location	R&D workers 1995	R&D workers 2011	Notes
Tatra	Kopřivnice	429	175	Foreign-owned in 2010, 83% production decline between 1995 and 2006
LIAZ	Jablonec n. N	301	0	Bankruptcy in 2001, plant closure in 2003
Avia	Praha	193	20	Foreign-owned in 2010, 96% production decline between 1995 and 2006, loss of most R&D competencies
Magneton	Kroměříž	93	20	Previously successful R&D negatively affected by failed domestic privatization and production decline
Motorpal	Jihlava	92	24	R&D and production of common rails transferred to Robert Bosch in the 1990s (failed joint venture)
Gumotex	Břeclav	55	21	A relatively successful Tier 3 supplier, R&D concentrates on the technical support of production
Motor Jikov	České Budějovice	48	6	The development of own engines terminated
Brano	Hradec n. M., Jablonec n. N.	38	118	R&D considered the most important source of competitiveness. One of the most successful domestic suppliers
PANAV	Senice na Hané	27	11	Effects of the collapse of the truck industry
Brisk Tábor	Tábor	25	22	R&D considered the most important source of competitiveness. A successful domestic supplier
Gumárny Zubří	Zubří	24	13	A shift from in house product development to product testing and the technical support of production
HŽP	Prostějov	15	6	Inability to keep up with Škoda Auto demands, a shift to aftermarket production
Total		1340	436	

Source: Company interviews

more realistically at 0.5% in 2007 compared with 2.3% for applied research and 97.1% for development (Eurostat 2011). These data show a particularly low share of applied research in Czechia compared to West European countries (France 31%, Spain 30%, Austria 21% and Britain 16%), and they underscore the overwhelming prevalence of lower level development activities in the Czech automotive R&D.

Conclusion

To what extent do we then see "the shift in the global distribution of innovation activities" (Schmitz and Strambach 2009: 232) in the context of the European automotive industry? Can we really argue that "the traditional division of competencies in the automotive industry, with the localization of knowledge-intensive modules of the value chain in core regions and labor-intensive activities in semi-peripheral regions, has lost its universal ability" (Winter 2010: 158)? Although I certainly agree that "the classical center–periphery model is neither inevitable, nor is it written in stone" (Layan and Lung 2004: 68), I have shown in this chapter, that despite the rhetoric of R&D globalization, countries located outside the automotive industry core in the vast majority of cases have not attracted sizeable higher-order R&D functions. The data presented show that despite the increasing role of ECE in European passenger car assembly, the position of ECE in the European automotive R&D continues to be disproportionately weak, as the automotive R&D remains concentrated in the West European automotive industry core, especially in Germany, without any signs of its diminishing. The Czech-based Škoda Auto and Romanian-based Dacia represent the best examples of a successful FDI-driven development of automotive R&D in ECE based on the strategic coupling of existing local R&D assets and strategic R&D needs of TNCs. However, the overall development of automotive R&D in ECE has so far been weak and has not altered the marginal position of ECE in the European automotive R&D division of labor. Consequently, the gap between the West European automotive industry core and Germany in particular, and ECE in automotive industry R&D remains very large. This situation underscores the peripheral nature of ECE automotive industry integration into the European automotive production system after 1990. While the standardized vehicle assembly and the production of components have dispersed to the ECE periphery mainly to exploit lower production costs and more flexible labor practices, strategic functions, including R&D, have remained highly concentrated in the West European core. The whole system is controlled from the core through the direct ownership of all ECE-based assemblers and most component suppliers by core-based TNCs. Without falling into the intellectual trap of developmental determinism, it would be unrealistic to expect that the existing European division of labor in automotive R&D will change any time soon (see also Kemeny 2011; Patel and Pavitt 1994). This is likely to be the case despite significantly lower R&D costs in ECE and ECE governments' efforts to attract more FDI in automotive R&D. As I have shown in this chapter, the degree of automotive R&D concentration in the European automotive industry core has tended to increase rather than decrease in the 2000s. The traditional reasons for this continuing concentration, such as scale and scope economies in R&D, synergy effects, better control over R&D results, tacitness, and cumulativeness, have been reinforced with a new automotive R&D organization related to modular production, favoring the co-location of ancillary R&D centers of modular suppliers close to R&D centers of lead firms.

The cases of Škoda Auto and Dacia suggest that the most successful automotive R&D development took place in ECE when core-based automotive Tier One lead firms decided to locate their regional R&D centers to ECE for their distinct global low cost brands (Škoda for VW and Dacia for Renault). These regional R&D centers then attracted both foreign and domestic automotive R&D because of the need for close R&D cooperation of both leading suppliers and various engineering firms with lead firms. Even with this success, the evidence shows that the scope of R&D development at Škoda Auto and Dacia has been limited. Furthermore, reproducing the experience of Škoda Auto and Dacia in ECE is unlikely unless another lead firm decides to locate the production and R&D of its global low cost brand into ECE. In the case of Czechia, neither Toyota Peugeot Citroën Automobile nor Hyundai, the other two assembly plants in the country, plan to establish any significant R&D in the country, which is in line with global strategies of Japanese and South Korean automakers (see Van Biesebroeck and Sturgeon 2010).

Although I expect a gradual increase especially in the routine and non-strategic low-level automotive R&D activities conducted in ECE, I do not envision that this growth will weaken the concentration of the strategic and most important automotive R&D in Western Europe in the near future. This gradual increase in automotive R&D in ECE will be mainly driven by foreign TNCs and their need to support both the growing car assembly and the production of components in ECE, as well as their need to lower costs of especially non-strategic lower-end standardized automotive R&D. ECE countries can actively affect these developments with long-term domestic policies that would make their economies more attractive for FDI in R&D, while improving their absorptive capacity to benefit from such FDI by increasing their indigenous R&D capabilities and improving governance (e.g. Fagerberg and Srholec 2008). The role of governmental educational policies to support the development of local firms' absorptive capacities that would attract FDI in R&D has been emphasized (Ernst 2008; Ernst and Kim 2002). In particular, the investment in and the expansion of tertiary education have been identified as the most important factor in attracting FDI in R&D and in fostering economic growth in more developed countries (Wang 2010). It is questionable, however, whether the ECE governments are capable of such long-term consistency in policy commitments as revealed by largely weak educational policies in the 1990s and 2000s.

The more detailed analysis of the Czech automotive R&D has demonstrated that while Czechia has by far the strongest automotive R&D within ECE, it suffers from similar weakness as the rest of ECE, including the almost complete control of automotive R&D by foreign TNCs and a weak domestic R&D. The most successful cases of automotive R&D development in ECE are examples of strategic coupling between the existing local R&D capabilities and the strategic needs of automotive TNCs. In the case of Czechia, both for Škoda Auto and Varroc (former Visteon-Autopal), foreign TNCs built upon the existing R&D capabilities and traditions. Both cases also show that a strong government policy and strong policies of domestic companies, which made the continuing R&D development a precondition for foreign acquisition, play an important role in the automotive R&D development in peripheral countries. I have argued that foreign ownership limits potential local and regional development effects of FDI in R&D by limiting the value capture potential from the automotive industry through value transfer abroad in the form of profits and dividends. Production grew more rapidly than R&D in the Czech automotive industry between 1995 and 2007, mainly because of the FDI-driven increase in the car assembly and components' manufacture. The significant increases in R&D employment and expenditures were also mainly driven by foreign TNCs. At the same time, the domestic automotive R&D capabilities diminished as the largest and most R&D competent domestic suppliers were taken over by foreign TNCs, and as automotive R&D shifted away from a larger-scale R&D, associated with the design of complete vehicles, to a smaller-scale, lower-level design and development activities. Despite the increases in the domestic automotive R&D employment and expenditures from 1995 to 2007, R&D of domestic firms continues to be very weak and excessively fragmented.

With some exceptions, the empirical evidence thus points towards predominantly truncation effects of automotive FDI in ECE. Despite some significant developments in the automotive R&D of ECE related to R&D internationalization, my analysis has shown that these changes have not altered the marginal position of ECE in the European automotive R&D, a situation that is likely to continue in the foreseeable future.

References

ACEA (2015) Facts about the automobile industry. European Automobile Manufacturers Association, Brussels

Aitken BJ, Harrison AE (1999) Do domestic firms benefit from direct foreign investment? Evidence from Venezuela. Am Econ Rev 89(3):605–618

Ambos B (2005) Foreign direct investment in industrial research and development: a study of German MNCs. Research Policy 34(4):395–410

Archibugi D, Iammarino S (2002) The globalization of technological innovation: definition and evidence. Rev Int Polit Econ 9(1):98–122

Asanuma B (1989) Manufacturer-supplier relationships in Japan and the concept of relation-specific skill. J Jpn Int Econ 3(1):1–30

Bathelt H, Malmberg A, Maskell P (2004) Clusters and knowledge: local buzz, global pipelines and the process of knowledge creation. Prog Hum Geogr 28(1):31–56

Bordenave G, Lung Y (1996) New spatial configurations in the European automobile industry. Eur Urban Reg Stud 3(4):305–321

Boschma RA (2004) Competitiveness of regions from an evolutionary perspective. Reg Stud 38(9):1001–1014

Boschma RA (2005) Proximity and innovation: a critical assessment. Reg Stud 39(1):61–74

Britton JNH (1980) Industrial dependence and technological underdevelopment: Canadian consequences of foreign direct investment. Reg Stud 14(3):181–199

Calabrese G (2001) R&D globalization in the car industry. Int J Automot Technol Manag 1(1):145–159

Cantwell JA, Dunning JH, Janne OEM (2004) Towards a technology-seeking explanation of U.S. direct investment in the United Kingdom. J Int Manag 10(1):5–20

Carrillo J, Lung Y, van Tulder R (2004) Cars, carriers of regionalism? Palgrave Macmillan, Houndmills
Carrincazeaux C, Lung YN, Rallet A (2001) Proximity and localisation of corporate R&D activities. Res Policy 30(5):777–789
Coe NM, Hess M (2011) Local and regional development: a global production network approach. In: Pike A, Rodríguez-Pose A, Tomaney J (eds) Handbook of local and regional development. Routledge, London, pp 128–138
Coe NM, Hess M, Yeung HWC, Dicken P, Henderson J (2004) 'Globalizing' regional development: a global production networks perspective. Trans Inst Br Geogr 29(4):468–484
Coe NM, Dicken P, Hess M (2008) Global production networks: realizing the potential. J Econ Geogr 8(3):271–295
CSO (2010a) Annual survey of economic subjects in selected industries (for the years 1998, 2002, 2005, 2006 and 2007). The Czech Statistical Office, Prague
CSO (2010b) Annual survey of research and development (for the period 1995–2007). The Czech Statistical Office, Prague
CSO (2016) R&D indicators. 2016 ed. The Czech Statistical Office, Prague
CzechInvest (1997) Škoda Automobilová a.s., part of the Volkswagen Group: CzechInvest Case Study. CzechInvest, Prague
CzechInvest (2010) Investment support promised for technology centers and business support services from June 2001 to 1st August 2009. CzechInvest, Prague
Dalton DH, Serapio MG (1999) Globalizing industrial research and development. U.S. Department of Commerce, Technology Administration, Office of Technology Policy, Washington, DC
Dannenberg J, Burgard J (2007) Car innovation 2015: a comprehensive study on innovation in the automotive industry. Oliver Wyman Automotive, New York
Dedrick J, Kraemer KL, Linden G (2010) Who profits from innovation in global value chains?: A study of the iPod and notebook PCs. Ind Corp Chang 19(1):81–116
Dias AVC, Salerno M (2004) International division of labour in product development activities: towards a selective decentralization? Int J Automot Technol Manag 4(2/3):223–239
Dicken P (1976) The multiplant business enterprise and geographical space: some issues in the study of external control and regional development. Reg Stud 10(4):401–412
Dicken P (2015) Global shift: mapping the changing contours of the world economy. Sage, London
Dunning JH, Wymbs C (1999) The geographical sourcing of technology-based assets by multinational enterprises. In: Archibugi D, Howells J, Michie J (eds) Innovation policy in a global economy. Cambridge University Press, Cambridge, pp 185–224
Edler J, Meyer-Krahmer F, Reger G (2002) Changes in the strategic management of technology: results of a global benchmarking study. R&D Manag 32(2):149–164
Ernst D (2002) Global production networks and the changing geography of innovation systems. Implications for developing countries. Econ Innov New Technol 11(6):497–523
Ernst D (2008) Innovation offshoring and Asia's electronics industry—the new dynamics of global networks. Int J Technol Learn Innov Dev 1(4):551–576
Ernst D, Kim L (2002) Global production networks, knowledge diffusion, and local capability formation. Res Policy 31(8–9):1417–1429
Etzkowitz H (2003) Innovation in innovation: the triple helix of university-industry-government relations. Soc Sci Inf Sur Les Sci Sociales 42(3):293–337
Etzkowitz H, Leydesdorff L (2000) The dynamics of innovation: from national systems and "Mode 2" to a triple helix of university-industry-government relations. Res Policy 29(2):109–123
Eurostat (2011) Structural business statistics: Annual detailed enterprise statistics—industry and construction. Eurostat
Eurostat (2016) Structural business statistics: Annual detailed enterprise statistics—industry and construction. Eurostat
Fagerberg J, Srholec M (2008) National innovation systems, capabilities and economic development. Res Policy 37(9):1417–1435

Filippaios F, Papanastassiou M, Pearce R, Rama R (2009) New forms of organisation and R&D internationalisation among the world's 100 largest food and beverages multinationals. Res Policy 38(6):1032–1043

Firn JR (1975) External control and regional development: the case of Scotland. Environ Plan A 7(4):393–414

Florida R (1997) The globalization of R&D: results of a survey of foreign-affiliated R&D laboratories in the USA. Res Policy 26(1):85–103

Florida R, Kenney M (1994) The globalization of Japanese R&D: the economic geography of Japanese R&D investment in the United States. Econ Geogr 70(4):344–369

Frigant V (2007) Between internationalisation and proximity: the internationalisation process of automotive first tier suppliers. Université Montesquieu Bordeaux, Bordeaux

Frigant V, Layan JB (2009) Modular production and the new division of labour within Europe: the perspective of French automotive parts suppliers. Eur Urban Reg Stud 16(1):11–25

Gassmann O, von Zedtwitz M (1998) Organization of industrial R&D on a global scale. R&D Manag 28(3):147–161

Gassmann O, von Zedtwitz M (1999) New concepts and trends in international R&D organization. Res Policy 28(2–3):231–250

Gereffi G (1999) International trade and industrial upgrading in the apparel commodity chain. J Int Econ 48(1):37–70

Gereffi G, Humphrey J, Sturgeon T (2005) The governance of global value chains. Rev Int Polit Econ 12(1):78–104

Gertler MS (2003) Tacit knowledge and the economic geography of context, or the undefinable tacitness of being (there). J Econ Geogr 3(1):75–99

Gerybadze A, Reger G (1999) Globalization of R&D: recent changes in the management of innovation in transnational corporations. Res Policy 28(2–3):251–274

Granstrand O (1999) Internationalization of corporate R&D: a study of Japanese and Swedish corporations. Res Policy 28(2–3):275–302

Havas A (2000) Changing patterns of inter- and intra-regional division of labour: Central Europe's Long and Winding Road. In: Humphrey J, Lecler Y, Salerno MS (eds) Global strategies and local realities; the auto industry in emerging markets. Palgrave Macmillan, Basingstoke, pp 234–262

Hayter R (1982) Truncation, the international firm and regional policy. Area 14(4):277–282

Henderson J, Dicken P, Hess M, Coe N, Yeung HWC (2002) Global production networks and the analysis of economic development. Rev Int Polit Econ 9(3):436–464

Howells J (1990a) The globalisation of research and development: a new era of change? Sci Public Policy 17(5):273–285

Howells J (1990b) The Internationalization of R&D and the development of global research networks. Reg Stud 24(6):495–512

Howells J (1990c) The location and organization of research and development: new horizons. Res Policy 19(2):133–146

Howells J (1996) Tacit knowledge, innovation and technology transfer. Tech Anal Strat Manag 8(2):91–106

Howells J (1999) Regional systems of innovation? In: Archibugi D, Howells J, Michie J (eds) Innovation policy in a global economy. Cambridge University Press, Cambridge, pp 67–93

Howells J (2002) Tacit knowledge, innovation and economic geography. Urban Stud 39(5–6):871–884

Humphrey J (2000) Assembler-supplier relations in the auto industry: globalisation and national development. Compet Chang 4(3):245–271

Humphrey J (2003) Globalization and supply chain networks: the auto industry in Brazil and India. Global Netw 3(2):121–141

Humphrey J, Memedovic O (2003) The global automotive industry value chain: what prospects for upgrading by developing countries. UNIDO, Vienna

Humphrey J, Schmitz H (2000) Governance and upgrading: linking industrial cluster and global value chain research. Institute of Development Studies, University of Sussex, Brighton
Humphrey J, Schmitz H (2002) How does insertion in global value chains affect upgrading in industrial clusters? Reg Stud 36(9):1017–1027
Humphrey J, Schmitz H (2004a) Chain governance and upgrading: taking stock. In: Schmitz H (ed) Local enterprises in the global economy: issues of governance and upgrading. Edward Elgar, Cheltenham, pp 349–381
Humphrey J, Schmitz H (2004b) Governance in global value chains. In: Schmitz H (ed) Local enterprises in the global economy: issues of governance and upgrading. Edward Elgar, Cheltenham, pp 95–109
Humphrey J, Lecler Y, Salerno MS (2000) Global strategies and local realities: the auto industry in emerging markets. Palgrave MacMillan, Basingstoke
Hymer S (1970) The efficiency (contradictions) of multinational corporations. Am Econ Rev 60(2):441–448
Hymer S (1972) The multinational corporation and the law of uneven development. In: Bhagwati JN (ed) Economics and world order. Macmillan, London, pp 113–140
ILO (2005) Automotive industry trends affecting component suppliers: report for discussion at the Tripartite Meeting on employment, social dialogue, rights at work and industrial relations in transport equipment manufacturing. International Labour Organization, Geneva
JAMA (2010) Common challenges, common future. Japan Automobile Manufacturers Association, Tokyo
Jensen C, Tragardh B (2004) Narrating the triple helix concept in "weak" regions: lessons from Sweden. Int J Technol Manag 27(5):513–530
Kaláb V (2011) Volkswagen's bonuses: Czechs will receive thousands of crowns, Germans thousands of euros. Lidové noviny. http://www.lidovky.cz (accessed 22 Mar 2011)
Kemeny T (2011) Are international technology gaps growing or shrinking in the age of globalization? J Econ Geogr 11(1):1–35
Konings J (2001) The effects of foreign direct investment on domestic firms—evidence from firm-level panel data in emerging economies. Econ Transit 9(3):619–633
Kuemmerle W (1997) Building effective R&D capabilities abroad. Harv Bus Rev 75(2):61–70
Kuemmerle W (1999) Foreign direct investment in industrial research in the pharmaceutical and electronics industries—results from a survey of multinational firms. Res Policy 28(2–3):179–193
Kumar N (2001) Determinants of location of overseas R&D activity of multinational enterprises: the case of US and Japanese corporations. Res Policy 30(1):159–174
Layan J (2000) The integration of peripheral markets: a comparison of Spain and Mexico. In: Humphrey J, Lecler Y, Salerno MS (eds) Global strategies and local realities: the auto industry in emerging markets. Palgrave Macmillan, Basingstoke, pp 16–41
Layan J-B, Lung Y (2004) The dynamics of regional integration in the European Car Industry. In: Carrillo J, Lung Y, van Tulder R (eds) Cars, carriers of regionalism? Palgrave Macmillan, Houndmills, pp 57–74
Le Bas C, Sierra C (2002) 'Location versus home country advantages' in R&D activities: some further results on multinationals' locational strategies. Res Policy 31(4):589–609
Leamer EE, Storper M (2001) The economic geography of the Internet age. J Int Bus Stud 32(4):641–665
Lefilleur J (2008) Geographic reorganization of the European automobile sector what role for the Central and East European countries in an enlarged European Union? An empirical approach. East Eur Econ 46(5):69–91
Liu WD, Dicken P (2006) Transnational corporations and 'obligated embeddedness': foreign direct investment in China's automobile industry. Environ Plan A 38(7):1229–1247
Liu WD, Yeung HWC (2008) China's dynamic industrial sector: the automobile industry. Eurasian Geogr Econ 49(5):523–548

Lundvall BA, Johnson B, Andersen ES, Dalum B (2002) National systems of production, innovation and competence building. Res Policy 31(2):213–231
Lung Y (2004) The changing geography of the European automobile system. Int J Automot Technol Manag 4(2/3):137–165
Lung Y, Volpato G (2002) Redesigning the automakers-suppliers relationships in the automotive industry. Int J Automot Technol Manag 2(1):3–9
Malecki EJ (1979) Locational trends in R&D by large U.S. corporations, 1965–1977. Econ Geogr 55(4):309–323
Malecki EJ (1980) Corporate organization of R and D and the location of technological activities. Reg Stud 14(3):219–234
Martin R (2010) Roepke lecture in economic geography-rethinking regional path dependence: beyond lock-in to evolution. Econ Geogr 86(1):1–27
Martin R, Sunley P (2006) Path dependence and regional economic evolution. J Econ Geogr 6(4):395–437
Massey D (1979) In what sense a regional problem? Reg Stud 13(2):233–243
Meyer-Krahmer F, Reger G (1999) New perspectives on the innovation strategies of multinational enterprises: lessons for technology policy in Europe. Res Policy 28(7):751–776
Miller R (1994) Global R&D networks and large-scale innovations: the case of the automobile industry. Res Policy 23(1):27–46
Moulaert F, Mehmood A (2010) Analysing regional development and policy: a structural-realist approach. Reg Stud 44(1):103–118
OICA (2016) World motor vehicle production by country and type, 1997–2015. Organisation Internationale des Constructeurs d'Automobile, Paris
Oinas P, Malecki EJ (2002) The evolution of technologies in time and space: from national and regional to spatial innovation systems. Int Reg Sci Rev 25(1):102–131
Patchell J (1993) From production systems to learning systems: lessons from Japan. Environ Plan A 25(6):797–815
Patel P, Pavitt K (1991) Large firms in the production of the world's technology: an important case of "non-globalization". J Int Bus Stud 22(1):1–21
Patel P, Pavitt K (1994) Uneven (and divergent) technological accumulation among advanced countries: evidence and a framework of explanation. Ind Corp Change 3(3):759–787
Patel P, Vega M (1999) Patterns of internationalisation of corporate technology: location vs. home country advantages. Res Policy 28(2–3):145–155
Pavlínek P (2002a) Domestic privatisation and its effects on industrial enterprises in East-Central Europe: evidence from the Czech motor component industry. Eur Asia Stud 54(7):1127–1150
Pavlínek P (2002b) Restructuring the Central and Eastern European automobile industry: legacies, trends, and effects of foreign direct investment. Post-Soviet Geogr Econ 43(1):41–77
Pavlínek P (2002c) Transformation of the Central and East European passenger car industry: selective peripheral integration through foreign direct investment. Environ Plan A 34(9):1685–1709
Pavlínek P (2003) Transformation of the Czech automotive components industry through foreign direct investment. Eurasian Geogr Econ 44(3):184–209
Pavlínek P (2004) Regional development implications of foreign direct investment in Central Europe. Eur Urban Reg Stud 11(1):47–70
Pavlínek P (2008) A successful transformation? Restructuring of the Czech automobile industry. Physica Verlag, Heidelberg
Pavlínek P (2012) The internationalization of corporate R&D and the automotive industry R&D of East-Central Europe. Econ Geogr 88(3):279–310
Pavlínek P, Janák L (2007) Regional restructuring of the Škoda Auto supplier network in the Czech Republic. Eur Urban Reg Stud 14(2):133–155
Pavlínek P, Ženka J (2011) Upgrading in the automotive industry: firm-level evidence from Central Europe. J Econ Geogr 11(3):559–586

Pavlínek P, Domanski B, Guzik R (2009) Industrial upgrading through foreign direct investment in Central European automotive manufacturing. Eur Urban Reg Stud 16(1):43–63
Reger G (2004) Coordinating globally dispersed research centres of excellence—the case of Philips Electronics. J Int Manag 10(1):51–76
Renault (2007) Renault expands international operations with new regional sites in Romania and Nordic Region. Renault Press Release
Renault (2010) Renault opens test center in Romania. Renault Press Release
Rodriguez-Pose A, Crescenzi R (2008a) Mountains in a flat world: why proximity still matters for the location of economic activity. Cambridge J Reg Econ Soc 1(3):371–388
Rodriguez-Pose A, Crescenzi R (2008b) Research and development, spillovers, innovation systems, and the genesis of regional growth in Europe. Reg Stud 42(1):51–67
Rutherford T, Holmes J (2008) 'The flea on the tail of the dog': power in global production networks and the restructuring of Canadian automotive clusters. J Econ Geogr 8(4):519–544
Santos TD (1970) Structure of dependence. Am Econ Rev 60(2):231–236
Schackmann-Fallis KP (1989) External control and regional development within the Federal Republic of Germany. Int Reg Sci Rev 12(3):245–261
Schmitz H, Strambach S (2009) The organisational decomposition of innovation and global distribution of innovative activities: insights and research agenda. Int J Technol Learn Innov Dev 2(4):231–249
Sheard P (1983) Auto-production systems in Japan—organizational and locational features. Aust Geogr Stud 21(1):49–68
Škoda Auto (2004–2015) Škoda auto annual reports, 2004–2015. Škoda Auto, Mladá Boleslav
Škoda Auto (2011) Škoda Auto annual report. Škoda Auto, Mladá Boleslav
Spencer JW (2008) The impact of multinational enterprise strategy on indigenous enterprises: horizontal spillovers and crowding out in developing countries. Acad Manag Rev 33(2):341–361
Storper M, Venables AJ (2004) Buzz: face-to-face contact and the urban economy. J Econ Geogr 4(4):351–370
Sturgeon TJ, Lester RK (2004) The new global supply base: new challenges for local suppliers in East Asia. In: Yusuf S, Altaf MAA, Nabeshima K (eds) Global production networking and technological change in East Asia. The World Bank and Oxford University Press, Washington, DC, pp 35–87
Sturgeon T, Van Biesebroeck J, Gereffi G (2008) Value chains, networks and clusters: reframing the global automotive industry. J Econ Geogr 8(3):297–321
Sturgeon T, Van Biesebroeck J, Gereffi G (2009) The North American automotive value chain: Canada's role and prospects. Int J Technol Learn Innov Dev 2(1/2):25–52
Torre A, Rallett A (2005) Proximity and localization. Reg Stud 39(1):47–59
UNCTAD (2005) World Investment Report 2005: transnational corporations and the internationalization of R&D. United Nations Conference on Trade and Development (UNCTAD), New York
Van Biesebroeck J, Sturgeon TJ (2010) Effects of the 2008–09 crisis on the automotive industry in developing countries: a global value chain perspective. In: Cattaneo O, Gereffi G, Staritz C (eds) Global value chains in a postcrisis world: a development perspective. The World Bank, Washington, DC, pp 209–244
Vernon R (1966) International investment and international trade in the product cycle. Q J Econ 80(2):190–207
Volpato G (2004) The OEM–FTS relationship in automotive industry. Int J Automot Technol Manag 4(2/3):166–197
von Zedtwitz M, Gassmann O (2002) Market versus technology drive in R&D internationalization: four different patterns of managing research and development. Res Policy 31(4):569–588
von Zedtwitz M, Gassmann O, Boutellier R (2004) Organizing global R&D: challenges and dilemmas. J Int Manag 10(1):21–49
Wang EC (2010) Determinants of R&D investment: the extreme-bounds-analysis approach applied to 26 OECD countries. Res Policy 39(1):103–116

Weterings A, Boschma R (2009) Does spatial proximity to customers matter for innovative performance? Evidence from the Dutch software sector. Res Policy 38(5):746–755

Winter J (2010) Upgrading of TNC subsidiaries: the case of the Polish automotive industry. Int J Automot Technol Manag 10(2/3):145–160

Yeung HWC (2007) From followers to market leaders: Asian electronics firms in the global economy. Asia Pac Viewpoint 48(1):1–25

Yeung HWC (2009a) Regional development and the competitive dynamics of global production networks: an East Asian perspective. Reg Stud 43(3):325–351

Yeung HWC (2009b) Transnational corporations, global production networks, and urban and regional development: a geographer's perspective on multinational enterprises and the global economy. Growth Change 40(2):197–226

Zander I (1999) How do you mean 'global'? An empirical investigation of innovation networks in the multinational corporation. Res Policy 28(2–3):195–213

Zhao Z, Anand J, Mitchell W (2005) A dual networks perspective on inter-organizational transfer of R&D capabilities: international joint ventures in the Chinese automotive industry. J Manag Stud 42(1):127–160

Chapter 5
Linkages and Spillovers

Introduction

In an increasingly globalized economy, and especially in less developed and middle-income economies, the role of TNCs is considered to be crucial for economic development (Jindra et al. 2009; Meyer 2004). Value creation is a fundamental precondition for successful economic development (Henderson et al. 2002; Coe et al. 2004) and TNCs can create or enhance opportunities for value creation by their decisions to invest in particular countries, regions and localities. Through the geographic diffusion of broadly defined technology, which in addition to production methods and technologies includes production organization and management (Görg and Greenaway 2004), FDI has direct and indirect effects on host economies. Direct effects include employment effects, trade effects, effects on capital formation and tax revenues. Indirectly, FDI may influence the industrial environment of host economies and the behavior and performance of host country firms in the form of spillovers from foreign-owned (henceforth foreign) firms through acquisition of skills, through imitation, competition, and exports (Blomström and Kokko 2001; Görg and Greenaway 2004; Dunning and Lundan 2008). In other words, the productivity and/or efficiency of host country firms may increase following the entry of foreign firms as foreign investors are unable to fully internalize their firm specific advantages, such as superior process and product technology and marketing skills, which may spill over to local firms (Blomström and Kokko 2001; Blomström et al. 2000; Dunning and Lundan 2008).

The aim of this chapter is to analyze linkages between foreign and domestic-owned (henceforth domestic) firms and spillovers from foreign to domestic firms in the Czech automotive industry. The contemporary automotive industry is typified by the high degree of vertical disintegration and, therefore, by strong backward linkages between lead firms (assemblers) and hundreds of their component suppliers organized in hierarchically structured production networks (Humphrey and Memedovic 2003). The automotive industry thus represents an excellent economic sector to study spillovers from foreign to domestic firms. With the 2015 production

P. Pavlínek, *Dependent Growth: Foreign Investment and the Development of the Automotive Industry in East-Central Europe*, DOI 10.1007/978-3-319-53955-3_5

of 1.3 million vehicles, the Czech automotive industry provides a relevant example of the automotive industry periphery that has been integrated into the European and global automotive production networks through large inflows of FDI since the early 1990s (Pavlínek, 2002a, c, 2003). However, despite the importance of the automotive industry for the Czech economy and the dominant role of FDI in the sector (Pavlínek 2012, 2015, 2008; Pavlínek and Ženka 2010, 2011), FDI's effects on domestic firms in the Czech automotive industry have not been systematically studied. In this chapter, I employ the qualitative research methodology to focus on backward linkages between TNCs' foreign subsidiaries and domestic suppliers through buyer-supplier relationships, because they are considered to be the most important channel through which spillovers develop (Javorcik 2004; Blalock and Gertler 2008; Ivarsson and Alvstam 2005). I have collected unique data about the effects of foreign investors on domestic automotive firms through a questionnaire completed by 317 foreign and domestic firms in 2009 and on site interviews with 100 automotive firms between 2009 and 2011. My main goal is to evaluate the extent to which linkages and spillovers from foreign to domestic firms have developed in the Czech automotive industry after its liberalization in the early 1990s and through which mechanisms they occur because the study of mechanisms of FDI spillovers has been neglected (Hallin and Lind 2012; Meyer 2004; Spencer 2008; Contreras et al. 2012). Specifically, I focus on three questions: First, how strong are the linkages between foreign and domestic firms and what kind of spillovers can be identified in the Czech automotive industry? Second, what are the effects of these linkages and spillovers on technological, organizational and strategic competences of domestic suppliers? Third, why are some domestic suppliers able to benefit from linkages with foreign firms to enhance their competitiveness and improve their position in the automotive value chain while others are unable to do so?

Theoretically and conceptually, my research draws on two strands of literature. First is vast literature on spillovers, linkages and effects of FDI on domestic firms and regional development (e.g. Aitken and Harrison 1999; Blomström and Kokko 2001; Hansen et al. 2009; Jindra et al. 2009; Britton 1980; Hayter 1982; Dicken 1976; Firn 1975; Amin et al. 1994; Phelps 1993). Second is literature on GPNs, GVCs and industrial upgrading (e.g. Henderson et al. 2002; Gereffi et al. 2005; Humphrey and Schmitz 2002; Kaplinsky 2000).

I argue that spillover effects from FDI at the firm level vary significantly across the Czech automotive industry and are strongly affected by differences in the capabilities and absorptive capacity of domestic firms and by the changing organization of the automotive industry. My analysis suggests that domestic firms were affected by horizontal and vertical spillovers in the 1990s and 2000s. Indirect horizontal and vertical spillovers were more important than direct vertical spillovers in the form of direct technology and knowledge transfer from foreign to domestic firms despite the integration of domestic firms into automotive GPNs through the development of supplier linkages with foreign firms. The importance of direct spillovers varies with the capabilities of domestic firms to exploit them and is related to the position of firms in the automotive value chain and the supplier hierarchy.

The chapter is organized as follows. I begin with a discussion of the relationship among FDI, linkages and spillovers in which I emphasize the importance of linkages between foreign and domestic firms for the potential development of spillovers. Next, I demonstrate how changes in the organization of the contemporary automotive industry undermined the position of domestic firms in automotive GPNs and with it the potential for spillovers from foreign to domestic firms. In the fourth section, I briefly analyze the general effects of FDI in the Czech automotive industry and I argue that FDI resulted in productivity spillovers but not necessarily in technology spillovers. In the fifth section, I present an empirical analysis of linkages between foreign and domestic firms based on my unique quantitative firm-level data. In the sixth section, I examine spillovers from foreign to domestic firms. I summarize the main findings of the chapter in the conclusion.

FDI, Linkages and Spillovers

After decades of research following the work of Caves (1974), there is no academic consensus about the benefits and drawbacks of FDI for host economies generally and for productivity of domestic firms in the form of spillovers specifically. This lack of consensus has been explained, for example, by the different ways in which FDI spillovers are measured. Differences in research design, methodology and data can influence research results (Barrios et al. 2011). While analyses using cross-sectional data tend to find statistically significant spillovers on productivity of domestic firms, panel data econometric techniques tend to find statistically negative or insignificant spillovers (Görg and Strobl 2001; Meyer 2004; Javorcik 2004). The lack of consensus on FDI spillovers also reflects the fact that FDI effects on host economies depend on a large number of different factors, such as FDI characteristics, the size of host country firms, the nature of vertical linkages between foreign and domestic firms, worker mobility, the technological gap between foreign and host country firms and the absorptive capacity of domestic firms (Smeets 2008; Görg and Greenaway 2004; Crespo and Fontoura 2007; Blomström and Kokko 2001; Havranek and Irsova 2011). Spillovers also differ within individual countries depending on the industry, the nature of operations, the mode of entry of foreign investors, the length of time since the original investment, the domestic or export market orientation of foreign firms, and other factors (e.g. Scott-Kennel 2007; UNCTAD 2001; Dicken 2015; Carrillo et al. 2004; Amin et al. 1994). Furthermore, Meyer and Sinani (2009) have argued that spillovers vary according to the level of economic development of host countries with very rich and very poor countries benefiting from inward FDI, while middle income economies being negatively affected by FDI. In contrast, according to Blomström and Kokko (2001), the poorest developing countries do not benefit from FDI spillovers but middle income economies do. There are also important differences within individual countries with more developed regions benefitting economically more from foreign subsidiaries than less developed regions (Dimitratos et al. 2009). Potential benefits of FDI for host economies thus strongly depend on the context of the individual countries and are, therefore, highly spatially variegated. Despite this lack of academic consensus on the effects of FDI in host economies, policy makers tend to assume generally positive FDI effects on host economies and host country firms, especially in terms of FDI's potential for technology and knowledge transfer (Hallin and Lind 2012; Harding and Javorcik 2011). This belief has translated into economic policies that are supportive of FDI in the majority of countries and in vast public expenditures to attract FDI in both more and less developed countries (UNCTAD 2012; Meyer 2004; Harding and Javorcik 2011).

In this chapter, I differentiate between productivity and technology spillovers. Productivity spillovers are defined as the effect of the presence of foreign firms on productivity in domestic firms (Görg and Strobl 2001) in the form of increased availability of information regarding more efficient production processes of foreign firms in a host economy. The presence of foreign firms also increases the pressure on domestic suppliers to become more efficient through productivity improvements in the form of better machinery and organization of production. Foreign firms typically have specific requirements on domestic suppliers in terms of the quality of supplied parts and components, such as technology audits and quality certificates, before they can start supplying foreign firms. Meeting these requirements increases the productivity and competitiveness of domestic firms, which can be achieved without the direct or indirect transfer of technological knowledge and know-how from foreign firms. Domestic firms thus become more efficient by imitating the process technologies of foreign firms while, at the same time, lacking innovation capabilities to further exploit, advance or develop these technologies. As such, productivity spillovers are especially related to process upgrading in domestic firms. Technology spillovers refer to the diffusion of technology and know-how from foreign to domestic firms (Hatani 2009) in such a way that will make them not only more efficient producers but also increase their innovation capabilities through the transfer of technological know-how. For example, new specialized software will allow domestic firms not only to contribute to cost reductions and increased efficiency but will also allow them to design and produce their own tools or molds they used to buy from other firms, which will increase the value-added of their production. Thus, technology spillovers, in addition to process upgrading, may also encourage product and functional upgrading in domestic firms. By distinguishing between productivity and technology spillovers I am trying to distinguish between more efficient production on one side and increased technological capabilities on the other side that would allow domestic firms to narrow the gap between them and foreign firms. I argue that more efficient production and the use of better technologies broadly defined do not necessarily increase the technological capabilities of domestic firms. At the same time, I recognize that productivity and technology spillovers are closely interrelated.

Spillovers from foreign to host country firms have two basic forms, horizontal and vertical. Horizontal spillovers are mostly unintentional spillovers to firms in the same industry, including competitors, while vertical spillovers are unintentional and intentional spillovers to domestic suppliers and customers (Hallin and Lind 2012;

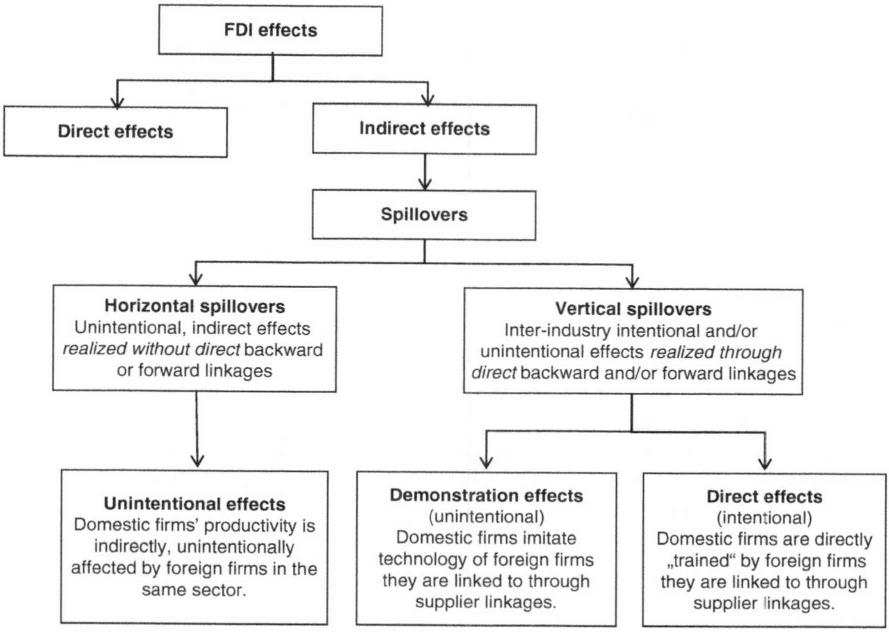

Fig. 5.1 The classification of spillovers. *Source*: Author

Blalock and Gertler 2008). Vertical spillovers to a large extent depend on the development and intensity of forward and backward linkages between TNCs' foreign subsidiaries and domestic firms through buyer-supplier relationships in the host economy (UNCTAD 2001; Giroud and Scott-Kennel 2009; Hansen et al. 2009). These forward and backward linkages may lead to intended and unintended spillovers of technologies, skills, various forms of knowledge and know-how from foreign to domestic firms (Blomström and Kokko 2001; Giroud and Scott-Kennel 2009; Fig. 5.1).

Linkages between foreign and domestic firms are thus an important precondition for vertical spillovers to occur (Blomström and Kokko 1998; Santangelo 2009; Scott-Kennel 2007; UNCTAD 2001; Görg and Strobl 2005). The impact of linkages on domestic firms could be both positive and negative, depending on what Cohen and Levinthal (1989) called a firm's 'learning' or 'absorptive' capacity (see also Cohen and Levinthal 1990; Girma 2005). Absorptive capacity refers to the ability of firms to "identify, assimilate and exploit knowledge from the environment" (Cohen and Levinthal 1989:569). It also includes the ability of firms to identify and exploit new scientific and technological knowledge generated by public research centers and universities (Cohen and Levinthal 1989). As such, absorptive capacity depends particularly on R&D capabilities of firms (Cohen and Levinthal 1989; Sturgeon et al. 2010) and it is enhanced by their R&D investment. Firms that conduct their own R&D are better at using and imitating external knowledge than firms without their own R&D, including better abilities to imitate externally available process or product innovations generated by other firms (Cohen and Levinthal 1989; Cohen and Levinthal 1990). Domestic firms that are able to absorb foreign technology and improve their overall competitiveness can benefit from their integration into GPNs through increased production, sales and employment (Scott-Kennel 2004; Ivarsson and Alvstam 2005). Such firms can also gradually improve their position in GPNs and GVCs through improved capabilities and functional upgrading (Humphrey and Schmitz 2002). Absorptive capacity is thus considered to be crucial for the ability of domestic firms to benefit from FDI (Ernst and Kim 2002; Meyer 2004; Kohli 2004) and upgrade their production and products or services to meet buyers' requirements (Dunning and Lundan 2008). Low technological and organizational capabilities of domestic firms may prevent them from absorbing foreign technology and from benefitting from the presence of foreign firms. This may result in negative consequences for domestic firms caused by FDI, such as crowding out effects, leading to the loss of competitiveness, downgrading and closure (Blomström and Kokko 1998; Görg and Greenaway 2004; Oetzel and Doh 2009; De Backer and Sleuwaegen 2003). Generally, the absorptive capacity of domestic firms as well as the number and intensity of linkages tend to increase with the overall level of development of host economies (Meyer and Sinani 2009; Dunning and Lundan 2008). However, large differences exist between different industries and different regions in the degree of linkages, especially in less developed economies (UNCTAD 2012).

The increasing integration of developing country suppliers into GPNs and GVCs, which are mostly organized by developed country lead firms, has not necessarily lead to the formation of strong linkages between foreign subsidiaries and domestic firms (e.g. Giuliani et al. 2005; Belderbos et al. 2001; Pavlínek 2004). The experience of weak linkages between foreign and domestic firms has also been the case of peripheral regions in developed countries (e.g. Schackmann-Fallis 1989; Tavares and Young 2006; Hewitt-Dundas et al. 2005; Crone 2002). Especially small domestic firms face high entry barriers to GPNs and GVCs (Nolan and Zhang 2002; Hatani 2009).

It has long been recognized by economic geographers and economists that (technology) spillovers are innately geographical (e.g. Jaffe et al. 1993) because the geographic proximity of economic actors increases the chances for spillovers by facilitating the flow of information, especially among firms with linkages within regional production systems (e.g. Florida 1996). In addition to localized patterns of codified knowledge, geographic proximity facilitates face-to-face contacts and the exchange of highly localized tacit knowledge (Storper and Venables 2004; Gertler 2003; Howells 2002; Howells 1996). The exchange of information and interactions of firms within clusters may increase firms' capabilities through processes of localized learning (Maskell and Malmberg 1999; Maskell and Malmberg 2007; Bathelt et al. 2004). The clustering of suppliers around assembly plants as well as the clustering of automotive R&D is typical for the contemporary automotive industry and has been well documented (e.g. Carrincazeaux et al. 2001; Frigant and Lung 2002; Sturgeon et al. 2008; Lung 2004). My previous research has identified such clustering of suppliers and R&D in the Czech automotive industry (Pavlínek and Janák 2007; Pavlínek 2012). Figures 5.2 and 5.3 suggest the importance of clustering in

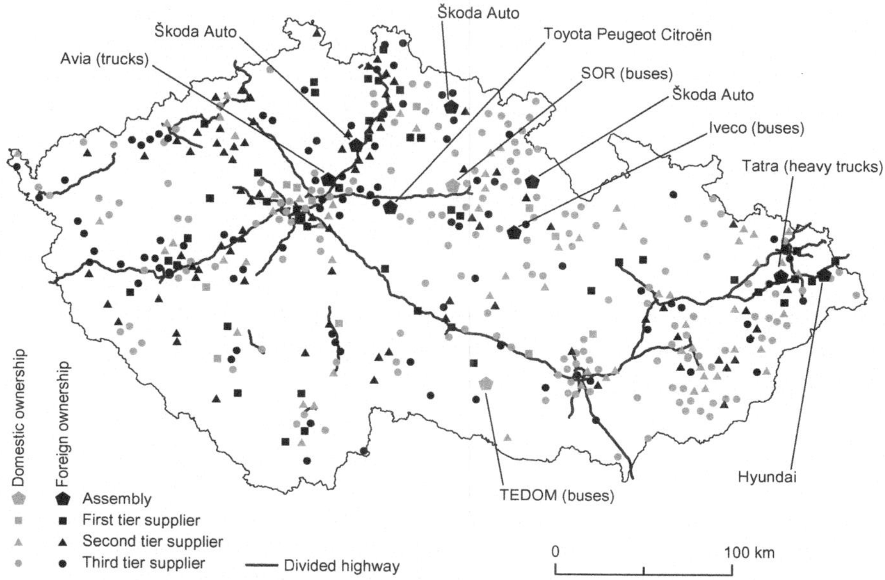

Fig. 5.2 The 2009 spatial distribution of foreign and domestic automotive firms in Czechia based on their position in the supplier hierarchy. *Source*: Author

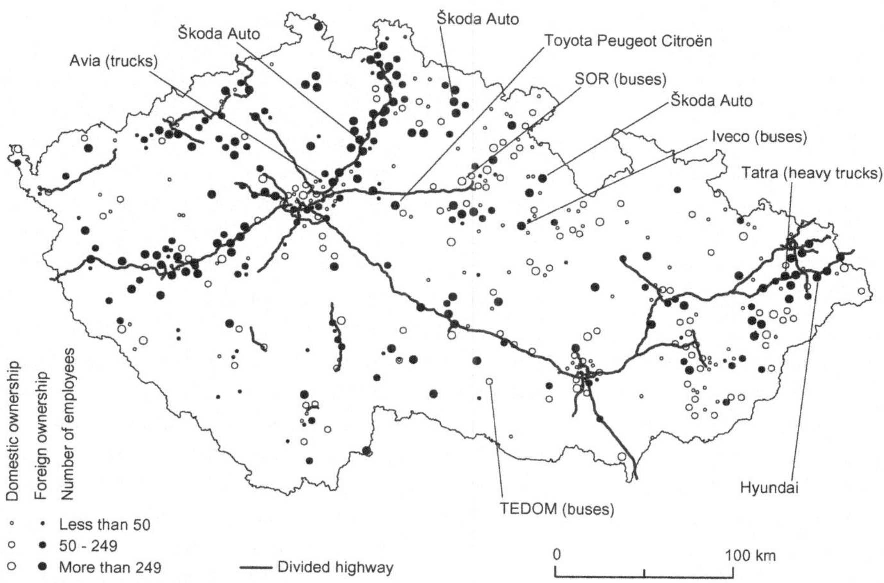

Fig. 5.3 The 2009 spatial distribution of foreign and domestic automotive firms in Czechia based on their number of employees. *Source*: Author

the Czech automotive industry around large passenger car assembly plants, in and around large cities, especially Prague, Pilsen and Brno, and along highways connecting Prague with Mladá Boleslav (the main Škoda Auto production complex) and with Pilsen and Germany. Both foreign and domestic firms are located in these clusters. Based on the previous research, we can thus assume that the clustering and agglomeration of automotive suppliers facilitate the development of spillovers between foreign and domestic firms in the Czech automotive industry.

Internationalization of the Automotive Supplier Industry and Its Consequences for Domestic Suppliers in Less Developed Countries

Before turning to the empirical analysis of linkages between foreign and domestic firms and spillovers in the Czech automotive industry, I will first investigate the position of domestic firms in automotive GPNs and review the general effects of FDI in the Czech automotive industry. In this section, I briefly demonstrate how the increasing globalization of the automotive industry has undermined the position of domestic suppliers in automotive GPNs. Consequently, the potential for linkages and vertical spillovers from foreign to domestic firms has been diminished.

The contemporary automotive industry represents a typical example of quasi-hierarchical (captive) value chains in which powerful lead firms organize and regulate vertical production networks of component suppliers (Humphrey and Schmitz 2004; Gereffi et al. 2005). Large assemblers (lead firms) set the basic parameters of automotive GPNs by wielding their corporate and market power. Lead firms define the architecture of the final product and of its crucial parts, select suppliers of modules and the most important components, set the schedule of their deliveries, and develop quality control mechanisms to be employed throughout the production network (Humphrey and Schmitz 2002; Humphrey and Schmitz 2004; Coe et al. 2004). During the 1990s, the largest core-based automakers invested heavily in new assembly plants located in the less developed "emerging" economies (Humphrey 2000; Sturgeon and Lester 2004). They were attracted by the profit-making potential of export-oriented low-cost production in peripheral regions such as Mexico and East-Central Europe, which are located close to automotive core markets and within regional trade agreements, and by potentially very large domestic markets in rapidly growing economies such as China and India (Liu and Yeung 2008; Liu and Dicken 2006; Van Biesebroeck and Sturgeon 2010; Humphrey et al. 2000; Pavlínek 2002c).

The geographic expansion of assembly operations and the contemporaneous development of modular design and production (Baldwin and Clark 1997; Frigant and Talbot 2005) compelled lead firms to increasingly demand global sourcing of certain components. Leading Tier 1 suppliers (sometimes referred to as Tier 0.5 suppliers) met this demand by rapidly internationalizing their operations through a wave of mergers, acquisitions and joint ventures in order to quickly develop their ability to supply lead firms wherever they assemble vehicles (Sturgeon and Lester 2004). These "global" suppliers have also become increasingly specialized in particular technologies and the production of distinct modules (Sadler 1999), and they significantly enhanced their R&D capabilities. As the differences in capabilities among suppliers increased, the entire supplier industry has been reorganized into distinct tiers (e.g. Humphrey and Memedovic 2003; Pavlínek and Janák 2007). Tier 1 suppliers are the most internationalized and supply modules and the most sophisticated components, which they co-design with lead firms. Tier 2 suppliers are less internationalized and supply lead firms and Tier 1 suppliers with less sophisticated and lower value-added components. Tier 3 suppliers are the least internationalized and supply low value-added, simple, standardized and slow-changing components in the entire GPN.

The internationalization and geographic expansion of leading suppliers and the restructuring of the supplier industry have had important consequences for domestic automotive suppliers in less developed countries. The widespread follow sourcing and the importance of long-term supplier relationships, based upon reputation and trust, favor existing core-based suppliers who are now required to supply lead firms in foreign locations wherever their high-volume final assembly takes place (Ivarsson and Alvstam 2005; Humphrey 2003). Domestic firms are typically ill positioned to compete with established foreign suppliers, which are often controlled by large TNCs and are experienced in delivering high quality components in a just-in-time regime in multiple foreign locations (Meyer 2004; Humphrey and Memedovic 2003). Experienced foreign suppliers also already possess management and quality expertise required by lead firms and capital to grow rapidly in foreign locations (Humphrey 2000). As a result, foreign lead firms often develop supplier networks through follow sourcing in less developed host countries consisting almost exclusively of their established foreign suppliers, including Tier 2 and Tier 3 suppliers. Because of high entry barriers, domestic firms find it almost impossible to enter such 'closed' supplier networks, and if they do, they play only a marginal role in them by delivering simple low value-added components (2009–2011 interviews; Barnes and Kaplinsky 2000). This situation prevents the development of supplier linkages between foreign and domestic firms and consequently prevents the development of vertical spillovers. In the context of the Czech automotive industry, this has been the case of Japanese and South Korean automotive lead firms, which relied on follow sourcing and almost totally excluded domestic companies from their production networks (2009–2011 interviews; see also Sturgeon and Lester 2004). Hatani (2009) has conceptualized such a situation as "spillover interception" in which spillovers from foreign to domestic firms fail to materialize in middle income economies despite high levels of FDI, and which has been supported by empirical evidence found in numerous studies (Meyer and Sinani 2009). Therefore, although FDI and linkages between foreign and domestic firms are a necessary precondition for vertical spillovers to develop, they do not guarantee that spillovers will occur (Saliola and Zanfei 2009).

Restructuring of the supplier industry has significantly reduced the number of suppliers (Sadler 1999). Domestic suppliers who survived the restructuring and consolidation of the supplier industry have become predominantly concentrated in the lowest tiers of the supplier hierarchy (Barnes and Kaplinsky 2000; Sturgeon and Lester 2004). Typically, there are only very few Tier 1 domestic suppliers, if any at all, in less developed countries (Pavlínek and Janák 2007). The number of domestic Tier 2 suppliers has also diminished as these were often taken over by foreign firms during their internationalization drive (Humphrey 2000; Humphrey 2003; Sturgeon and Lester 2004). Although the performance of domestic suppliers tends to improve with their integration into GPNs (UNCTAD 2001), they usually lack the necessary size and resources to engage in product and process innovation at the scale required by lead firms (Aller et al. 1999; Pavlínek 2012). Therefore, they tend to specialize in the supply of simple standardized components. Their incorporation into automotive GPNs is based mainly on their low production costs. In such cases, there may be little or no knowledge transfer from foreign to domestic firms even if the domestic firms supply large volumes of components and materials to foreign firms (Saliola and Zanfei 2009). In many less developed countries, domestic suppliers lack basic capabilities, such as process and project management capabilities or know-how and engineering capabilities, that limit their integration into automotive supplier networks (Lockstrom et al. 2011). In such a situation, even a long-term presence of foreign firms in host countries may not lead to the increase in linkages with domestic firms (Saliola and Zanfei 2009).

The continuous cost-cutting pressure and the emphasis on product quality throughout automotive GPNs stimulate process and product upgrading among suppliers (Humphrey and Schmitz 2002; Humphrey and Schmitz 2004). As long as domestic suppliers participate in GPNs, these cost-cutting and quality demands are favorable for the development of vertical spillovers since foreign firms might be willing to help their domestic suppliers achieve desired quality and price of supplied components through sharing some of their broadly defined technology. Spillovers may improve the position of domestic firms in automotive GPNs. More capable and competitive domestic firms could help decrease the dependence of the automotive industry on foreign capital in less developed countries. They can also increase their value creation, enhancement, and capture that are crucial for regional development (Coe et al. 2004; Henderson et al. 2002). Ultimately, this may help enhance the competitive position of the entire economy in the international division of labor. However, the increasing globalization of the automotive industry has led to a decreasing role of domestic suppliers in automotive production networks (Barnes and Kaplinsky 2000; Humphrey 2000, 2003; Humphrey and Salerno 2000; Humphrey and Memedovic 2003). Consequently, the potential for vertical spillovers has tended to diminish in host economies.

Still, it is difficult to make any general conclusions about automotive suppliers in less developed countries since the nature of the automotive industry and the related opportunities for domestic suppliers depend on a number of different factors, including market size, institutional factors and the distance from developed country markets (Sturgeon and Van Biesebroeck 2011). However, I think it is safe to conclude that the recent changes in the organization and functioning of automotive GPNs have been unfavorable for the integration of domestic suppliers into these networks. Domestic suppliers tended to be increasingly excluded from the existing GPNs or were unable to integrate in cases of newly developed supplier networks. Such a situation tends to weaken backward linkages between foreign firms and domestic suppliers and undermines the potential for spillovers. On a more general level, it has been argued that changes in the sourcing strategies of automotive TNCs tended to undermine engineering and design capabilities of less developed countries (Humphrey 2000, 2003). To investigate these issues in a specific context, I will turn to the analysis of FDI, linkages and spillovers in the Czech automotive industry.

FDI Effects in the Czech Automotive Industry

In this section, I argue that large inflows of FDI into the Czech automotive industry in the 1990s and 2000s resulted in strong productivity spillovers but not necessarily in technology spillovers from foreign to domestic firms. I contend that the position of firms in automotive GVCs and GPNs affects the development of spillovers from foreign to domestic firms.

My previous work on FDI in the Czech automotive industry, and in East-Central Europe as a whole, highlighted the crucial role of FDI in its post-1990 restructuring (e.g. Pavlínek, 2002a, b, c) and upgrading (Pavlínek et al. 2009, 2012; Pavlínek and Ženka 2011). As of 2011, foreign investors invested more than USD10 billion in the narrowly defined Czech automotive industry (NACE 29) making it, together with the real estate sector, the third largest recipient of FDI in Czechia after the banking industry and the wholesale-retail industry (CNB 2012). By 2008, there were 225 foreign automotive firms employing 135,827 workers in the broadly defined automotive industry.[1] Foreign firms dominate the sector, accounting for more than 90% of turnover, value-added, profit, income taxes, tangible assets and R&D expenditures (Table 5.1).

The post 1990 economic liberalization and subsequent FDI exposed domestic firms to foreign competition, which introduced much higher standards for the quality of supplied components, quality-management practices, and the timing of delivery (Pavlínek, 2002b, 2003). To quickly achieve new standards, Volkswagen (VW) organized the restructuring of the supplier base of its newly acquired Czech assembler Škoda Auto through follow sourcing and upgrading its domestic suppliers in the early 1990s. Škoda Auto actively encouraged foreign takeovers of its pre-1991 domestic suppliers to transfer foreign technology from foreign (mostly VW's) suppliers. By 2005, 94 joint ventures had been established between Škoda Auto's domestic and foreign suppliers in Czechia and Slovakia (the vast majority of them in Czechia) and foreign suppliers built 58 new factories to supply Škoda Auto (Pavlínek 2008). Mergers, acquisitions and newly built foreign factories were not limited to Škoda Auto suppliers but affected the entire Czech automotive components industry. In the process, the most capable domestic suppliers were taken over by foreign firms. For VW, foreign acquisitions and joint ventures represented the fastest and most efficient way of transferring foreign technology to the Czech auto-

[1] In addition to NACE 29 firms, the broadly defined automotive industry includes firms from other industrial sectors that are involved in the automotive value chain, such as suppliers from the plastic industry, rubber industry, electrical equipment, and iron and steel industry.

Table 5.1 Basic indicators of the domestic and foreign firms in the broadly defined Czech automotive industry, 2008

	Domestic	Foreign	Domestic (%)	Foreign (%)
Number of firms	250	225	52.6	47.4
Employment	37,125	135,827	21.5	78.5
Turnover (billion CZK)	62.3	730.0	7.9	92.1
Value-added (billion CZK)	15.4	144.8	9.6	90.4
Profit (billion CZK)	0.7	22.8	3.0	97.0
Wages (billion CZK)	8.7	60.1	12.7	87.3
Income taxes (billion CZK)	0.8	7.4	9.2	90.8
Tangible assets (billion CZK)	16.3	193.2	7.8	92.2
R&D expenditures (billion CZK)[a]	0.6	9.0	6.1	93.9

Notes: Includes firms with more than 20 employees, financial indicators are in constant prices
Source: Author' calculations based on various databases
[a]2007 data

motive industry. At the same time, Škoda Auto educated its domestic suppliers who remained in domestic hands about the ways of achieving new standards. All its suppliers had to undergo a quality system certification process and pass Škoda Auto's regular quality audits in order to continue supplying. Automotive suppliers have to continuously upgrade their production through better technology, more efficient work organization and management practices in order to survive. Especially lower tier suppliers who supply simple low value-added standardized components can be relatively easily replaced if they are unable to keep up with the relentless competitive pressure in the automotive industry and the ongoing price squeeze by lead firms (Ernst and Kim 2002). Those Škoda suppliers who could not upgrade quickly were replaced by foreign suppliers (Pavlínek 2003; see also De Backer and Sleuwaegen 2003). About two-thirds of original pre-1989 Škoda suppliers stopped supplying Škoda Auto in the 1990s (Pavlínek 2008).

Although horizontal spillovers were especially negative for the domestic firms that were forced to exit the automotive industry, the exit of uncompetitive domestic firms was a necessary part of the restructuring and upgrading of the domestic automotive industry that increased its overall competitiveness and without which it could not have survived in the long run. Crowding out effects of FDI in the Czech automotive industry also need to be understood in the context of changes in the global automotive industry that tended to marginalize domestic suppliers in automotive GPNs (Barnes and Kaplinsky 2000; Humphrey 2000; Humphrey 2003). Those few domestic suppliers in the narrowly defined automotive industry, who survived strong crowding out effects of FDI in the 1990s, benefitted from the rapidly growing automotive production in Czechia and also from exports. In addition to the crowding out of domestic firms, FDI thus strongly encouraged process and product upgrading of those who survived through productivity spillovers (Pavlínek and Ženka 2011) and indirect spillovers in the form of increased requirements and competition from foreign firms. However, it does not necessarily mean that technological knowledge has been transferred along with the productivity spillovers

(Hatani 2009). I will address this issue in the empirical analysis of spillovers in the Czech automotive industry.

During the 2008–2009 economic crisis, lower-tier suppliers (both domestic and foreign) were further squeezed by assemblers and forced to lower their prices by 10–20% (interview July 8, 2011). Consequently, 15 suppliers went bankrupt or closed their automotive plants in Czechia and four plants were relocated abroad during, and immediately after, the economic crisis (Pavlínek 2015). These enormous price pressures contribute to process upgrading but make it extremely difficult for automotive suppliers to engage in functional upgrading (Pavlínek and Ženka 2011). The economic crisis thus contributed to the further marginalization of domestic suppliers in the automotive supply chain.

These crowding out effects of FDI need to be understood in the context of trade and FDI liberalization and institutional changes related to the political-economic transformation of the 1990s (see Drahokoupil 2009; Pavlínek 2002b). Government policies affected potential spillovers from foreign to domestic firms especially in the early 1990s. During the negotiations of the terms of joint venture between Škoda and VW in 1991, the government openly supported the development of linkages between foreign and domestic firms by securing the temporary protection of Škoda's domestic suppliers. After Škoda's takeover, existing domestic suppliers were granted a transition period during which they continued to supply Škoda but had to gradually achieve VW's quality standards (Pavlínek 2008). Between 1992 and 1998, however, the government failed to openly support the development of linkages between foreign and domestic firms. In the absence of an explicit industrial policy, the government FDI policies were either completely absent (1992–1997) or limited to the indiscriminate attraction of FDI (1998–2001) (Pavlínek and Ženka 2011). After 2000, the government began promoting linkages between foreign and domestic firms and links between firms (both domestic and foreign) and universities. Since 1999, CzechInvest, the state investment promotion agency, has operated the "Supplier Development Program" in order to foster links between foreign and domestic firms and attract more foreign investors in the Czech automotive industry. It consists of the provision of a database of Czech-based (both domestic and foreign) automotive suppliers, including a list of their products and capabilities; the arrangement of links between Czech-based suppliers and incoming foreign investors; and the identification of potential domestic firms suitable for mergers and acquisition (CzechInvest 2014). Between 2002 and 2013, the government together with the EU spent EUR 42.5 m to support the formation and operation of about 60 regional cluster organizations in various industries. These clusters had to have at least 15 members, 60% of them SMEs, and had to include a university and/or research institute. The Moravia-Silesia automotive cluster is the only cluster formed in the automotive industry. It supports innovation activities, competitiveness and export capabilities of its 62 members (domestic and foreign firms, engineering services providers, universities, technical high schools and a regional development association of producers), through inter-firm cooperation and close links to state and regional institutions (MIT and CzechInvest 2013). My survey of 274 automotive firms revealed that only 29% of them were actively involved in some form of cooperation with other stakeholders, such as organized partnerships or clusters. The poor participation of automotive firms has thus limited the potential benefits of these programs in the Czech automotive industry.

Backward Linkages Between Foreign Firms and Domestic Suppliers

My analysis of spillovers in the Czech automotive industry is based on detailed firm-level data collected through personal interviews with senior managers of selected automotive firms and a survey of Czech-based automotive firms. I have drawn on a database of 490 Czech-based automotive firms with 20 or more employees in the broadly defined automotive industry (CSO 2009) to conduct a survey in 2009, which yielded a response rate of 65% (317 firms). The survey provided firm-level data about linkages between domestic and foreign suppliers in Czechia. Together with Pavla Žížalová and Jan Ženka, I carried out the interviews with 100 foreign and domestic automotive firms between December 2009 and August 2011 (Table 5.2). The interviews, in which foreign and domestic firms were targeted with different questions, collected more detailed information about spillovers than the survey and are, therefore, the main source of data for my analysis presented here. A large number of surveyed and interviewed firms at different positions of the automotive value chain yielded a highly representative sample. In-depth interviews allowed me to investigate factors behind spillovers and mechanisms through which they occur. Therefore, in addition to the identification of different types of spillovers, my qualitative data allowed me to examine their consequences for technological, organizational and strategic competences of domestic suppliers and explain why only

Table 5.2 Basic characteristics of the interviewed and surveyed firms compared to the total database

	Interviewed firms	Surveyed firms	Total database
Total number of firms	100	317	490
Domestic firms	38	162	228
Foreign firms	62	155	262
Assemblers	6	7	8
Tier 1	19	42	52
Tier 2	32	102	149
Tier 3	43	166	281
Small size	8	41	51
Medium size	33	143	233
Large size	59	133	206
Average size	1056	488	364

Note: Size categories of firms: small firms less than 50 employees, medium-size firms 50–250 employees, large firms more than 250 employees
Source: Author' 2009 survey and 2009–2011 interviews, CSO (2009)

Table 5.3 The average share of the total volume of automotive supplies sourced by Czech-based foreign firms (in %)

	Number of firms	Per cent share of total supplies from		
		Domestic firms	Czech-based foreign firms	Abroad
Total	62	12.6	10.9	76.5
Tier 1	14	13.7	10.8	75.5
Tier 2	21	15.4	7.7	76.9
Tier 3	22	7.0	7.9	85.1
Assemblers	5	20.0	32.0	48.0

Source: Author' 2009–2011 interviews

certain domestic suppliers have been able to benefit from spillovers. I have classified Czech-based suppliers into tiers based on the sophistication and value-added of supplied components while ignoring their degree of internationalization and their size as criteria for their classification. As opposed to some recent studies (e.g. Giroud et al. 2012), I differentiate between Czech-based foreign firms and domestic firms and analyze their supplier linkages to evaluate the effects of FDI on domestic firms. This distinction is very important since, as I have already shown, foreign firms and domestic firms play very different roles in contemporary automotive supplier networks because of the widespread use of follow sourcing by lead firms.

I have argued that the development of vertical spillovers depends on the existence and intensity of linkages between foreign and domestic firms. Therefore, the starting point of my empirical analysis is the evaluation of linkages between foreign and domestic firms. Czech-based foreign firms were asked during interviews to estimate to what extent they source components and materials from domestic firms, other Czech-based foreign firms and from abroad. I want to emphasize that these figures are based on qualified estimates of respondents rather than the precise data. In most cases, firms do not differentiate among Czech-based suppliers according to their ownership structure. Still, I believe that these qualified estimates are an important source of information about the extent of linkages between domestic and foreign firms. The results, which are summarized in Table 5.3, show a low share of parts and components sourced from domestic suppliers (13.5%) and a high share sourced from abroad (76.0%). Overall, Czech-based foreign firms sourced 86.5% of their total supplies from other foreign firms supplying both from abroad and from Czechia. This relatively low share of domestic suppliers of the total supplies to Czech-based foreign firms is also supported by the survey data. 98 out of 146 surveyed foreign firms (67.1%) reported the share of supplies from domestic firms to be less than 25%. Only 21 foreign firms (14.4%) estimated that more than 50% of their total supplies were sourced from domestic suppliers, while almost two-thirds (94 firms) were sourcing more than 50% of their total supplies from abroad (Table 5.4).

However, 40% (25) of interviewed foreign firms, all of them greenfield investors, reported that the share of domestic suppliers in their total supplies increased since their investment, and 35% (22) reported an increase in supplies from Czech-based foreign firms. This would support the arguments about the gradual development of

Table 5.4 The distribution of the total volume of automotive supplies sourced by Czech-based foreign firms

Share of supplies (%)	Domestic firms		Czech-based foreign firms		Foreign firms	
	Number of firms	%	Number of firms	%	Number of firms	%
0	22	15.1	49	33.6	13	8.9
1–24	76	52.1	54	37.0	17	11.6
25–49	27	18.5	28	19.2	22	15.1
50–74	17	11.6	10	6.8	40	27.4
75–99	2	1.4	3	2.1	49	33.6
100	2	1.4	2	1.4	5	3.4
Total	146	100.0	146	100.0	146	100.0

Source: Author' 2009 survey

linkages between foreign and domestic firms and the increasing embeddedness of foreign investors in host economies with time (e.g. Dunning and Lundan 2008; Dicken 2015). At the same time, however, seven large formerly domestic firms that were taken over by foreign investors, including assemblers such as Škoda Auto, Avia and Tatra, reported a significant decrease in the share of domestic suppliers of their total volume of supplies. This decrease reflects their integration into GPNs after their foreign takeovers and the importance of centralized sourcing strategies of TNCs. In the process, many traditional domestic suppliers were replaced with the established foreign suppliers of their new foreign owners. In some cases, production increases following the foreign takeover required increases in supplies that under-capitalized small- and medium-sized domestic suppliers were unable to meet. Consequently, their overall share of supplies decreased, or they were replaced by foreign suppliers.[2] The share of domestic suppliers also decreased because many of them were taken over by foreign firms and, with the change of ownership, became foreign suppliers.

According to my data, foreign Tier 3 suppliers account for 44% of all foreign automotive suppliers located in Czechia. A low share of supplies sourced by foreign Tier 3 firms from domestic suppliers underscores the fact that their assembly operations of simple standardized components were most often set up to exploit lower labor costs in Czechia, rather than to tap into the local manufacturing expertise. Since simple standardized components are not usually supplied in a just-in-time regime, the proximity of Tier 3 suppliers to assembly operations in Western Europe is less important than low production costs (Pavlínek and Janák 2007; Frigant and Lung 2002; Klier and Rubenstein 2008). The majority of parts and components for foreign Tier 3 suppliers are now supplied from low-cost countries, particularly China and India, where production costs are significantly lower than in Czechia. As a result, foreign Tier 3 suppliers tend to have only tenuous, if any, linkages

[2] 13.5% of the interviewed domestic firms lost their former domestic customers after these were taken over by foreign firms (2009–2011 interviews).

Table 5.5 Strengths and weaknesses of domestic firms according to Czech-based foreign firms

Strengths	No. of firms	%	Weaknesses	No. of firms	%
Geographic proximity	25	59.5	Product quality	16	39.0
Flexibility	20	47.6	Size	8	19.5
Product prices	12	28.6	Reliability	8	19.5
Communication	5	11.9	Product prices	8	19.5
Transportation costs	3	7.1	Instability	4	9.8
Product quality, know-how	3	7.1	Managerial skills	3	7.3
			Technology	3	7.3
			Financial resources	2	4.9
			Productivity	2	4.9

Notes: 42 foreign firms listed at least one strength and 41 foreign firms listed at least one weakness of domestic firms. Each firm could list more than one strength and weakness of domestic firms
Source: 2009–2011 interviews

with domestic automotive firms (Table 5.3). At the same time, the main reason behind a low share of domestic suppliers in supplying Tier 1 foreign firms is the relative lack of domestic firms capable of supplying more sophisticated, high-quality components at the price and quantity required by Tier 1 firms (2009–2011 interviews). A small average size of domestic automotive firms (149 workers) compared to foreign firms (604 workers) in 2008 (Table 5.1) makes it difficult for domestic suppliers to produce components and parts in volumes required by high volume assemblers and Tier 1 suppliers. As a result, the majority of these components are also supplied from abroad and by Czech-based foreign suppliers (Table 5.3). At least theoretically, therefore, domestic firms should be in the best position to supply foreign Tier 2 suppliers. However, even in this case, domestic suppliers do not account for a significantly higher share of supplies of foreign firms as they have had increasing difficulties to compete with imports from both lower-cost and more developed countries. A director of a Tier 2 domestic supplier argued in 2011:

> Our prices always keep on going down. What cost 10 euros ten years ago costs 4 euros now. However, the greatest decrease was in the past three years during the economic crisis when we got really squeezed by assemblers. More or less, we were included in global sourcing together with the Chinese and Indians, and assemblers squeezed everything out of us that was left (interview, July 8, 2011).

Additional reasons for a low share of domestic supplies to foreign firms are suggested in Table 5.5. According to foreign suppliers, the most important advantages of domestic suppliers include their geographic proximity, flexibility and low prices. At the same time, the lower quality of their products, together with their smaller size, lower reliability and less competitive prices compared to foreign suppliers are considered to be their most important disadvantages. Suppliers from more developed countries often supply higher quality components at competitive prices despite higher labor costs because of their use of advanced technologies and more efficient, less labor intensive production processes compared to domestic firms.

Table 5.6 Reasons for sourcing supplies from abroad by Czech-based foreign firms

	Centralized sourcing		Unavailability in Czechia		Low quality in Czechia		
		%		%		%	Total firms
Total	40	64.5	40	64.5	25	40.3	62
Assemblers	4	80.0	4	80.0	2	40.0	5
Tier 1	8	57.1	11	78.6	5	35.7	14
Tier 2	11	52.4	12	57.1	9	42.9	21
Tier 3	17	77.3	13	59.1	9	40.9	22

Note: Each firm could list more than one reason for sourcing supplies from abroad
Source: 2009–2011 interviews

According to Czech-based foreign firms, the two most important reasons for a low share of supplies sourced from domestic suppliers are the unavailability of particular parts, components and materials in Czechia and the centralized sourcing by foreign lead firms (Table 5.6). This means that Czech-based foreign firms have no or very limited influence on where their most important supplies are sourced from. When they have a choice, they choose suppliers that meet their price, quality and quantity requirements. The majority of interviewed managers argued that whether suppliers were foreign or domestic was not an important selection criterion. Tier 3 foreign firms are most affected by centralized sourcing and, therefore, have the weakest linkages with domestic firms (compare with Table 5.3). Even if domestic suppliers are competitive, because of their small or medium size, they are often unable to meet the requirement of centralized sourcing to supply the entire production network of a particular foreign firm. For Tier 1 suppliers, the most important reason for sourcing supplies abroad is their unavailability in Czechia. Examples include electronic components or parts made of advanced plastic materials.

Technology spillovers from foreign to domestic firms should potentially contribute to process and product upgrading of domestic firms, which, over time, should be reflected in the gradually increasing quality and sophistication of supplied components by domestic firms. How did linkages between foreign and domestic firms influence domestic firms from the point of view of foreign firms? More than two-thirds of foreign firms argued that their requirements on domestic suppliers were higher than the Czech-industry standards at the beginning of their supplier relationship, especially in terms of quality of supplied parts and components. In 60% of the cases, domestic suppliers were asked to meet specific requirements before they could start supplying foreign firms, especially to undergo technology audits and obtain quality certificates (Table 5.7). Approximately half of the respondents argued that both the quality (25 responses) and the sophistication (29 responses) of parts and components supplied by domestic suppliers increased over years in response to the increased quality and sophistication requirements of their customers. This empirical evidence points to strong productivity spillovers especially at the beginning of supplier relationships between foreign and domestic firms. However, according to foreign firms, no domestic suppliers have upgraded to the extent that would allow them to improve their position in the supplier hierarchy. Not surpris-

Table 5.7 Requirements on domestic suppliers by Czech-based foreign firms.

	Yes		No	
		%		%
Higher requirements on domestic suppliers than was the domestic industry standard at the beginning of the supply relationship[a] in terms of	38	67.9	18	32.1
Quality of parts/components	29	51.8		
Production technology	15	26.8		
Timing of delivery	8	14.3		
Domestic suppliers asked to meet specific requirements before they could start supplying	35	60.3	23	39.7
Quality certificate	19	32.8		
Technology audit	18	31.0		
Increase in parts/components quality	14	24.1		
New production technologies	6	10.3		
New machinery	2	3.4		

Notes: These were standard requirements in the automotive industry abroad. Each firm could list more than one from the list of requirements
Source: 2009–2011 interviews
[a]Only at the beginning of investment

ingly, 59% of foreign firms argued that foreign suppliers supply more sophisticated and complex products than domestic suppliers.

The analysis of foreign firms has revealed their limited linkages with domestic firms. While these data suggest that domestic firms only play a marginal role in supplying Czech-based foreign firms, it does not mean that most domestic automotive firms do not supply foreign firms. The low share of domestic suppliers in supplying Czech-based foreign firms corresponds with their low share of the total turnover, value-added and other financial indicators of the Czech automotive industry (Table 5.1). Both the survey and company interviews show that the vast majority of domestic automotive firms are involved in supplier linkages with foreign firms. Ninety-two percentage of the interviewed domestic companies supply foreign firms. Therefore, we need to turn to domestic firms for a better understanding of the nature of linkages between foreign and domestic firms and their consequences for spillovers.

Spillovers and FDI Effects on Domestic Firms

In the next step, I have analyzed interviews with 37 domestic firms about their linkages with foreign firms and spillovers. My sample included 20 firms that existed during the centrally planned economy before 1990 and 17 firms that were established after 1990. Five firms were small (less than 50 employees), 20 were medium-sized (50–250 employees), and 12 were large (more than 250 employees). More

Table 5.8 General effects of the entry and operation of foreign firms in the Czech automotive industry on domestic firms according to domestic firms

General FDI effects	Yes	%	No	%
New customers among foreign firms	26	70.3	11	29.7
Increased competition in the labor market	17	45.9	16	43.2
Increased direct (product) competition	12	32.4	25	67.6
Decreased share of the domestic market	6	16.2	25	67.6

Note: N = 37. Not all interviewed firms answered all questions
Source: 2009–2011 interviews

than half (21 firms, 57%) where classified as Tier 3 suppliers, 11 (30%) were Tier 2 firms, 4 (11%) were Tier 1 firms and there was also one small assembler of buses. Generally, higher tier suppliers are in a better position to benefit from linkages than lower tier suppliers (UNCTAD 2001). My interview questions were designed to identify horizontal and vertical spillovers based on direct and indirect relationships between foreign and domestic firms.

Overall, 49% of interviewed domestic firms argued that they were positively affected by the entry and operation of foreign firms in the Czech automotive industry, while 19% believed that they were affected negatively and 38% of firms believed that the entry of foreign firms had no effect on them at all. Increased sales, because of new customers among Czech-based foreign firms, was by far the most important positive effect of foreign firms on domestic firms, cited by 70% of domestic firms. In several cases, domestic firms were established to take advantage of the increased demand for parts and components generated by the entry of foreign firms. The increased competition for workers in the local labor market was the most important negative effect of foreign firms on domestic firms cited by 46% of interviewed domestic firms. Only about one-third of domestic firms were negatively affected by product competition from Czech-based foreign firms (Table 5.8).

Less than half of the interviewed domestic firms were affected by technology spillovers (Table 5.9). The most important technology spillovers included learning about new technology, new methods of quality management and new organizational and management methods. Domestic firms could experience these spillovers either directly or indirectly. Direct effects refer to the direct active help of foreign firms to domestic firms. Examples include a foreign firm providing production technology to a domestic firm or training managers of domestic firms in quality management. Indirect (demonstration) effects refer to a situation in which domestic firms learned about new technology indirectly from foreign firms, for example, through observation during visits of foreign firms. Indirect spillovers, especially in the form of demonstration effects, played much more important role than direct effects. Technology transfer through workers previously employed by foreign firms affected only 16% of the interviewed domestic firms (Table 5.9).

Overall, one-third of the interviewed domestic firms experienced some direct spillovers from foreign firms, suggesting the limited significance of direct spillovers for domestic firms (Table 5.10). Direct spillovers took place especially in those cases when foreign firms were interested in sourcing components and parts from

Table 5.9 Technology spillovers from foreign to domestic firms in the Czech automotive industry

	No. of firms	%	Indirect effect	%	Direct effect	%
Learning about new technology	16	43.2	15	40.5	4	10.8
Learning about new quality management systems	14	37.8	12	32.4	2	5.4
Learning about new organizational and management methods	12	32.4	10	27.0	4	10.8
Access to new components/parts	10	27.0	9	24.3	2	5.4
Technology transfer through workers previously employed by foreign firms	6	16.2				
Learning about new marketing methods	2	5.4	1	2.7	1	2.7
Firms affected by technology spillovers	17	45.9				

Note: N = 37. Each firm could be affected by both indirect and direct effect
Source: 2009–2011 interviews

Table 5.10 Direct spillovers from foreign to domestic firms in the Czech automotive industry

	No. of firms	%
Quality certificates advise	5	13.5
Management training	4	10.8
Provision of technology (license, sale, etc.)	4	10.8
Blue-collar workers training	3	8.1
Production organization advise	3	8.1
Production inputs	2	5.4
Suppliers connections	2	5.4
Domestic firms with direct spillovers	12	32.4

Note: N = 37
Source: 2009–2011 interviews

domestic firms and domestic firms needed help to achieve the required quality and efficiency of production. These requirements significantly affected domestic firms because 62% of the interviewed domestic firms had to meet such specific requirements before they could start supplying foreign firms. These prerequisites were important especially in the early and mid-1990s when the linkages between domestic and foreign firms began to form and when domestic firms had no prior experience with supplying foreign firms. The most frequent requirement of foreign firms, before entering into the supply relationship with domestic firms, was the possession of an international quality certificate and technological audits (30% of domestic firms). Other requirements, together listed by 32% of domestic firms, included demands to improve the quality of particular parts or components, timing of deliveries and lowering their prices.

The most important negative spillovers experienced by domestic firms were related to increased competition on the local labor market because of the entry of foreign firms. These include the loss of workers because of poaching by foreign firms (40.5% of the interviewed domestic firms), followed by the necessity to increase wages in order to keep up with foreign firms and stay competitive in the labor market (24.3%). These negative spillovers are place specific and are strongly affected by the distance decay effect within particular clusters of automotive production. Additionally, 13.5% of the interviewed domestic firms were negatively affected by the loss of supplier contracts due to the takeover of former Czech customers by foreign firms. No domestic firm reported a worsened access to credit because of the presence of foreign firms, and 27% of the interviewed domestic firms did not experience any negative spillovers from foreign firms.

Absorptive Capacity of Domestic Firms

How can we explain the limited significance of technology and direct spillovers from foreign to domestic firms in the Czech automotive industry? One possible explanation is the low absorptive capacity of domestic firms (Carrillo et al. 2004). Although absorptive capacity is a "fuzzy concept" which cannot be empirically measured directly, I use R&D employment of domestic firms and their cooperation with universities and public research institutes as proxy measures to evaluate their absorptive capacity (Humphrey and Oeter 2000). The R&D employment in domestic automotive firms increased from 292 in 1997 to 585 in 2007 and their R&D expenditures grew by 158%, suggesting an increasing absorptive capacity of domestic automotive firms (CSO 2009). However, a closer look at the data reveals that out of 250 domestic firms in the broadly defined automotive industry only 69 (28%) employed any R&D workers, 38 (15%) employed more than 3 R&D workers and 14 (6%) employed more than ten in 2007 (CSO 2009). The fact that almost three-fourths (72%) of domestic automotive firms employed no R&D workers suggests their low absorptive capacity (see also Pavlínek 2012).

Out of 37 interviewed domestic firms, 18 (49%) employed R&D workers and an additional 6 (16%) reported workers in design and engineering, 14 (38%) employed three or more R&D workers and 7 (19%) employed 10 or more. The fact, that 35% of the interviewed domestic firms did not employ any R&D workers and an additional 27% employed only one or two suggests a low absorptive capacity of the majority of domestic firms. The information collected during interviews also revealed that a majority of the domestic firms had no links with universities and public research institutes. Ten of the 37 interviewed domestic firms (27%) cooperated with Czech universities on R&D activities in the form of joint R&D projects, product testing and measurements, and by supporting selected university students in an effort to recruit them. Only one interviewed domestic supplier cooperated with a public research institute on joint research projects supported by national R&D programs. The interview data were further supported by the information collected by the survey according to which 19% (31 of 163) surveyed domestic automotive firms were engaged in some form of R&D cooperation with universities. I argue that the low absorptive capacity of the majority of domestic firms contributes to limited spillovers from foreign to domestic firms and that differences in absorptive capacity contribute to differences in abilities of domestic firms to benefit from potential spillovers from foreign firms.

Classification of Domestic Suppliers Based on Spillovers

In my approach, I combine both the experience of foreign firms with domestic suppliers and the experience of domestic suppliers with foreign firms to investigate spillovers from foreign to domestic firms. My field work suggests that domestic suppliers are a highly variegated group of firms with different capabilities and a different absorptive capacity whose relationships with foreign firms vary as well as their abilities to benefit from potential spillovers (see also Klier and Rubenstein 2010; Sturgeon and Van Biesebroeck 2009; Kohli 2004). During my interviews, I could clearly see that some suppliers have been able to benefit from spillovers while others have not. Therefore, treating domestic automotive firms as a homogeneous group obscures the complex reality and may lead to generalizations that do not necessarily apply to a significant number of domestic firms. To address this problem, I have categorized domestic firms into four distinct groups based on my interview data about spillovers from foreign firms. These four categories are related to the type of product, the firm's position in the GPN, production and R&D capabilities, and spillover effects (Table 5.11).

The table suggests that there are only a few (11%) domestic Tier 2 and Tier 1 innovation-oriented and relatively highly capable suppliers (Category 3), including domestic engineering service providers. These firms have a high absorptive capacity and are, therefore, able to benefit from spillovers. All domestic firms classified in this category were affected by horizontal spillovers, especially through demonstration effects in terms of learning about new management systems and new technology, access to new technology, and through increased market opportunities provided by Czech-based foreign subsidiaries and through exports. Supplier linkages played an important role in transferring information and knowledge from foreign firms about quality requirements and new delivery systems. The majority of these domestic firms have begun to internationalize their production by setting up subsidiaries abroad. For example, according to the director of a large domestic supplier (2300 workers) of door and cockpit systems, R&D is its most important source of competitiveness. In 2011, it employed 150 R&D workers. Since the early 1990s, the company has learned "everything" from foreign firms through supplier linkages, although it did not receive any direct technical, management, financial or procurement assistance from foreign firms. Its turnover increased ten times between 1990 and 2011. Today, it supplies all of the major assemblers with the exception of Nissan and Hyundai/Kia. It is one of the very few domestic suppliers that have tentatively begun to internationalize by setting up small subsidiaries in Russia, China and South Africa. It is also one of the very few domestic companies that, according to its

Table 5.11 Categorization of domestic firms based on spillover effects in the Czech automotive industry

	Category 1 (N = 10, 27%)	Category 2 (N = 21, 56.8%)	Category 3 (N = 4, 10.8%)	Category 4 (N = 2, 5.4%)
Type of product	Standardized, simple, low value-added parts based on detailed customer specifications (e.g. castings), products designed by customers	Higher value-added and more complex products/components that may be partly based on in-house development (e.g. bearings, engine components, bus and truck chassis)	Final parts/components based on in house know-how and R&D	Final parts/components that may be based on in-house know-how and R&D
Position in GPN	Captive Tier 3 suppliers	Tier 3 and Tier 2 suppliers	Tier 2 and Tier 1 suppliers	Tier 2 and Tier 3 suppliers
R&D activities and absorptive capacity	None or only technical support of production and/or simple technical construction Firms with R&D workers: 20% College-educated workers: 5.2%	Mostly technical development and engineering focused on incremental process and product development Firms with R&D workers: 48% College-educated workers: 16.0%	Development of new products, material development, engineering, process innovation Firms with R&D workers: 100% College-educated workers: 21.9%	Product development, production process development Firms with R&D workers: 50% College-educated workers: 10.7%
Capabilities	Operational • Basic manufacturing skills • Quality control • Maintenance and procurement capacity	Duplicative • Expansion of production through investment • Purchase and use of external technologies	Adaptive and innovative • Adaptation and improvement of external technologies • Development of new technical, engineering and design skills • New products and processes developed through formal R&D activities	Duplicative • Expansion of production through investment • Purchase and use of external technologies

Spillover effects	"Passing by" Only a *potential* for spillovers through: • Demonstration effects: access to new technology and quality control • Direct effects through purchasing/leasing technology Missing endogenous competencies and absorptive capacity to fully benefit from the inclusion in GPNs. Supplier assets and capabilities do not match the needs of TNCs	Enhancement Mixture of different spillovers through: • Demonstration effects: access to new technology, organizational, management and marketing methods; references • Direct effects: management training, support in search for new suppliers	Interactive Prevalence of demonstration/ indirect spillovers through: • Pressure put on quality, delivery and in-house development • Co-design with customers Complementarity and coupling between the supplier and opportunities provided by links with foreign investors and the integration into GPNs	Negative Predominantly negative direct spillovers through: • Direct competition • Employee poaching

Source: Author

director, improved its position in the supplier hierarchy from Tier 3 to Tier 2 in the past twenty years (interviews on June 24, 2005 and August 8, 2011).

A small group of capable domestic firms (5%; Category 4) has been strongly affected by negative direct horizontal spillovers, especially in terms of employee poaching and direct product competition. Still, these firms have survived FDI's crowding out effects by switching to new products and new markets. For example, a domestic supplier of fuel injectors for diesel engines has been negatively affected by a foreign Tier 1 firm that set up three subsidiaries to produce fuel injection systems in the same town in order to tap into the domestic firm's skilled labor force and low labor costs in the 1990s. Its three subsidiaries were generously supported by government investment incentives for every newly created job and by tax holidays. They actively recruited workers of the domestic firm by offering higher wages and openly preferring them to other job applicants. By 2005, they were employing about 5000 workers in the region. Out of these, about 3000 workers were trained by and formerly worked at the domestic firm. The domestic firm lost its most qualified and skilled workers despite substantially increasing wages. It also lost its market share to its foreign competitor and was forced to completely abandon supplying the automotive industry. In order to survive, it has specialized in the production of injection pumps and fuel injection systems for agricultural and construction machinery. Its employment dropped from 6000 workers in 1989 to 1900 in 2011 and the number of R&D workers declined from 92 to 25 between 1995 and 2011. R&D capabilities and the related absorptive capacity of the domestic firm were crucial in switching to new products and new markets (interviews on July 11, 2005 and April 11, 2011).

About one-fourth (27%) of the interviewed domestic suppliers (Category 1) is unable to benefit from direct vertical spillovers because of their low capabilities and low capacity to effectively absorb knowledge from foreign firms (Ernst and Kim 2002). These Tier 3 suppliers have low competencies that are limited to simple manufacturing and assembly operations and they supply standardized, simple, low value-added parts and components based on detailed customer specifications. The absence of R&D functions in 80% of these firms and a low share of college educated workers are important indicators of their low absorptive capacity (Cohen and Levinthal 1990; Giroud et al. 2012). The low absorptive capacity of these domestic firms prevents them from exploiting potential direct spillovers from foreign firms which, in turn, prevents them from narrowing their gap behind foreign firms. As a result, these domestic suppliers experience the "spillover interception" (Hatani 2009). For example, a Czech-based subsidiary of a foreign Tier 1 firm (AB) outsourced the low-volume production of its older spare parts to a medium-size domestic firm, which was established in 2000 and employed 60 workers at the time of the interview. AB also helped the domestic firm to launch the production of these spare parts by providing its old production line, helping to organize the production, assisting with achieving the quality certificate, and by providing the administrative support. It also helped the domestic firm to establish links with its existing suppliers. In other words, the domestic firm benefited from the direct knowledge transfer from AB in the form of technical assistance, the provision of various information and administrative assistance (see Giroud et al. 2012). Consequently, its number of employees increased 12 times, its revenues 13 times, but its value added only 2.7 times between 2000 and 2010. At the same time, however, despite this help, the domestic supplier has failed to develop its own know-how, it has been unable to fully absorb the technology provided by AB and has remained strongly dependent on AB, which buys more than 90% of its output. AB taught its domestic supplier how to use its technology to produce spare parts but since it is too advanced for the domestic firm, it does not fully understand its know-how and it does not engage in any R&D activities on its own. In other words, technology has been transferred, which significantly increased AB's productivity (productivity spillovers), but technological knowledge has not, indicating the absence of technology spillovers. Although the domestic firm has learned a lot through its cooperation with AB and it has been growing, it remains a typical captive Tier 3 supplier producing simple standardized low value-added spare parts and remains highly dependent on AB, its key customer (interview on March 25, 2011; see also Gereffi et al. 2005).

Tier 3 and Tier 2 suppliers who supply various automotive parts and components that are *partly* based on their in-house process and product development represent the most numerous category of the interviewed domestic suppliers (57%; Category 2). These suppliers have employed foreign technology and invested in the expansion of production in order to tap into the increased demand for automotive components in Czechia and abroad. Their higher absorptive capacity, which is also indicated by a higher presence of R&D functions (in 48% of the firms in the category), allowed them to benefit from various horizontal and mainly indirect vertical spillovers through backward linkages with foreign firms and through demonstration effects. They gained a valuable experience by supplying foreign firms, which they used to win contracts to supply other foreign firms both in Czechia and abroad. Overall, they have been able to keep up with competition through process and product upgrading in their particular tier but unable to improve their position in the supplier hierarchy. Some of these domestic firms benefited from direct vertical spillovers from foreign firms. For example, a large domestic supplier of metal castings (300 employees) received direct knowledge transfer from foreign firms in order to meet their requirements after it was selected to supply them. Prior to the start of the supplier relationship, foreign firms sent their experienced process engineers to the domestic firm for up to 1 week to improve its production processes in order to ensure 100% reliability of their future supplier. Although foreign firms offered this help free of charge, any resulting savings were split between the domestic firm and the foreign firm providing help. The domestic firm learned how to improve the quality of its products, the reliability of its machinery and how to streamline its production through supplier linkages with foreign firms. At the same time, it has been actively upgrading its production processes and its products in order to increase its competitiveness. The domestic firm designs its own machinery and it has gradually shifted from the production of castings to work pieces and preassembled simple modules that now account for 20% of its output (interview on December 17, 2009). However, it is important to note that such examples of direct knowledge transfer from foreign to domestic firms have been mentioned very rarely during my interviews (Table 5.10), suggesting that, overall, they do not play a very important role in the Czech automotive industry.

Conclusion

My analysis has identified diverse spillover effects from foreign to domestic firms in the Czech automotive industry. Although econometric studies have mostly found either statistically insignificant or negative horizontal spillovers from foreign to domestic firms in East-Central Europe (Djankov and Hoekman 2000; Görg et al. 2006; Jarolím 2000; Kinoshita 2001; Konings 2001), my firm-level qualitative data suggest that both positive and negative horizontal spillovers have affected domestic firms. Negative horizontal spillovers, especially in the form of increased competition and increased quality requirements, led to strong crowding out effects that forced the majority of domestic firms to be either acquired or form joint ventures with foreign firms or exit the automotive industry in the 1990s. The domestic firms that survived these challenges benefited from positive horizontal spillovers, especially from demonstration effects, imitation and increased access to both domestic and international markets to upgrade their products and processes and become integrated in automotive GPNs. This suggests that negative horizontal spillovers played the most important role after the entry of FDI but may only be temporary, although some negative horizontal spillovers, such as employee poaching and increased labor market competition, continue to negatively affect domestic firms. It also suggests that positive horizontal spillovers affected those domestic firms that survived the original restructuring of the 1990s (see also Kosová 2010). Overall, at least in terms of the extent of impact, horizontal spillovers in the form of increased product and labor market competition, quality requirements, demonstration effects and market access have played a more important role than vertical spillovers in the Czech automotive industry after 1990 because they affected the vast majority of domestic automotive firms. This finding challenges the conclusion of Geršl (2008:243), who found vertical spillovers to be "much more important" than horizontal spillovers in the Czech manufacturing industry as a whole.

Vertical spillovers from foreign to domestic firms were more selective than horizontal spillovers. My analysis of linkages between foreign and domestic firms revealed that Czech-based foreign firms source 86.5% of their total supplies from other foreign firms both from abroad and from Czechia and only 13.5% from domestic suppliers. The most important reasons for a low share of supplies from domestic firms include the centralized sourcing by automotive TNCs, the unavailability of particular materials or parts in Czechia and often a low quality of supplies by domestic suppliers. These reasons tend to outweigh the advantages of geographic proximity, flexibility and often lower prices of domestic firms. However, a low share of domestic suppliers does not mean that linkages between foreign firms and domestic firms are weak because the low share of domestic suppliers corresponds with their low share of the total output of the Czech automotive industry. Almost all interviewed domestic firms were to a greater or lesser extent integrated into automotive GPNs through their supplier linkages with foreign firms, which is the basic precondition for the development of vertical spillovers. My data point to strong productivity spillovers from foreign to domestic firms especially at the beginning of their supplier relationships. This is because, in most cases, foreign firms imposed higher requirements on domestic firms with respect to quality and sophistication of supplied parts and components than was the industry standard in Czechia. However, despite the integration of domestic firms into GPNs and strong supplier linkages between domestic and foreign firms, I have found that only less than half of the interviewed domestic firms reported any technology spillovers from foreign firms and only one-third experienced direct technology spillovers. In other words, while linkages between foreign and domestic firms are an important precondition for vertical spillovers to occur, there is no guarantee that vertical spillovers will actually develop in the presence of these linkages. One plausible explanation of weak vertical spillovers from foreign to domestic firms is the low absorptive capacity of domestic firms, which is suggested by a high share of domestic firms with no R&D capabilities and by the weak links of domestic firms with universities and public research institutes.

I acknowledge the limitations of my analysis that has focused on the existing domestic firms. A part of the explanation of weak direct horizontal spillovers may lie in the fact that the majority of most capable domestic suppliers were taken over by foreign firms in the 1990s and 2000s. These former domestic firms benefited from direct transfers of technology and know-how from their new foreign owners. At the same time, I did not investigate domestic firms that did not survive and that might have experienced strong negative spillovers from foreign firms. My focus on the existing domestic firms would thus tend to underestimate the real extent of both positive and negative FDI effects on domestic firms.

My research suggests that the failure to consider the heterogeneity of domestic firms may lie behind many inconclusive results of various analyses about spillovers from foreign to domestic firms as these effects can significantly differ among different firms or groups of firms. Consequently, it makes it almost impossible to generalize the effects of spillovers on technological, organizational and strategic competences of domestic firms as a whole. Therefore, instead of treating domestic firms as a homogeneous group, I classified them into four basic types. My classification shows large differences in the capabilities and absorptive capacity of domestic firms, which significantly influence their ability to benefit from spillovers.

My research also shows how the particular nature of GPN influences the potential of domestic firms to benefit from linkages and spillovers in the form of improving their overall position in the value chain. In our case of the quasi-hierarchical value chain, even direct positive spillovers did not help domestic firms improve their position in the supplier hierarchy. As a result, the vast majority of domestic automotive firms remain locked in subordinate positions as Tier 3 and Tier 2 suppliers in automotive GPNs dominated by foreign lead firms. Consequently, despite high levels of FDI, domestic firms continue to lag behind foreign firms (Peter et al. 2012) with limited chances to significantly improve their position in the automotive value chain and become major competitive players in the Czech and European automotive industry. Given this inability to close the gap between themselves and foreign firms and given the contemporary nature of the global automotive industry and limited spillovers from foreign firms, the marginalized and vulnerable position of domestic automotive suppliers of less developed countries in the automotive GPNs is likely to persist in the foreseeable future.

References

Aitken BJ, Harrison AE (1999) Do domestic firms benefit from direct foreign investment? Evidence from Venezuela. Am Econ Rev 89(3):605–618

Aller RA, Ubillos JB, Beldarrain VC, Garcia JCL (1999) New tendencies in inter-firm relations in the automotive industry and their impact on European periphery suppliers—lessons from Spain. Eur Urban Reg Stud 6(3):255–264

Amin A, Bradley D, Howells J, Tomaney J, Gentle C (1994) Regional incentives and the quality of mobile investment in the less favoured regions of the EC. Prog Plann 41(Part 1):1–112

Baldwin CY, Clark KB (1997) Managing in an age of modularity. Harv Bus Rev 75(5):84–93

Barnes J, Kaplinsky R (2000) Globalization and the death of the local firm? The automobile components sector in South Africa. Reg Stud 34(9):797–812

Barrios S, Gorg H, Strobl E (2011) Spillovers through backward linkages from multinationals: measurement matters! Eur Econ Rev 55(6):862–875

Bathelt H, Malmberg A, Maskell P (2004) Clusters and knowledge: local buzz, global pipelines and the process of knowledge creation. Prog Hum Geogr 28(1):31–56

Belderbos R, Capannelli G, Fukao K (2001) Backward vertical linkages of foreign manufacturing affiliates: evidence from Japanese multinationals. World Dev 29(1):189–208

Blalock G, Gertler PJ (2008) Welfare gains from foreign direct investment through technology transfer to local suppliers. J Int Econ 74(2):402–421

Blomström M, Kokko A (1998) Multinational corporations and spillovers. J Econ Surv 12(3):247–278

Blomström M, Kokko A (2001) Foreign direct investment and spillovers of technology. Int J Technol Manag 22(5–6):435–454

Blomström M, Kokko A, Zejan M (2000) Foreign direct investment: firm and host country strategies. MacMillan Press, New York, NY

Britton JNH (1980) Industrial dependence and technological underdevelopment: Canadian consequences of foreign direct investment. Reg Stud 14(3):181–199

Carrillo J, Lung Y, van Tulder R (2004) Cars, carriers of regionalism? Plagrave Macmillan, Houndmills

Carrincazeaux C, Lung YN, Rallet A (2001) Proximity and localisation of corporate R&D activities. Res Policy 30(5):777–789

Caves RE (1974) Multinational firms, competition, and productivity in host-country markets. Economica 41(162):176–193

CNB (2012) Přímé zahraniční investice za rok 2010 (Foreign direct investment in 2010). Czech National Bank, Prague

Coe NM, Hess M, Yeung HWC, Dicken P, Henderson J (2004) 'Globalizing' regional development: a global production networks perspective. Trans Inst Br Geogr 29(4):468–484

Cohen WM, Levinthal DA (1989) Innovation and learning – the 2 faces of R- and-D. Econ J 99(397):569–596

Cohen WM, Levinthal DA (1990) Absorptive-capacity – a new perspective on learning and innovation. Adm Sci Q 35(1):128–152

Contreras OF, Carrillo J, Alonso J (2012) Local entrepreneurship within global value chains: a case study in the Mexican automotive industry. World Dev 40(5):1013–1023

Crespo N, Fontoura MP (2007) Determinant factors of FDI spillovers—what do we really know? World Dev 35(3):410–425

Crone M (2002) Local sourcing by multinational enterprise plants: evidence from the UK regions and the implications for policy. Environ Plann C Gov Policy 20(1):131–149

CSO (2009) Annual survey of economic subjects in selected industries, 2009th edn. The Czech Statistical Office, Prague

CzechInvest (2014) Partnership opportunities. http://www.czechinvest.org/en/partnership-opportunities

De Backer K, Sleuwaegen L (2003) Does foreign direct investment crowd out domestic entrepreneurship? Rev Ind Organ 22(1):67–84

Dicken P (1976) The multiplant business enterprise and geographical space: some issues in the study of external control and regional development. Reg Stud 10(4):401–412

Dicken P (2015) Global shift: mapping the changing contours of the world economy. The Guilford Press, New York, NY

Dimitratos P, Liouka I, Young S (2009) Regional location of multinational corporation subsidiaries and economic development contribution: evidence from the UK. J World Bus 44(2):180–191

Djankov S, Hoekman B (2000) Foreign investment and productivity growth in Czech enterprises. World Bank Econ Rev 14(1):49–64

Drahokoupil J (2009) Globalization and the state in Central and Eastern Europe: the politics of foreign direct investment. Routledge, London

Dunning JH, Lundan SM (2008) Multinational enterprises and the global economy. Edward Elgar, Cheltenham

Ernst D, Kim L (2002) Global production networks, knowledge diffusion, and local capability formation. Res Policy 31(8–9):1417–1429

Firn JR (1975) External control and regional development: the case of Scotland. Environ Plann A 7(4):393–414

Florida R (1996) Regional creative destruction: production organization, globalization, and the economic transformation of the Midwest. Econ Geogr 72(3):314–334

Frigant V, Lung Y (2002) Geographical proximity and supplying relationships in modular production. Int J Urban Reg Res 26(4):742–755

Frigant V, Talbot D (2005) Technological determinism and modularity: lessons from a comparison between aircraft and auto industries in Europe. Ind Innov 12(3):337–355

Gereffi G, Humphrey J, Sturgeon T (2005) The governance of global value chains. Rev Int Polit Econ 12(1):78–104

Geršl A (2008) Productivity, export performance, and financing of the Czech corporate sector: the effects of foreign direct investment. Finance Uver Czech J Econ Finance 58(5–6):231–247

Gertler MS (2003) Tacit knowledge and the economic geography of context, or the undefinable tacitness of being (there). J Econ Geogr 3(1):75–99

Girma S (2005) Absorptive capacity and productivity spillovers from FDI: a threshold regression analysis. Oxf Bull Econ Stat 67(3):281–306

Giroud A, Jindra B, Marek P (2012) Heterogeneous FDI in transition economies—a novel approach to assess the developmental impact of backward linkages. World Dev 40(11):2206–2220

Giroud A, Scott-Kennel J (2009) MNE linkages in international business: a framework for analysis. Int Bus Rev 18(6):555–566

Giuliani E, Pietrobelli C, Rabellotti R (2005) Upgrading in global value chains: lessons from Latin American clusters. World Dev 33(4):549–573

Görg H, Greenaway D (2004) Much ado about nothing? Do domestic firms really benefit from foreign direct investment? World Bank Res Obs 19(2):171–197

Görg H, Hijzen A, Murakozy B (2006) The productivity spillover potential of foreign-owned firms: firm-level evidence for Hungary. The University of Nottingham, Nottingham

Görg H, Strobl E (2001) Multinational companies and productivity spillovers: a meta-analysis. Econ J 111(475):F723–F739

Görg H, Strobl E (2005) Spillovers from foreign firms through worker mobility: an empirical investigation. Scand J Econ 107(4):693–709

Hallin C, Lind CH (2012) Revisiting the external impact of MNCs: an empirical study of the mechanisms behind knowledge spillovers from MNC subsidiaries. Int Bus Rev 21(2):167–179

Hansen MW, Pedersen T, Petersen B (2009) MNC strategies and linkage effects in developing countries. J World Bus 44(2):121–130

Harding T, Javorcik BS (2011) Roll out the red carpet and they will come: investment promotion and FDI inflows. Econ J 121(557):1445–1476

Hatani F (2009) The logic of spillover interception: the impact of global supply chains in China. J World Bus 44(2):158–166

Havranek T, Irsova Z (2011) Estimating vertical spillovers from FDI: why results vary and what the true effect is. J Int Econ 85(2):234–244

Hayter R (1982) Truncation, the international firm and regional policy. Area 14(4):277–282

Henderson J, Dicken P, Hess M, Coe N, Yeung HWC (2002) Global production networks and the analysis of economic development. Rev Int Polit Econ 9(3):436–464

Hewitt-Dundas N, Andreosso-O'Callaghan B, Crone M, Murray J, Roper S (2005) Selling global, buying local? What determines the sourcing patterns of multinational plants in Ireland? Reg Stud 39(2):225–239

Howells JRL (1996) Tacit knowledge, innovation and technology transfer. Technol Anal Strateg Manag 8(2):91–106

Howells JRL (2002) Tacit knowledge, innovation and economic geography. Urban Stud 39(5–6):871–884

Humphrey J (2000) Assembler-supplier relations in the auto industry: globalisation and national development. Comp Change 4(3):245–271

Humphrey J (2003) Globalization and supply chain networks: the auto industry in Brazil and India. Global Netw 3(2):121–141

Humphrey J, Lecler Y, Salerno MS (2000) Global strategies and local realities: the auto industry in emerging markets. Palgrave MacMillan, Basingstoke

Humphrey J, Memedovic O (2003) The global automotive industry value chain: what prospects for upgrading by developing countries. UNIDO, Vienna

Humphrey J, Oeter A (2000) Motor industry policies in emerging markets: globalisation and the promotion of domestic industry. In: Humphrey J, Lecler Y, Salerno MS (eds) Global strategies and local realities; the auto industry in emerging markets. Basingstoke, Palgrave Macmillan, pp 42–71

Humphrey J, Salerno MS (2000) Globalisation and assembler – supplier relations: Brazil and India. In: Humphrey J, Lecler Y, Salerno SM (eds) Global strategies and local realities: the auto industry in emerging market. Palgrave Macmillan, Basingstoke, pp 149–175

Humphrey J, Schmitz H (2002) How does insertion in global value chains affect upgrading in industrial clusters? Reg Stud 36(9):1017–1027

Humphrey J, Schmitz H (2004) Chain governance and upgrading: taking stock. In: Schmitz H (ed) Local enterprises in the global economy: issues of governance and upgrading. Edward Elgar, Cheltenham, pp 349–381

Ivarsson I, Alvstam CG (2005) The effect of spatial proximity on technology transfer from TNCs to local suppliers in developing countries: the case of AB Volvo in Asia and Latin America. Econ Geogr 81(1):83–111

Jaffe AB, Trajtenberg M, Henderson R (1993) Geographic localization of knowledge spillovers as evidenced by patent citations. Q J Econ 108(3):577–598

Jarolím M (2000) Foreign direct investment and productivity of firms. Finance Uver 50(9):478–487

Javorcik BS (2004) Does foreign direct investment increase the productivity of domestic firms? In search of spillovers through backward linkages. Am Econ Rev 94(3):605–627

Jindra B, Giroud A, Scott-Kennel J (2009) Subsidiary roles, vertical linkages and economic development: lessons from transition economies. J World Bus 44(2):167–179

Kaplinsky R (2000) Globalisation and unequalisation: what can be learned from value chain analysis? J Dev Stud 37(2):117–146
Kinoshita Y (2001) R&D and technology spillovers through FDI: innovation and absorptive capacity. Centre for Economic Policy Research, London
Klier T, Rubenstein J (2008) Who really made your car? Restructuring and geographic change in the auto industry. W.E. Upjohn Institute for Employment Research, Kalamazoo, MI
Klier TH, Rubenstein JM (2010) The changing geography of north American motor vehicle production. Cambr J Reg Econ Soc 3(3):335–347
Kohli A (2004) State-directed development: political power and industrialization in the global periphery. Cambridge University Press, Cambridge
Konings J (2001) The effects of foreign direct investment on domestic firms—evidence from firm-level panel data in emerging economies. Econ Trans 9(3):619–633
Kosová R (2010) Do foreign firms crowd out domestic firms? Evidence from the Czech Republic. Rev Econ Stat 92(4):861–881
Liu WD, Dicken P (2006) Transnational corporations and 'obligated embeddedness': foreign direct investment in China's automobile industry. Environ Plann A 38(7):1229–1247
Liu WD, Yeung HWC (2008) China's dynamic industrial sector: the automobile industry. Eurasian Geogr Econ 49(5):523–548
Lockstrom M, Schadel J, Moser R, Harrison N (2011) Domestic supplier integration in the Chinese automotive industry: the buyer's perspective. J Supply Chain Manag 47(4):44–63
Lung Y (2004) The changing geography of the European automobile system. Int J Auto Technol Manage 4(2/3):137–165
Maskell P, Malmberg A (1999) The competitiveness of firms and regions—'Ubiquitification' and the importance of localized learning. Eur Urban Reg Stud 6(1):9–25
Maskell P, Malmberg A (2007) Myopia, knowledge development and cluster evolution. J Econ Geogr 7(5):603–618
Meyer KE (2004) Perspectives on multinational enterprises in emerging economies. J Int Bus Stud 35(4):259–276
Meyer KE, Sinani E (2009) When and where does foreign direct investment generate positive spillovers? A meta-analysis. J Int Bus Stud 40(7):1075–1094
MIT and CzechInvest (2013) Cluster organizations in the Czech Republic. Ministry of Industry and Trade and CzechInvest, Prague
Nolan P, Zhang J (2002) The challenge of globalization for large Chinese firms. World Dev 30(12):2089–2107
Oetzel J, Doh JP (2009) MNEs and development: a review and reconceptualization. J World Bus 44(2):108–120
Pavlínek P (2002a) Restructuring the Central and Eastern European automobile industry: legacies, trends, and effects of foreign direct investment. Post Soviet Geogr Econ 43(1):41–77
Pavlínek P (2002b) The role of foreign direct investment in the privatisation and restructuring of the Czech motor industry. Post Communist Econ 14(3):359–379
Pavlínek P (2002c) Transformation of the central and East European passenger car industry: selective peripheral integration through foreign direct investment. Environ Plann A 34(9):1685–1709
Pavlínek P (2003) Transformation of the Czech automotive components industry through foreign direct investment. Eurasian Geogr Econ 44(3):184–209
Pavlínek P (2004) Regional development implications of foreign direct investment in Central Europe. Eur Urban Reg Stud 11(1):47–70
Pavlínek P (2008) A successful transformation? Restructuring of the Czech automobile industry. Physica Verlag, New York, NY
Pavlínek P (2012) The internationalization of corporate R&D and the automotive industry R&D of East-Central Europe. Econ Geogr 88(3):279–310
Pavlínek P (2015) The impact of the 2008–2009 crisis on the automotive industry: global trends and firm-level effects in Central Europe. Eur Urban Reg Stud 22(1):20–40

Pavlínek P, Domanski B, Guzik R (2009) Industrial upgrading through foreign direct investment in Central European automotive manufacturing. Eur Urban Reg Stud 16(1):43–63
Pavlínek P, Janák L (2007) Regional restructuring of the Škoda auto supplier network in the Czech Republic. Eur Urban Reg Stud 14(2):133–155
Pavlínek P, Ženka J (2010) The 2008–2009 automotive industry crisis and regional unemployment in Central Europe. Cambr J Reg Econ Soc 3(3):349–365
Pavlínek P, Ženka J (2011) Upgrading in the automotive industry: firm-level evidence from Central Europe. J Econ Geogr 11(3):559–586
Peter KS, Svejnar J, Terrell K (2012) Foreign investment, corporate ownership, and development: are firms in emerging markets catching up to the world standard? Rev Econ Stat 94(4):981–999
Phelps NA (1993) Branch plants and the evolving spatial division-of-labor: a study of material linkage change in the northern region of England. Reg Stud 27(2):87–101
Sadler D (1999) Internationalization and specialization in the European automotive components sector: implications for the hollowing-out thesis. Reg Stud 33(2):109–119
Saliola F, Zanfei A (2009) Multinational firms, global value chains and the organization of knowledge transfer. Res Policy 38(2):369–381
Santangelo GD (2009) MNCs and linkages creation: evidence from a peripheral area. J World Bus 44(2):192–205
Schackmann-Fallis KP (1989) External control and regional development within the Federal Republic of Germany. Int Reg Sci Rev 12(3):245–261
Scott-Kennel J (2004) Foreign direct investment: a catalyst for local firm development? Eur J Dev Res 16(3):624–652
Scott-Kennel J (2007) Foreign direct investment and local linkages: an empirical investigation. Manag Int Rev 47(1):51–77
Smeets R (2008) Collecting the pieces of the FDI knowledge spillovers puzzle. World Bank Res Obs 23(2):107–138
Spencer JW (2008) The impact of multinational enterprise strategy on indigenous enterprises: horizontal spillovers and crowding out in developing countries. Acad Manage Rev 33(2):341–361
Storper M, Venables AJ (2004) Buzz: face-to-face contact and the urban economy. J Econ Geogr 4(4):351–370
Sturgeon T, Van Biesebroeck J, Gereffi G (2008) Value chains, networks and clusters: reframing the global automotive industry. J Econ Geogr 8(3):297–321
Sturgeon TJ, Gereffi G, Rogers KB, Fernandez-Stark K (2010) The prospects for Mexico in the North American automotive industry: a global value chain perspective. Actes GERPISA 42:11–22
Sturgeon TJ, Lester RK (2004) The new global supply base: new challenges for local suppliers in East Asia. In: Yusuf S, Altaf MAA, Nabeshima K (eds) Global production networking and technological change in East Asia. The World Bank and Oxford University Press, Washington, DC, pp 35–87
Sturgeon TJ, Van Biesebroeck J (2009) Crisis and protection in the automotive industry: a global value chain perspective. In: Evenett SJ, Hoekman BM, Cattaneo O (eds) Effective crisis response and openness: implications for the trading system. World Bank, Centre for Economic Policy Research, London, pp 285–305
Sturgeon TJ, Van Biesebroeck J (2011) Global value chains in the automotive industry: an enhanced role for developing countries? Int J Technol Learn Innov Dev 4(1–3):181–205
Tavares AT, Young S (2006) Sourcing patterns of foreign-owned multinational subsidiaries in Europe. Reg Stud 40(6):583–599
UNCTAD (2001) World investment report 2001: promoting linkages. United Nations, New York, NY

UNCTAD (2012) World investment report 2012: towards a new generation of investment policies, United Nations conference on trade and development (UNCTAD). United Nations, New York, NY

Van Biesebroeck J, Sturgeon TJ (2010) Effects of the 2008–09 crisis on the automotive industry in developing countries: a global value chain perspective. In: Cattaneo GG, Staritz C (eds) Global value chains in a postcrisis world: a development perspective. The World Bank, Washington, DC, pp 209–244

Chapter 6
The State and the Development of the Automotive Industry

Introduction

The state has played a key role in the industrialization of less developed countries (Kohli 2004), including the development of the automotive industry (Dicken 2015; Humphrey and Oeter 2000). Its crucial importance for the automotive industry was most recently demonstrated in both developed and developing countries during the 2008–2009 economic crisis (Van Biesebroeck and Sturgeon 2010; Klier and Rubenstein 2010; Stanford 2010; Sturgeon and Van Biesebroeck 2009). Along with investment strategies of global automotive lead firms, state policies played an important role in the rapid development of the automotive industry in less developed 'emerging' economies since the early 1990s (Sturgeon et al. 2008; Carrillo et al. 2004; Humphrey et al. 2000; Humphrey and Oeter 2000). The fastest growth took place in countries with rapidly growing new demand and potentially very large domestic markets, such as China, India and Brazil (Liu and Yeung 2008; Liu and Dicken 2006; Van Biesebroeck and Sturgeon 2010), and in 'integrated peripheral markets', which are less developed countries located in peripheral areas surrounding traditional core regions of automotive production, such as Mexico and ECE (Pavlínek 2002; Sturgeon et al. 2010; Layan 2000). Integrated peripheral markets have been typified by 'hands off' industrial policies, dependence on foreign direct investment (FDI) and by integration into core-based production networks (Humphrey and Oeter 2000). Core-based lead firms invested heavily in these peripheral regions in assembly operations because of low production costs, geographic proximity to large affluent core markets, and also because of their inclusion in large regional economic blocs, such as the European Union (EU) and the North American Free Trade Agreement. While the role of lead firms in these processes has been emphasized and analyzed, much less attention has been given to the role of state strategies beyond the provision of investment incentives, although exceptions exist (e.g. Liu and Dicken 2006; Liu and Yeung 2008; Humphrey and Oeter 2000; Drahokoupil 2008, 2009a).

P. Pavlínek, *Dependent Growth: Foreign Investment and the Development of the Automotive Industry in East-Central Europe*, DOI 10.1007/978-3-319-53955-3_6

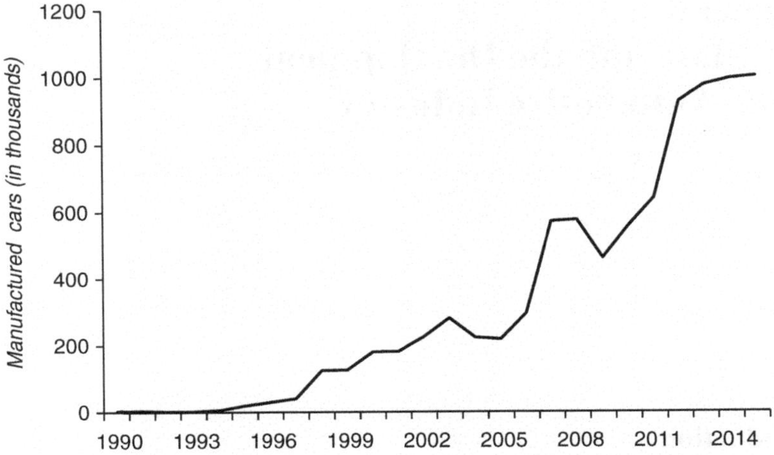

Fig. 6.1 Passenger car production in Slovakia, 1990–2015. *Source*: Based on data from OICA (2016) and ZAP (2000)

The goal of this chapter is to analyze the role of the state in the development of the automotive industry in Slovakia, which represents an excellent example of a peripheral country that has been integrated into European automotive production networks since the early 1990s. Driven by FDI inflows of €2.9 bn in the automotive industry between 1990 and 2014 (NBS 2015), the annual assembly of passenger cars increased from less than 3000 units in 1993 to one million units in 2015 (Fig. 6.1) (ZAP 2000; OICA 2016). Slovakia became the 14th largest producer of automobiles in the world in 2015 and the largest producer of cars per capita (184 per 1000 inhabitants in 2015). FDI-driven export-oriented expansion of the automotive industry contributed to rapid economic growth, especially between 2000 and 2007 (OECD 2012). Slovakia recorded the fastest GDP growth per capita in the OECD during 2001–2011 and it significantly narrowed the income gap relative to the more developed half of the OECD countries from more than 60% to almost 40% (Fig. 6.2) (OECD 2013).

In this chapter, I seek to move beyond the uncritical praise by the state, media, supranational organizations and consulting firms of FDI-driven development of the Slovak automotive industry (e.g. Sario 2013; Jakubiak et al. 2008; EY 2010) and provide a more critical reading of the role of the state in these processes. I show that the state's role was instrumental in the growth of the Slovak automotive industry. Although its post-1990 development has been driven by FDI, I argue that the state played an important role in making it possible by creating highly favorable conditions for foreign capital in Slovakia. In the process, the dependence of Slovakia on the externally controlled automotive industry has sharply increased (Table 1.3). By 2014, foreign capital controlled 98% of the automotive industry, measured by a percentage of production value (Eurostat 2016). As of 2012, 80% of automotive suppliers were foreign-owned and 93.5% of technologies were imported (ZAP

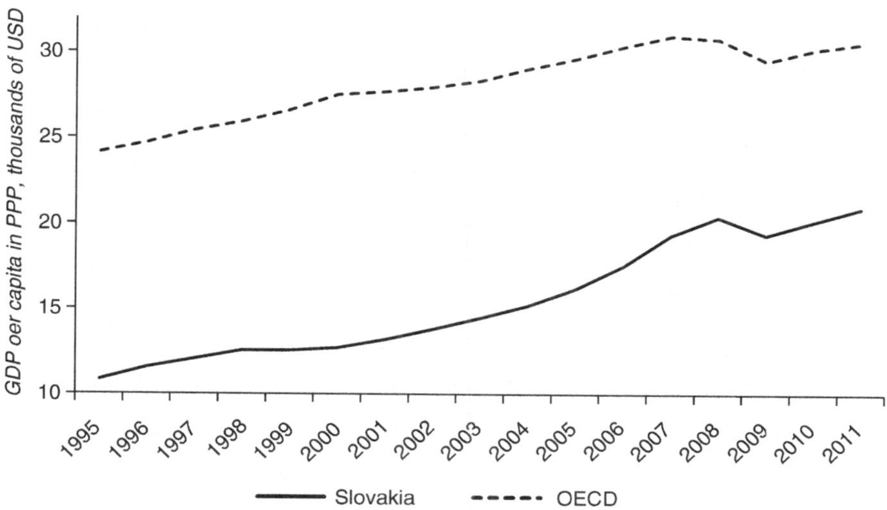

Fig. 6.2 GDP per capita in USD in purchasing power parity in OECD countries and Slovakia, 1995–2011. *Source*: Based on data from OECD (2012)

2013; Luptáčik et al. 2013). In 2012, the automotive industry accounted for 26% of Slovak exports and 20% of it imports (ZAP 2013).

Theoretically and conceptually, this chapter draws upon analyses of ECE in International Political Economy (e.g. Shields 2008; Drahokoupil 2009a), studies of external dependency and truncation in Economic Geography (e.g. Dicken 1976; Britton 1980), and on GVC and GPN perspectives (e.g. Gereffi et al. 2005; Henderson et al. 2002). Empirically, in addition to secondary sources, the chapter draws on a 2010 survey of 299 Slovak-based automotive firms with 20 or more employees which yielded a response rate of 44% and on 50 on-site interviews conducted with Slovak-based automotive firms between 2011 and 2015, plus a 2005 interview at Volkswagen (VW) Slovakia.

The chapter begins with a discussion of the state and the automotive industry development in ECE. Second, I briefly discuss the role of the state in the development of the Slovak automotive industry during the state socialist period. Third, I analyze the changing role of the state in the automotive industry during the post-1993 independence. Fourth, I present case studies of the role of the state in attracting and accommodating three foreign assembly firms: VW, PSA Peugeot-Citroën (PSA) and Kia. Fifth, based on firm-level interviews, I present an evaluation of state policies in the automotive industry by foreign and domestic firms. Sixth, I consider limits of the state-foreign capital nexus for a successful economic development in Slovakia. Finally, I summarize the main results in the conclusion.

The State and the Development of the Automotive Industry in East-Central Europe

Since the early-1990s, neoliberal export-oriented strategies of economic development became the new orthodoxy in less developed economies, including the former state socialist countries of ECE (Harvey 2005; Bohle 2006; Gowan 1995; Gereffi 2013). The automotive industry is a prime example of such strategies that are based upon attracting large inflows of FDI to finance and restructure the existing industries, build new industrial capacity and promote domestic automotive production. Despite questions about the appropriateness of automotive industry-centered strategies in contemporary economic development (Humphrey 2000), countries around the world continue to lure automotive transnational corporations (TNCs) to set up new production within their territories (Liu and Dicken 2006). In this intensifying competition, ECE countries have capitalized on the needs of core-based TNCs to geographically expand into ECE markets and increase their global competitiveness by offshoring labor intensive production to lower-cost peripheral locations. In addition to its market potential and low production costs, ECE is attractive because of its proximity to affluent Western European markets, its inclusion in the EU, flexible labor policies, low labor militancy, and weak labor unions. In other words, ECE has become one of the latest 'spatial fixes' sought by TNCs for the absorption of surplus capital (Harvey 2006, 2010).

The state has played an important role in making this spatial fix possible during ECE's transition from "state socialism to neoliberalism" (Shields 2008: 447). In the absence of sufficient domestic capital and after the failure of national-oriented strategies of the early 1990s (Drahokoupil 2008), neoliberal strategies of industrial development prevailed in ECE. Restructuring of the state through the processes of transnationalization (Shields 2004, 2008; Vliegenthart 2009) opened up national economies for penetration by foreign capital. A part of domestic political elites, variously labeled as a 'comprador administration' (Baran 1957), 'comprador fraction of the bourgeoisie' (Poulantzas 1973), 'comprador intelligentsia' (Eyal et al. 1997), 'comprador class' (Vliegenthart 2010) or 'comprador service sector' (Drahokoupil 2009b), aligned their interests with those of foreign capital and gained political influence, which they used to successfully promote FDI-friendly policies across ECE. In other words, they "helped to translate the structural power of transnational capital into tactical forms of power that enabled agential power to work in sync with the interests of the multinationals" (Drahokoupil 2009a: 3). By the late 1990s, ECE states have become competition states (Cerny 1997), which are typified by state strategies that rely on foreign capital as a primary vehicle for increasing national economic competitiveness and by pursuing FDI-driven industrialization and restructuring strategies (Drahokoupil 2008, 2009a, b). ECE competition states have competed over mobile FDI by creating favorable conditions for the entry and operation of TNCs in their national economies, including various investment incentives, tax provisions, education policies, and industrial relations. These competition states are typified by 'inward investment regimes' (Phelps and Wood 2006) or 'investment promotion machines' (Drahokoupil 2008) that are subnational territorial coalitions which *ad hoc* mobilize social actors at local, regional and national scales, with the goal to attract particular foreign investors and promote their interests in a particular locality, region and country (see also Phelps 2000, 2008). Thus, FDI and industrial policies in ECE have been primarily driven by the imperative to accommodate the needs of foreign capital and, in particular, the needs of large 'strategic' (or flagship) investors, whose interests are represented by the comprador sector in domestic politics. The goal of these policies has been to improve or maintain a country's competitive position in transnational flows of FDI, which is important not only for attracting new investments but also for stabilizing the existing ones. Although individual countries might be attempting to actively shape their industrial structure by attracting FDI into particular sectors of the economy, they only have a chance to succeed if these sectors are attractive to foreign TNCs and in line with their transnational investment strategies.

Bargaining powers of states have declined especially in less developed countries because of the liberalization of FDI policies and relinquishing certain controls over their national economies to supranational organizations (Phelps and Raines 2003; Phelps 2008). Bargaining powers of ECE states with foreign TNCs over FDI terms have been further undermined by small domestic markets and intense competition from neighboring countries with similar factor endowments (see Liu and Dicken 2006). Automotive TNCs exploited this relative weakness of ECE countries by engaging in regulatory arbitrage, playing countries off against one another with the goal of securing the best possible terms for their investment (Kolesár 2006, 2007). Consequently, automotive TNCs were able to "secure exceptionally favorable terms of entry into the region" (Bartlett and Seleny 1998: 320). Regulatory arbitrage may lie behind the decreased economic benefits of FDI for host economies because it can lead to 'corporate capture' of national and local institutions and resources, in which the state and regional governments act in the context of an asymmetrical power relation with respect to foreign capital and, consequently, end up serving the interests and needs of foreign TNCs at the expense of domestic firms and population (Phelps 2000, 2008). In this situation, the state provides resources to lower investment costs of incoming flagship investors and tailors investment incentives to their specific needs. Typically, the state agrees to finance and build customized infrastructure, such as highway links, railway terminals or supplier parks; secures customized assembly and provision of land for greenfield production complexes; and finances labor force training. Additional signs of corporate capture include: state agencies, regional and local politicians place interests of flagship investors above those of domestic firms and local residents; flagship investors may develop a disproportionate influence over state economic, education and training policy-making to serve their specific needs; the state agrees not to allow other investors to locate in the proximity of a flagship investor in order to lessen competition for labor in the local labor market; and there are few positive regional development impacts of FDI beyond newly created jobs (Phelps 2000, 2008). In the words of UNCTAD (1998: 103): "When governments compete to attract FDI, there will be a tendency to overbid… The effects can be both distorting and inequitable since the costs are ultimately borne by the public and hence represent transfers from the local community to the ultimate owners of the foreign investment."

At the same time, however, the EU local content regulations, combined with co-location imperatives of assembly plants and suppliers in the contemporary modular assembly processes (Sturgeon and Lester 2004), forced automotive lead firms to develop supplier networks in ECE. Lead firms pressured established foreign suppliers to follow them into ECE and also forced the most capable domestic suppliers to upgrade in order to meet the lead firms' quality and timing requirements or be excluded from supplier networks (e.g. Pavlínek et al. 2009; Pavlínek 2003). Territorial embeddedness of foreign investors in host economies through the development of supplier networks generates potentially significant economic benefits by increasing the value from production in host economies and also by generating spillovers that may increase the competitiveness of domestic firms (Pavlínek and Žížalová 2016). For example, as we could see in Chap. 1, Slovakia attracted 128 investments in new automotive supplier plants between 1997 and 2015 and ECE as a whole attracted more than 1200 (EY 2010; ERM 2016). These potentially large economic benefits of territorial embeddedness make foreign-owned automotive assembly plants extremely desirable in the eyes of national governments and increase their willingness to engage in competitive bidding with other countries in order to attract them.

However, the state-based competition over FDI in ECE has been mostly of the 'low-road' variety "on the basis of low wages, docile labour and low taxes, which perpetuate an inability to upgrade to an economic base of higher skill and higher wages" (Malecki 2004: 1104). In 1997, Ellingstad (1997) warned that a 'maquiladora syndrome' might be developing in ECE. According to Ellingstad (1997), the maquiladora economy is typified by export-oriented manufacturing; low wages that do not match increases in productivity; lower worker productivity and skills than in home countries of foreign investors; high value-added components for the assembly that are either imported or produced locally by other foreign firms; the assembly of often high-tech, high quality goods with a relatively high value added; high regional concentration of export-oriented manufacturing; and by large regional development disparities. Overall, the maquiladora strategy promotes the development of "low-wage, low or medium-skill, low value-added manufacturing" with limited chances of upgrading in the foreseeable future (Ellingstad 1997: 9). Although Bernaciak and Šćepanović (2010: 141) argued that "by the late 1990s, regional industry had largely recovered from the "maquiladora syndrome", a number of indicators suggest otherwise, including low real wages despite substantially increased productivity, weak unions, high unemployment (14% in Slovakia in 2013), a persistent wage gap between ECE and Western Europe (Fig. 6.3), imports of high value-added components or their production by foreign-owned suppliers rather than domestic firms, the weak development of higher value-added non-production functions (Table 6.1), and the intensification of uneven development because of FDI (Pavlínek 2004).[1] Nölke

[1] The average monthly wage in the Slovak automotive industry was €992 in 2012 (Luptáčik et al. 2013). A CEO of a foreign firm that has produced in Slovakia since 1993 remarked: "We are here

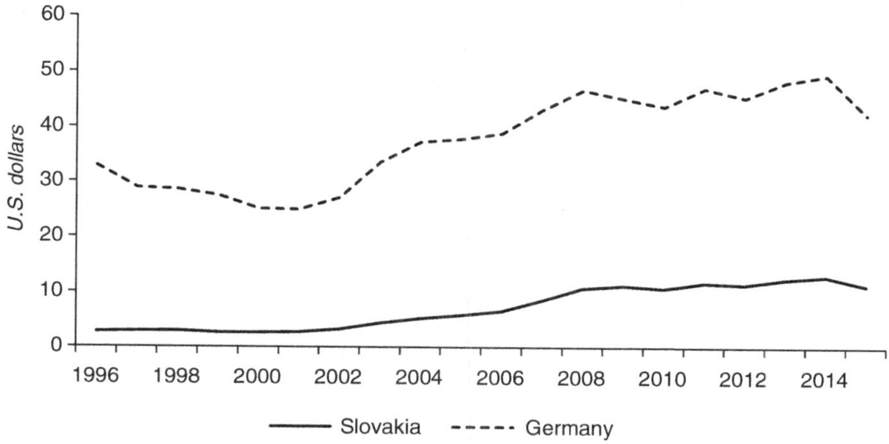

Fig. 6.3 Hourly compensation costs in manufacturing in Slovakia and Germany, 1996–2015. *Note*: Compensation costs include direct pay, social insurance expenditures, and labor-related taxes. *Source*: Based on data from Conference Board (2016)

Table 6.1 Selected functions conducted in foreign-owned automotive industry subsidiaries in Slovakia

	Parent company abroad		Slovak subsidiary		No answer	
	No.	%	No.	%	No.	%
Decisions about what products will be produced	54	93.1	3	5.2	1	1.7
Strategic planning	53	91.4	5	8.6	0	0.0
Investment decisions	50	86.2	8	13.8	0	0.0
Market research	50	86.2	8	13.8	0	0.0
Price setting for produced goods	49	84.5	9	15.5	0	0.0
Marketing of subsidiary products	48	82.8	8	13.8	2	3.4
R&D, design	46	79.3	8	13.8	4	6.9
Supplier selection	43	74.1	14	24.1	1	1.7
Sale and after-sale services	25	43.1	31	53.4	2	3.4
Product distribution	20	34.5	38	65.5	0	0.0
Organization of production	7	12.1	50	86.2	1	1.7
Accounting	7	12.1	51	87.9	0	0.0

Note: N = 58
Source: 2010 survey conducted by the author

and Vliegenthart (2009) argued that FDI-driven industrial development strategies have increased

just because of [low] wages (interview on June 14, 2011). According to OECD (2013: 27), "the domestic value added content of Slovak exports is very low by international comparison."

ECE's external dependence on foreign capital to such an extent that it has led to the emergence of a 'dependent market economy' as a distinct type of capitalism in ECE.

Economic geographers have analyzed the effects of FDI on national and regional economies since the 1970s (e.g. Firn 1975; Dicken 1976; Britton 1980; Hayter 1982). The early studies have concluded that in addition to external dependency, FDI-driven industrial development has long-term structural costs for less developed regions and countries in the form of truncated development. Truncated firms are defined as "subsidiaries and branch plants, which rely on their foreign based parent companies for various services and functions and whose autonomy is circumscribed by head-office dictates" (Hayter 1982: 277). Instead of upgrading and catching up with more developed economies, truncation tends to exacerbate industrial and technological underdevelopment of host economies by developing routine capital-intensive and low-skill industrial activities, while high-skill and control functions remain concentrated in core regions/countries (Hayter 1982; Britton 1980). However, with the introduction of post-Fordist production methods since the late 1970s, there has been significant geographical reorganization of industrial activities by TNCs (Dicken 2015), including changes in the relationship between TNCs and local areas (Dicken et al. 1994). Therefore, we need to consider the possibility that the conclusions of the truncation literature may no longer be as relevant in the early twenty-first century as they were in the 1970s and 1980s.

FDI-driven dependent development often results in rapid industrialization and fast economic growth. Certain ECE economies, such as those of Slovakia and Poland, have recorded some of the fastest rates of economic growth in Europe since 2000 (OECD 2013), which could be largely attributed to FDI-driven extensive industrial development. In this type of economic development, ECE became specialized in labor intensive manufacturing, while control, R&D and other higher value-added functions, such as marketing and branding, remained concentrated in the global economic core. None of the three large foreign-owned automotive assembly plants in Slovakia have any R&D functions and their other higher value-added functions are extremely limited. Strategic planning, marketing, investment decisions, supplier selection, product pricing and distribution, sale and after sale services are all located abroad in the home countries of their foreign owners (2011–2015 interviews). The 2010 survey of 299 Slovak-based automotive firms, which was conducted by the author and which yielded a response rate of 44% (133 firms), showed that a similar situation exists among foreign-owned component suppliers in Slovakia. Subsidiary functions and competencies were reported by 58 foreign firms. The results, which are summarized in Table 6.1, confirm that the vast majority of foreign subsidiaries have limited non-production functions and that most strategic functions, such as strategic planning, investment decisions, product decisions, marketing and R&D are overwhelmingly concentrated abroad. In other words, the majority of foreign firms in the Slovak automotive industry do not engage in high value-added activities that remain concentrated abroad and, as such, they fit the notion of truncated branch plants. The survey results thus suggest that external ownership makes it less likely that higher value-added activities are developed in Slovak-based foreign automotive firms and are in line with the conclusions of the truncation literature on FDI effects in peripheral regions of developed countries (Britton 1980; Hayter 1982; Dicken 1976; Firn 1975). Although high value-added functions and competencies might gradually develop in some subsidiaries over time (Dicken 2015; Amin et al. 1994), the evidence from both Western Europe and ECE suggests that functional upgrading in foreign-owned branch plants has so far typically been very limited and uneven (Amin et al. 1994; Phelps 1993; Pavlínek and Ženka 2011). Furthermore, truncation is also unfavorable for the development of a strong domestic automotive sector because it "necessarily implies that foreign investment replaces or preempts economically viable indigenous development" (Hayter 1982: 277).

In this mode of dependent development, value enhancement and value capture tend to be low (Smith et al. 2002). In the case of Slovakia, labor costs account for only 7% of the total cost of automotive assembly (Bella 2013) and tax holidays further lower the potential for value capture. At least in this respect, the situation in ECE is reminiscent of peripheral regions in developed countries that were analyzed by the truncation literature. It is not surprising that the truncation effects of FDI in ECE were documented in the 1990s and 2000s (Grabher 1994, 1997; Pavlínek 2004, 2012). Consequently, the 'catching-up' process of ECE with the economic core and upgrading to a better position in the European automotive industry division of labor are likely to be limited despite the rapid FDI-driven industrialization of the 2000s.

GPN and GVC approaches in particular have argued that successful regional and national economic development can be achieved through the active insertion of regions and countries into externally organized production networks and value chains (Coe et al. 2004; Henderson et al. 2002; Gereffi et al. 2005; Gereffi 1999). For example, it has been argued that automotive branch plants located in peripheral regions are being transformed into 'performance/networked branch plants' that are embedded in local economies, have greater operating and even strategic autonomy and, as such, can gradually upgrade their functions and position in GPNs (Pike 1998; Dawley 2011). GVC and GPN perspectives have emphasized the possibilities for upgrading in peripheral regions through the coupling of local, regional and national assets with the strategic needs of TNCs (Coe et al. 2004; MacKinnon 2012). The state plays an important role in building and maintaining regional and national assets in the form of particular labor skills, knowledge, regional institutions and FDI policies that attract foreign capital. There is evidence from East and Southeast Asia supporting these arguments (Yeung 2009, 2013). Nevertheless, (Dicken et al. 1994: 40–41) remind us that "the prospects for greater local embeddedness of TNCs created by the new organizational forms appear to be limited to a minority of favoured places." Even performance plants located in peripheral regions have been susceptible to closure and corporate rationalization (Dawley 2007), which suggests the continuing validity of the truncation argument. In the context of the automotive industry generally and of the ECE automotive industry specifically, the GVC/GPN perspectives seem to be unduly optimistic because firm-level upgrading, especially among domestic firms, has mostly been limited to process upgrading (Pavlínek et al. 2009; Pavlínek and Ženka 2011; Pavlínek 2012). Empirical evidence from ECE and other less developed countries also points to the decreasing role of domestic firms in automotive value chains, which are increasingly dominated by foreign firms (Barnes and Kaplinsky 2000; Humphrey 2000, 2003).[2] Examples of successful strategic couplings in the ECE automotive industry are an exception rather than a rule (Pavlínek 2012), while the newly developed dependence on foreign capital and truncation effects are widespread (Table 6.1).

A review of existing research thus suggests that state industrialization strategies based on large inflows of FDI are problematic because FDI represents a double edged sword. It can lead to rapid industrialization and economic growth in host economies but at the expense of truncation, foreign control and dependent development. What follows is an empirical analysis of the role of the state in the development of the Slovak automotive industry, which supports my argument about the crucial role of ECE competition states in making the FDI-driven development of the automotive industry possible, despite their relatively weak bargaining position with foreign automotive TNCs.

The State and the Pre-1990 Development of the Slovak Automotive Industry

Before turning to the post-1990 period, I will briefly summarize the role of the state in the development of the Slovak automotive industry during the state socialist period (1948–1989), because the pre-1990 context strongly influenced state attitudes and policies toward the automotive industry after 1990.

No automotive industry had existed in Slovakia prior to World War Two (WWII) despite the fact that former Czechoslovakia had a long tradition of automotive manufacturing starting in the 1890s (Pavlínek 2008: 34–36). All pre-WWII Czechoslovak automobile production took place in Czechia. This spatial pattern slowly began to change during the state-directed industrialization of Slovakia after WWII (Pavlínek 1995; Smith 1998). The Czech-based truck makers established several branch plants in Slovakia starting in the early 1950s.[3] The government also decided about transfers

[2] For example, when asked whether domestic Tier 2 and Tier 3 suppliers meet Kia's quality and timing of delivery requirements, a Kia Slovakia manager replied: "The problem is not that they would not meet some criteria, the problem is that they virtually do not exist. Even suppliers of our suppliers are foreign-owned or JVs and are rarely domestic firms" (interview on June 20, 2011). 80% of 274 Slovak-based component suppliers are foreign-owned (ZAP 2013) but foreign-owned suppliers are on average much larger than domestic ones.

[3] Avia, the producer of medium-weight trucks, built a subsidiary in the town of Žilina in 1952, originally to conduct general repairs and the servicing of its cars in Slovakia, and later to produce truck superstructures and connecting shafts. Tatra, the heavy off-road truck maker, established branch plants in Bánovce nad Bebravou (assembly and the production of components) in 1957 and Čadca (components) in 1958. Liaz, the producer of heavy road trucks, set up subsidiaries in Zvolen in 1971 (final assembly and the production of components) and Veľký Krtíš (engine assembly, main LIAZ truck and engine repair shop) also in 1971 (Pavlínek 2008).

of several automotive firms from Czechia to Slovakia.[4] However, the final assembly continued to be concentrated in Czechia. In the second half of the 1960s, the federal government contemplated strategies to increase the production of passenger cars. Slovak politicians demanded that it allocated investment for the construction of a new assembly plant in the Slovak capital Bratislava. Although Slovakia had an available labor force and underutilized manufacturing facilities built during the post-WWII industrialization drive (Studeničová and Uhrík 2009), its automotive industry tradition, technical expertise and labor force experience and skills were limited. In the middle of 1971, after several failed proposals, the construction of the Bratislava Automotive Works (BAZ) was approved. A member of the board of directors of VW Slovakia explained the decision as follows (interview on July 21, 2005):

> Before 1989, there was a kind of rivalry between Czechia and Slovakia. The Slovaks argued that because there were three [passenger car] assembly factories in Czechia [at Mladá Boleslav, Vrchlabí and Kvasiny], there should also be at least one in Slovakia. Mr. Husák, who was Slovak and was the president [of Czechoslovakia] and the general [Communist] party secretary at that time, was able to strongly influence the decision making process. So, an artificial decision was made to build an assembly plant in Bratislava. It was a political decision which was irrational. It was decided that the factory had to be in the capital city of Bratislava despite its non-existent automotive tradition, which was not considered to be important. Everything was built too big here, although the BAZ factory complex had no production program. Consequently, the BAZ ended up with large empty factory buildings.

At the same time, the Czechoslovak federal government had decided to abandon the previously approved project for the assembly expansion at the Škoda complex in Czechia and transfer it to BAZ because it could not afford to finance both projects. However, the planned assembly of the Škoda 720 at BAZ was never launched because high investment costs undermined the support of the federal government (Dufek 2004; Studeničová and Uhrík 2009). The construction of the BAZ factory complex continued in the 1970s and 1980s but without a clear plan about what automobiles would be assembled there.[5]

The development of BAZ before 1990 thus illustrates the total dependence of the automotive industry on shifting state policies during the state socialist period. It also suggests that the Slovak government was eager to develop the automotive assembly in Slovakia for several decades before the 1993 independence. In this context, the

[4] For example, the relocation of production of light commercial vehicles from Vrchlabí to Trnava (TAZ—Trnavské automobilové závody) in 1973 and the transfer of production of special tractors from Zetor Brno to Martin (ZŤS—Závody ťažkého strojárstva) in 1978. The production of mopeds and motorcycles with engines below 1000 cm^3, including R&D of new products, was relocated from Prague's Jawa company to Považské strojárne in Považská Bystrica in western Slovakia in 1955 (Pavlínek 2008).

[5] The low-volume assembly of Škoda cars (the Garde) was transferred from Škoda to BAZ in 1982 but it was phased out in 1987 after only 3480 cars were assembled. All components for the assembly had to be transported from Škoda's main plant in Czechia where the assembly was much more economical. BAZ also produced front axles for Škoda but its production was plagued by serious quality problems (Studeničová and Uhrík 2009; ZAP 2000; interview with a Member of the Board of Directors, VW Slovakia, July 21, 2005).

post-socialist and post-independence state attitudes and policies were to a significant extent path-dependent by building on Slovak efforts to develop the automotive industry during the state socialist period.

The State and the Automotive Industry in Slovakia After 1990

Immediately after the collapse of state socialism, the Czechoslovak federal government was deciding on the course of future development and privatization of the automotive industry. In June 1990, it approved the "Automotive industry strategy" and decided to seek foreign investors for state-owned automotive assembly plants (Studeničová and Uhrík 2009). Eventually, the Czech and Slovak national governments independently selected German VW for joint venture (JV) agreements with Czech-based Škoda and Slovak-based BAZ (Pavlínek and Smith 1998).

Throughout the early and mid-1990s, Slovakia was not perceived as a favorable destination for foreign investors because of perceived uncertainty related to the establishment of the new independent country, weak investment incentives and shifting privatization and FDI policies mired in low transparency and corruption (Smith and Ferenčíková 1998; Jakubiak et al. 2008; Javorcik and Kaminski 2004). During this period, the Slovak government pursued an inward-oriented strategy of economic development that supported large domestic firms and was hostile to FDI (Pavlínek and Smith 1998; Drahokoupil 2009a). The failure of this policy to generate a sustainable economic growth, combined with the domestic pressure from the emerging comprador sector and the external pressure from the EU, the International Monetary Fund (IMF) and the World Bank to open up to FDI (Medve-Bálint 2014), paved the way for an alternative approach based on attracting large FDI inflows (Drahokoupil 2008).[6] In its various reports, the IMF, for example, repeatedly urged the Slovak government to speed up privatization and open up to FDI in the late 1990s: "Accelerated privatization of telecommunications and of other companies held by the State would convey an important message about the new government's open attitude to foreign investors…" (IMF 1998 cited in Marcinčin 2000b: 309). In its report prepared for the consultations with the Slovak government, the IMF (1999a) considered macroeconomic instability, high corporate income tax rate, the lack of tax incentives compared to neighboring countries, and the government's privatization policy that discriminated against foreign investors in favor of domestic managerial groups, as main reasons for low FDI in Slovakia. And in 1999, the IMF pressed on:

> For the revitalization of the banking and corporate sectors it is most important to accelerate their restructuring and privatization. Delayed addressing of these serious economic issues

[6] Slovakia signed the European Association Agreement in October 1993 (effective on February 1, 1995), applied for the EU membership on June 27, 1995, became an EU member on May 1, 2004, and adopted the Euro currency on January 1, 2009.

would undoubtedly threaten the economic stability of Slovakia and reduce its chances for an early integration into Western Europe" (IMF 1999b cited in Marcinčin 2000a: 335).

A shift away from the inward-oriented development strategies promoting national capitalism and the changing attitude to FDI was reflected in the "Program for the Development of the Automotive Industry in Slovakia" approved by the nationalist government in July 1998 (Vestník 1998) just before it was replaced by a 'reformist' (neo-liberal) government in October 1998 following the September 1998 elections. The Program defined the vision, strategy and goals of the development of the automotive industry until 2010. It set three basic goals: (1) securing the sufficient supply of vehicles necessary for the development of the Slovak economy, while achieving a positive trade balance with automotive products; (2) increasing the automotive output and restructuring the related industries, especially manufacturing, electronic, iron and steel, rubber and plastic industries; and (3) increasing the integration of Slovakia in the global economy through the automotive industry. Each of these basic goals had specific targets attached. For example, the automotive industry output was supposed to grow by 20% annually until 2000, by 15% between 2001 and 2005 and by 12% between 2006 and 2010. The government required the automotive industry to create 15,000 new jobs and invest 60–80 bn Slovak crowns ($1.7–2.3 bn), mainly through FDI ($1.4–1.8 bn) by 2010.[7] The Program included detailed production goals for individual producers, such as trebling the output of VW Slovakia by 2010 and attracting at least one additional passenger car assembly plant of a global lead firm that would assemble 100–150 thousand units annually in Slovakia. There were also annual production goals for the assembly of trucks (2000–3000 units), buses (500–800 units), light commercial vehicles (2000 units) and the components industry, whose output was to quadruple by 2010. The domestic technological investment was supposed to account for 15–20% of the total technological investment in the automotive industry and the rest was to be secured through FDI. Slovakia was to start exporting automotive technologies mainly to other ECE countries as well as develop and start exporting business services for the automotive industry (Vestník 1998).

Although the Program mainly relied on foreign capital for its financing, it called for state financial support of the automotive industry exports, employment, restructuring and regional development. It stressed the importance of state incentives for foreign investors, including lower taxes and the removal of trade barriers. It also declared state support for automotive R&D in Slovakia, labor force training and educational programs to train the labor force for the automotive industry, active seeking and attracting foreign investors, the development of infrastructure and of integrated information systems (Vestník 1998). The Slovak Ministry of Economy became responsible for the entire Program, which was coordinated by the government's plenipotentiary for the development of the automotive industry and further advised by the Council for the Development of the Slovak Automotive Industry.

[7] All conversions of the Slovak koruna used in this chapter are based upon official exchange rates for a particular year published by the Slovak National Bank at http://www.nbs.sk/en/statistics/exchange-rates/en-kurzovy-listok.

During its annual evaluation of the Program, the Slovak government specified tasks to be completed by individual ministries in a given time period in support of the Program. In other words, the state put in place a battery of policies designed to develop the automotive industry through FDI by global assemblers and component suppliers.

The goals for the development of the automotive industry set in the Program could only be achieved through large inflows of FDI, which required a radical opening of the domestic economy to foreign capital. In 1999, the government approved a "Strategy of the support of FDI entry" (Medžová 1999), which was a reaction to and the emulation of the generous system of investment incentives introduced in Czechia in 1998 (Drahokoupil 2009a). Investors investing at least €5m (€2.5m in regions with high unemployment rates) in setting up new manufacturing operations in Slovakia with at least 75% of foreign ownership were offered 5 years of tax holidays. They had to export at least 60% of output and could qualify for 50% lower taxes on their profits for an additional 5 years, provided they invested an additional €5m (€2.5m in regions with high unemployment rates) (Medžová 1999). The corporate tax rate was lowered from 40% to 29%. In 2003, the government introduced a 19% flat tax and an employer-friendly flexible labor code (Fisher et al. 2007; Bohle and Greskovits 2006; Duman and Kureková 2012). This radical turn in the treatment of foreign TNCs by the state was strongly influenced by the lobbying efforts of various organizations on behalf of foreign capital included in the comprador sector, such as the American Chamber of Commerce in Slovakia, by bilateral negotiations with foreign TNCs, and by the introduction of a 'race to the bottom' in tax regimes, labor protection and investment incentives for foreign capital in ECE (Bohle 2006).

Although the Program seemed to be very ambitious when it was introduced in 1998, many of its goals, such as the employment, investment and total output targets of passenger cars, were achieved much faster than the government had anticipated. This was the outcome of the extensive growth of the automotive industry after 2000 that was driven by large inflows of FDI that were strongly supported by investment incentives. By the end of 2010, FDI stock in the Slovak automotive industry (NACE 29) reached €2.3 bn ($3.1 bn) (NBS 2015), which was almost twice the volume targeted by the government in 1998, and the output of passenger cars was 557 thousand units compared to the plan of 340–390 thousand units (Vestník 1998; Fig. 6.1). In 2005, the government argued that the "rapid pace of growth [of the automotive industry] was only made possible by very thoughtful strategic measures of the Slovak government" and it called for further support of this growth through lower tax payments and levies on foreign investors (SEM 2005). Increasing labor shortages in the rapidly growing automotive industry forced the government to restructure the state-run system of vocational training and initiate changes in the structure of educational programs in state universities. It argued that universities "must permanently adjust their curricula to the needs of the automotive industry and closely cooperate with the industry" (SEM 2005). At the same time, the state support for the development of the indigenous automotive industry was virtually non-existent. While the pre-1998 state support targeted large domestic enterprises in basic industries, such as petrochemicals, chemicals, metals and the energy sector and ignored the needs of small and medium enterprises (SMEs) (Beblavý 2000), the post-1998 governments also failed to introduce any policy supporting the development of domestic SMEs (Duman and Kureková 2012).

In order to further illustrate the role of the state in the development of the Slovak automotive industry, the next section provides short case studies of the role of the state in attracting four passenger car assembly plants to Slovakia after 1990: VW, PSA, Kia and Jaguar Land Rover.

The Competition State and Flagship Investments by Foreign Assemblers in Slovakia

VW Slovakia

Throughout the 1990s, the development of the Slovak automotive industry was closely linked to the VW investment at BAZ. In the early 1990s, the Slovak government was in charge of selling BAZ to a foreign investor. However, the interest of foreign investors in BAZ was very limited. Since VW was preoccupied with its effort to secure the JV agreement with Škoda in Czechia, it was not originally interested in BAZ. Therefore, in the second half of 1990, the Slovak government was negotiating the sale of BAZ with General Motors (GM), which proposed to produce 200,000–300,000 gearboxes annually at BAZ. However, the negotiations broke down because the Slovak government refused to grant a substantial investment subsidy requested by GM (interview at VW Slovakia, June 14, 2011). Slovak officials approached VW again following its selection for JV with Škoda in Czechia. VW proposed to assemble 30,000 automobiles annually at BAZ, produce gearboxes and reorganize the automotive supplier network in Slovakia. Since the Slovak government was especially eager to launch vehicle assembly in Slovakia, it accepted VW's proposal. The JV agreement was signed in May 1991. VW bought 80% stake at BAZ for 48m German marks (USD29m) and promised to invest an additional 800m (USD480m) to set up assembly for 30,000 cars annually, 200,000 gearboxes and employ 1500 workers. VW bought the remaining 20% in 1994 to become the sole owner of VW Bratislava, which was renamed to VW Slovakia in 1999 (Studeničová and Uhrík 2009; interview at VW Slovakia, June 14, 2011).

One of the most important reasons why VW bought BAZ was a potential to increase its cost competitiveness by developing low-cost export-oriented production in Slovakia based on large labor cost differences between Germany and Slovakia (Pavlínek and Smith 1998). In the early and mid-1990s, Slovak labor costs were at less than 10% of German labor costs and in 1996, hourly compensation costs in Slovakia ($2.73) were at 8.3% of those in Germany ($33.22) (USBLS 2013). Despite the narrowing of the wage gap between Slovakia and Germany in the 1990s and 2000s, large labor cost differences continue to persist. In 2001, the Slovak labor costs per unit of production in the automotive industry were at 15.1% of the EU-15 average and lowest in Central Europe (Schönwiesner 2005). In 2014, the average hourly compensation costs in the production of motor vehicles and other transport equipment were still 76.8% lower in Slovakia ($14.77) than in Germany ($63.59) (Conference Board 2016) (Fig. 6.3). Despite the claims that "the advantage of cheap labor no longer exists in the automotive industry" (Bella 2013), wage differences between the core and periphery are the "key to North-to-South offshoring" (Baldwin 2013: 31) and automotive firms try to minimize increases in wages and keep them as low as possible (Freyssenet and Lung 2000). VW Slovakia is no exception and low wages continue to be extremely important for its competitiveness. In 2014, for example, the VW management proposed a 4% cut in workers' salaries despite the low average monthly wage (€1400 in 2013) and €170m profits earned by VW Slovakia in 2013 (SME 2014).

The first VW Passat was assembled at the end of 1991, the assembly line production of the Passat Variant started in 1992 and the assembly of gearboxes was launched in 1994 (VW 2010). However, the output grew slowly to 41,000 cars in 1997. VW let the Slovak government know that it would not substantially increase its production unless taxes were lowered to make Slovakia competitive with the neighboring countries, such as Hungary and Poland, where VW was heavily investing in the second half of the 1990s. The Slovak government swiftly reacted and offered tax breaks to foreign investors in the middle of 1998, but in such a way that only VW qualified for them (Studeničová and Uhrík 2009). The tax allowance for VW amounted to €31.2m in 1999 (Jakubiak et al. 2008). After taxes were lowered, VW relocated the assembly of the Golf Synchro from Germany to Slovakia to lower its production costs. As the most sophisticated Golf model, the Synchro required a larger labor input than more standardized Golf models and, therefore, benefited from low labor costs in Slovakia. Subsequently, the output of VW Slovakia tripled in 1998 (to 125,000 units) compared to 1997. The successful assembly of the Synchro let to further production increases and by 2003, VW was assembling 281,000 passenger cars in Slovakia (interview at VW Slovakia, June 14, 2011).

The state strongly supported this growth by approving investment incentives for VW to build a new components factory in the city of Martin (€9.6m between 1998 and 2000) (Zamkovský 1999; Vagac 2000). In 1999, the Ministry of Construction was mandated to coordinate the preparation of conditions for the construction of 1000 new apartments in the Bratislava region, primarily for the employees of VW and its suppliers. The Transportation Ministry became responsible for increasing the capacity of the Devínska Nová Ves railway station in order to meet the needs of the rapidly growing production at VW Slovakia. It was also responsible for building the highway connection to VW at the estimated cost of 1 bn Slovak crowns (€330m) (Vagac 2000). The state also supported and heavily subsidized the location of foreign suppliers in Slovakia, especially through the construction of supplier parks (Table 6.2). Based on the 2001 law on industrial parks, the government was allowed to pay up to 70% of their construction costs in certain areas (Bohle and Greskovits 2006). Two supplier parks (Lozorno and Küster) were built close to VW Slovakia for its crucial suppliers after VW selected its Bratislava factory for the assembly of luxury SUVs for the VW Group (the VW Touareg, Audi Q7 and Porsche Cayane).

Table 6.2 Investment incentives provided by Slovakia for flagship investments by VW, PSA and Kia

VW Slovakia	PSA Slovakia	Kia Slovakia
80% of BAZ sold to VW for USD29m in 1991	Land for the factory site and its infrastructure (€152m)	Direct state incentives (€328m)
Tax allowance granted in 1998 (€31.2m in 1999)	Tax holidays	Highway construction to Žilina (€700m)
Subsidies for the construction of the components factory in the city of Martin (€9.6m 1998–2000)	€1640 subsidy for each newly created job	€1750 subsidy for each created job
Construction of 1000 new apartments in the Bratislava region for VW workers	€11.3m for worker training	State-funded worker training
Increase in the capacity of the Devínska Nová Ves railway station	Help with the recruitment of workers	Construction of a new railway terminal
Highway connection to VW Bratislava (€330m)	Help with the construction of housing for workers	Reconstruction of the airport at Dolný Hričov
Provision of land and infrastructure for the construction of two supplier parks (Lozorno and Küster)	Establishment of a French school in Trnava	English language school for children of South Korean employees
Investment incentives to expand production (€14.3m in 2009 and long-term tax holidays)	Education geared towards the needs of PSA at the Trnava technical school	A new health center, training center and police station in Žilina
		1000–1200 new apartments in Žilina
		Luxury houses close to Bratislava for South Korean managers
		The Construction Law amended
		The same incentives given to Hyundai Mobis
		No other assembler allowed to locate within 100 km from the Kia factory

Note: No information about investment incentives provided by Slovakia for Jaguar Land Rover was available at the time of writing
Sources: Zamkovský (1999), Vagac (2000), VW (2013), PSA (2003), Kia (2004)

In 1997, VW had only four direct and nine indirect suppliers located in Slovakia (Javorcik and Kaminski 2004) and the vast majority of components were supplied from abroad (Pavlínek and Smith 1998). By 2004, 17 VW principal suppliers were located in these two supplier parks (2005 interview). In 2009, VW Slovakia succeeded in the VW concern-wide competition to assemble the smallest VW passenger cars (the VW Up!, Škoda Citigo and Seat Mii) which started in 2011. The state provided €14.3m in investment incentives in addition to long-term tax holidays. VW invested €308m to increase the production capacity of VW Slovakia to 400,000 units, added 1500 jobs and doubled its output (419,888 cars in 2012 compared to 210,441 in 2011) (VW 2013). With a strong support from the state, VW Slovakia thus successfully developed as a low-cost assembler within the VW corporate production network.

State policies towards VW Slovakia contributed to the development of the competition state. By the early 2000s, Slovakia was able to compete with other ECE countries in attracting large FDI projects, which was demonstrated by the decisions of PSA and Kia to build their assembly plants in Slovakia. Both investments illustrate the active role of the Slovak state in the development of the automotive industry and its willingness to aggressively engage in the 'race to the bottom' with its Central European neighbors over flagship automotive investment projects.

PSA Peugeot-Citroën Slovakia

In November 2002, PSA announced a plan to build a €700m assembly plant with the annual capacity of 300,000 small passenger cars in ECE, mainly because of 75% lower labor costs compared to France (Schönwiesner 2002). The announcement started a bidding war among Czechia, Hungary, Poland and Slovakia over the investment. Eventually, Hungary and Poland lost because of high labor costs compared with Slovakia and also because of the poor quality of infrastructure at the proposed site at Radomsko in Poland (Trend 2003). Czechia was disqualified because PSA was already building a JV factory with Toyota (TPCA) at Kolín and also because of the poor quality of infrastructure and unresolved past environmental liabilities at the proposed factory site close to the city of Žatec (iDnes 2003). PSA chose the Slovak offer and its proposed Trnava site. The total value of investment incentives was limited to 15% of the original investment by EU regulations. Slovakia offered €152m in the form of the land for the factory site and its infrastructure, tax holidays, a €1640 subsidy for each newly created job and €11.3m for worker training. The state also promised to help with worker recruitment, education geared towards the needs of PSA at the Trnava technical school, the construction of housing for workers, and the establishment of a French school in Trnava (PSA 2003). The combination of investment incentives, low labor costs and high unemployment rate in the Trnava region (around 13%) were the most important factors favoring Slovakia in addition to Trnava's automotive tradition, well developed infrastructure and its proximity to the capital Bratislava (Table 6.2). At the time of negotiations, the government did "the maximum to accommodate the wishes and needs of PSA" (interview at PSA Slovakia, June 17, 2011).

Kia Slovakia

The Slovak competition state, along with its investment promoting machines led by the Sario state investment agency, was even more aggressive in attracting Kia's investment. In 2002 and 2003, Czechia, Hungary, Poland and Slovakia were considered by the Hyundai Automobile Group for a $1.5 bn investment by its Kia subsidiary. In November 2002, the Hyundai top management began to negotiate with politicians of these four countries but kept them guessing about its selection process. In April 2003, it was unofficially reported that Czechia was no longer one of the candidates (SME 2003) but in August 2003, it was reported that the decision about the factory location would be made between Hungary and Czechia, with Czechia being the frontrunner (Kremský 2003). At that point, the Slovak minister of Economy traveled to South Korea to personally present a new attractive package of investment incentives to the management of Kia, "an offer which was impossible to refuse" according to a highly ranked former official at the Slovak Ministry of Economy (Kolesár 2007: 59). Kia obviously used the late Slovak offer to attempt to exert bigger incentives from Hungary and Czechia. Both countries complained that the size of incentives sought by Kia violated EU and national regulations and exceeded the expected benefits of the investment (Kolesár 2007; Pavlínek 2008). This suggests that Slovakia was overbidding and ended up paying too much for the investment.[8] In November 2003, Kia officially narrowed its selection to Poland and Slovakia and eventually selected Slovakia on March 2, 2004. The size of the investment incentives was the decisive factor, in combination with low labor costs and low labor militancy. Kolesár (2006: 44) has argued that "most of my interviewees confirmed that Slovakia offered Kia everything the Korean investor had asked for and that was the primary reason why Kia Motors decided to invest in the country." The Polish Economic Ministry secretary complained that Poland lost to Slovakia despite the Polish offer of a "staggering" $200m (€158m) in investment incentives (Janoška et al. 2004).

The original size of the Kia investment was €700m. The value of direct state incentives offered by Slovakia was €178m (HN 2005).[9] Additional indirect incentives included the construction of a highway to Žilina at the cost of €700m, the construction of a supplier park and a new railway terminal, the reconstruction of the airport at Dolný Hričov, an English language school for children of South Korean employees, a new health center, a training center, a police station, 1000–1200 new apartments in Žilina, and luxury houses close to Bratislava for South Korean managers (HN 2005). Kia received €1750 for each created job and Slovakia paid for the training of newly hired Kia workers. Slovakia was also obliged to provide the same

[8] Slovakia paid $86,000 per job created by Kia, compared to $50,000 per job created by PSA Slovakia, $48,000 by Hyundai in Czechia and $37,000 by TPCA in Czechia (Kolesár 2007).

[9] By 2005, the value of direct state incentives provided to Kia increased by €150m (77.5%) above the initial commitment because Kia increased its planned production capacity by 50% from 200,000 to 300,000 units annually and also because of the "incompetent management by the Slovak Economic Ministry" (HN 2005).

investment incentives to Hyundai Mobis, Kia's principal supplier. It also promised to give similar incentives to other Kia suppliers, provided the state had enough money to do so. The state agreed not to allow any other assembler to locate within 100 km from the Kia factory and not to change laws for the duration of the investment in such a way "that would endanger economic benefits of the state support for Kia". It also promised not to change its tariff policy, defend the investment incentives for Kia with the European Commission and defend Kia's interests in any potential dispute (Kia 2004). Slovakia simply provided everything Kia asked for (Kolesár 2007). At the same time, Kia was to receive all of the incentives even if it did not complete all of the investments listed in the contract. In that case, Slovakia had no right to demand any additional investment from Kia or return of any investment incentives with the exception of those required by the Slovak and EU law (Kia 2004). The contract is thus extremely one-sided, suggesting a very asymmetrical power relationship between Kia and the state, and it represents an example of corporate capture in Slovakia (Phelps 2000, 2008).

In 2005, Slovakia won another regulatory arbitrage over the €500m investment by South Korean Hankook Tire by offering €105m or 21% of the total value of the investment. In this case, however, the government did not approve the investment agreement after strong criticism from Slovak entrepreneurs and politicians that the country would be paying too much (€90,000) for each newly created job. Slovakia then offered lower incentives (€25,000 per job or 6% of the total value of the investment), which Hankook refused and, instead, built the factory in Hungary, which offered €56m in direct incentives (12% of the value of the investment) (Kolesár 2006). The case of Hankook Tire suggests three important conclusions: First, investment incentives do matter despite the fact that TNCs and competition states tend to downplay their importance in location decisions compared to other factors. The size of investment incentives was obviously the most important factor in the final location decision of Hankook Tire between Slovakia and Hungary. Second, the Slovak competition state had reached its limit with the Kia investment and the state recognized that attracting FDI at any cost might be counterproductive. Third, states can ultimately limit the power of TNCs and the comprador sector on their territories but often at the expense of foreign capital exit.

Jaguar Land Rover

Ten years after the case of Hankook Tire, Slovakia was successful in the 2015 bidding war over the new assembly factory of Jaguar Land Rover (JLR). In the spring of 2015, the Indian-owned British-based JLR decided to build a factory to assemble its luxury SUVs and four-wheel-drive cars in Central Europe. Czechia, Hungary, Poland and Slovakia were originally considered for the $1.5 billion investment but as one of the negotiators argued, "Jaguar Land Rover did not care too much about geographical location. They just wanted the best deal" (Foy and Sharman 2015). Slovakia was eliminated from this group first, followed by Hungary and then

Czechia. Poland became the favorite by offering strong investment incentives and three potential factory sites in the industrial region of lower Silesia with the existing networks of automotive suppliers and large labor force. The location choice eventually narrowed to Jawor near Wroclaw. At that point, and as was the case with the Kia investment, Slovakia re-entered the bidding war with an attractive investment offer. The Slovak law on providing incentives to large foreign investors was changed in order to allow for the increase in investment incentives to JLR and its key suppliers at the site at Nitra that was designated as the first strategic industrial park in Slovakia. The prime Minister of Slovakia, Robert Fico, personally met JLR executives and "told them that if there was anything that they required, they only needed to ask him [because] Slovakia wanted to be the most competitive country" (Foy and Sharman 2015). Poland refused to offer more to JLR because it felt that it had offered very competitive investment incentives. Poland's economy minister suggested that Slovakia was overbidding for the JLR investment by saying that "we do not fight for every investment regardless of how high the price is ... we do not need to overpay (Foy and Sharman 2015). The Polish Ministry of Economy argued: "Slovaks offered an extremely high direct state support and we could not accept this level of state support because it would mean that both parties would unevenly share profits and costs [of this investment]" (SME 2015). The Slovak government refused to disclose the incentives offered to JLR. Although it reportedly offered the maximum permissible EUR 130 million in direct incentives according to EU legislation, the total cost of attracting JLR for Slovakia, including the cost of preparing the industrial park at Nitra, might be EUR 600 million (LN 2016). The annual capacity of the JLR plant will be 150,000 vehicles and it will employ 2800 workers. Construction began in September 2016 and assembly is expected to start at the end of 2018 (JLR 2016).

Beyond Assemblers: State Policies from the Perspective of Component Suppliers

As we could see, VW, PSA and Kia strongly benefitted from investment incentives and, therefore, it is not surprising that they positively evaluated the state automotive industry policy during 2011 interviews. In addition to investment incentives, they stressed the importance of the flat tax and the adoption of the euro currency. Still, the assemblers, along with the OECD (2012), would like to see the creation of "as flexible labor markets as possible" and the restructuring of the education system so that it would better reflect the "market demand for labor" (interviews at VW Slovakia, Kia Slovakia and PSA Slovakia on June 14, 16 and 20, 2011). However, it has been argued that the state offered large investment incentives to foreign TNCs at the expense of taxpayers and SMEs (Zamkovský 2001; Bohle and Greskovits 2006). Indeed, after 1998, when Slovakia began to vigorously compete for automotive FDI, the state withdrew from the welfare system and from the support of domestic firms (Duman and Kureková 2012), spending on education in Slovakia has

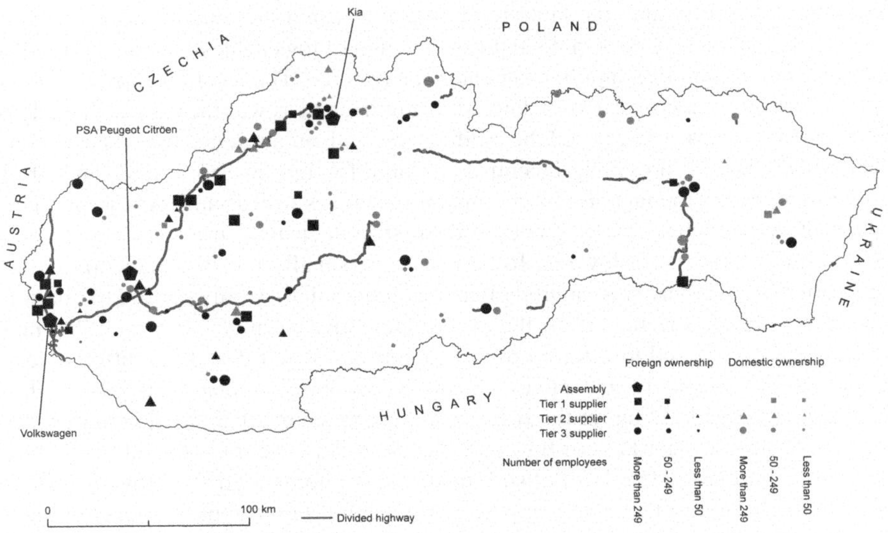

Fig. 6.4 The location of interviewed automotive firms in Slovakia. *Source*: Author

been one of the lowest among the OECD countries (OECD 2013), and the state support for domestic research has been erratic.[10]

Therefore, in the next step, the chapter looks beyond large TNC assemblers in order to gain a broader perspective on how the Slovak-based automotive firms evaluate state policies towards the automotive industry. It draws on 50 on-site interviews with automotive firms conducted in Slovakia between 2011 and 2015 with 22 domestic-owned (henceforth domestic) firms and 28 foreign-owned (henceforth foreign) firms, including VW, PSA and Kia (Fig. 6.4). The interviewed firms are a representative sample selected from the database of 299 Slovak-based automotive firms in terms of size, ownership and the position in the supplier hierarchy. The interviews were conducted with directors or top managers and covered various questions related to the operation and development of automotive firms in Slovakia. Foreign firms were asked whether the state economic and industrial policies help them develop or at least maintain the strategic assets because of which they have invested in Slovakia. Domestic firms were asked a similar question, whether the state economic and industrial policies help them improve or at least maintain their competitive advantages. The results are summarized in Tables 6.3 and 6.4.

Of the 45 answers, 12 respondents (27%) evaluated the state policy towards the automotive industry positively, 26 (58%) negatively, and seven evaluations (16%) were neutral, highlighting both positive and negative aspects of the state policy. Of

[10] The Slovak Science Foundation (Agentúra na podporu vedy a výskumu) had to cancel general calls for proposals in 2003, 2008, 2009 and 2013 because the national government did not allocate any money for basic research in the national budget. In 2011, financing of successful projects was cut by more than 50% (Hajduch 2014).

Table 6.3 Evaluation of state economic and industrial policy by the interviewed by automotive firms, 2011–2015

	Total		Foreign subsidiaries		Domestic firms	
	No.	%	No.	%	No.	%
Positive	12	26.7	7	25.9	5	27.8
Negative	26	57.8	13	48.1	13	72.2
Neutral	7	15.6	7	25.9	0	0.0
Total	45	100.0	27	100.0	18	100.0

Note: Five firms (four domestic firms and one foreign subsidiary) did not answer the question
Source: Author's 2011–2015 interviews

Table 6.4 Negative and positive aspects of state economic and industrial policy according to the interviewed automotive firms, 2011–2015

	Total answers	%	Foreign	%	Domestic	%
Negative						
Weak educational system	16	25.8	12	36.4	4	13.8
Investment incentives to large TNCs	7	11.3	2	6.1	5	17.2
Inflexible labor laws	6	9.7	3	9.1	3	10.3
Bureaucracy	4	6.5	2	6.1	2	6.9
High taxes	3	4.8	1	3.0	2	6.9
Corruption	3	4.8	0	0.0	3	10.3
No help to small firms	2	3.2	1	3.0	1	3.4
Euro	1	1.6	0	0.0	1	3.4
No help at all	1	1.6	1	3.0	0	0.0
Positive						
Investment incentives to large TNCs	6	9.7	6	18.2	0	0.0
Subsidy for a specific project	6	9.7	0	0.0	6	20.7
Euro	2	3.2	2	6.1	0	0.0
Infrastructure: highways	2	3.2	0	0.0	2	6.9
Flat tax	1	1.6	1	3.0	0	0.0
Stable country	1	1.6	1	3.0	0	0.0
Labor market policy	1	1.6	1	3.0	0	0.0
Total	62	100.0	33	100.0	29	100.0

Notes: Number of firms included: 40. Each firm could list more than one answer. Six domestic firms and four foreign subsidiaries did not list any specific reasons
Source: Author's 2011–2015 interviews

the 18 domestic firms who replied to the question, five (28%) viewed the effects of state economic policies positively and 13 (72%) negatively. Among foreign firms, seven of 27 responses (26%) were positive, 13 (48%) were negative and seven (26%) were neutral (Table 6.3). A less critical view of state policies by foreign compared to domestic firms could be attributed to the fact that many foreign firms strongly benefited from investment incentives, which some firms appreciated, while criticizing other aspects of state policies. In many cases, however, foreign firms failed to mention incentives and emphasized negative aspects of state policies.

Table 6.4 highlights the positive and negative views of state economic and industrial policies by interviewed firms as well as different views by foreign and domestic firms. By far, foreign automotive firms are most concerned about the quality of the Slovak labor force and the failure of the state to adequately educate the workforce to satisfy the needs of automotive firms. The weak education system was highlighted by 36% of foreign firms and 14% of domestic firms, suggesting a greater problem with the quality of workforce for foreign than domestic firms. Domestic firms might be better accustomed to the existing quality of the local labor force and, therefore, do not perceive it to be a major problem. Respondents complained about difficulties to find skilled workers on the labor market and the lack of practical skills possessed by graduates from state schools at all levels. Quotes from four different interviews highlight the problems felt by foreign firms:

> We need a high share of skilled workers for our operations, and I am not talking about operators, but technicians and engineers. Here, I would need more brains, more people thinking how they can better perform, improve processes and machines. And I am struggling with that. And that would be the two factors my parent company would need to be successful in Slovakia. Definitely it would be preferable to get it locally, to start with the base where people are trained, where they have the automotive industry spirit. But this is not the case (interview with CEO of foreign firm, June 23, 2011).

> The problem is the support from the government. It is very formal and difficult to follow. The government is not providing the conditions we need. We have problems to find enough employees, the unemployment rate is very low, especially in this area, in Bratislava and it is the same for Košice. More importantly, in my opinion, the labor force training is not good in Slovakia, the training after school, so that they [young workers] would have the training in factories and not [just] the theoretical training. I would pay for that. And that is missing here (interview with CEO of foreign firm, June 22, 2011).

> A long-term problem of the Slovak education system is that it does not reflect labor market demand. What is missing here are technically-oriented workers with university degrees, and, of course, workers with the vocational and high school technical training. The existing demand is not absolutely covered… Certainly, we feel that the education system is not adequately supported by the government (interview at a vehicle assembly firm, June 22, 2011).

> The government should be really investing in the qualification of students, qualification of workers, or it would be a mess. The problem is really, what is the benefit of purchasing from Slovak companies today? I can buy cheap products somewhere else but I can't find good products here (interview with CEO of foreign firm, June 23, 2011).

Increasing labor shortages in the rapidly growing automotive industry forced the government to restructure the state-run system of vocational training and initiate changes in the structure of educational programs in state universities in the mid-2000s. The government argued that universities "must permanently adjust their curricula to the needs of the automotive industry and closely cooperate with the industry" (SEM 2005). This quote points to corporate capture in the area of education and training policy-making but no positive outcomes of these state efforts were acknowledged by automotive firms during 2011–2015 interviews.

The second most cited criticism of state policies was the provision of investment incentives for large foreign TNCs, which ranked as the most important for domestic firms who felt that the support of foreign investors was often provided at the expense of domestic firms. The third major criticism was the perceived inflexible labor law, especially in terms of hiring and firing workers according to the momentary needs of firms, and the inability of firms to use short-term employment contracts. Additional negative views included high taxes, corruption, no help provided to small firms, and the strong euro, which is undermining the competitiveness of domestic products in foreign markets. Among the positive aspects of state economic and industrial policies, foreign firms most appreciated investment incentives, while domestic firms most often highlighted the importance of state subsidies for their specific projects. Two respondents emphasized the importance of the euro for their firms and the improving transportation infrastructure (Table 6.4). For example, a CEO of a foreign firm argued on June 16, 2011:

> I do not know of any foreign automotive firm that would regret its investment in Slovakia. They get tax holidays and subsidies for each created job. The state is smart to primarily support assemblers and few key suppliers. These key firms received extremely good investment incentives.

Limits of the State-Foreign Capital Nexus

The long-term goal of the state is to improve Slovakia's position in automotive GPNs through industrial upgrading. It should be achieved through the development of automotive R&D (SEM 2005), which seems to be a typical approach towards the automotive industry in less developed economies. As Humphrey and Oeter (2000: 55) argued "governments expect to generate investment and employment in labour-intensive activities in the short term, and hope that eventually higher-skilled jobs will also be created."

Firm-level interviews confirmed that Slovakia is attractive for the FDI-driven development of R&D activities because of its low R&D labor costs (2011–2015 interviews). However, the limited supply of R&D labor force is viewed as a major constrain. A director of the foreign-owned supplier of plastic parts in Slovakia argued during an interview on June 23, 2011, "we [foreign investors] are all struggling with [low] technical competencies and knowledge of university graduates." More importantly, given the overwhelming dependence of the Slovak automotive industry on foreign capital, the state effort to develop strategic automotive R&D in Slovakia is likely to succeed only if it is in line with the strategic need of automotive TNCs. So far, automotive lead firms have engaged in the very limited internationalization of their R&D into ECE (Pavlínek 2012). Given these constraints, the development of a larger-scale and strategic automotive R&D beyond more routine R&D is likely to be difficult to achieve in Slovakia. Industry-financed expenditures on

R&D decreased in Slovakia from 0.65% of GDP in 1995 to 0.2% of GDP in 2010 (OECD 2013) and Slovakia fell more behind many advanced and emerging countries because its industrial R&D investment did not keep up with the extensive growth of automotive production during the 2000s.

The dependence of the automotive industry development in Slovakia on strategic needs of foreign TNCs is obvious from the fact that the annual production targets specified by the government in 1998 (Vestník 1998) for the assembly of trucks, buses and light commercial vehicles have not been achieved. This illustrates that the state policy has only been successful as far as it has met strategic needs and goals of large automotive TNCs. High volume production of passenger cars and labor intensive assembly of special models could especially benefit from the combination of cheap labor force and investment incentives to develop the low-cost production in integrated peripheral markets. So far, automotive TNCs have not shown any interest in the assembly of trucks, buses and light commercial vehicles in Slovakia.

On the surface, state policies for the development of the automotive industry in Slovakia look extremely successful. FDI in the automotive industry has strongly contributed to capital formation, exports, the balance of payments and employment. For example, in 2012, the narrowly defined automotive industry (NACE 29) directly employed 60,828 workers (compared to 6000 in 1993) and it generated an additional 140,000 jobs indirectly (Luptáčik et al. 2013). However, despite the FDI-driven economic growth, the unemployment rate has remained one of the highest among OECD countries and the concentration of automotive FDI in western Slovakia, where 74% of all automotive firms are located, has contributed to uneven development. As of 2011, Slovakia recorded the highest regional inequalities at the TL2 level among OECD countries (OECD 2012). It is also questionable to what extent large investment incentives contribute to a self-sustaining growth (Amin et al. 1994). More importantly, this growth has been achieved at the expense of subordinating state policies and decision-making to those of foreign capital. Bella (2013) has argued: "Volkswagen and Kia do not care about the enforceability of law or the administrative maze [in Slovakia] because any government minister is as far away from them as the nearest phone and they manage to negotiate a service from the state they need." State industrial policies have been driven by the needs of foreign capital, resulting in foreign-capital dependent development (Nölke and Vliegenthart 2009) and corporate capture (Phelps 2000), in which automotive lead firms achieved a disproportionate influence over the government decision making and its economic policies.

Conclusion

There is no doubt that Slovakia has experienced extremely successful growth of the automotive industry when measured by its rapidly increased output and exports. This chapter has demonstrated that the state and its policies towards foreign capital have played an important role in this growth by opening the domestic economy to

FDI and by successfully competing over large FDI projects with generous investment incentives and low taxes. It has also illustrated the power of automotive lead firms to exert the best possible investment terms from the states through regulatory arbitrage among countries with similar factor endowments.

The development of extensive spillovers from foreign to domestic firms, which would drive the upgrading and development of a strong domestic automotive sector, could justify FDI-driven industrialization policies and large state expenditures spent on attracting foreign lead firms. At the moment, the lack of available data makes it impossible to evaluate the extent of spillovers in the Slovak automotive industry but "the spillover effect on domestic companies in the [automotive] sector is likely to be very limited" (Šipikal and Buček 2013: 479). Experience from other integrated peripheral markets, such as Mexico, suggests that the development of capabilities of local suppliers is a long term process that takes decades (Sturgeon et al. 2010). Furthermore, the current configuration of the global automotive industry has not been favorable for the extensive development and upgrading of domestic firms beyond process upgrading (Barnes and Kaplinsky 2000; Humphrey 2000, 2003). In other words, a strong development of the domestic automotive industry that would justify large state expenditures spent on attracting foreign firms, lower the dependence of the Slovak automotive industry on foreign capital, and stabilize the supplier network in Slovakia will be difficult to achieve. The future success of the automotive industry in integrated peripheral markets, such as Slovakia, will continue to depend on FDI and the transfer of foreign technology. However, the wage competitiveness of Slovakia, its distinct advantage in the 1990s and early 2000s, has been eroded as Central European currencies devalued during and after the 2008–2009 economic crisis (OECD 2012) and Slovakia has increasingly been threatened by relocations of the most cost-sensitive labor intensive activities to lower-cost countries (Pavlínek 2015).[11]

Firm-level interviews suggested that a long-term state investment in higher education and vocational training is important for maintaining and improving the competitiveness of Slovak-based automotive firms and it is crucial for the development of higher value-added functions in both foreign subsidiaries and domestic firms. Since local value creation is based on high knowledge activities stemming from both domestic and foreign firms, the development of these competencies would help Slovakia upgrade its position in automotive GPNs from being a predominantly automotive industry subcontractor based on cheap labor to a knowledge-based automotive producer with innovative globally-oriented foreign and domestic firms. As we could see, however, while the state has been willing to offer generous incentives to foreign firms to invest in Slovakia, its investment in vocational training and higher education has been inadequate to meet the labor needs of automotive firms. Similarly, the state support of R&D and of the development of innovative domestic firms has been inadequate. So far, the state has mainly pursued quick FDI-based

[11] By 2015, Slovak hourly compensation costs in manufacturing ($11.26) exceeded those of Poland ($8.53), Hungary ($8.25) and Czechia ($10.29) (Conference Board 2016).

policy fixes rather than a long-term policy focusing on the development of strategic assets that could attract FDI in higher value-added functions.

External control and the dependence on foreign capital and technology represent the greatest weaknesses of the FDI-driven industrialization. An overwhelming foreign ownership means that ultimate decisions about the industry are made abroad by TNC headquarters in the context of their global operations. Sturgeon and Van Biesebroeck (2011: 201) have recently argued with respect to Mexico: "Clearly, the fate of an [automotive] industry in a small, regionally embedded country like Mexico is tied to factors that lie largely outside the control of the state or of local firms." State industrial policies in Slovakia have been to a large extent subordinated to the needs of foreign capital, leading to corporate capture, which may limit the abilities of the state to pursue independent industrial development policies. Large investment incentives and low corporate taxes undermined the ability of the state to adequately finance domestic research, education and the support of domestic firms. Ultimately, therefore, the rapid development of the automotive industry in Slovakia, ECE as a whole, as well as other integrated peripheries, needs to be attributed to a successful spatial fix by global automotive lead firms. The rapidly increased automotive output and exports tell us more about the successful offshoring of automotive technologies and production models by German, French, South Korean and other foreign firms to Slovakia than they do about the capabilities of the domestic automotive industry (Baldwin 2011). Based on the experience of other peripheral regions, it is unlikely that foreign lead firms will strongly develop higher value-added functions in Slovakia. In the long run, value transfer in the form of profit repatriation by foreign firms will likely exceed the invested foreign capital and the profit seeking behavior of foreign firms will not necessarily coincide with long-term state development goals. For example, since foreign automotive firms have been most interested in low-cost production in Slovakia, they will be interested in maintaining the wage gap between Slovakia and Western Europe, while the state should strive to close this gap in order to increase the standard of living of its population. Under this situation, it will be difficult for Slovakia and other ECE countries to substantially improve their peripheral position in the European and global automotive industry division of labor and join the core areas of the automotive industry in order to fully benefit from its rapid FDI-driven development since the early 1990s.

References

Amin A, Bradley D, Howells J, Tomaney J, Gentle C (1994) Regional incentives and the quality of mobile investment in the less favoured regions of the EC. Prog Plan 41(Part 1(0)):1–112

Baldwin R (2011) Trade and industrialisation after globalisation's 2nd unbundling: how building and joining a supply chain are different and why it matters. Working paper 17716

Baldwin R (2013) Global supply chains: why they emerged, why they matter, and where they are going. In: Elms DK, Low P (eds) Global value chains in a changing world. WTO Publications, Geneva, pp 13–59

Baran PA (1957) The political economy of growth. Monthly Review Press, London

Barnes J, Kaplinsky R (2000) Globalization and the death of the local firm? The automobile components sector in South Africa. Reg Stud 34(9):797–812

Bartlett D, Seleny A (1998) The political enforcement of liberalism: bargaining, institutions, and auto multinationals in Hungary. Int Stud Q 42(2):319–338

Beblavý M (2000) Industrial policy. In: Marcinčin A, Beblavý M (eds) Economic policy in Slovakia 1990–1999. Center for Social and Media Analysis, Research Center of the Slovak Foreign Policy Association and Institute for Economic and Social Reforms, Bratislava, pp 228–263

Bella T (2013) Zabije nás nakoniec úspech našich automobiliek? SME. http://ekonomika.sme.sk/c/7028263/zabije-nas-nakoniec-uspech-nasich-automobiliek.html. Accessed 28 Dec 2013

Bernaciak M, Šćepanović V (2010) Challenges of upgrading: the dynamics of east Central Europe's integration into the European automotive production networks. Indust Bezieh 17(2):123–146

Bohle D (2006) Neoliberal hegemony, transnational capital and the terms of the EU's eastward expansion. Cap Class 30(1):57–86

Bohle D, Greskovits B (2006) Capitalism without compromise: strong business and weak labor in Eastern Europe's new transnational industries. Stud Comp Int Dev 41(1):3–25

Britton JNH (1980) Industrial dependence and technological underdevelopment: Canadian consequences of foreign direct investment. Reg Stud 14(3):181–199

Carrillo J, Lung Y, van Tulder R (2004) Cars, carriers of regionalism? Palgrave Macmillan, Houndmills

Cerny PG (1997) Paradoxes of the competition state: the dynamics of political globalization. Gov Oppos 32(2):251–274

Coe NM, Hess M, Yeung HWC, Dicken P, Henderson J (2004) 'globalizing' regional development: a global production networks perspective. Trans Inst Br Geogr 29(4):468–484

Conference Board (2016) International comparisons of hourly compensation costs in manufacturing, 1996–2015. The Conference Board, New York

Dawley S (2007) Making labour-market geographies: volatile 'flagship' inward investment and peripheral regions. Environ Plan A 39(6):1403–1419

Dawley S (2011) Transnational corporations and local and regional development. In: Pike A, Rodriguez-Pose J, Tomaney J (eds) Handbook of local and regional development. Routledge, London, pp 394–412

Dicken P (1976) The multiplant business enterprise and geographical space: some issues in the study of external control and regional development. Reg Stud 10(4):401–412

Dicken P (2015) Global shift: mapping the changing contours of the world economy. The Guilford Press, New York

Dicken P, Forsgren M, Malmberg A (1994) The local embeddedness of transnational corporations. In: Amin A, Thrift N (eds) Globalization, institutions and regional development in Europe. Oxford University Press, Oxford, pp 23–45

Drahokoupil J (2008) The investment-promotion machines: the politics of foreign direct investment promotion in central and eastern Europe. Eur Asia Stud 60(2):197–225

Drahokoupil J (2009a) Globalization and the state in Central and Eastern Europe: the politics of Foreign direct investment. Routledge, London

Drahokoupil J (2009b) The politics of the competition state: the agents and mechanisms of state transnationalization in Central and Eastern Europe. In: Bruszt L, Holzhacker R (eds) The transnationalization of economies, states, and civil societies: new challenges for governance in Europe. Springer, New York, pp 135–155

Dufek J (2004) Příběh Škody Favorit: Osudy automobilové výroby v socialistickém Československu. Dějiny a Současnost 26(4):12–16

Duman A, Kureková L (2012) The role of state in development of socio-economic models in Hungary and Slovakia: the case of industrial policy. J Eur Publ Policy 19(8):1207–1228

Ellingstad M (1997) The maquiladora syndrome: Central European prospects. Eur Asia Stud 49(1):7–21

ERM (2016) European restructuring monitor. European Foundation for the Improvement of Living and Working Conditions

Eurostat (2016) Structural business statistics: annual detailed enterprise statistics—industry and construction. Eurostat.

EY (2010) The central and eastern European automotive market: industry overview. Ernst & Young, Stuttgart

Eyal G, Szelenyi I, Townsley E (1997) The theory of post-communist managerialism. New Left Rev 222:60–92

Firn JR (1975) External control and regional development: the case of Scotland. Environ Plan A 7(4):393–414

Fisher S, Gould J, Haughton T (2007) Slovakia's neoliberal turn. Eur Asia Stud 59(6):977–998

Foy H, Sharman A (2015) How Slovakia overtook Poland in factory race. Financial Times November 17, 2015.

Freyssenet M, Lung Y (2000) Between globalisation and regionalisation: what is the future of the motor industry? In: Humphrey J, Lecler Y, Salerno MS (eds) Global strategies and local realities; the auto industry in emerging markets. Palgrave Macmillan, Basingstoke, pp 72–94

Gereffi G (1999) International trade and industrial upgrading in the apparel commodity chain. J Int Econ 48(1):37–70

Gereffi G (2013) Global value chains in a post-Washington consensus world. Rev Int Polit Econ 21(1):9–37

Gereffi G, Humphrey J, Sturgeon T (2005) The governance of global value chains. Rev Int Polit Econ 12(1):78–104

Gowan P (1995) Neo-liberal theory and practice for Eastern Europe. New Left Rev 213:3–60

Grabher G (1994) The disembedded regional economy: the transformation of east German industrial complexes into western enclaves. In: Amin A, Thrift N (eds) Globalization, institutions and regional development in Europe. Oxford University Press, Oxford, pp 177–195

Grabher G (1997) Adaptation at the cost of adaptability? Restructuring the eastern German regional economy. In: Grabher G, Stark D (eds) Restructuring networks in post-socialism: legacies, linkages, and localities. Oxford University Press, Oxford, pp 107–134

Hajduch M (2014) Najhoršia udalosť slovenskej vedy za rok 2013. SME. http://tech.sme.sk/c/7085219/najhorsia-udalost-slovenskej-vedy-za-rok-2013.html. Accessed 2 Feb 2014

Harvey D (2005) A brief history of neoliberalism. Oxford University Press, Oxford

Harvey D (2006) The limits to capital. Verso, London

Harvey D (2010) The enigma of capital and the crises of capitalism. Oxford University Press, Oxford

Hayter R (1982) Truncation, the international firm and regional policy. Area 14(4):277–282

Henderson J, Dicken P, Hess M, Coe N, Yeung HWC (2002) Global production networks and the analysis of economic development. Rev Int Polit Econ 9(3):436–464

HN (2005) Mikloš sa bude snažiť minimalizovať zvýšenie výdavkov štátu na projekt Kia. HNonline SK. http://hnonline.sk/c1-16912480-miklos-sa-bude-snazit-minimalizovat-zvysenie-vydavkov-statu-na-projekt-kia. Accessed 9 Sept 2013

Humphrey J (2000) Assembler-supplier relations in the auto industry: globalisation and national development. Compet Change 4(3):245–271

Humphrey J (2003) Globalization and supply chain networks: the auto industry in Brazil and India. Glob Netw J Transnatl Aff 3(2):121–141

Humphrey J, Oeter A (2000) Motor industry policies in emerging markets: globalisation and the promotion of domestic industry. In: Humphrey J, Lecler Y, Salerno MS (eds) Global strategies and local realities; the auto industry in emerging markets. Palgrave Macmillan, Basingstoke, pp 42–71

Humphrey J, Lecler Y, Salerno MS (2000) Global strategies and local realities: the auto industry in emerging markets. Palgrave Macmillan, Basingstoke

iDnes (2003) Jahn: Vyděláme i na Peugeotu v Trnavě. iDnes. http://ekonomika.idnes.cz/jahn-vydelame-i-na-peugeotu-v-trnave-dbt-/ekoakcie.aspx?c=A030115_104810_ekoakcie_klu. Accessed 6 Nov 2013

IMF (1998) Slovak Republic: recent economic development. International Monetary Fund, Washington, DC

IMF (1999a) Slovak Republic: selected issues and statistical appendix. International Monetary Fund, Washington, DC, http://www.imf.org/external/pubs/ft/scr/1999/cr99112.pdf

IMF (1999b) Final report on the visit of representatives to Slovakia, January 27. International Monetary Fund, Washington, DC

Jakubiak M, Kolesar P, Izvorski I, Kurekova L (2008) The automotive industry in the Slovak Republic: recent developments and impact on growth. Working Paper No. 29. Commission on Growth and Development, Washington, DC. The International Bank for Reconstruction and Development/The World Bank

Janoška J, Roman S, Martin J, Juraj H (2004) Investičné stratégie automobiliek: Kórejčanov presvedčili nižšie dane a mzdy. Trend. http://www.etrend.sk/trend-archiv/rok-/cislo-Marec/investicne-strategie-automobiliekkorejcanov-presvedcili-nizsie-dane-a%C2%A0mzdy.html. Accessed 6 Nov 2013

Javorcik BS, Kaminski B (2004) The "EU factor" and Slovakia's globalization: the role of foreign direct investment. Finance Úvěr Czech J Econ Finance 54(9–10):456–472

JLR (2016) Jaguar Land Rover begins construction of Slovakian plant. Press release, 13 Sept. 2016

Kia (2004) Investičná zmluva týkajúca sa navrhovanej výstavby závodu na montáž automobilov v Žiline, Slovenská republika [Investment contract between Kia Motors Corporation, Slovakia and the city of Žilina]

Klier TH, Rubenstein JM (2010) The changing geography of north American motor vehicle production. Camb J Reg Econ Soc 3(3):335–347

Kohli A (2004) State-directed development: political power and industrialization in the global periphery. Cambridge University Press, Cambridge

Kolesár P (2006) Race to the bottom? The role of investment incentives in attracting strategic automotive foreign direct investment in Central Europe. Central European University, Budapest

Kolesár P (2007) Vzťah nadnárodných korporácií a národných vlád v strednej Európe: Konkurencia krajín V4 pri získavaní zahraničných investícií [The relationship of transnational corporations and national governments in Central Europe: the competition of V4 countries over foreign investment]. Masarykova Univerzita, Brno

Kremský P (2003) Do Česka mieri ďalšia automobilka. Trend. http://firmy.etrend.sk/firmy-nefinancny-sektor/do-ceska-mieri-dalsia-automobilka.html. Accessed 11 Sept 2013

Layan J (2000) The integration of peripheral markets: a comparison of Spain and Mexico. In: Humphrey J, Lecler Y, Salerno MS (eds) Global strategies and local realities: the auto industry in emerging markets. Palgrave Macmillan, Basingstoke, pp 16–41

Liu WD, Dicken P (2006) Transnational corporations and 'obligated embeddedness': foreign direct investment in China's automobile industry. Environ Plan A 38(7):1229–1247

Liu WD, Yeung HWC (2008) China's dynamic industrial sector: the automobile industry. Eurasian Geogr Econ 49(5):523–548

LN (2016) Slováci začnou vyrábět jaguary za dva roky. V září se začne stavět továrna. Lidovky. http://byznys.lidovky.cz/tiskni.aspx?r=firmy-trhy&c=A160816_133605_firmy-trhy_ELE. Accessed 25 Aug 2016

Luptáčik M, Habrman M, Lábaj M, Rehák Š (2013) The importance of automotive industry for the Slovak economy: empirical results. University of Economics in Bratislava, Department of Economic Policy, Bratislava

MacKinnon D (2012) Beyond strategic coupling: reassessing the firm-region nexus in global production networks. J Econ Geogr 12(1):227–245

Malecki EJ (2004) Jockeying for position: what it means and why it matters to regional development policy when places compete. Reg Stud 38(9):1101–1120

Marcinčin A (2000a) Enterprise restructuring. In: Marcinčin A, Beblavý M (eds) Economic policy in Slovakia 1990–1999. Center for Social and Media Analysis, Research Center of the Slovak Foreign Policy Association and Institute for Economic and Social Reforms, Bratislava, pp 320–357

Marcinčin A (2000b) Privatization. In: Marcinčin A, Beblavý M (eds) Economic policy in Slovakia 1990–1999. Center for Social and Media Analysis, Research Center of the Slovak Foreign Policy Association and Institute for Economic and Social Reforms, Bratislava, pp 292–319

Medve-Bálint G (2014) The role of the EU in shaping FDI flows to east Central Europe. J Common Mark Stud 52(1):35–51

Medžová A (1999) Stratégia podpory vstupu zahraničných investícií je len o málo konkrétnejšia ako balíček ekonomických opatrení. E-Trend. http://www.etrend.sk/trend-archiv/rok-/cislo-Marec/strategia-podpory-vstupu-zahranicnych-investicii-je-len-o-malo-konkretnejsia-ako-balicek-ekonomickych-opatreni.html. Accessed 12 Apr 2013

NBS (2015) Priame zahraničné investície, 2013 [Foreign direct investment, 2013]. National Bank of Slovakia, Bratislava

Nölke A, Vliegenthart A (2009) Enlarging the varieties of capitalism: the emergence of dependent market economies in east Central Europe. World Polit 61(4):670–702

OECD (2012) Slovak Republic 2012. OECD, Paris

OECD (2013) Slovak Republic: fostering an inclusive job-rich recovery. OECD "Better Policies" Series, Paris

OICA (2016) World motor vehicle production by country and type, 1997–2015. Organisation Internationale des Constructeurs d'Automobile, Paris

Pavlínek P (1995) Regional development and the disintegration of Czechoslovakia. Geoforum 26(4):351–372

Pavlínek P (2002) Transformation of the Central and East European passenger car industry: selective peripheral integration through foreign direct investment. Environ Plan A 34(9):1685–1709

Pavlínek P (2003) Transformation of the Czech automotive components industry through foreign direct investment. Eurasian Geogr Econ 44(3):184–209

Pavlínek P (2004) Regional development implications of foreign direct investment in Central Europe. Eur Urban Reg Stud 11(1):47–70

Pavlínek P (2008) A successful transformation? Restructuring of the Czech automobile industry. Physica Verlag, Heidelberg

Pavlínek P (2012) The internationalization of corporate R&D and the automotive industry R&D of East-Central Europe. Econ Geogr 88(3):279–310

Pavlínek P (2015) The impact of the 2008–2009 crisis on the automotive industry: global trends and firm-level effects in Central Europe. Eur Urban Reg Stud 22(1):20–40

Pavlínek P, Smith A (1998) Internationalization and embeddedness in east-central European transition: the contrasting geographies of inward investment in the Czech and Slovak republics. Reg Stud 32(7):619–638

Pavlínek P, Ženka J (2011) Upgrading in the automotive industry: firm-level evidence from Central Europe. J Econ Geogr 11(3):559–586

Pavlínek P, Žížalová P (2016) Linkages and spillovers in global production networks: firm-level analysis of the Czech automotive industry. J Econ Geogr 16(2):331–363

Pavlínek P, Domanski B, Guzik R (2009) Industrial upgrading through foreign direct investment in Central European automotive manufacturing. Eur Urban Reg Stud 16(1):43–63

Phelps NA (1993) Branch plants and the evolving spatial division-of-labor: a study of material linkage change in the northern region of England. Reg Stud 27(2):87–101

Phelps NA (2000) The locally embedded multinational and institutional capture. Area 32(2):169–178

Phelps NA (2008) Cluster or capture? Manufacturing foreign direct investment, external economies and agglomeration. Reg Stud 42(4):457–473

Phelps NA, Raines P (2003) The new competition for inward investment: companies, institutions and territorial development. Edward Elgar, Cheltenham

Phelps NA, Wood A (2006) Lost in translation? Local interests, global actors and inward investment regimes. J Econ Geogr 6(4):493–515

Pike A (1998) Making performance plants from branch plants? In situ restructuring in the automobile industry in the United Kingdom. Environ Plan A 30(5):881–900

Poulantzas N (1973) On social classes. New Left Review I/78: 37–54.

PSA (2003) Zmluva o investičnej spolupráci [Investment contract between PSA, Slovakia and the city of Trnava]

Sario (2013) Automotive industry. Slovak Investment and Trade Development Agency, Bratislava

Schönwiesner R (2002) Stred Európy bojuje o ďalšiu automobilku. Trend. http://firmy.etrend.sk/firmy-nefinancny-sektor/stred-europy-bojuje-o-dalsiu-automobilku.html. Accessed 9 Sept 2013

Schönwiesner R (2005) Najlepší pomer produktivity a miezd nájdu automobilky na Slovensku. Trend. http://ekonomika.etrend.sk/svet/najlepsi-pomer-produktivity-a-miezd-najdu-automobilky-na-slovensku.html. Accessed 5 June 2013

SEM (2005) Rozvoj automobilového priemyslu ako generátor hospodárskeho rastu priemyslu a jeho reštrukturalizácie. Slovak Ministry of Economy, Bratislava

Shields S (2004) Global restructuring and the Polish state: transition, transformation, or transnationalization? Rev Int Polit Econ 11(1):132–154

Shields S (2008) How the east was won: transnational social forces and the neoliberalisation of Poland's post-communist transition. Glob Soc 22(4):445–468

Šipikal M, Buček M (2013) The role of FDIs in regional innovation: evidence from the automotive industry in western Slovakia. Reg Sci Policy Pract 5(4):475–490

SME (2003) Viaceré automobilky mapujú možnosti investovania v SR. SME. http://ekonomika.sme.sk/c/859987/viacere-automobilky-mapuju-moznosti-investovania-v-sr.html. Accessed 4 Nov 2013

SME (2014) Volkswagen chce znížiť platy, odborárov zaskočil. SME. http://ekonomika.sme.sk/c/7074289/volkswagen-chce-znizit-platy-odborarov-zaskocil.html. Accessed 28 Jan 2014

SME (2015) Automobilka Jaguar Land Rover príde na Slovensko. http://ekonomika.sme.sk/c/7958224/automobilka-jaguar-land-rover-pride-na-slovensko.html. Accessed 12 Aug 2015

Smith A (1998) Reconstructing the regional economy: industrial transformation and regional development in Slovakia. Edward Elgar, Cheltenham

Smith A, Ferenčíková S (1998) Inward investment, regional transformations and uneven development in eastern and Central Europe: enterprise case-studies from Slovakia. Eur Urban Reg Stud 5(2):155–173

Smith A, Rainnie A, Dunford M, Hardy J, Hudson R, Sadler D (2002) Networks of value, commodities and regions: reworking divisions of labour in macro-regional economies. Prog Hum Geogr 26(1):41–63

Stanford J (2010) The geography of auto globalization and the politics of auto bailouts. Camb J Reg Econ Soc 3(3):383–405

Studeničová M, Uhrík J (2009) Od tankov k Tuaregu. Verbis, Bratislava

Sturgeon TJ, Lester RK (2004) The new global supply base: new challenges for local suppliers in East Asia. In: Yusuf S, Altaf MAA, Nabeshima K (eds) Global production networking and technological change in East Asia. The World Bank and Oxford University Press, Washington, DC, pp 35–87

Sturgeon TJ, Van Biesebroeck J (2009) Crisis and protection in the automotive industry: a global value chain perspective. In: Evenett SJ, Hoekman BM, Cattaneo O (eds) Effective crisis response and openness: implications for the trading system. World Bank, Centre for Economic Policy Research, London, pp 285–305

Sturgeon TJ, Van Biesebroeck J (2011) Global value chains in the automotive industry: an enhanced role for developing countries? Int J Technol Learn Innov Dev 4(1/2/3):181–205

Sturgeon T, Van Biesebroeck J, Gereffi G (2008) Value chains, networks and clusters: reframing the global automotive industry. J Econ Geogr 8(3):297–321

Sturgeon TJ, Gereffi G, Rogers KB, Fernandez-Stark K (2010) The prospects for Mexico in the north American automotive industry: a global value chain perspective. Actes du GERPISA 42(June):11–22

Trend (2003) Je rozhodnuté: PSA postaví nový závod v Trnave. Trend. http://firmy.etrend.sk/firmy-nefinancny-sektor/je-rozhodnute-psa-postavi-novy-zavod-v-trnave.html. Accessed 9 Sept 2013

UNCTAD (1998) World investment report 1998: trends and determinants. United Nations, New York

USBLS (2013) International comparisons of hourly compensation costs in manufacturing, 1996–2012: time series tables. August 9, 2013 ed., U.S. Bureau of Labor Statistics, Division of International Labor Comparisons.

Vagac L (2000) The automotive industry in the Slovak Republic. South-East Eur Rev Labour Soc Aff 2:143–172

Van Biesebroeck J, Sturgeon TJ (2010) Effects of the 2008–09 crisis on the automotive industry in developing countries: a global value chain perspective. In: Cattaneo O, Gereffi G, Staritz C (eds) Global value chains in a postcrisis world: a development perspective. The World Bank, Washington, DC, pp 209–244

Vestník (1998) Program rozvoja automobilového priemyslu SR (program for the development of the automotive industry in the SR). Vestník Minist Hospod SR 3(2):9–18

Vliegenthart A (2009) From employee governance to corporate governance: transnational forces and the polish corporate governance debates since the 1980s. In: Bruszt L, Holzhacker R (eds) The transnationalization of economies, states, and civil societies: new challenges for governance in Europe. Springer, New York, pp 61–82

Vliegenthart A (2010) Bringing dependency back in: the economic crisis in post-socialist Europe and the continued relevance of dependent development. Hist Soc Res Hist Sozial 35(2):242–265

VW (2010) Volkswagen Slovakia: 2010 Čísla a fakty. VW Slovakia, Bratislava

VW (2013) Volkswagen Slovakia: facts and figures. VW Slovakia, Bratislava

Yeung HWC (2009) Regional development and the competitive dynamics of global production networks: an east Asian perspective. Reg Stud 43(3):325–351

Yeung HWC (2013) Governing the market in a globalizing era: developmental states, global production networks and inter-firm dynamics in East Asia. Rev Int Polit Econ 21(1):70–101

Zamkovský J (1999) Globalizácia a Slovensko: Prípad vládneho Programu rozvoja automobilového priemyslu. CEPA, Bratislava

Zamkovský J (2001) Ako sa loví plachá zver pod Tatrami: prípad BMW. CEPA, Bratislava

ZAP (2000) Slovak Republic automotive industry: statistics – yearbook 2000. The Automotive Industry Association of the Slovak Republic and the Slovak Chamber of Commerce and Industry, Bratislava

ZAP (2013) Základné informácie o automobilovom priemysle a jeho význame pre SR. The Automotive Industry Association of the Slovak Republic, Bratislava

Chapter 7
Conclusion

The automotive industry has developed rapidly in ECE since the early 1990s and has become integrated into the European and global automotive production networks through FDI and trade by foreign automotive TNCs. As a result, the ECE output of cars quadrupled between 1990 and 2015. The production of automotive components expanded even more rapidly for both the assembly operations in ECE and exports. This rapid growth of the automotive industry helped in overcoming the industrial decline of the 1990s, that followed the collapse of state socialism, and contributed to the economic recovery across ECE after 1995. In the process, hundreds of thousands of jobs were created. By 2015, the automotive industry employed more than seven hundred thousand workers across ECE. Because of its rapid growth, the automotive industry has significantly increased its share of industrial employment, production, exports, GDP and FDI in ECE. These and other economic indicators point to the successful development of the automotive industry and its increasingly important role in ECE economies. Not surprisingly, ECE politicians and economists alike have praised the development of the automotive industry as an unqualified success and the ECE countries have vigorously competed over each new automotive investment by foreign TNCs with generous investment incentives.

Against this backdrop, this book has engaged in a detailed and more critical analysis of the processes related to the FDI-driven development of the automotive industry in ECE that tend to be overlooked or marginalized in the conventional analysis. My focus has been on long-term consequences of this development at the firm level, in the regional context, and on the ECE's position in the international division of labor. My analysis drew on firm-level information and data collected directly from individual firms through firm-level questionnaires and extensive firm-level interviews with both foreign-subsidiaries and domestic firms in Czechia and Slovakia. My goal has been to understand how the processes related to FDI-driven development of the automotive industry actually operate on the ground and in individual firms in ECE.

As we could see, FDI, which exceeded €35 billion as of 2015, has been fueling the export-oriented growth of the automotive industry in ECE. All car assembly

P. Pavlínek, *Dependent Growth: Foreign Investment and the Development of the Automotive Industry in East-Central Europe*, DOI 10.1007/978-3-319-53955-3_7

factories, engine and transmission plants, along with the most important components suppliers are foreign-owned. Drawing on the work of David Harvey, we can consider the development of the automotive industry in ECE and in integrated peripheries as a whole to be one of the latest manifestations of spatial fixes in the global automotive industry in its constant search for profits and lower production costs. ECE has been attractive for foreign TNCs because of the combination of several factors: significantly lower production costs than in Western Europe, which are mainly based on lower labor costs; membership in the European Union, which allows for tariff-free access to the large West European market; and geographic proximity, combined with a relatively good quality infrastructure, which lower transportation costs.

I have argued that despite a number of factors that influence the location decisions of foreign TNCs, the relative geographic location of individual ECE countries and their distance from Western Europe explain the distribution of automotive FDI between 1990 and 2015. Countries such as Bulgaria that are located further away from Western Europe have been much less successful in attracting automotive FDI despite their lower wages and lower taxes than countries directly bordering Western Europe, such as Czechia, Hungary, Poland and Slovakia. I have argued that ECE will continue to be attractive for automotive FDI in the foreseeable future as long as production costs, especially labor costs, remain significantly lower in ECE than in Western Europe, assuming that other favorable factors, such as EU membership and low taxes, remain in place. This explains why the drop in FDI inflows during the 2008–2009 economic crisis has only been temporary. These and other factors, such as large sunk costs, also explain why the ECE automotive industry is not in danger of large-scale relocations of production "further east" as some authors have argued. The 2008–2009 economic crisis showed that the only exception is the most labor-intensive manual assembly of standard components that do not have to be delivered just-in-time, such as cable harnesses for standard models of cars.

FDI has also transformed the supplier industry in ECE as more than twelve hundred new factories for the production of automotive components were built across the region between 1997 and 2015. We could also see that compared to the foreign-owned automotive sector, the domestic sector is very weak. This weakness is the outcome of several factors. In those countries that had a relatively well-developed auto supplier industry before 1990, such as Czechia, the best domestic suppliers were taken over by foreign firms in the wave of acquisitions in the 1990s. Those domestic firms that were unable to upgrade and failed to meet the strict conditions for domestic suppliers set by Western firms had to exit the automotive industry. Domestic firms that were not taken over by foreign firms and were able to upgrade in order to meet the quality and delivery requirements tend to be positioned at the bottom of the supplier hierarchy and supply low value-added simple components, usually as Tier 3 suppliers.

Large inflows of FDI have contributed to significant upgrading in the ECE automotive industry. Process upgrading has been most widespread among both foreign subsidiaries and domestic firms since it is a basic precondition for their continuing competitiveness. Product and especially functional upgrading have been much more selective. Product upgrading has generally been limited to the most important Tier 1 suppliers and assembly firms. Similarly, functional upgrading, measured by R&D employment, has mostly been limited to a small group of large foreign subsidiaries.

FDI has contributed to the development of the distinct division of labor between ECE and Western Europe in the automotive industry. In order to benefit from ECE's lower production costs, foreign TNCs have been primarily interested in setting up production sites across ECE from which they could serve the EU market. Higher value-added and strategic functions have been developed much more slowly across ECE and only to a limited extent as they are typically conducted in the home countries of automotive TNCs. I have demonstrated this division of labor and the slow development of higher value-added functions in ECE by analyzing the development of automotive R&D. My analysis has shown that despite the "R&D globalization" rhetoric, the actual internationalization of corporate R&D activities has been slow in the automotive industry and that the organizational structure of the contemporary automotive industry is not favorable for the large-scale internationalization of automotive R&D. The empirical data from ECE show that while it has become a popular region for the development export-oriented automotive production by foreign TNCs, the development of automotive R&D has lagged considerably behind. The greater automotive R&D conducted in Czechia and Romania are notable exceptions that could be explained by the presence of regional R&D centers of Škoda Auto and Dacia, which are distinct brands within the VW Group and Renault, respectively. I have argued that the development of R&D in Škoda Auto and Dacia is the outcome of strategic coupling between regional assets and strategic needs of TNCs. Still, the scope of R&D conducted in these two regional R&D centers is limited and other foreign assemblers do not conduct any R&D in ECE. There has been a gradual increase in R&D employment among suppliers in ECE but these are typically routine and non-strategic low-level automotive R&D activities attracted by either low-cost R&D labor or by the necessity to support the existing production. Automotive R&D is generally controlled by foreign TNCs as R&D functions in domestic firms tend to be either non-existent or very limited. The prospects for the future development of automotive R&D in ECE are constrained not only by the organization of automotive R&D by TNCs, but also by the limited availability of highly skilled automotive R&D workforce in ECE because of the weak educational policies of ECE governments after 1990.

Because technology transfer is considered to be one of the most important potential long-term benefits of FDI in less developed countries, I have investigated the long-term development effects of automotive FDI in ECE through the analysis of spillovers from foreign subsidiaries to host country firms. I have identified horizontal and vertical spillovers from foreign subsidiaries to host country economies and investigated them in the context of the Czech automotive industry. Horizontal spillovers were important especially in the 1990s after the initial opening to FDI and affected domestic firms both positively and negatively. However, my focus was on supplier linkages between foreign subsidiaries and domestic firms because they are the most important precondition for the development of vertical spillovers of broadly defined technology from foreign subsidiaries and its transfer to host economies. My analysis of vertical spillovers in the Czech automotive industry has suggested that they have been much more selective than horizontal spillovers and had only a limited and uneven impact on domestic firms despite the fact that the vast majority of domestic automotive suppliers have been involved in supplier relationships with foreign subsidiaries. While productivity spillovers have been strong and reflected in process upgrading of domestic firms, technology spillovers have generally been weaker and have been reported by less than half of interviewed domestic firms. Furthermore, only one-third of interviewed domestic firms have experienced direct technology spillovers from foreign subsidiaries despite being involved in supplier relationships with them. The low absorptive capacity of domestic firms, which is related to their limited automotive R&D capabilities, is one of the most important reasons for weak technology spillovers. Many domestic automotive suppliers have therefore been unable to benefit from potential spillovers and others have been able to benefit only partially. My research has also shown that the ability to benefit from spillovers has not helped domestic firms to improve their position in the supplier hierarchy.

This book has shown that ECE governments have played an extremely important role in the development of the automotive industry after 1990 by opening up national economies to flows of foreign capital, creating favorable conditions for FDI, and accommodating its needs. Since the late 1990s, ECE countries have engaged in the 'race to the bottom' by vigorously competing over automotive FDI through various investment incentives. I have argued that, ultimately, the 'race to the bottom' leads to the decreasing of potential benefits of FDI for host economies and to corporate capture, in which states often serve the needs of foreign capital at the expense of meeting other important needs. Slovakia provides a telling example of how ECE governments have willingly engaged in the 'race to the bottom' by developing the competition state. It has had the most aggressive investment promotion regime in ECE and its automotive industry is the most controlled by foreign capital of all ECE countries (Table 1.3). I have argued that while this reliance on FDI for industrial development generally and the automotive industry specifically has been successful in creating jobs, increasing exports and contributing to GDP, it has not been without potentially significant long-term development costs.

The question of the long-term development effects of the growth of the automotive industry in ECE has been reoccurring throughout this book. I have argued that the overwhelming foreign ownership and control is the underlying structural feature of the automotive industry in ECE, which has resulted in its truncated development. We could see that truncated development is the outcome of the financial, technological and managerial dependency of the ECE automotive industry on foreign capital, in which ECE has become narrowly specialized in the assembly of cars and the production of components, while higher value-added nonproduction functions have mostly been conducted in corporate headquarters and parent enterprises abroad. Foreign ownership has contributed to the transfer of value from ECE through various profit shifting strategies, such as profit repatriation and transfer pricing. Value capture in ECE has been further limited by low corporate taxes and tax holidays that have been provided to foreign investors by ECE governments. The overwhelming foreign ownership and control of the automotive industry and the low capabilities of many domestic suppliers have made it difficult for domestic firms to become integrated in the automotive production networks. The low level of integration of the automotive industry with host country economies has limited the potential for technology transfer from foreign subsidiaries to host country firms, which has undermined one of the most important long-term potential benefits of FDI.

Overall, the growth of the automotive industry in ECE has been the outcome of the successful spatial fix by foreign TNCs rather than the outcome of indigenous industrial development. For struggling ECE economies it has represented a relatively easy and rapid way to generate the desperately needed industrial employment and exports following the industrial collapse of the early 1990s. ECE countries are clearly determined to continue with the same FDI-driven strategy for the continuing development of the automotive industry in the future. It will work as long as wages in ECE remain low compared to Western Europe and ECE remains locked in the peripheral position of the European automotive industry production system.

Index

P. Pavlínek, *Dependent Growth: Foreign Investment and the Development of the Automotive Industry in East-Central Europe*, DOI 10.1007/978-3-319-53955-3

The manufacturer's authorised representative in the EU is Springer Nature Customer Service Centre GmbH, Europaplatz 3, 69115 Heidelberg, Germany. If you have any concerns regarding our products, please contact ProductSafety@springernature.com

Printed and bound by CPI Group (UK) Ltd, Croydon, CR0 4YY
25/09/2026
02222869-0008